WEYERHAEUSER ENVIRONMENTAL BOOKS

William Cronon, Editor

Weyerhaeuser Environmental Books explore human relationships with natural environments in all their variety and complexity. They seek to cast new light on the ways that natural systems affect human communities, the ways that people affect the environments of which they are a part, and the ways that different cultural conceptions of nature profoundly shape our sense of the world around us.

Making Mountains

New York City and the Catskills

DAVID STRADLING

UNIVERSITY OF WASHINGTON PRESS

Seattle & London

Making Mountains is published with the assistance of a grant from the Weyerhaeuser Environmental Books Endowment, established by the Weyerhaeuser Company Foundation, members of the Weyerhaeuser family, and Janet and Jack Creighton.

University of Washington Press
P.O. Box 50096, Seattle, WA 98145, U.S.A.
www.washington.edu/uwpress

Library of Congress Cataloging-in-Publication Data

Stradling, David.
    Making mountains : New York City and the Catskills / David Stradling.
        p.   cm. — (Weyerhaeuser environmental books)
    Includes bibliographical references and index.
    ISBN-13: 978-0-295-98747-7 (cloth : alk. paper)
        1. Catskill Mountains (N.Y.)—Relations—New York (State)—New York.   2. New York (N.Y.)—Relations—New York (State)—Catskill Mountains.   3. Rural-urban relations—New York (State)—Case studies.   4. Landscape—New York (State)—Catskill Mountains—History.   5. Human ecology—New York (State)—Catskill Mountains—History.   6. Catskill Mountains (N.Y.)—Environmental conditions.   7. Haynes family.   8. Catskill Mountains (N.Y.)—Biography.   9. Mountain life—New York (State)—Catskill Mountains—History.   10. Catskill Mountains (N.Y.)—Social life and customs.   I. Title.
    F127.C3S77   2007
    303.48'27473807471—dc22   2007019376

Cover photo: Catskill Mountain House, engraved by J. R. Smith, ca. 1830. Library of Congress, Prints & Photographs Division, LC-USZC4–3360.

To the memory of

Glentworth Butler Haynes

1906–1995

Contents

Foreword   ix

Preface: The Haynes Family of Haynes Hollow   xv

Acknowledgments   xxv

Introduction: Types of the Permanent and Unchanging   5

1. A Natural Resource   20

2. Envisioning Mountains   46

3. The Mountain Hotels   76

4. Making Wilderness   109

5. Mountain Water   140

6. Moving Mountains   177

7. A Suburb of New York   209

   Epilogue: Whose Woods These Are   240

   Notes   253

   Bibliographical Essay   289

   Index   306

Foreword

In a City's Mountain Shadow

William Cronon

Ask almost any modern American to name the most celebrated wild places in the United States today, and you're likely to be given a list of sublime landscapes lying far to the west of the Mississippi River: Yosemite, Yellowstone, Grand Canyon, and a few others. Together, these might seem to suggest that the long American love affair with wilderness began in the Far West—and yet it would be hard to imagine a more misleading conclusion. In fact, one could argue with considerable force that Americans in the eighteenth and early nineteenth centuries first learned the symbolic language for appreciating the wild beauty of their national landscape from English and European writers and artists depicting places like the Alps and the Lake District. Niagara Falls was certainly the single most sought-after natural wonder in the early years of the new American republic. Thoreau's perambulations in the vicinity of Walden Pond helped create the literary models that would eventually be applied to far wilder western places. And the success during the second half of the nineteenth century in designating the Adirondack Mountains as "forever wild" in the New York State Constitution was unquestionably among the earliest and most influential efforts at protecting a wild mountain landscape, setting aside a territory so vast that even today it rivals all other U.S. wilderness preserves outside Alaska. Whatever we may think today, the American love of wilderness was born well east of the Mississippi River.

Among the eastern places most central in shaping subsequent American attitudes toward wilderness, arguably none has been more important—or, ironically, less known to most U.S. citizens today—than New York's Catskill Mountains. Located just a hundred miles north of Manhattan, they are perhaps best remembered as the site where Washington Irving had his eighteenth-century character Rip Van Winkle fall magically asleep for twenty years, awakening to discover a post-revolutionary world far different from his own time. As wealthy New Yorkers began to make excursions up the Hudson River from their metropolitan homes, they sought out these rolling, forested mountains. Although the Catskills are low by western standards—the loftiest is a mere 4,180 feet high—their precipitous rise from the Hudson creates a stunning backdrop for travelers in the valley below.

It was thus no accident that the Catskills became the single most influential place in the United States for promulgating new romantic ideas of nature. For the romantics, sublime landscapes like the Catskills—with their soaring peaks, steep chasms, foaming cataracts, and violent storms—were the best places on the planet to experience God's presence in the earthly creation. Beginning in the 1820s with the immensely influential work of Thomas Cole, these mountains became the subjects of countless paintings depicting the beauties of wild nature. Collectively known as the Hudson River School, artists like Cole, Frederic Edwin Church, Sanford Robinson Gifford, and Jasper Cropsey created a rich tradition of landscape painting unlike anything seen before in either Europe or the United States. The Hudson River School introduced the visual iconography of romantic nature to American audiences—and more often than not the physical embodiment of that nature was just upstream from New York City in the Catskill Mountains.

One reason for this was the founding in 1824 of the famed Catskill Mountain House. Constructed on a high promontory looking down thousands of feet to the Hudson River, with a beautiful pair of lakes perched high in the valley behind the hotel and a famous waterfall a little to its south, the Mountain House provided the food, lodgings, and other amenities that made it relatively easy for New York artists, writers, and intellectuals—and the elite tourists who followed them—to sojourn in mountain country that might otherwise have seemed too daunting and uncomfortable. Some of Thomas Cole's most famous canvases were painted within just a mile or two of the Mountain House, and more than one of them depicted the hotel itself, so stunning was its appearance amid the surrounding peaks. The Mountain House remained in business for more than a century, and during its early decades it helped define traditions of romantic tourism that would eventually spread from coast to coast. Although it closed its doors in 1941 and was eventually burned to the ground in 1963 by the state of New York in an astonishing failure to recognize its architectural and cultural significance as the most influential mountain resort hotel in U.S. history, the Mountain House still stands in memory as a symbolic benchmark not just for the Catskills, but for the entire American landscape.

The disproportionate role of the Catskills in shaping nineteenth-century American ideas of wild nature was a direct result of their special relationship to New York City, which emerged during this same period as the dominant metropolitan center for the country as a whole. Because it was so easy for urban elites to travel to and sojourn in these mountains, the Catskills were among the earliest examples of a wilderness landscape that gained symbolic significance by seeming to stand in opposition to the city, even as their economy, social life, and cultural meanings were increasingly influenced by the myriad interconnections that bound city and mountains ever closer together. It was not just that wealthy tourists, artists, and intellectuals spent so much time and money in the Catskills; it was that local residents found their own economic opportunities shaped by these urban visitors and also influenced by the demands of nearby urban markets. Although Manhattanites might feel a world away from New York City when they gazed down on the Hudson from the veranda of the Mountain House, in fact their very presence at the hotel was evidence that it was not nearly so distant from the city as they liked to imagine.

It is this relationship between the city and its nearby mountains that David Stradling has taken as his subject in *Making Mountains: New York City and the Catskills*. Himself the descendant of rural residents of the Catskills, Stradling is an urban environmental historian whose first book, *Smokestacks and Progressives*, was a study of urban air pollution during the opening decades of the twentieth century. (He has also contributed to this series a superb collection of documents entitled *Conservation in the Progressive Era* that anyone interested in that subject will enjoy reading.) Long persuaded that environmental historians have paid too little attention to the city, being biased instead toward agricultural landscapes and wilderness areas, Stradling decided that it might be helpful to demonstrate the many ways in which even seemingly wild places have historically been tied to the urban areas that helped establish their cultural importance. He rightly concluded that there were few better places to demonstrate the value of this insight than the Catskills, and the result is this fine book on a wild mountain landscape whose past is inexplicable if one fails to explore the ways in which Catskill history is bound up with that of New York City.

Because the Catskills have changed so much over the course of American history, there are many phases and chapters in Stradling's story, and many colorful characters, starting with his own grandfather, Glen Haynes, who opens the book by providing an opportunity for the author to revisit his childhood roots in these mountains. Stradling then turns to the colonial period to trace the early Dutch and English settlement of the Hudson and its nearby mountains, noting the local economic cycles of boom and bust as farms were established and various commodities were harvested from Catskill hillsides. Logging operations and tanneries stripped the mountains of trees, and quarries harvested stone to provide building materials for the city.

It was into mountains already profoundly shaped by agriculture and industry that early nineteenth-century writers like Washington Irving and painters like Thomas Cole eventually arrived and began the Catskills' transformation into icons of romantic nature. Soon came tourist amenities like the Mountain House and its lesser-known competitors, and with them the jobs and economic services to supply creature comforts for urban visitors who were willing to spend generously to assure that their encounter with a perceived wilderness did not mean too great a separation from good food and drink and a comfortable bed. By the end of the nineteenth century, the Catskills were home to John Burroughs, a nature writer so celebrated that in his day he rivaled Henry David Thoreau and John Muir, even though his fame has not endured so successfully as theirs in the twentieth century. Burroughs was a close friend of many of the leading industrialists and captains of industry of his day, and many of them sought him out in his Hudson Valley home to partake of the wilderness beauty he described so eloquently in his writings.

By the twentieth century, the Catskills were undergoing still other transformations that were no less tied to New York City. As the growing metropolis cast an ever-wider net to supply water for its millions of residents, the Catskills inevitably came to be perceived at least in part as an urban watershed, with reservoirs and elaborate pipelines designed to keep an underground torrent of mountain water flowing toward Manhattan Island. At the same time, New Yorkers began to seek experiences in the mountains that focused as much on music and vaudeville entertainment as on romantic nature and outdoor recreation. The summer camps of the Borscht Belt were the result, with a complex ethnic geography expressing the changing immigrant populations of the city. By the 1960s, the Catskills had famously become a retreat for folk artists like Bob Dylan, and ultimately became the site of the most famous outdoor concert in the history of rock and roll, known by the Catskill community near which it was held: Woodstock. Like many other natural areas on the outskirts of major cities, the Catskills in the late twentieth century saw growing concerns about sprawl, with heated debates about the value of government zoning regulations that might limit subdivisions and development in the mountains.

Throughout these many waves of historical change, the Catskills and their residents remained apart from the city even as their lives and communities became inextricably bound to their urban visitors, customers, and neighbors to the south. David Stradling tells this complex story with great clarity and energy, narrating the history of this mountain landscape as a contribution to rural and urban history, and always with the intention of demonstrating that city and country have a single unified past if only we make sure we understand the ways they have influenced each other over time.

As a result, *Making Mountains* has implications far beyond the Catskills, for two quite different reasons. The first is that it was in the Catskills that Americans learned to love their mountains. The traditions established on these Hudson Valley slopes would come to have ramifying implications, now largely forgotten, for places like Yosemite and Yellowstone and Grand Canyon that are today far better known. To understand the cultural traditions that now shape our experience of western wilderness, one really should make a pilgrimage to experience the wondrous view of the Hudson from the site where the Catskill Mountain House once stood.

David Stradling's second message is no less compelling. Although places like the Catskill Mountains have long been assigned a symbolic role as polar opposites of the city—as landscapes whose natural beauty is inherently in tension with the urban landscapes against which we so often counterpose them—in fact these symbols of city and country, of humanity and nature, were forged by the same history and gain their most profound meanings only in relationship to each other. It was New York artists and intellectuals who helped teach their fellow citizens the many meanings of nature in the paintings and essays that depicted these mountains, and it was residents of the Catskills who welcomed urban visitors into their communities to help them experience the life of these mountains. Those who have made their homes in places like the Catskills have long depended on urban markets for their livelihoods, just as city dwellers have long looked to the mountains for the retreats they believe will reconnect them to the earth and thereby make their lives more meaningful. Although we often see the two as profoundly separate places, the city and its mountains share a common history. By helping us realize that the Catskills and New York City can only be understood relative to each other, David Stradling reminds us that the same lesson applies with equal force to all human communities and the natural environments that surround and sustain them.

Preface

The Haynes Family of Haynes Hollow

U p in New York State's Catskill Mountains where the population has always been thin, certain family names lie thick on the land. Generations stayed close to familial homesteads, and over time their names attached to certain features, some natural, like streams and mountains, others cultural, such as roads and hamlets. In the central Catskills of Ulster County, for example, Winchell Road runs up Winchell Hill, Haynes Hollow Road approaches Haynes Mountain, and before the waters of the Ashokan Reservoir rose to cover them, a boarding business run by the Bishops, called Bishop Falls House, sat near Bishop Falls. It is common in rural America for familial names to cluster on the landscape, and so perhaps this observation should convey no special meaning. After all, the names alone tell us little about how these families lived here; they tell us little about how the Catskills might be different from other rural places.

But if you travel up Haynes Hollow Road, still unpaved more than a century after having been blazed up the steep grade, by the time you reach a surprisingly level patch of land along a high ridge you may have a new appreciation of what it meant to be a Haynes living in Haynes Hollow, along Haynes Hollow Road, just beneath the summit of Haynes Mountain. To the Haynes family, those names held special meanings—about an intention to stay in the mountains, to own the land they lived upon, and to succeed there for themselves and their children. The names tell us how connected to this place that family really was, and so perhaps these names can help connect us to the larger story of the Catskills.

Most of the family names that lie on the Catskill landscape make quieter statements, for they appear on small blocks of stone carved to mark the final resting places of mountain residents. One of these stones sits at the grave shared by Glentworth and Gladys Haynes at the Mount Tremper Rural Cemetery, a little over ten miles from Haynes Mountain as the crow flies. Hayneses had lived in the Catskills for a hundred years when Glen was born in 1906. He grew up in the mountains and would love them always, but as it turned out he was the last of his family to be born in the Catskills. Most likely he will be the last to be buried there, too.

When I can, I visit the Haynes gravesite, for these are my grandparents who lie buried in this mountain soil. I knew them well in life, having visited them once or twice a year at their Kingston home, just outside the Catskills. We traveled through the mountains together, and on a couple occasions we visited my grandfather's boyhood home in Highmount, just a few miles from Haynes Hollow. While there, I am certain I heard much about the Grand Hotel, which sat on the hill above his old home, and about how my grandfather's family made money in various ways from the tourists who came there. But we did not need to be in Highmount to hear about life in the Catskills, for my grandfather was a wonderful storyteller, and his stories were almost always set in the mountains, when he was a boy. And so, even though I have never lived in the Catskills, I had reason to know more about these mountains than most outsiders even before I began work on this book about their history. Given my grandfather's love of this region, when he passed away I felt compelled to learn even more.

I grew up far from the Catskills, in Cincinnati, and after living in upstate New York for five years, I went farther away to graduate school, where I wrote a book about industrial cities. Afterwards, I began this project thinking I might study some rural place where I could investigate issues of land use, natural resource exploitation, and the growth of the conservation movement. I quickly decided to research the Catskills, in part because of my personal ties, but also because I knew these mountains to have a rich cultural history, from the Hudson River landscape paintings to the Woodstock Festival. The Catskills have been a playground to the masses of New York, as well as the stomping grounds of some extraordinary individuals, from Thomas Cole to John Burroughs to Bob Dylan. The Adirondacks, the other New York mountain range, have received lots of attention from historians, both academic and popular, and so initially I thought I might write a corrective history, one that gave the Catskills their due, placing them within the grand narrative of our nation's tourism and conservation history.[1] After all, this mountain region has been remarkably important to America's cultural and environmental history. Its topography inspired the quintessential nineteenth-century landscape images; its tourist industry helped set national expectations for American vacationing. In turn, it was the home of the nation's greatest land-scape painter, one of its most popular nature writers, and its finest folk musician.

I began this project, then, assuming that tucked in these prominent biographies there must be powerful Catskills stories that had yet to be told. After years of research, however, I've finally come to believe that my grandfather's story says as much about the changing nature of the Cat-skills as any of these more famous biographies. I have put him up front because his life so thoroughly reflects the themes of this book: the blend-ing of city and country that occurred in the mountains, and the chang-ing relationship Americans have had, here and elsewhere, with the countryside and with nature itself.

Tracking the Haynes family through the six generations that they resided in these mountains can tell us much about life in the Catskills, and how New York City's growth influenced both Catskills families and landscapes. Three generations of Haynes had made their living in the mountains more or less unconnected to the city, farming in the Dry Brook Valley, where Judson Haynes and his brother had settled around 1800 and into which Haynes Hollow runs.[2] But, in an evolving and complex relationship, the growing city encouraged changes in the lives of Catskills residents. This became particularly evident in the life of Edgar Haynes, who, after having worked in the employ of the Ulster and Delaware Rail-road in the early 1870s, opened a summer hotel, Haynes House, in Oliv-erea, where the family hoped to capitalize on the growing tourist industry by putting up guests drawn to nearby Slide Mountain and other Catskills peaks. By the 1880s, thousands of New York City tourists made the short trip to the mountains, and boardinghouses and hotels, like Haynes House, sprung up throughout the region and, along with the carriage roads and hiking trails, helped create a tourist landscape in the mountains. Thus, mak-ing the Catskills landscape and the region's distinctive culture became a collaborative effort: a process that mixed the capital, labor, interests, and ideas from both the city and the country.

But there is more to this city-country relationship than just the shared responsibility for the mountain environment, for in this story, too, is evidence of how the growth of American cities encouraged new types of interaction with nature, with the countryside. Over the course of the nineteenth century and into the twentieth, more Americans expe-rienced country landscapes as tourists and came to know nature primarily through leisure, as visitors. Although this was a broad, sweeping process, it operated through the lives of individuals, as is made especially clear in the life of Glen Haynes, one of Edgar's grandsons. Despite being born and raised in the Catskills, Glen moved to the city, assuring that his relationship with the mountains would change—that he would think of them in new ways. Because he made his living outside the mountains, Glen could develop a conservative view toward the region, one that emphasized the conservation of natural resources and the preservation of the unique Catskills culture and landscape. This type of thinking was representative of the reconception of nature that lay at the core of an evolving environmental consciousness that still holds so much influence over the countryside.

Glen was born in Highmount, where his parents, Clair and Grace Haynes, had moved several years earlier in the hopes of making a living from the thriving tourist industry. Clair operated a taxi service and opened a souvenir shop and ice cream parlor near the Ulster and Delaware train station, which delivered thousands of summer tourists, most of them from New York City. The Hayneses came to know many of the seasonal tourists quite well, and when their second son was born, they named him after a wealthy Brooklyn physician, Glentworth Butler, who owned a summer home in Highmount and with whom the Haynes family had a long relationship.[3]

The young Glen helped his parents in their various tourist-related enterprises, but even before the Great Depression tourism in Highmount and nearby Pine Hill had begun to decline. Before the stock market crash of 1929, Glen sought work in New York City. Writing home from his 95th Street apartment that spring, Glen described his job at the Pennsylvania Hotel, across from Penn Station, and his adventures in the city, where he took in movies and visited the zoo. With a population of nearly seven million people, New York City could hardly be less like Glen's Highmount home. Hoping to make his mother feel more at ease about his absence, Glen suggested that she would "more than likely see me Sunday after next getting off that 4:15 bus" in Pine Hill, a reassurance that also indicated how connected these two very different places actually were.[4]

Though the easy transportation to and from the city allowed frequent trips back to the mountains, Glen stayed many years in New York, where he and his wife Gladys, born on a Delaware County farm, started their family. Glen took more promising work on the other side of Penn Station, at the 8th Avenue post office, where he sorted mail. Eventually, Glen found a postal position on the Ulster and Delaware Railroad, which allowed him to move his family to Kingston, within sight of the mountains. When the Ulster and Delaware ceased operations, Glen sorted mail on West Shore trains as they traveled from Weehawken to Albany. After his shift, Glen rode the train home, to the Kingston station. Although his work kept him away from his wife and his daughter Gail for long hours during the week, nearly every weekend he took his family to the mountains, to visit relatives, pick berries, swim, ski, or simply rest in the cool air around the Ashokan Reservoir aerators, where fountains shot city-bound waters into the air before they entered the Catskill Aqueduct. So, for Glen the countryside had become a place of leisure, a place to escape the demands of everyday life in the city, just as it had for all of those tourists who had traveled up to Highmount earlier in the century. Glen and Gladys lived long lives in Kingston, and kept strong ties to the mountains, but they both died in Cincinnati near the home of their daughter.

Even in this quick telling, the story of the Haynes family reveals much about changes taking place in the Catskills over the course of the last two centuries, many of them related to the growing importance of New York City. Judson made a living on the land, like many immigrants to the Catskills area. By the time his grandson Edgar tried to make it on his own, summer boarders would supplement a modest farm income. Edgar's son Clair relied almost entirely on summer visitors to support his family. He owned land, about five acres, but he was not a farmer, an occupation that became increasingly rare in the mountains over the twentieth century. The growing role of New York City in Catskills' lives is most evident in Glen's story. Limited opportunities in the Highmount area forced him to move away from home. Like so many other Americans fleeing rural stagnation in the 1920s, he chose the most logical destination to seek a brighter future—the city itself. It is one of the great storylines in American history—country boy comes to the big city. We imagine his awe at the size of the place, the buildings, the crowded sidewalks; we imagine his awkwardness in making his way in foreign territory, unfamiliar with urban customs and the pace of city life. We feel his loneliness and isolation, his pining for the comforts of his country home.[5]

Still, Glen succeeded in the city, and, though we ought not make too much of this success, perhaps it tells us something about his preparation for city life as he grew up in the mountains. Surrounded by forests and open lands, as a child Glen was also surrounded by city folk, at least during the summer months. He grew up accustomed to their habits, their dialects, their demands. Some of the tourists, those who came year after year, he knew quite well. He formed great, lasting friendships. He grew up enjoying the Grand Hotel orchestra, and, I imagine, he had occasion to partake of the fine foods served to the guests. Since the city was just about four hours away, by age twenty-three, when he finally moved to New York, he had visited several times before, including stays at the Brooklyn home of his good friend Jimmy Butler, son of Glen's namesake. When Glen did arrive in the city seeking work, he was not actually alone. His older brother already lived in the city, as did so many families he had come to know while working around the hotel. He even carried a letter of introduction from *Brooklyn Daily Eagle* editor Herbert Foster Gunnison, who had come to know Glen during many years of summer vacations in Highmount. In other words, life in the Catskills had prepared Glen well for life in the city. He had a taste for what it could offer, he had a sense of its culture, and he had a safety net of friends and family to help him navigate his new life.[6]

Still, Glen returned to the mountains, at least to the degree that he thought he could, no doubt encouraged by his wife, who, raised in dairy country, never felt at home in the city or even in the New Jersey suburbs where they lived for a time. Eventually, regular trips back into the mountains from Kingston kept them connected to home. They showed off their Catskills to their daughter and their two grandsons, of which I am the younger, and late in life Glen espoused a preservationist attitude, supporting efforts to protect the Catskills, to keep the mountains as he had always known them. Glen's great-great-great-grandfather had come to the mountains expecting to change them, to clear the land and make a living there; Glen left the mountains to make a living and then hoped his Catskills would stay the same forever.

In addition to the visits I made growing up, I passed through the Catskills frequently in the 1980s and 1990s, taking several different routes. Most often I traveled on Route 28, through, or near, the villages of Fleischmanns, Highmount, and Pine Hill, on my way from Colgate University to Kingston. The mountains were beautiful, I thought, but the cultural landscape was in shambles mostly, cluttered with listing, unpainted buildings. For variety, sometimes I took the more northerly route, 23a, through Prattsville, Hunter, and Tannersville, where the economy looked more lively, due to the ski industry, but still unsteady, as tourist towns often appear in the off-season. Tellingly, I never stopped at the most famous spots in the region—the Catskill Mountain House overlook and

Kaaterskill Falls. Once among the most visited rural places in America, by the 1980s they were so little talked about that I knew nothing of them, even though I drove within a few miles of both. Eventually I took the more southerly Route 17, through Liberty and Livingston Manor, when I began to visit my future wife in Westchester County. On Route 17, I saw less of the region, other than the hills, as the four-lane highway kept me farther from towns, farther from the older cultural landscape—except the fading billboards advertising the region's fading hotels. Together these three roads represent the three major routes through the Catskills region, both currently and historically, and so collectively my trips gave me a sense of the region's diversity and its prosperity, or lack thereof.

During all this traveling through the mountains, I came to believe that the Catskills reveal their history more readily than most American places, for the countryside holds ample evidence of a long economic decline. Hotel ruins punctuate the landscape, as do small towns that have failed to shrink fast enough to keep pace with their declining fortunes. Riding through Fleischmanns, Highmount, and Pine Hill, I couldn't tell if these places had ever been prosperous, but I knew they had been busier. As I trained to be an environmental historian, I began to read in this landscape the themes of the American past, laid out in the second-growth forests that replaced farm fields in the region's valleys, the wilderness preserves that topped the highest peaks, and the massive reservoirs that supplied pure water to a faraway city. Here was physical evidence of agriculture's decline in eastern America, the successful movement to preserve wild places for the use of an increasingly urban population, as well as the imposition of the city upon the country to supply a basic human need. The more I learned, the better I became at finding evidence of the past in more than just the hotel ruins and declining towns.

While my training encouraged me to find evidence of change in the landscape, I have come to realize that most urban visitors are unlikely to engage in the same activity. Every scene in the country suggests stasis to urban eyes, even though every one contains clues to the waves of change that have rushed through these mountains. Perhaps the peace and quiet of the country are enough to convince visitors from more hectic places that nothing much happens in the country—ever. What follows provides ample evidence that this is clearly not the case. This place has a long and, I think, a fascinating history.

My own family's history may seem an odd place to begin a book that primarily concerns the cultural causes of environmental change and evolving ideas about rural landscapes. Environmental histories more commonly begin with a purely descriptive chapter that sets the scene, acquaints readers with the place under study.[7] Here readers learn of the flora and fauna, the soils and topography, even the climate. At the very least readers learn the boundaries of the place. Sometimes Native Americans occupy the landscape portrayed in this setting, but often it poses momentarily unchanged by human intrusion, Eden before the fall. Unlike many regional environmental histories, then, this one does not begin with that physical description of the place, except only in the most general way with the brief accounts of the three routes through the mountains. The definition of the Catskills has changed so dramatically over the last three centuries that to offer some presettlement description would be difficult. Indeed, just where the Catskills are has long been a matter of controversy and, more surprisingly, remarkable change. Differing definitions have developed over time, including those created by the city's water supply maps, which demarcate watersheds above their dams; the state's Department of Environmental Conservation maps, which reveal the "Blue Line" that surrounds the Catskill Park; and the state's 1970s Catskill Study boundaries, which included much more than just the mountainous region in Ulster, Greene, Sullivan, Delaware, and Schoharie counties. History has so frequently and thoroughly changed the Catskills that descriptions can hold only for an era, not for all time. In one of the most dramatic changes, twentieth-century urban tourists caused the Catskills to move, at least in common conception, toward the city, actually out of the mountains to the foothills of Sullivan County. Indeed, mention the Catskills to New Yorkers today, as I frequently have in the process of researching this book, and invariably they will assume you are referring to the region known as the Borscht Belt, the Jewish Catskills resort area around Monticello and Liberty. No doubt a tourist in the 1850s would be dumbfounded by a late twentieth-century definition of the Catskills, which prominently featured a region fully outside the mountains. Clearly the Catskills have long been a cultural construction as much as a geological feature.

Beginning with the Haynes genealogy allows me to avoid this problem of defining the Catskills, and to make an additional very important point. My family's history suggests the difficulty of assigning responsibility for the changes that took place in the mountains. Obviously local residents shaped the mountains, clearing fields, farming, building villages, and making a living in a variety of ways. In arguing that New York City residents helped make and remake the mountains—both environmentally and culturally—I do not intend to diminish the importance of these local actors. But urbanites, especially from New York City, made a series of demands on the region, each of which initiated changes in the mountains. At some point in my research I concluded that I would write a book about the power of the city over the country, assuming that the lives of individuals would help illustrate the inequality of the relationship. Reality proved much more complex, since so many individuals mixed the two places so thoroughly in their own lives, as clearly evidenced in the life—and even the name—of Glen Haynes. For two centuries, many country folk have moved to the city, for part of the year or some portion of their lives, often trying to make the money that could save their mountain homes. Conversely, city folk have gone to the mountains, for part of the year or parts of their lives, until the mountains felt like home. More than just disembodied economic and cultural ties link these two places; they are joined by countless biographies—some unknown, such as that of Glen Haynes, but some quite famous, such as those of financier Jay Gould and naturalist John Burroughs, both born in the town of Roxbury, on the western edge of the Catskills, and both of whom spent considerable time away in the city. These individual and familial connections between the two regions—city and country—blur the distinction between insiders and outsiders. What is most important in the story that follows, however, is that this mixing of lives represents a blending of city and country. As this mixing occurred, in a very real sense the Catskills became an integral part of the urban landscape. This landscape is the result of a long, often contentious collaboration between city and country, one in which new ideas of nature and the countryside took hold.

Acknowledgments

I have accumulated a great number of debts in the course of researching and writing this book. Many people aided my research, including friends like Will Sears, who let me stay with him in Washington as I worked at the Library of Congress; Brian and Debra Perrotto, who kept me company when the libraries closed in Albany; and David and Susan Beattie, who put me up in Olive as I wandered around the Catskills. Among those who helped me in archives, museums, and libraries were Shirley McGrath and Raymond Beecher of the Greene County Historical Society, Dean M. Rogers of the Vassar College Rare Books and Archives, Jerold Pepper at the Adirondack Museum, Nancy Dean and Brenda Marston at Cornell University Rare Books and Manuscripts, and Carl Peterson and Mike Poulin at Colgate University's Case Library.

Evelyn Bennett of the Town of Shandaken Historical Society in Pine Hill stayed late as I read through the *Pine Hill Sentinel,* creating a lasting, happy memory for me as I showed her references to my great-grandfather in the paper. I also received enthusiastic support from Linda Wurm and Andrew Dresser at the Zadock Pratt Museum, where I was treated to lunch and lively conversation. (I was very saddened to hear that Andrew passed away before I could finish this book.) Although we only spoke on the phone, John Mundt was particularly kind in allowing me to use the wonderful library of the Anglers' Club of New York (where Mary O'Malley made me an excellent lunch—one senses from the free lunches that people really understand how tight historians' budgets can be!).

Special thanks to James D. Folts at the New York State Archives, whose detailed knowledge of the collections held in Albany is stunning. He is a model of professionalism and efficiency, making research at the State Archives a joy. Nina Postupack and Salvatore Greco of the Ulster County Clerk's Office located and arranged for me to purchase the single most important source I used in writing this book—the Ashokan Reservoir Transcripts, which are truly a treasure. Sylvia Rozzelle, Olive's town clerk, was especially helpful to me and has done a great service to her community in seeking out and storing documents related to the history of that fascinating place.

I also relied on archivists, librarians, curators, and volunteers whose names remain unknown to me, including those at the New York Public Library, Library of Congress, Kingston Public, Sullivan County Historical Society, the Ontario & Western Historical Society, Haines Falls Public Library, Phoenicia Library, the Thomas Cole National Historic Site at Cedar Grove, Olana (Frederick Church's home), and the New York State Historical Association Library.

I received important summer research funding from the New Jersey Institute of Technology, where I taught at the outset of this project, and from the University of Cincinnati's University Research Counsel. The Taft Memorial Fund here at U.C. also provided a summer research grant, as did the National Endowment for the Humanities. Any views, findings, conclusions, or recommendations expressed in this book do not necessarily reflect those of the National Endowment for the Humanities. I also received a Larry J. Hackman Research grant to facilitate the use of the collections at the New York State Archives.

I talked with many, many Catskills residents as I conducted my research (and vacationed) in the mountains, including Bob Gildersleeve, who walked with me and my family through the woods around Kaaterskill Falls, and Tom Alworth, who talked with me about the Catskills Center for Conservation and Development and our mutual appreciation for John Burroughs. I would also like to thank Diane Galusha, who chatted with me about the book and read chapter 5 and the epilogue, improving both.

Several others have aided with the writing of this work, including Phil Terrie, who read the chapter on wilderness and made it better, and Michael Kudish, who read the first chapter very closely, catching some errors and sharpening some prose. David Soll, just embarking on his own Catskills project, read chapter 5 and prevented me from making embarrassing errors. My former colleague Linda Przybyszewski read some of my Catskills work and offered helpful suggestions. My good friend and valued colleague Wendy Kline also read large parts of the manuscript and offered suggestions and much-needed encouragement. Several of our graduate students have also helped along the way, including Dan Glenn, Aaron Cowan, and Dawn Spring.

The most important aid I received in writing this book came from Karl Jacoby, Peggy Shaffer, and Bill Cronon. Karl and Peggy commented on the entire draft, and their suggestions were critical to improving this work. Bill's editing, guidance, and encouragement vastly improved the book and kept me on task. Karl, Peggy, and Bill all understood that I had found a topic worthy of an important book, and they each encouraged me to give this topic its due. I hope I have at least partly succeeded. At the University of Washington Press, Julidta Tarver is the model of academic editing. Her colleague Kerrie Maynes provided skilled copy editing, catching more errors than I care to admit and significantly improving the book. Although so many people have helped me along the way, any shortcomings in the work are wholly my responsibility.

My deepest debt is to my family, Jodie, Sarah, and Nina, who forgave my absences and distractions over the last seven years. Jodie has always been my first editor, and, though she does not think so, she is my most important reader, the one who gives me confidence as well as advice. Thanks too to my mother, Gail Stradling, who helped me find materials related to her father and grandfather, and discussed this project with relatives she knows better than I. In part, this book is an apology to my grandfather, Glen Haynes, for the many times I failed to listen and learn from him as he told stories about his young life in the mountains. I was too young myself to understand how much I could take from them. Though I can never replace the stories I lost when he died, I have tried to write a narrative in which he would have found much that was familiar, and from which he would have taken some pride.

Making Mountains

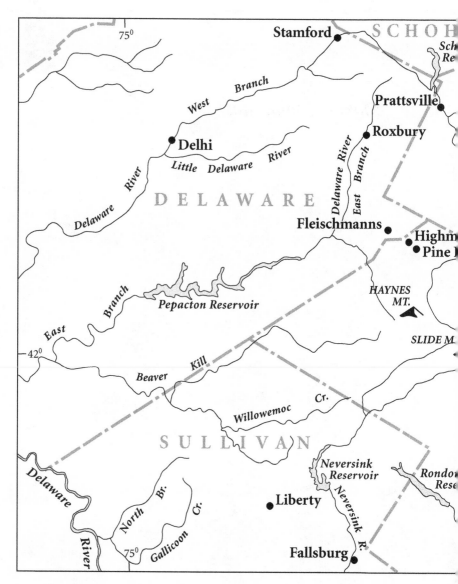

Map 1 The Catskills region.

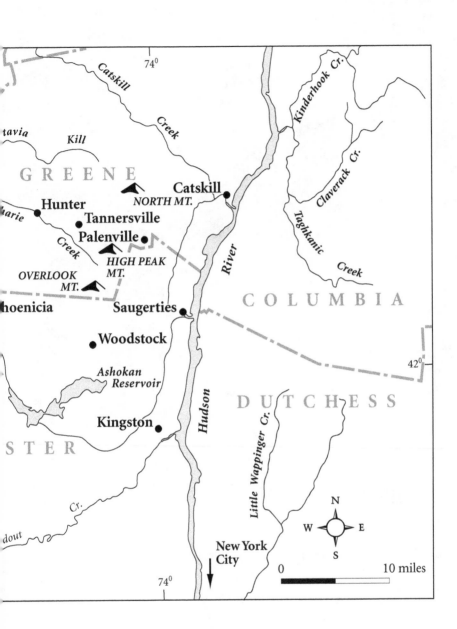

Introduction

Types of the Permanent and Unchanging

The hills and the mountains grow old and pass away in geologic time as invariably as the snow bank in spring, and yet in our little life they are the types of the permanent and unchanging.

—John Burroughs, 1922

The everlasting hills! They are here to stay. How they speak to the eternity of Him who laid their foundations. Kingdoms pass away; tribes, nations, dynasties flow along like these balling streams, but the great mountains, solemn, sublime and silent, are here always.

—Reverend Irenaeus Prime, 1884

John Burroughs was the most popular nature writer of his time. Though he traveled widely and wrote on a great variety of topics and places, he was a Catskills native, and his many essays on those mountains spanned his more than half-century career, from the 1860s into the 1920s. Through his long life, Burroughs moved back and forth from the mountains and a number of places that served as his home, including Washington, DC, and Riverby, his long-time estate on the banks of the Hudson. On his trips back to the Catskills, he found ample evidence of change in the mountains. Abandoned and run-down bark-peeler's cabins gave him shelter during his youthful backwoods tramps; impoverished and run-down farms saddened him as he approached his life's end. One need not be as observant as Burroughs to perceive the waves of change that washed over the mountains. The great stands of hemlock receded, as did most of the Catskills forests. Farms filled the valleys, and then they too mostly receded. Great hotels dotted the mountains, and, along with other lodgings, provided summer retreats for thousands of urban tourists. The hotels too receded over time, though mostly after Burroughs himself had passed. Ironically, then, late in life, as Burroughs reflected back on his Catskills boyhood, his thoughts turned to the permanence suggested by the mountains themselves. People had come and gone, left their marks here and there, left ruins that evidenced their lives, but the mountains were everlasting. As Burroughs looked out over a rapidly changing landscape, where agriculture was increasingly failing, the mountains, he thought, were "permanent and unchanging." In that, at least, he took some comfort.

It is just this kind of thinking, so common over the past two centuries, that hides so much human history in the mountains. Regularly, tourists passing through the mountains literally overlooked farm fields, gazed into woodlots beyond, and declared the site a perfect wilderness. Many hikers commented on the trackless wilderness they explored in the mountains, failing to dwell on the wide, worn paths that led them through it. Some visitors stood on a wooden platform and watched wild torrents fall, then failed to mention the dam that held back the waters until let loose for the display, or even the platform that allowed the viewers the finest perspective for such a poetic demonstration of nature's sublimity. Tourists waded by the thousands into mountain streams and declared them pure and sweet. Indeed, so many visitors to the region, over so long a period, commented on the wild nature of the mountains, on their very permanence, that we might mistake their accumulated testimonies as evidence of actual stasis in the Catskills. Most comments on the everlasting nature of the hills came from visitors, who, unlike Burroughs, had never made a home in the mountains. They were unlikely to see changes taking place in the Catskills over time, but when they did, they were likely to lament them.

This book is mostly about the mountains, about changes taking place in the Catskills economy and landscape. Despite this rural focus, the changes described here happened largely because of changes taking place at some distance, in the city. To understand what happened in the Catskills, one must explain why so many New Yorkers came to the mountains and saw them as they did—so incompletely, so inaccurately. Why were they unlikely to see evidence of change in the mountains? More important, why did so many city residents come to regret those changes they did see in the countryside?

New York City grew explosively in the nineteenth century, drawing new residents from both Europe and rural America. They came in such large numbers because city life was better than country life in fundamental ways, especially in economic prospects and cultural amenities. The city offered education, social connections, and the opportunity to rise. But city life was so evidently worse than country life, too, particularly as cities continued to grow. The impure air, suspect water, crowd diseases, the crowds themselves—all of this could be offensive, even threatening, especially to the city's growing middle class. Over time city residents would work to solve the problems of urbanity, and they would meet with some success, but even if the city's water became more reliable, its odors less offensive, its streets less foul, some urban flaws simply could not be overcome. The city remained crowded, loud, chaotic, and overwhelmingly unnatural as compared to the country. These defects in urban living became important topics of conversation in a nation that took great pride in its rural birth, in the character of its farmers, in the productivity of its farms.

The flaws of the city constituted an important aspect of the growing disparity between city and country, but even taken together they did not constitute the most obvious difference between those two types of places. During the nineteenth century, the city, at its core and its edges, became the place where Americans accepted change, even celebrated it. Cities readily displayed the nation's economic growth and prosperity. In particular, New York City's physical structure changed dramatically, especially during the long period of stunning growth that began in the 1820s, with new buildings, ever grander in size and appointments, appearing in new architectural styles. The latest technologies, so bright and fast, so dizzyingly effective, came together in the city, helping to remake continually America's urban culture and economy. Despite occasional laments about what was lost as the old gave way to the new, the city became the place of change. Acceptance of an ever-changing city was facilitated by awareness that some places would remain the same—church sanctuaries, living rooms, and the countryside. That rural America would remain as it always had been decreased urban trepidation about what might come next in the city. And so, the undeniable draw of urbanity and its irreparable flaws placed dual pressures on rural America, draining its vitality by luring away its people, and creating expectations of what the countryside should be, what it should remain.

Nineteenth-century city dwellers could conceive of the countryside as static because they were increasingly removed from it. This distance between city and country was much more than geographical, of course. The city changed so thoroughly, became so different from the countryside, that even frequent urban visitors to rural landscapes failed to accurately interpret what they saw. Outside the city, urban eyes were drawn to static scenes, to rusticity, to quaintness, to soothing natural prospects.

Even the many ruins that dotted the countryside by the late 1800s—the unmended milldams, the unused mills, the empty tanneries, and the ghost towns around them—projected timelessness to urban eyes. In reality, of course, the ruins marked not just the passage of time but the passing of an era. Still, urban pens and brushes reinforced images of stasis, raising the expectation that the rural landscape should always serve to calm the anxious urban crowds. And so, distance from the countryside allowed city residents to create new abstractions of nature and rural landscapes. They idealized rural places, how they appeared and what purposes they served, a process that so evidently took place in the Catskills.[1]

By the mid-1800s, tourism had become the predominant means by which urbanites experienced nature. Demographic growth and industrialization had created increasingly unnatural cities, forcing residents to seek nature outside their communities. At the same time, city residents increasingly took vacation trips to the countryside, as wealth spread and culture more readily accepted such pursuits of leisure. Tourism further encouraged the idealization of rural landscapes, as city residents began to associate work with the metropolis, and leisure and consumption with the country. In touring rural America, using it as a foil for urban life, middle-class city residents developed new conceptions of nature and the countryside more generally. By late century, even those who accepted and encouraged change in the city, those of progressive politics, would have a remarkably conservative relationship to the countryside. There they would demand preservation—the preservation of both rural lands and rural cultures, the preservation of their idealized retreats. In other words, the modern environmental consciousness, which favored preservation of rural, natural places, had long incubated in urban America, intensifying as demographic growth, industrialization, and technological innovation transformed the metropolis.

The extensive literature on the Catskills reveals a growing fascination with the wild in the mountains, especially in the wealth of passionate prose written by and for urban tourists in the second half of the 1800s. Romanticism inspired much of the writing, which was laced with references to God's power in nature and, in turn, nature's power over its human observers. Still, the era's romantic notions of nature and its purple prose do not fully explain the bald hyperbole of the descriptions. Writers commonly compared the Catskills to Europe's most beautiful mountains. In 1884, historian J. B. Beers wrote that the Catskills "contain within their bounds probably more varied and beautiful scenery than can be found outside of Switzerland," conceding, however, that the New York mountains may not be as sublime. Writing in 1881, lithographer Henry Schile considered the term "American Switzerland" much deserved by the Catskills. "For him who has seen, and is acquainted with, the black forests and Switzerland, and who has viewed the Catskills," he declared, "the difference will be but one of the historical aspects of the country." For the benefit of his New York readers, Schile concluded, "It seems as if the gods, in all their inscrutable wisdom had ordained that this great city should grow up in the vicinity of the Catskills, that it might have within easy reach, a place of recreation unsurpassed in the splendor of its scenery."[2]

Actually, Schile got it backwards. As the great city of New York grew, it became clear that the mountains would have to grow as well. A rather unassuming cluster of mountains—beautiful yes, but nowhere rising above 4,204 feet—would have to carry comparisons with Switzerland's Alps, where the tallest peak is fully 11,000 feet higher. Did people really think North and South mountains resembled the Matterhorn or the Jungfrau? Much has been made of the young nation's search for cultural security—some area in which comparisons with Europe were favorable. The landscape, the American expanse, its variety and beauty could serve that purpose. Americans could substitute great natural history for human history.[3] America had no castles, no massive cathedrals, no ruins of empires past, but it had big trees, long rivers, and glorious mountains. While surely this assessment of America's cultural need is accurate, it does not explain why so many writers fixated on the Catskills. With the Rockies well known, the Smokies close at hand, and the Adirondacks more spectacular, why did so many writers choose the lowly Catskills as America's standard-bearer?

The answer to this riddle lay just a hundred miles downstream, where the growing city of New York, like the nation as a whole, needed to announce its importance. It would be the nation's metropolis and, eventually, the world's. Through the middle decades of the 1800s, in the words of historian David Scobey, "the city grew from a leading port to the organizing center of American capitalism."[4] In the same way that the continent's wild nature, its great expanses and spectacular elevations, became central to Americans' fledgling nationalism, so too would a spectacular hinterland legitimize New York City's position as the nation's most important city, even though it did not hold the nation's capitol. Thus, claiming to have its own Alps just up the river was part of New York City's larger claim to national significance. Just as important, these exaggerated imaginings of the Catskills reveal just how thoroughly urbanites could idealize the mountains and how much influence the city would have over conceptions of the Catskills.

To truly understand the rich history of the Catskills, one must travel back and forth between the city and the mountains, following the paths set by Thomas Cole, John Burroughs, Bob Dylan, and literally millions of other individuals. The Catskills have played an important role in the history of the nation's tourism and the development of the modern environmental consciousness precisely because of the city more than a hundred miles to the south. Not only have the people of the city helped shape the Catskills, they have done so repeatedly, even constantly. Since the 1820s, the mountains have served variously as an extractive site for natural resources, a wilderness icon, a vacationland, the best source of fresh water, an ideal spot for a second home, and the very representation of constancy in an ever-changing world. Thus, over the past two hundred years, the mountains have filled many different needs for urbanites, and to do so the mountains have had to change, both in conception and reality.

A wide variety of documents point to the importance of the city-country relationship in the making of the Catskills, including works of fiction by the city's authors, masterful mountain landscapes painted for the city's customers, engineering studies of mountain watersheds conducted by the city as it searched for a new water supply, and a massive catalogue of tourist literature written for urban vacationers. So varied are the connections between the mountains and the city, that the history of the Catskills might serve as a confirmation of William Cronon's argument in *Nature's Metropolis*, which blurs the distinctions between city and country, noting that the history of Chicago (or any city) must be told in conjunction with those of the landscapes that have supported urban growth. *Nature's Metropolis* emphasizes economic connections—the connections of the capitalist market that drew together very distant places, and in the process transformed both. Like so many environmental histories, *Nature's Metropolis* describes waves of transformation—destruction and degradation, from the environmentalist perspective—wrought by the expansion of the capitalist market. In the end, Cronon reminds us that although our culture holds city and country as polar opposites, they have in fact created each other and are thus intimately linked.[5]

Environmental historians, including Cronon, have generally described the expansion of the capitalist market in geographical terms, and so they follow frontiers as they move across landscapes. Like *Nature's Metropolis*, many foundational texts in environmental history catalogue and explain environmental decline, including Cronon's earlier work, *Changes in the Land*, and the seminal works of Donald Worster, *Dust Bowl* and *Rivers of Empire*, all of which describe how the nation's growing capitalist economy diminished the natural environment.[6] Through these and other works, environmental history provides a series of declension narratives with a powerful political message: economic growth has come with a staggering environmental cost. In other words, with some exceptions, the field of environmental history has told a series of stories about the arrival of the market and the damage it has wrought. Unfortunately, all too often, then the story stops.

To understand what happens next, what becomes of a place after the initial transformations wrought by market connections, I have employed a different methodology. Instead of an examination of a series of places designed to determine the scope of New York City's relationship with the country around, this book is a deep history of the city's complex relationship with one relatively small area. Thus, what follows is a series of thematic chapters—which are also roughly chronological—that trace the shifting relationship between the city and the mountains, the growing importance of tourism in America's interaction with nature, and the development of a preservationist ethic. In the first decades of the 1800s, the mountains began supplying a series of natural resources to the market. While the region's butter, timber, and bluestone found their way to many destinations, in one industry—tanning—the New York City-Catskills connection was nearly complete, and the business transformed mountain forests before the midcentury. Although agriculture and natural resource extraction have both persisted in the mountains, by the latter half of the nineteenth century, their importance to the Catskills economy had receded. These industries did encourage new uses of the mountains, however, by literally opening up the region, with paths, roads, and railroads, all of which would allow a growing legion of urban tourists to make their way into the mountains and into the woods. Struggling agriculture and industry would provide picturesque scenes and romantic ruins for touring literati and artists. In turn, authors like Washington Irving and James Fenimore Cooper helped create new, powerful images of the mountains. Even more important, landscape painters, following the lead of Cole, provided their largely urban market with myriad Catskills canvases, each conveying the inspirational power of the mountains. Altogether, artists of pen and brush created popular cultural associations. As tourists flocked to the Catskills, most arrived in a place with which they had some familiarity, at least through fictional tales and idealized landscape imagery. To meet the needs of the tourist market, both locals and outsiders created a new landscape of hotels, trails, carriage paths—an infrastructure of tourism. By the late 1800s, the Catskills' utility for urban tourism had become so evident that the state protected the forestlands, eventually declaring them "wild forever" to satisfy city residents who demanded some wilderness easily accessible to the city. Almost simultaneously, the ever-growing demand for water sent civil engineers to the mountains, where in the twentieth century two supply systems would transform the relationship between New York City and the mountains forever.

In the chapters that follow, then, the complex relationship between New York and the mountains carries the narrative down long digressions, and at points these departures may seem to move well beyond the central themes concerning the connections between city and country that shaped Catskills landscapes. But the accumulation of these stories—from Rip Van Winkle's long sleep, Cole's brilliant landscapes, Burroughs's tramps, the Ashokan Reservoir's construction, Jews' bungalow summers, and Dylan, The Band, and *Music from Big Pink*—represents the real weight of the New York–Catskill relationship. All this and more embodies the making of one of America's distinctive places, one built through a collaboration of country and city, of local and urban hands, capital, and ideas. The accumulation of these stories—the history of the Catskills— also describes the construction of a culture, at once adamantly rural, even in conflict with the city, and beholden to the metropolis that has made the Catskills among the most celebrated mountains in our nation's history.

A number of historians have set out to describe the relationship between city and country, and most have labeled it in one way or another "imperial." Cultural historian Raymond Williams produced an early classic on the subject in 1973, in which he describes the changing images of the country and the city in English literature. Williams clearly reveals how much of the relationship between city and country lies outside market connections, how much is cultural, found in the pages of literature, in the ideas that help define places. This theme is remarkably strong in Catskills history, where a changing urban culture cast new meanings and values upon rural places. The Catskills have long occupied an important place in New York City's powerful cultural hinterland, and over time, urbanites have placed heavy cultural demands upon the mountains, especially through a long love affair with Hudson River art in the mid-1800s and through a growing appreciation for second-home ownership in the late 1900s. Quite simply, the deepest and most lasting changes that have occurred in the mountains reflect the evolution of the city's culture, especially changing tastes and values, and not innovations within the economy. As Marjorie Hope Nicolson wrote in her seminal work on the development of mountain aesthetics, "we see in Nature what we have been taught to look for, we feel what we have been prepared to feel."[7] Urban culture taught New Yorkers to look to the mountains for inspiration—and health, and repose, and retreat.

Raymond Williams hoped to do much more in his work than reveal the changing nature of the cultural relationship between city and country. His argument goes well beyond literature, to the imperial imperatives of capitalism that reshaped both city and country. For Williams, the culture that emanated from industrial cities was just part of the larger imperialism that described the urban relationship to the countryside.[8] And so Williams' argument has much in common with Cronon's, for in both the growing city primarily represents the power of the capitalist market to reorganize society, to reorder the landscape. In this articulation, then, the city is caught within economic imperatives as surely as the county, but other historians describe the relationship in a way that places the city—and its powerful residents—in command. In his comprehensive history of water in California, Norris Hundley describes in detail the "urban imperialism" that brought water to the growing cities of Los Angeles and San Francisco.[9] Gray Brechin goes further in his discussion of "Imperial San Francisco," describing that city's ability to acquire energy and water. "As a city grows," Brechin notes, "so does both its reach and its power to transform the nonhuman world on which its people depend." This growing "urban Maelstrom," as Brechin calls it, pulls toward itself a larger and larger hinterland, reordering the countryside around. For Brechin the process occurs largely at the hands of the city's elite, the powerful, the wealthy, and the "thought shapers" who encouraged, directed, and profited from the city's growth.[10]

The imperial stories Hundley and Brechin tell involve control of the hinterland's resources and the accumulation of wealth in the city, but of course the city-country relationship is more complex than that. In his study of twentieth-century tourism in the American West, Hal Rothman describes a growing imperial relationship created largely by urban tourists moving through rural landscapes. "Tourism is the most colonial of colonial economies," he concludes. "When tourism creates sufficient wealth, it becomes too important to be left to the locals. Power moves away from local decision makers," and at the same time, the tourist landscape, altered to suit the expectations of the tourists, loses its authenticity. In this way, according to Rothman, tourism in the West has been a "devil's bargain" for rural communities that had hoped tourist development would bring wealth but not change.[11]

Much of the Catskills history that follows might be used to support these imperial models. Surely the "thought shapers" of New York, like those of Brechin's San Francisco, had remarkable influence over the Catskills, and New York's imperial reach over Catskills water was no less certain than that of Hundley's Los Angeles and San Francisco. And, though beyond the scope of Rothman's work, the Catskills might fit comfortably with his argument concerning the "devil's bargain" of tourism, for few American landscapes have been so transformed to suit the needs of tourists. In these ways, and in others, a real imbalance of power has existed between New York City and the Catskills counties. Catskills natives have not always been victims in this relationship, as many of them grew quite wealthy from New York money, but rarely could they compete with metropolitan power. Generally, only those who anticipated or acceded to urban demands benefited from them. Those who resisted generally lost, even if only in the long run.

Not surprisingly, if one wanted to describe an imperial relationship between the city and the country—between New York and the Catskills— the best story to tell would be that of the water supply. The rapid and consistent growth of New York in the nineteenth century sent city leaders in search of a new, more reliable water supply—twice. Although nothing about the city's growth specifically required that the Catskills supply the water, demographics more or less demanded the redefinition of some significant space as municipal watershed. In the words of geographer Matthew Gandy, the Catskills became part of "a giant metabolic urban system," a system forced to expand to meet the needs of the city's growing population. Gandy argues that capitalism lay at the center of the city's imperial ambitions, but any coastal city of millions must have its thirst slaked by some distant water supply, capitalism or no capitalism. In this instance, and others, the very "urbanness" of the city created demands on the country around it. As the city grew, it could better provide certain resources for its residents, especially cultural and economic resources. At the same time, the city's deficiencies grew all the more apparent. Heightened urbanism—with its population density and intensive land use—sent city residents to the countryside in search of a different set of resources: pure water, fresh air, open space, and solitude. All this and more New Yorkers found in the Catskills. This represents, I think, imperialism of a sort.[12]

Although this imbalance of power has been evident to me throughout my work, I have never been wholly comfortable with the imperial model, and certainly not a model that places the city's elite or its capitalist profit motive as the prime mover of change in the mountains. This model simply leaves too much out; it reflects only part of what happened in the Catskills over the last two hundred years, and perhaps not even the greater part. Early in this project, as I explored this imperial theme, I found myself categorizing important actors as Catskills locals or city folk. I soon grew suspicious of that task's value, however. After all, was long-time Catskill resident Thomas Cole a local, despite having come to the mountains only in his mid-twenties? Was Sanford Gifford more genuinely local because he was born and raised in the Hudson Valley? Was Asher Durand less so because he spent most of his time in the city and tramped through the Catskills mostly in the summer? And what of their paintings—Hudson River landscapes with their own styles and strengths but clearly of the same artistic moment— could they be dissected in some way, attributed partly to the mountains that inspired them and partly to the city where they found their market?

These landscape paintings might symbolize the long and complex relationship between the city and the mountains, for the canvases contain a remarkable blending of urban and rural. Their compositions reflected urban ideas and met urban demands, but they were evidently of the country as well. Just as in the painted landscapes, so too are urban and rural blended in the actual Catskills. What follows is the long history of that blending process, of a landscape shaped by many hands, many minds— some urban, some rural, many that were both. And so this work reveals no conspiratorial power of the city over the country—no real empire. Although the actions of the city's residents and its government have at times caused harm, resentment, and jealousy in the Catskills, just as often urban contributions—everything from pieces of literature to second homes—have gone through a process of naturalization, in which the Catskills culture has accepted the changes, in essence making them native. This naturalization has been especially evident in the instance of the greatest imposition of the city in the mountains—the building of the reservoirs. They have become much more than reminders of the dislocation they caused; they are now, and have long been, important parts of the Catskills landscape: naturalized lakes, native and beautiful, worthy of local pride. These reservoirs are just part of a landscape—and a culture—wrought by collaboration between city and country that blended the ideas, interests, and actions of a wide variety of people from New York and the mountains. This relationship has had its conflicts, imbalances, and even injustices, but it is this collaboration that has made the mountains—and continues to do so.

Before beginning this story, I must make two concessions. First, this book is about the relationship between New York City and the Catskills, but it says very little about the former. In the chapters that follow I say only enough about changes in the city to make sense of the ripples that they sent through the mountains. This may disappoint some readers hoping to learn more about the city itself, but I do believe my focus on the mountains makes sense. Certainly the Catskills influenced the city—especially by sending particular products to urban markets, by shaping the experiences of urban tourists, and by giving up so many of its people who migrated to New York in search of work. However, in a city—especially one as large as New York—one sees the contributions of a thousand places, in the bodies of immigrants, the steel of its buildings, the produce in its markets, etcetera. Although Catskills bluestone colored the city's walks, Catskills scenery covered gallery walls, and Catskills natives lived out city lives, these important contributions might be easily lost in the cultural and economic confluence of the city. And, just as important, they pale in comparison to the changes the city brought to the mountains. Thus, because the relationship was so uneven, this book is primarily about the Catskills.

The second concession concerns how I have conceived of "the city." At times in this book, this phrase refers specifically to New York, or even more specifically to New York's municipal government, as is the case when I discuss the city's acquisition of mountain valleys for the construction of reservoirs. At other times, however, "the city" must represent something less specific. For instance, the cultural images and expectations that helped shape the Catskills came less specifically from New York City than from the nation's broader culture. Thus, in these instances the power of "the city" to remake the mountains really involved the development of a powerful urban culture, one that influenced New Yorkers, Philadelphians, and residents in hundreds of American cities and villages. The influence of New York's writers and artists, and the sheer number of tourists who seasonally fled Manhattan, clearly gave that city a special role in both shaping the nation's urban culture and the mountains, but we cannot forget that residents of other cities also played a role in remaking the Catskills. Thus, at times this story is about "The City"—as New Yorkers are wont to call their home; at other times this is a story about "the city"—a type of place where Americans increasingly lived.

The thematic chapters that follow trace the long collaboration that has created the Catskills landscape, and while the narrative of necessity covers a diversity of topics, one particular theme builds throughout— the theme that opened this introduction. Throughout the nineteenth and twentieth centuries Americans have increasingly accepted the notion that rural culture is static—and that rural landscapes should be static too. During the century of the city's most dramatic growth and industrialization, from about 1830 to 1930, more and more New Yorkers experienced nature through tourism, a process that encouraged the growth of a preservationist ethic. As the city changed seemingly daily, experiencing what historian Max Page describes as "a dynamic upheaval of the urban landscape," New Yorkers were increasingly forced to seek evidence of their culture's past outside the city's boundaries.[13] As developers demolished the old to make way for the new, Manhattan shed evidence of its own history. As early as the late 1800s, New Yorkers hungry for the comfort of the American past sought connections to the nation's history in the city's hinterland. In the mountains, urbanites wearied by the uncertainty of continual change found comfort in the familiar American scenes of everlasting hills, forever wild forests, and the nation's rural past. Visitors erroneously assumed that the constant changes at work in the city had not reached so deep into the woods, that by the Catskills' very distance from the city, the ruggedness of the environment, or by the foresight of conservationists, this natural place survived, untouched. As they commented on the mountains' "everlasting beauty," they reinforced the idea that the Catskills represented original wildness, unchanged by human hands. In an ever-changing world, the mountains—any mountains, not just the Catskills—represented permanence, just as Burroughs had declared as he reminisced about his own mountain boyhood. Ironically, given how much change New Yorkers have encouraged in the Catskills over the past two hundred years, the most lasting influence of city residents has come through the demand that the mountains and their forests stay the same, so that they might continue to connect urbanites to a more settled, more natural, and, especially since September 11, 2001, less frightening past.

While economic and demographic growth made it difficult for the city to accumulate ruins, or even to retain living landmarks of previous eras, the countryside retained its relics, some of which decayed only at the rate demanded by the weather. As rural upstate New York suffered through its long, uneven depression, ongoing now for more than a century, the countryside grew increasingly dissimilar to the city. In the city, the old quickly gave way to the future; in the country, when relics finally succumbed, they tended to give way to the past, seemingly returning the landscape to its pre-settlement appearance. The Catskills landscape is full of "used to be": this used to be the Overlook Hotel; this used to be a tanning village; this used to be a dairy farm. More important, the forests that once again occupy the great majority of the Catskills landscape represent timelessness, the landscape of the east's Edenic past. Urban visitors can easily believe that the past has been preserved in the Catskills, and most rural places, in a way that it generally has not been in the city. Indeed, this theme has become so strongly believed that historian David Walbert has argued, "Even ruralites have, over time, unthinkingly accepted this equation of the rural with the past, for they have been and remain unable to define rurality on their own terms."[14] But I think there is more to rural residents' acceptance of this seemingly urban conception of the countryside. Country residents, especially those in agricultural communities, have long expressed great pride in their survival on the land and their overriding desire to pass along a lifestyle and the landscape that sustains it to another generation. There is an inherent conservatism in those sentiments, one that encourages a type of conservationism too. So if there is a growing interest in holding the rural landscape in stasis, it may come from a confluence of interests from both city and country.

The mountain landscape hides much more of its past than most visitors suspect. It gives only hints of the Catskills lives, the comings and goings, the booms and busts that rolled through the mountains. In the city, new buildings rise to replace those demolished, and by their mere presence they encourage us to forget what came before. In the mountains, forests are no less successful in hiding the past. Like the mountains themselves, the forests are the "types of the permanent and unchanging," symbols of stasis. And from all but the most knowledgeable visitors, these forests conceal a deep human history in the Catskills.

—ᴠᴠ— *Chapter 1* —ᴠᴠ—

A Natural Resource

Civilization seemed to have done little more than to have scratched this rough,
shaggy surface of the earth here and there.

—John Burroughs, 1894

One is struck by the lack of majestic trees like those of many Maine forests. Along
the mountain roads the wood is mainly of the second growth; the axe has done
its work—the lumber is too near civilization not to be needed.

—Philip Quilibet, 1877

In the decades following the American Revolution, settlers moved
into the Catskills unconcerned with the markets of New York City. Too
distant in the days of carriages and too small a market for most agricultural products until after the War of 1812, New York City played no role
in the decision of the first farmers to seek land in the mountains. For a
generation, sometimes more, they produced almost entirely to fill local
needs. In this way, the earliest history of the Catskills, the first effort to
remake the mountains, from wooded valleys to productive farms, had
essentially nothing to do with the small city at New York Harbor. What's
more, life in the small city was not all that dissimilar to life in the country, despite the former's dedication to commerce. In 1800, New York's
60,000 residents lived clustered on the tip of Manhattan, and most could
easily escape the city's confines by crossing the Hudson to the open spaces
of New Jersey, by traveling up to the sparsely inhabited reaches of the
island, or even by taking to sea.[1]

If Catskills settlers thought nothing of New York's growing commerce
when they took to the mountains, few of them intended to remain aloof
from spreading agricultural markets altogether, and over time the influence of the city would be felt in the Catskills. Indeed, market participation was the goal of most settlers, for only through trade might they
accumulate some wealth, purchase land, build finer homes, and live better lives. Early surplus trading remained close to home due to poor transportation, but the object of trade was to find the best price. From the
very beginning of Catskills settlement, merchants and farmers could

generally find the best prices in New York City. And so, what at first was truly a rural endeavor to make a living in an upland frontier gradually became an effort to sell for greater profit to a market more than 100 miles downstream. Even as early as the 1820s the city affected the mountains, its growing market encouraging settlers and entrepreneurs to find some means to make money from the land, to find something to sell to the city down the river. In the nineteenth century, Hudson River sloops, then steamers and canal barges, and then railroads, allowed mountain residents to ship out various products urbanites might require. These market connections transformed the region's agriculture, at first creating a greater demand for export items, but then creating the economic conditions under which mountain farmers could not compete. Just as important, market connections created opportunities for numerous nonagricultural, extractive industries. Over time, the Catskills provided several natural resources to the city—from butter to bluestone, from tanbark to barrel hoops. Altogether these various enterprises, and many others that supported the Catskills economy, had a transformative effect on the mountain environment, most particularly in extensive deforestation and the disturbance of the area's streams and rivers. The market connections that brought Catskill agricultural products, stone, wood, and tanned leather down to the city thus united local hands and city money, an early and important component in the collaborative effort to remake the mountains.

The Hudson River Valley near the Catskills has had a long human history. Home of the Lenni-Lenape, Mohawks, and Mahicans at the time of European arrival in the 1600s, the Hudson Valley has supported agriculture for perhaps one thousand years. While Native American agricultural settlements in the mountains themselves were sparser than those in the surrounding Hudson, Mohawk, and Delaware valleys, Indians did make use of the mountains, for hunting and fishing trips particularly. Some lower-elevation locations in the mountains may have helped sustain Native Americans for up to four thousand years, especially as seasonal hunting grounds.[2] This Native American occupancy is remembered largely through names on the landscape, including Esopus, Neversink, Pepacton, and Pakatakan, but in all other ways evidence of Native American occupation has long since disappeared.

In the late 1600s, Dutch and then English colonists settled in the flat lands between the Hudson and the mountains, but the imposing eastern range of the Catskills generally prevented movement further west.

European settlers began to arrive in the mountains in significant numbers only after the American Revolution. Many of them came from Connecticut and other New England states, where the supply of good agricultural land could no longer keep pace with demographic growth.[3] Others came south from the Albany area, in search of cheap land in the western Catskills, particularly along the Schoharie Creek and the two branches of the Delaware. They found some locations ready for farming, as Indian clearings gave fortunate settlers a head start on the hard work of making a farm. Still, those hoping to find good farmland in the mountains generally did not, and those who stayed in the higher elevations tended to combine agriculture with a number of other pursuits to make their livings. In this way, the stinginess of the soil and the shortness of the growing season contributed to the development of other industries, including the tanning and bluestone businesses that flourished in the 1800s. Farm families continually searched for additional income, working as bark peelers for tanners or as quarrymen or cartmen when they could.

This pattern persisted through the early 1900s, as families produced whatever they could to stay on the land. Alonzo Hungerford, of the Shokan area, lived a fairly typical life working among the Catskills. Most of Hungerford's income came from his work as a farmhand, but he also labored at another man's quarry periodically. In 1893, he gained ownership of a fourteen-acre woodlot from Zadock Boice, the operator of a sawmill at Bishop Falls, who had already taken the large timber from the property. Hungerford would use the land for many purposes, including taking out cordwood, saplings to make barrel hoops, and even bluestone from a small quarry. Like so many others in the mountains, for so many generations, the Hungerford family pieced together a living, making products for the market, like bluestone and hoops, when they could, and selling their labor when they could not.[4]

Despite the impediments, agriculture gained a stronger foothold in the mountains than one might suspect. In 1819, Henry Dwight toured the Catskills hoping to describe the relatively unknown region's geology. Dwight ascended the very steep Kaaterskill Clove and as he continued westward he was surprised by what he found. The town of Hunter, which Dwight estimated as having 500 to 600 residents, was already producing good crops, and he judged that the land in the Schoharie Valley, in which Hunter lay, was "very luxuriant the first year or two after it is cleared." What's more, with manure Dwight expected production would improve. In the meantime, even more forest would be cleared, with settlers already hard at work "converting their trees into lumber," and the region replete with fine mill seats along fast-flowing streams. During Dwight's summer visit, Hunter seemed to hold much promise as an agricultural community.[5]

Just a year later, a surveyor noted the considerable "improvement" of lands further west in the Schoharie Valley, in an area that would eventually become part of Jewett Township. While the upland lots remained unoccupied, the flatter, more accessible lots had substantial clearings, especially along the area's many streams. Near the East Kill, just north of the Schoharie, Abel Mix had "improved" about 50 of his 125 acres, which is to say he had prepared them for farming by removing trees and stumps. Nearby, Charles Kelsey had cleared "a great part" of his 105-acre lot, made particularly valuable by its proximity to two public roads. Just as important, Kelsey's land lay near Zadock Brown's gristmill and sawmill on the East Kill, both of which would provide critical services to the frontier farming community. Brown had already constructed a frame house near the mills, a sure sign of his early success.[6]

The flats along the Schoharie, the Esopus, and the two branches of the Delaware invited early settlement, but the process of "improving" valleys through agriculture would continue for decades in the less accessible reaches of the mountains. As late as the 1870s, squatters continued to eke out a living by clearing the property of the region's many absentee owners. Abram Kelly, for example, had cleared 20 acres near the Beaver Kill in Hardenburgh, even taking the time to build both a log house and a barn on land he did not own. He kept cattle, using the manure to fertilize his fields of potatoes and buckwheat, two of the most common crops in the region. Kelly had also planted an apple orchard—clearly the action of a man who hoped to stay awhile to reap the benefits of his labors. Each spring Kelly also tapped surrounding maple stands to make sugar and syrup. He had fenced a garden, using the abundant fieldstone, and also cut hay from a sizable meadow of his own creation. In other words, despite the fact that Kelly did not own the land, he conducted an agriculture common to the region, one that relied on multiple crops and, particularly, on grass-fed cattle.[7]

By the 1870s, dairying filled the fertile mountain valleys along the larger rivers and their smaller tributaries.[8] Lithographer Henry Schile lamented the completeness of the transformation around Hunter during his visit in 1881. "It is a pity that the farmers of this neighborhood could not appreciate the value of the beautiful forests that once flourished here," he wrote. But, of course, the farmers did appreciate the value of the forests, not just for their beauty, as Schile would have them, but also for their utility. At perhaps the peak of agricultural settlement in the mountains, New York's 1875 census found nearly half of the Town of Woodstock's acreage "improved," the forest removed. Of the improved acreage, however, only 14 percent was plowed, while nearly 40 percent was mowed for hay and 46 percent kept as pasture. Neighboring Olive Township was about 46 percent agricultural land, with only about 22 percent of this under plow. Each mountain township had its own agricultural pattern, set by topography and soil quality mostly, but no town had more land under plow than in pasturage, a formula that limited the intensity of Catskills farming and the density of the population.[9]

Pasturage dominated Catskills agriculture for two reasons. First, the steepness of the terrain and its rockiness made row crops difficult to grow and not particularly productive when attempted. Pastures and hay fields, however, could easily replace forests on the more modest mountainside grades, at least up to about 2,200 feet.[10] Second, thousands of horses lived in the mountains, particularly for use in the extractive industries. Both tanning and bluestone quarrying required great herds of horses. Horses also aided in the young tourist industry, carrying vacationers to and from railroad stations and on scenic drives. All of this activity, this large number of animals, required food, providing farmers with a ready market for pasture lands and pressed hay. As early Catskills historian Harry Haring claimed, "Every hillside that held any soil became a hay field. Every level spot was planted with corn or oats."[11]

Of the exported agricultural goods, butter led the way in the second half of the 1800s, as railroads provided better access to the New York City market. Even the very mountainous Shandaken Township managed to produce 94,000 pounds of butter in 1875, while the most isolated of all Ulster County townships, Hardenburgh, with a total population of just 671, produced a remarkable 74,000 pounds of butter. This level of production suggests the importance of butter as a means of securing cash in an agricultural region that had very little to export. Too far from the city to send unprocessed milk, most mountain farm families turned the vast majority of their market-bound milk into butter. By the late 1800s, the region's railroads had built their own creameries in an effort to develop freight business, and then hired men to work them, marking a shift in labor from women in the home to men in a plant.[12]

Nineteenth-century city residents did drink considerable quantities of Catskills milk, but they generally did so while visiting the mountains.[13] Indeed, fresh milk and other agricultural products were among the most important attractions for city folk coming to the country in the second half of the 1800s. Just as tourism increased the need for local horses, it also increased demand for dairy cows and chickens in the mountains' farming communities, and for any number of fresh fruits and vegetables. In 1900, the proprietors of the Bishop Falls House, a small boardinghouse run on the Bishops' family farmstead, issued a pamphlet advertising their newly expanded, thirty-five-room house: "An excellent table supplied with fresh vegetables, poultry and eggs, maple syrup, milk, butter and so forth." Clearly agriculture provided critical support for the local tourist industry, and vice versa.[14]

Since most farm families did not produce primarily for the urban market, Catskills farmsteads reflected a great diversity of production. Jefferson Roosa's Esopus Valley farm at the turn of the century might serve as an example. Roosa, his wife, and his three daughters worked a ninety-seven-acre farm, where they raised corn, oats, buckwheat, rye, and potatoes. The animals on the farm—eight cows, two horses, a large flock of chickens, and some pigs—consumed all of the grains, as well as the timothy and clover hay Roosa cut from about twenty acres. Roosa estimated that in 1906 the cows produced $50 in milk each, which he sold to a creamery near the Ulster and Delaware's Shokan station. He sold eggs in the market, too, earning a total of $224, and eleven hogs earned him $111 in that same year. In total, the Roosa farm sold just over $900 worth of products, a modest income supplemented by two of his girls' summer labor at the Mohonk House, a popular resort several miles away. The most important product of the Roosa farm, however, was not what made it to market, but what stayed at home, sustaining the family of five with a remarkably varied diet. Despite the short growing season, the garden plots of the region's farms produced sweet corn, tomatoes, cucumbers, radishes, beets, lettuce, string beans, peas, et cetera, while fruit trees produced cherries, pears, peaches, plums, and, most abundantly, apples. Of all of the products of the farm economy, then, only a small portion made it to market, mostly in the form of butter, eggs, apples, and pork.[15]

In an effort to improve agriculture in the Delaware's East Branch valley, which would have required greater market production, a number of farmers organized the Catskill Mountain Agricultural Society, holding its first fair in Margaretville in August 1889. Not coincidentally, the names

of several society officers are also the names of some of the valley's settlements, including Allaben and Griffin (of Griffin's Corners, now called
Fleischmanns). Also listed among the eleven vice presidents was Judson
Haynes, who was part of the third generation of Hayneses trying to make
a living along Dry Brook. Named for his grandfather who had arrived
in Dry Brook around 1800, Judson farmed 433 acres in an area known
as Haynes Hollow.[16]

Support for the Margaretville fair came not just from the farmers in
the region, but also from agricultural dealers in New York City. A pamphlet announcing the fair, and the society itself, contained advertisements
for four commission merchants based in the city, two of them with offices
on Chambers Street near city hall. Each claimed to be specialists in butter, but they listed other products as well, including eggs, poultry, and
cheese, all of which made their way out of the mountains in this era, particularly on the Ulster and Delaware Railroad. No doubt conflicts over
prices and quality could sour relations between Catskills farmers and the
city's commission merchants, but these two different groups of market
participants had at least one identical interest, made clear by the merchants' support of the Agricultural Society: both wanted to see more
Catskills products sold in New York City markets. This confluence of
interests lay at the heart of the collaboration between city and Catskills
residents; both groups hoped to grow wealthier from the relationship.[17]

Despite the early signs of success and the concerted efforts of merchants
and husbandmen, few Catskills farms were successful for long. The gradual nineteenth-century expansion of agricultural lands was followed
by a similarly gradual decline. All the same, the agricultural economy
and the rural culture it created remained central to the American self-
conception, even in the East, where more than just Catskills farms failed
in the face of competition from the Midwest. Even those many Americans who left the country for the city generally took with them fond memories of their rural experiences, and those who shared those memories
helped confirm the nation's belief in the value of a rural life, especially
the connection to nature it afforded.

One of the nation's most important rural memoirists was John Burroughs, born in 1837 on a Delaware Country farm on a hillside above the
Delaware's East Branch. John's great-grandfather, Ephraim, had settled
near Stamford shortly after the Revolution. One of his sons, Eden, moved

south, establishing a farmstead on the slopes of a small mountain called Old Clump. One of Eden's sons, Chauncey, cleared his own farm on the southern slope of Old Clump, where he would help raise ten children and many crops on 350 acres. One of those children, John, would grow up enthralled by his birthplace, ever thankful of his agricultural childhood and the long hours he spent outdoors, in nature. By the time he purchased his father's farm in 1913, however, he had become an internationally known nature writer and only secondarily a farmer. His beloved Catskills, both their wildness and their agriculture, were among his most popular topics.[18]

When Chauncey and his wife Amy ran the farm, the Burroughs family relied on dairy production, keeping about thirty cows and shipping butter to the village of Catskill by wagon, and thence to New York City by boat. But, as was typical of the region's agriculture in the mid-1800s, the farm remained diversified, producing a variety of products for home use and for the market. Each spring the men participated in sugaring, tapping maples and evaporating the sap in large kettles. The family also kept sheep, primarily for homespun wool, made by Amy. The most forgotten aspect of Catskills agriculture, sheep were once abundant enough to support several regional woolen mills in the nineteenth century. Sheep could graze on steep hillside pastures, just as they did on Old Clump. Still, as John Burroughs noted after he returned to the farm, mountainous Delaware County was "grazing country," where the dairy cow thrived, and "her products" were "the chief source of the incomes of the farms."[19]

Burroughs was not the only well-known personality to write of his childhood home in Delaware County. Jay Gould, who grew up in Roxbury and went to school with Burroughs, wrote a lengthy history of Delaware County, the first major accomplishment in a life full of them. While much of the text glorified the many conflicts that punctuated the region's movement toward its cultivated and civilized condition— the Indian wars, the American Revolution, and the anti-rent wars of the 1840s—Gould also lamented the passing of the region's frontier state. "We should like to be transported back to those good old times, were it only for a day or two," Gould wrote in 1856, "just to breakfast on those delicious trout . . . and sup on choice bits of dried elk-meat." Despite brief passages such as these, Gould expended little prose exploring the lives of the region's farmers, and later in life he wasted little time pining for the rural life he left behind as a very young man. Still, these telling phrases, written even before Gould had left rural New York for the city, suggest how common the lament had become for simpler times and abundance now lost, even to those who still lived in the country.[20]

A better description of Catskills culture came from the somewhat less famous Candace Wheeler, raised on a Delhi farm along the other branch of the Delaware River. Late in life, she reminisced about her Catskills childhood after a long, successful career in textile design, and like Burroughs she lauded the strength of her rural roots, to which she had at least partly returned through the purchase of a second home in a cottage community outside Haines Falls. Like Burroughs, Wheeler praised the work of her mother, whom she aptly called a "domestic manufacturer," for it was her mother who made the butter for sale at market, just as Amy Burroughs did for forty years. Sounding even more like her friend Burroughs, Wheeler declared, "It was the farm that unconsciously taught us the book of Nature, the love of which has been one of the richest of my life acquirements." By the time Wheeler wrote in the early 1900s, many Americans longed to read the "book of Nature," though they were increasingly less likely to do so on a farm. Still, the pining for a rural past, as in the memoirs of Catskills emigrants, became a central thread in the developing preservationist ethic in urban America.[21]

Though some Catskills sons and daughters had moved away from agriculture and the mountains, others stayed and persisted. And lucrative or not, Catskills agriculture had led to significant deforestation. However, another industry played a more obvious role in the transformation of the mountain environment. The Catskills were rich in hemlock, a species with particularly dark-hued foliage. Combined with the frequent hazes that hung over the mountains, the dark foliage of the hemlocks supplied a peculiar tint to the landscape, suggesting a name for the Catskills—the Blue Mountains—as early travelers called the range seen from the Hudson River. The dark woods may also have given the mountains a reputation as a mysterious land and encouraged the development of rich local mythology. Dense, old-growth hemlock stands created remarkably dark understories, providing perfect settings for many a story of mystery and magic. As Harry Haring noted, "the peculiar nature of standing hemlock" made "the forest shadowy and ghostly."[22]

These hemlock forests attracted more than just the pens of fiction writers and poets; they drew the attention of tanners, always in search of new sources of tannin, a chemical found in the bark of hemlock and oaks and integral to the treatment of hides in the making of leather. Transporting bulky bark over long distances for the extraction of tannins was economically untenable, so by the early 1800s leather manufacturers in New York City, concentrated in an area in Manhattan called the Swamp, established trade routes that delivered untreated hides to ports along the Hudson.[23] At Kingston, for example, sixty to eighty hides could be strapped to a wagon for transport up into the mountains, closer to the hemlocks. The tanned hides, of course, returned to the city along the same route. Although tanning took place in many New York counties, by 1835 about 40 percent of the state's tanning took place in the Catskill region.[24]

Small tanneries opened in the Catskills as early as 1800, but the industry expanded rapidly after 1817, when Jonathan Palen built a tannery on Kaaterskill Creek just below the not-yet-famous Kaaterskill Clove and not far from the docks in Catskill. Taking advantage of both ample hemlock and waterpower, essential for grinding bark, Palen built a successful business that apparently operated into the 1850s. By that time dozens of other tanneries had opened in the area, spreading further into the mountains. J. W. Kiersted operated a tannery in the Kaaterskill Clove itself, just downstream from the great falls. Another, smaller operation helped clear the hemlocks farther up the clove in Haines Corners, near Haines Falls.[25] Another tannery opened in the vicinity of the aptly named Tannersville. Farther into the mountains still, Colonel William Edwards opened his large New York Tannery in 1817 along the Schoharie Creek. As the village of Edwardsville (now called Hunter) grew around the tannery, the trees disappeared, leading to a largely denuded valley. Although the tannery burned twice in the 1830s, Edwards rebuilt it both times, indicating the continuing value of the operation. After the tannery had consumed the usable hemlock nearby, Edwards opened a "bark road" through Stony Clove. The bark thus supplied helped keep the tannery prosperous through 1849, a year that saw it tan 26,000 hides.[26]

By 1825, Greene County produced more leather than the rest of the state. In that year, Zadock Pratt opened his famed tannery along the Schoharie in a place later to be called Prattsville. In 1824, Pratt had visited the region, about twenty-five miles from the Hudson River, and declared it "a perfect wilderness." It was also a fine location for a massive tannery, despite the great distance from the port at Catskill. Pratt already had considerable experience in the business, for he had worked in his father's small tannery as a boy and had opened tanneries in partnership with his brothers in Lexington. Stepping out on his own, Pratt constructed "an immense wooden building" in the spring of 1825 that would hold three hundred vats for soaking hides. He constructed a mill capable of grinding more than a cord of bark an hour, and over the course of a year his tannery could consume 6,000 cords of bark.[27]

Like other tanners in the Catskills, Pratt conducted his business through large firms in the Swamp. A good relationship with Swamp merchants, including Gideon Lee and Company, which supplied Pratt's first hides, allowed Pratt to work on credit and share profits with his downstate partners. He marketed all of his leather in New York City, a place he visited regularly to maintain business connections, and where merchants in the Swamp offered the best prices.[28] His hides came through the port at Catskill and over the mountains, after having originated in San Juan, Oronoco, Montevideo, and Buenos Aries, among other places. These South American and Caribbean hides were even less expensive than regionally supplied cattle skins, and their transport over such great distances speaks to the magnitude of the industry created in the Catskills and New York City—only the economies of scale created by great volume could make such extensive transportation economical.[29]

By all accounts, particularly his own, Pratt was an innovator in his field, conducting experiments which allowed him to gradually improve his processes. Pratt tinkered with concentrations of the "oozes" in which the hides soaked and with the length of time they should spend in each stage of the process. Eventually, Pratt produced more leather per hide in this way, increasing his profitability. An accounting of Pratt's manufacturing system appeared in *Hunt's Merchants' Magazine* in 1847, offering a detailed description of the work and of the volume of material the tannery had consumed. A good indication of Pratt's pride in his accomplishments and his desire for publicity, the article included statistics concerning his tannery, summarizing materials used over twenty years in the business. During its operation, the tannery consumed ten square miles of hemlock forest, taking 120,000 cords of bark. At an estimated four trees to the cord, Pratt's tannery alone consumed 480,000 hemlocks from 1825 to 1845. The tannins from this bark tanned nearly 500,000 hides over those years, most of them used to produce shoe soles in the city.[30]

Even though the Prattsville tannery was large by industry standards, it employed on average just fifty-eight men, with perhaps twelve of these working as teamsters between Catskill and the tannery. In the 1850s, tanneries in Ulster and Sullivan counties employed on average just nineteen men, most of them engaged in the difficult, semiskilled work of grinding bark and handling the hides at various stages. Thus, tanneries were generally small operations, but they also employed many other people, particularly in the seasonal work of peeling bark. The *Merchants' Magazine* estimated that two hundred men owed their livelihood to the Pratt establishment. Even excluding all of the indirect workers and contract bark peelers, Pratt's monthly payroll in the 1840s ran about $1,120, a considerable sum for a backcountry village.[31]

Regardless of efficiency or innovation, Pratt's tannery was destined to meet the same fate as all such establishments in the mountains. It would exhaust proximate hemlock bark and gradually become too expensive to operate. By 1842, Pratt sought arrangements to procure bark from as far away as Roxbury, reserving the right to cut the timber owned by John Rickard in that town. Eventually, Pratt had to go too far to find bark, and the tannery ceased operations in 1845. After his tannery's closing, Pratt succinctly described the pattern repeated over and over in the mountains: "No more bark can be had in my vicinity. The land is cleared up for ten miles around, the tannery, 26 years old, is worn out and rotted down." Pratt's first great tannery had closed, but he continued in the business, opening other tanneries in New York and Pennsylvania, even operating one with Jay Gould, the greatest businessman to come out of the mountains.[32]

Throughout the mountains the transformation of the hemlock forests was staggering and rapid. Each spring bark peelers set out into the woods, when actively dividing cambium created a weak layer between the bark and the wood, making that the only time of the year that the peeling could take place. Often working in gangs, the men created shelters in the woods using the hemlock logs. Women cooked and cleaned in the larger camps, where the peelers stayed for a month or more. A good peeler could make two cords of bark a day, felling hemlocks and peeling the bark off only the trunk below the first branch. Peelers stacked up the usable bark, often leaving the rest of the fallen trees to rot on the forest floor. Later in the year, in the fall or winter, the collected bark traveled by wagon or sled along rough "bark roads" toward the tanneries. Some bark peelers remained in the forests in the winter, making shingles of the hemlock in isolated hemlock log cabins.[33]

Bark peelers rarely left behind extensive clear-cuts, taking only the hemlocks with enough girth to make their felling worth the effort and leaving very young trees standing. However, the peelers also left behind considerable debris, including all the branches of felled trees, and some-times even the thicker trunks, all of which created a serious fire hazard when it dried. Not surprisingly, forest fires escalated in the late 1800s, often fueled by the wasteful debris of bark peelers or loggers. These blazes could completely denude the forest, creating large openings that looked like clear-cuts and had significant ecological consequences. The fires shifted species populations, allowing sun-loving plants to flourish in burned sections, and giving competitive advantages to trees that could sprout from stumps. Many fires came before, but in the three decades after 1880, at least twenty-nine forest fires burned in Ulster and Greene counties. With their similar history of logging and bark peeling, the Adirondacks also became the home of great fires, including dozens of fires in 1903 that burned a total of 600,000 acres and sent yellow smoke all the way to New York City, signaling the dire need for better fire pre-vention in the state's forests, including the Catskills.[34]

Much has been made of the wasted wood created by the tanning indus-try, some of which fueled the fires, but peelers did use some of the timber, even rafting hemlock down the Delaware to more distant markets, despite the wood's poor reputation as lumber. Hemlock gained wide use in the construction of Catskills homes and other buildings, including the tanneries' many structures. Even Pratt's large home, now a museum in Prattsville, reveals its sturdy hemlock beams. Some hemlock lumber went into the creation of plank roads in the region, where crudely milled lum-ber laid side by side offered a bumpy ride, but one generally free of muddy quagmires. The most important such road ran from Kingston up the Esopus Valley and on to Pine Hill, roughly the route that the Ulster and Delaware Railroad would take later in the century.

In 1853 and 1854, Mortimer Strong toured tanneries for the Market Fire Insurance Company, hoping to determine which establishments were good insurance risks for his company. He inspected 282 operations over two years, most of them in New York State, with a few others in Penn-sylvania, which would soon become the center of the tanning industry in the east. Tanneries had a habit of burning down, even when fully oper-ational, given their completely wooden construction and the use of fires to warm water and sometimes to run steam engines. Tanneries were more likely to burn as they approached the ends of their usefulness, when own-ers became careless with their diminishing investment or engaged in arson to gain one last profit from their businesses through insurance settlements. Even though Strong visited ten counties in New York State, Greene, the center of the state's industry just a decade before, was not among them. The state census for 1855 showed just nine tanneries left in the county, and given the propensity of failing tanneries to burn, Strong's employer no doubt assumed Greene's few remaining tanneries represented poor risks.[35]

Strong visited twenty-two tanneries in Ulster County, where his notes reveal an average age of over thirteen years for the buildings. One of the largest, in Shokan, opened in 1833 and by the time Strong visited, the Hoyt Brothers of New York City owned it. Significantly, this was just one of very few tanneries for which Strong identified city ownership. While in some cases Strong may have failed to ascertain or report absentee ownership, this was not a trivial issue to the inspection process. Strong took into account the character and vigilance of proprietors, and no doubt an ownership based outside the region would have warranted comment in the report. Thus, the industry appears to have had two separate fields of capital investment: one based in the Swamp and the other in the mountains. The paucity of direct downstate investment in mountain tanneries may reflect a lack of interest among the city's firms in undertaking such ephemeral operations. In the mountains, however, the tanneries appeared to be great opportunities, if not for investing, then for work. While visiting the Dewittville Tannery along the Neversink River, Strong noted that the "men of this valley . . . derive their chief support from [the tanneries]." Later that same day, Strong visited another facility farther upstream, accessed by a nearly completed plank road, noting that bark would be plentiful for some years to come.[36]

The industry had also moved southward into Sullivan County, where Strong's notes revealed how industrialists moved right along with the industry. Firms that began in the business in Greene or Ulster County, including that of the Palen family, owned several of the thirty-eight tanneries Strong visited in Sullivan. According to Strong, the Palens' new enterprise, the Fallsburg Tannery, "had a reputation of being wealthy," no doubt derived from the family's previous successes. The movement of owners like the Palens and Zadock Pratt reflected the fluidity of rural capital and, more important, indicated the draining of wealth out of the Catskills as soon as the tanning industry began to falter.[37]

As one would expect, the tanneries Strong visited in Sullivan County tended to be younger than those in Ulster County, averaging just nine years in age, with an even younger median age of six years. In all of the counties Strong visited, the age of the tanneries generally correlated with the price they paid for bark. Newer establishments, closer to fresh hemlock stands, paid as little as $2.50 per cord. Older tanneries could pay much more. At the Eaton Tannery, established in 1833 in Gilboa, Schoharie County, not far from Pratt's old mill, Strong reported that the hemlock was very scarce, costing the owner $3.50 per cord. The owner expected to run the tannery for another one and a half years, "then give up the business up here as it will end the bark." Although this tannery, and another in Gilboa run by the same man, were not prospective clients, Strong wanted to make clear that the character of the men was in no way responsible for the closing of the tanneries: "They are good careful men but their work is done here."[38]

Decades of cutting left permanent changes in the forest. The most dramatic change involved the hemlock itself, for although it remained in the mountains, observers would come to associate the species with particular environments—very steep hillsides, ravines, and swampy areas. Many came to assume that hemlocks naturally preferred these types of environments, even though they remained in abundance here only because the difficulty of the terrain made them unattractive to the bark peelers. Forest historian Michael Kudish has estimated that in total the Catskills tanning industry consumed more than 7.5 million hemlocks, or 164 square miles of forest, and never again would the species occupy the forests in great stands as it had before the tanning industry swept through.[39]

The ephemeral industry left behind clearly altered forests, but the tanneries themselves altered the environment too, not just by creating around them towns of workers and their families but by creating dams, mills, mill ponds, and countless gallons of tanning liquid—poetically called "juices"—that invariably went downstream when no longer of use.[40] By 1854, T. Addison Richards, in the mountains writing about the region's tourism, complained about the adverse effects of the tanneries, noting that the industry "destroys the beauty of many a fair landscape—discolors the once pure waters—and, what is worse than all, drives the fish from the streams!"[41] Similarly, Ernest Ingersoll commented more than twenty years later that the Esopus Creek was a mountain stream "such as the painters go to Scotland to find," adding, however, "or rather it was before the forests on its banks were felled and its waters were befouled by the refuse from the tanneries, mills, and villages which, attracted by its bark and lumber, have grown up on its banks."[42]

Many of the villages that developed around the sites of large tanneries were as impermanent as the industry itself, though some residents struggled to prevent this fate. Zadock Pratt in particular spent considerable energy in an attempt to ensure that his village would persist, even prosper, after the tannery ceased operation. He founded a town that grew to nearly 2,000 inhabitants and boasted of other industries, including gristmills and sawmills, but also woolen factories, which were rarer in the mountains. Skilled workers operated a printing press, repaired machinery, and manufactured barrels and cabinets. Pratt himself hoped that once cleared of hemlock, the Schoharie Valley would sustain a thriving dairy industry. He even operated a dairy near his tannery as an example to others in the area.[43]

In many locations, however, when the tanneries closed, the settlements around them closed too. Samsonville, the site of General Henry A. Samson's large tannery, was once an important town. In 1854, the Samson Tannery employed seventy men, processing a remarkable 31,000 hides a year. By 1930, Haring declared Samsonville nearly a ghost town; it had never found a replacement for the jobs lost when the tannery closed. Not surprisingly, then, the collapse of the industry brought declines in population, as some people moved away from their mountain homes, perhaps following their source of income southward. The Town of Hunter's population dropped from 1,849 in 1850 to 1,564 in 1875. More dramatically, Lexington fell from 2,263 to 1,314, and the once-vibrant Prattsville dwindled from 1,989 to 1,121. After approximately fifty years of settlement, in some cases even less, parts of the Catskills were already failing, with agriculture too thin to support much growth, and the voracious tanning business too fleeting to establish much of anything permanent.[44]

In an apparent reference to Greene County's Kiersted Tannery, author Charles Rockwell reported in 1873, "There are the decayed and decaying ruins of what was once a busy and thrifty village of tanners in the wild ravine of the Cauterskill Clove, nearly opposite the Laurel House." In 1896, the *Shoe and Leather Reporter* reminded its readers that the "romantic region" of the Catskills was actually a "Used-Up Tannery District," where nothing remained "but the ruined vats." These vats and other deteriorating tannery remains became part of the Catskills' first set of ruins, dilapidated buildings scattered along waterways, attracting the comments of the occasional tourist or artist.[45]

In his many essays on the Catskills, some of which recount his long hikes through the mountains, John Burroughs observed the many ways in which the tanning industry altered mountain forests. During his adventures, Burroughs sought out "the inevitable bark road," using the rough passages through the woods as a means to navigate the otherwise dense forest.[46] He and his companions also sought out shelter in bark peelers' cabins, and in one instance, in the Neversink Valley in 1869, he spent the night in an old barkmen's stable, grateful for the shelter during a heavy rain. During this particular trip, Burroughs found a mixture of structures in the woods, including the ruins of a shingle shop, with neglected shingles still housed. He also found evidence of continued bark peeler's work—a recent clearing near Biscuit Brook.[47] In addition to the eased transportation and occasional shelter, Burroughs, and many tourists who would visit the region in subsequent decades, made good use of the older bark clearings where edible berries proliferated in the sunshine— including blackberries, which he called "an important item in the woods." In just this way, the ephemeral tanning industry, along with the concomitant but longer-lived agricultural industry, opened up the region to visitors and shaped the landscape they would come to see. The mountain landscape of picturesque ruins, wide paths through the woods, and romantic clearings came to represent an ideal tourist environment and helped set urban conceptions of nature and the countryside.[48]

Although tanning was the most famous, it was not the only forest product industry in the Catskills. Some of the other industries followed directly on the heels of the bark peelers. Since hemlock cannot grow from the stump, cleared forests gave way to mostly different species, including hardwood saplings. After several years of growth, the saplings could be cut, and then, using a sharp, two-handled drawknife, men could strip the slender trunks into hoops for barrels. Hoop making grew in the 1850s and peaked around 1885, flourishing where tanning had recently declined. In 1886, Burroughs reported on the importance of hoops in Ulster County. "Every team that went by had a load or was going for a load of hoops," he wrote. With the collapse of the tanning industry, the region turned dramatically toward hoops, even fighting the winter's cold by using "hoop-shavings or discarded hoop-poles" as fuel. Burroughs found hoops used in barter and determined that no one had money "until he sold his hoops," indicating that at least for a brief period hoops functioned much the way butter did over a longer period: they were a means of entry into the cash economy. In this part of Ulster County, Burroughs saw "big hoops, little hoops, hoops for kegs, and firkins, and barrels, and hogsheads, and pipes; hickory hoops, birch hoops, ash hoops, chestnut hoops, hoops enough to go around the world." Although not as lucrative as tanning, hoop making did provide some supplemental income for families staying behind as the tanning industry fled, and at least briefly gave hope to the region's economy.[49]

Furniture factories also sprang up in the Catskills in the second half of the 1800s. In 1855 Horace Baldwin opened his Hunter furniture business, and by 1868 the success of the enterprise allowed him to open a larger chair factory, one employing 200 women and children who made the seating.[50] Also in Hunter, the old Edwards tannery (closed by 1857) took on new tenants, as first a bedstead factory and then an ash-rim manufacturer occupied parts of the main building. Furniture manufacturers took advantage of both the available labor and the growing hardwood saplings, easily shaped into a number of products. Haring claimed that the industry peaked in the 1880s, when more than forty furniture factories operated in the Catskills.[51] Other, smaller forest products industries included cooperage mills, making barrel staves and heads, and at least two excelsior mills produced the wood shavings used in packing. As in most eastern forestlands, then, Catskills wood made its way into the market in a variety of forms.[52]

Although forests fell through most of the Catskills for a variety of reasons, only in certain locations did forests support lumber production for more than the local market. For much of the nineteenth century, the eastern slopes of the Catskills were at least partially protected from lumbering due to transportation issues. Since the timber industry relied on water for the floating of logs down to mills and markets, lumbermen selected their forests based largely on access to water routes. The Esopus was too populated with mills along its length to float out logs, which would have posed too great a risk to the river's many milldams. Other streams, such as the Kaaterskill and Plattekill, were simply too small and precipitous to reliably float timber. These rivers did provide power for sawmills, however, which were nearly ubiquitous along mountain streams, and which generally produced only for the local market.

On the western slope of the Catskills, however, the Delaware River allowed lumbermen to float timber in rafts down to market. As early as the late 1790s, settlers along both branches of the Delaware were rafting valuable white pine to Philadelphia, providing important economic stimulus to the region. By the 1830s, more than 2,000 rafts a year floated down the Delaware, though not all of them originated in the mountains. Still, even as high as Margaretville, lumbermen could tie their logs together along the East Branch, where they awaited spring freshets, created by heavy rains and melting snow packs, to carry them southward. Candace Wheeler remembered the "periodical excitement" of the freshets in Delhi, during which she sat along the West Branch and watched the "adventurous raftsmen" negotiate the high waters. The lumber industry grew rapidly in the 1800s, leading to the settlement of a number of timber towns, including Deposit, so named because it was a fine location to drop logs awaiting spring floods, and Lumberville, which changed its name to Arena after the rafting industry declined.[53]

On the way downstream the men guided the rafts using two large oars, one at the front and the other at the rear. At Hancock, where the two branches of the Delaware join, the widened river allowed rafts to be strung together, creating a stable platform capable of carrying not just the raftsmen but family and friends too. Indeed, the rafts provided a means of carrying other wood products to market, including hardwoods that required the aid of softwoods to float. These "top loads" could include other products as well, including butter and bluestone.[54]

As early as the 1830s, Deposit, on the West Branch, had become an important stop on the way down to Philadelphia's lumber market. Here loggers could sell their timber to Martial Hulce, who then rafted it down the Delaware. Hulce sold the wood in Philadelphia, where he also did his banking, but he then traveled to New York City to buy the goods he would sell in his Deposit store. His receipts from the 1830s show early summer purchases of silks, cloth, guns, shears, pins, utensils, and any number of other goods, acquired in lower Manhattan, especially in the thriving markets on Pearl and Water streets. In some years he followed the spring visit to New York with another in the fall, when a second rainy season could allow another raft trip south. Although Philadelphia provided the market for the western Catskills lumber, Hulce's relationship with Manhattan stores reveals how important New York's remarkable variety of goods and reasonable prices had become to Hulce's livelihood and the region's economy.[55]

By the turn of the twentieth century, the limited supply of accessible, valuable pine had long since given out, and lumbermen had turned to other species, including the less valuable hemlock. As axes pushed the forests away from the rivers that could float out logs, lumbering waned in the Catskills, even in Delaware County, outcompeted by the distant but very accessible forests of the South. One observer of the Delaware River noted in 1898, "Few rafts are now run either on the West or East branches." The virgin stands closest to the Delaware, and even some of its tributaries, such as the Beaver Kill and the Mill Brook, had been removed. As easy access to large trees declined, the Catskills became an importer of lumber, particularly of Carolina yellow pine, commonly used in house construction.[56]

In 1877, Philip Quilibet noted in New York's *Galaxy* magazine, "One is struck by the lack of majestic trees like those of many Maine forests. Along the mountain roads the wood is mainly of the second growth; the axe has done its work—the lumber is too near civilization not to be needed."[57] This deforestation must have been obvious, but oddly, Quilibet's observations notwithstanding, few nineteenth-century visitors commented on the "work of the axe" in the mountains, perhaps because the landscape always retained a considerable amount of forest land, particularly compared to the agricultural landscapes closer to the Hudson and the urban landscapes from which most visitors came. In this very fundamental way, city landscapes, so devoid of trees, would help shape urban conceptions of the countryside, which would appear so heavily forested in contrast. Urban visitors saw rural landscapes incompletely, their eyes drawn more to the forests than the fields.

Though Quilibet clearly understood the urban market's role in diminishing the forests, he failed to speculate on the environmental consequences of deforestation. With farmers using cleared lands for grazing, and with second-growth forests quickly filling voids in unfarmed areas, few observers issued more than aesthetic complaints about the disturbed woodlands. However, especially destructive floods in the mid-1800s, reported mostly due to the damage they wrought to mills and milldams, may have resulted from one of the consequences of deforestation— unusually high storm runoff. In 1869, the "Big Pumpkin Flood" of the Delaware inundated farms, floating away produce (including pumpkins), livestock, and, significantly, hundreds of rafts of lumber awaiting a less violent freshet. While one need not look for an unnatural reason for flashy mountain rivers to carry away obstructions, undoubtedly deforestation encouraged unusual flooding that year, since the bare hillsides failed to retain precipitation as the forests once had.[58]

Meanwhile, the development of another forest industry—the exportation of Christmas trees—undoubtedly had a negligible effect on the mountain ecology. As early as 1851, as the nation increasingly adopted the tradition of bringing an evergreen tree into the home at Christmas time, Catskills farmers began to export balsam firs for sale in the city. According to one widely accepted story, Mark Carr became the first person to bring trees into the city for sale, sledding them down to Manhattan and setting up on the corner of Vesey and Greenwich streets. His initial success eventually led to the annual export of some 200,000 young evergreens from the mountains by the late 1800s, and farmers who struggled to produce traditional agricultural products turned to planting fields of evergreens to supply this growing market.[59]

It is hardly surprising that a well-forested land would send to market a wide variety of wood products, but the Catskills may be better known for another natural resource export: bluestone. This distinctive, blue-hued sandstone runs very close to the surface through much of the Catskills. Although sandstone quarries dotted central New York from the Hudson River to Lake Erie, the Catskills became famous for this fine, colored stone, with "bluestone" initially referring to the stone quarried in Ulster County, though later the term would be used more broadly to describe any flagging used in eastern cities, especially New York. At first the industry developed close to the Hudson, to which the heavy bluestone traveled via wagon. This required the construction and maintenance of good roads, some of which were partially paved with bluestone. It also required great skill from teamsters carrying heavy loads down steep grades.[60] The cost of overland transportation limited the spread of the industry until 1869, when the Ulster and Delaware Railroad connected points in the Esopus Valley to the port in Kingston. Thereafter the Catskills townships sent flagging, curbs, mantles, and other cut stone to New York and many other cities and villages, and bluestone became the region's second great export industry.[61] The stone was particularly suitable for sidewalks, since it would not wear smooth and become slippery, and New York's beautiful and functional sidewalks were well known. Of course, most city residents were probably unaware of this connection to the Catskills, and one industry journal noted, "New Yorkers walk day by day over the smoothest bluestone sidewalks in the world, yet, if asked where they come from, the majority say, 'I'm blessed if I know.'"[62]

The thickness of the bluestone varied, as did its quality, but it was nearly ubiquitous in the mountains and foothills in all the Catskills counties. In 1879, *The Manufacturer and Builder* raved about Hudson River quarrying, noting, "The supply is practically inexhaustible, while the business is really in its infancy." The journal estimated that that year the Hudson River would carry more than $1 million in stone down to the city.[63] Despite the great volume of trade that developed in the 1870s, most bluestone quarries were quite small, operated by individuals or families, with only a few very large quarries run by corporations. Capital investments in these quarries tended to be slight, often just involving the handheld tools the men used, such as sledges, wedges, and pry bars, with some operators even renting out wagons for the periodic hauling of stone to rail stations. Very few operations used extensive machinery, though some used blasting powder to clear away topsoil and unwanted stone. But with bluestone so widely found, most quarrymen would not bother digging too deep to reach marketable stone, preferring to simply move to more fertile ground when the "top" grew too burdensome to remove. Moving from site to site was the norm for quarry workers, given the ease with which new quarries could be opened, and given that most men did not own the land on which their quarries sat, working them instead on a contract basis for property owners.[64]

Larger quarries used horse-driven derricks to swing the heaviest stones onto wagons. This was an important tool for those hoping to extract the most valuable stone—unbroken flagging. Smaller pieces of stone found markets as curbing, mantles, and other decorative stone, and eventually a market developed even for crushed bluestone, suitable for making macadam roads. By 1890, perhaps 20,000 men worked in the various aspects of the bluestone business in the Catskills region. Many of them were skilled workers, particularly in Ulster County, where men cut much of the stone before shipping it down the Hudson. One author claimed, "Through the quarrying country every hillside is dotted with the cottages of the quarrymen, and every valley has its little hamlet that has grown up about the quarries."[65] Still, like most other industries in the mountains, quarrying was seasonal, and many men worked in it only during breaks from other work, such as farming.[66]

Some dealers purchased stone at stations along the Ulster and Delaware and milled it before loading train cars bound for New York. The Ulster and Delaware Bluestone Company operated a mill at the Allaben station as early as 1891, and it operated another mill at West Hurley. By 1900, the Hudson River Bluestone Company operated two mills, one in Kingston and another in Brodhead's Bridge, another Ulster and Delaware station. Most of the stone that came down to the Hudson was only "quarry dressed" however, and it would be milled either on the waterfront or even when reaching its downriver destination.[67] While the largest bluestone dealers had offices in New York City or Philadelphia, clearly the industry's focus was in the mountains and along the Hudson River ports nearest the Catskills, all of which had facilities for handling stone barges, including the very small village of Malden. Here, and at the other ports, men cut stone into desired shapes, sometimes polished it, and loaded it onto barges headed downstream to New York or more distant ports, particularly in New England.[68]

Quarries were scattered about the mountains, but careful observers noted their cumulative effect on the landscape. Since most quarries were small and short-lived, operators rarely concerned themselves with rock wastes, called "rubbish," which simply accumulated at the quarry, adding to the sense of disruption caused by the digging and blasting. Some quarries developed directly in streambeds, where erosion had exposed seams of high-quality stone. John McCaffery's quarry used a flume to contain the Sawkill River as he quarried its bed. The Van Kleek and Dudrey quarry near Brodhead's Bridge worked along the Esopus Creek, dumping its waste stone directly into the creek bed.[69] Making special reference to Ulster County, Philip Quilibet noted in 1877 that the presence of bluestone "causes the face of nature in these parts to be scarred with many a quarry."[70]

The bluestone industry flourished until the late 1890s, when the less-expensive Portland cement began to replace bluestone in flagging and sidewalks. In his 1903 study of the industry, Harold T. Dickinson noted that the Greene and Ulster quarry region already showed signs of retreat. Near Saugerties, in one of the most productive regions, Dickinson estimated "not one half as many men as formerly are working now." All the same, his map of the region showed dozens of quarries still in operation, and new quarries continued to open, particularly as old ones gave out, often under the weight of their own rubbish piles.[71] Still, as with other fleeting industries in the mountains, the decline of quarrying brought a changing landscape. Like the ephemeral tanning industry, bluestone quarrying rarely led to significant capital accumulation in the mountains, even in the form of machinery or other physical plants. Capital remained fluid, labor remained flexible, and together they left little more than modest holes all around the region. Hundreds of abandoned quarries dotted the region, and in some cases the industry's collapse meant the near abandonment of nearby towns. By 1930, one observer found that "nearly all" the quarry towns had "shriveled up," including the once-vibrant village of Stony Hollow, the first Ulster and Delaware station outside of

Kingston, which had all but disappeared. Malden, too, with its mill closed, lost its reason for being. Thus, as the bluestone industry failed, it left yet another set of ruins on the landscape.[72]

Although some bluestone is still quarried in and around the Catskills, like tanning and hoop making before it, the prosperous lifespan of quarrying was relatively short. Agriculture, on the other hand, was slower to mature and slower to fade. From the very beginning Catskills agriculture faced serious problems. The region's farmers found themselves outcompeted by more fertile regions with longer growing seasons, especially as the Erie Canal greatly expanded New York City's agricultural hinterland and bypassed the Catskills region. After 1825, farms much further from the city could more cheaply send their products to market via water routes than could the farms of the mountain townships, a disparity only partly rectified by railroads later in the century. Although constant competitive pressures stunted Catskills farming, the decline in mountain agriculture began in earnest during the agricultural depression of the 1920s. When the Great Depression of the 1930s exacerbated the situation, many farmers stopped producing for the market. Thousands of former agricultural acres reverted to state ownership through targeted purchases and tax sales, and the land itself generally reverted to forests—the natural ruins of yet another fading industry.

Casual observers have often overlooked the cumulative effects of these natural resource industries in the mountains. Certainly the forests of the Catskills recovered, and even if some species have become more common and others scarcer than in presettlement forests, the mountains are again, and have been for some time, a well-wooded land. Indeed, some areas never lost their original forest cover, including much of the high mountain range running from Panther, through Slide, to Peekamoose, where Michael Kudish has estimated the high elevations have protected nearly twenty-five square miles of first-growth forest. Journalist Lucy C. Lillie proclaimed in 1883, "Progress has come sweeping over the country . . . but it can never destroy what nature has reared [in the Catskills]." Lillie concluded her *Harper's Monthly* essay with a poetic appraisal of nature's persistence in the Catskills: "No intrusion seems to disturb the solemnity of the peaks and gorges, the sweetness of the mountain streams, the innumerable brooks and torrents."[73] Two years later, John Burroughs could stand atop Slide Mountain, the highest peak in the Catskills at 4,180 feet, and look out over an expansive wilderness. "All was mountain and forest on every hand," he wrote. "Civilization seemed to have done little more than to have scratched this rough, shaggy surface of the earth here and there."[74]

Despite Lillie's assessment and the view from Slide Mountain, most places in the mountains had been touched by the late 1800s, some by the heavy hand of industry, others by the hands of farmers, loggers, and quarrymen attempting to eke out a living in a stingy landscape. The Catskills looked very different than they do today, with hay fields on hillsides, bark clearings deep in the forests, and cow pastures surrounding modest farmsteads. Photographs from this era reveal the extent of the deforestation, as entire valleys lay in pasturage, and even the large summer homes of urbanites rested in open fields with ample vistas. Milldams, providing power to gristmills, sawmills, and other industry, impeded the flow of all the region's sizeable waterways. In the late 1800s, these dams—both in use and in ruins—were still common along mountain streams.

All of the natural resource industries created temporary booms, in economic activity and in population, and then just as surely ended in busts, with entire villages disappearing right along with the opportunities. What was left, a landscape of ruins—abandoned farm fields slowly filling with saplings, unrepaired milldams broken by spring floods, poorly built tanneries listing with age, and mile after mile of "wood roads" stretching through second-growth forest—was itself a product of these market connections, perhaps even the most important product. As J. B. Jackson theorized in "The Necessity for Ruins," this landscape served a role in memorializing the American past, a "bygone domestic existence and its environment." In the Catskills, urban tourists, who would come in increasing numbers in the late nineteenth century, could seemingly visit the past, a very reassuring trip from the chaos of constantly changing New York. In the mountains they could surround themselves with evidence of the quintessential American struggle—settler versus wilderness, the struggle of the frontier. Ruins dotted the ideal romantic landscape, providing evidence of work, but not necessarily work underway. This landscape, rich with evidence of temporary successes and inevitable failures, of arrivals and departures, gave an aura of romance to a region better known for the triumphs of nature than those of its residents. The ruins left by agriculture and extractive industries thus provided more than just evidence that the Catskills were indeed a much-altered landscape, remade much more completely than observers like Lillie were likely to admit; they also provided the fodder for a new way of viewing the mountains, as a remnant of a distant past. As early as the mid-1800s, urban visitors to the countryside, distanced from the rural struggle for success, could look fondly upon the ruins that evidenced failure, and think mostly how wonderful it must have been to live so close to nature.[75]

The long decay of so much of the built landscape in the mountains reveals the fleeting nature of capital accumulation in the country—in stark contrast to the ongoing accretion of wealth in the city. An interest in building better farms and better lives brought mountain residents into the market, but ultimately most of them left scant reminders of their success. Meanwhile, in the city, merchants, bankers, insurance men, and others accumulated wealth in enviable amounts. Through their relationships with the Catskills and hundreds of other rural regions both near and far, they built trading houses, warehouses, office buildings, stylish residences of granite and brick and of bluestone, too. One might easily walk through midcentury Manhattan and marvel at the obvious accumulation of wealth—evident in so many grand edifices. Remarkably though, much like the tanneries, sheds, barns, and ramshackle farmsteads of the Catskills, these buildings too would largely disappear from the landscape. The weight of failure would not pull them down, however. Rather, the equally powerful force of continued success would replace them with even grander edifices.

—∽— *Chapter 2* —∽—

Envisioning Mountains

Where the cow is, there is Arcadia.

—John Burroughs, 1886

Hail! Hail ye mountain solitudes ye wilds
untrodden by the city crowd!
I come to dwell with you.

—Thomas Cole, 1835

Early Catskills settlers worked hard to transform the mountains into a productive landscape, as did subsequent generations of farmers, bark peelers, lumbermen, and quarrymen. Yet in the 1830s and 1840s, as more New Yorkers learned of the mountains, they tended not to hear about the mundane struggles for livelihood. And as more New Yorkers traveled to see the Catskills, they brought with them a set of images and expectations that had little to do with the industriousness of the local residents and the fields they had cleared. For, simultaneous to the market's encouragement of agriculture and industry in the mountains, the Catskills gained special status in New York City's literary and artistic hinterland. From 1820 through the remainder of the century, the Catskills captured the attention of traveling writers and artists, many of them participating in the rich urban culture developing in Manhattan. They created the words and images that framed the countryside and produced idealized portraits of country life and landscape. They created cultural associations, freighting the landscape with meaning—meaning that had essentially nothing to do with the residents already there and at work. While most of these increasingly important cultural images came from outside the mountains, they were encouraged and marketed by local entrepreneurs. Even as many Catskill residents struggled to build an agricultural community, some worked to build a romantic reputation for the mountains, making use of largely urban art. Collectively, this art created new expectations about what the Catskills should be, and, eventually, what these mountains should remain.

The stories of history, and the personalities and events that appear within them, gathered only slowly in the Catskills. In stark contrast, the rich lands along the Hudson, and the many Dutch towns from New York to Albany, collected the tales of Henry Hudson, the Dutch explorer who in 1609 sailed up the river in a ship called *Half Moon;* the accounts of the American Revolution, in which Hudson Valley battles proved critical; and the stories of nearly 200 years in between. As late as the 1820s, however, the Catskills were still sparsely populated, their Euro-American history just beginning. Without this history, without the cultural associations that might attract visitors, very few tourists sought out the Catskills in the first decades of nineteenth century. According to Sarah Hale, the editor of *American Ladies' Magazine,* the traveler sought scenes that could "awaken remembrances," places with significance in literature or history. Hale determined that the American countryside failed to attract the "sentimental traveler" for "want of intellectual and poetic associations with the scenery he beholds." She complained, "Genius has not consecrated our mountains" (presumably with poetry) and "No fairies nor lovers have made our valleys their places of resort." According to Hale, this explained why Americans were much more likely to travel through the Old World than Europeans were to tour the United States. "We want writers who can throw enchantment around rural scenes and life," she concluded. In this passage, Hale neatly articulated how literature and art might combine with tourism to remake rural landscapes, to cast new stories, "enchantment," on already occupied places.[1]

Ironically, even as Hale wrote in 1835, this process was well under way in the Catskills, as authors and artists created the cultural associations that would help attract tourists for generations. One of the earliest pieces came from a man of science rather than art, though he clearly saw the artistic potential of the mountains. Henry Dwight entered the mountains in 1819 in search of scientific knowledge, hoping to describe the geography and topography of a rather large, blank spot on the map. After ascending the eastern mountain ridge, the only part of the mountains seen from the Hudson, Dwight was surprised to find the farming town of Hunter. He also found a "sublime display of nature's workmanship," the spectacular beauty of the region's many cloves and falls. Upon returning from his journey, he mentioned the mountains "to more than fifty persons," but he had not "met with more than five or six" who knew of the Catskills' beauty.[2] The mountains, so completely unknown outside themselves, were still a land of mystery. However, just ten years after Dwight's visit, most Americans could surely recall two significant tales of the mountains, and they might just as surely fail to mention that the events they described had never really happened. By 1830, if the residents of the growing cities around New York Harbor knew just a little about the Catskills' past, it likely came from fiction.

Geoffrey Crayon told one of these stories in 1820, though he said he had found it in the papers of Diedrich Knickerbocker, who had recently passed away. Of course, both Crayon and Knickerbocker were creations themselves of Washington Irving, the New York author who, using the pseudonym Knickerbocker, had written a fanciful history of his state, published in 1809. The well-received *History of New-York* gave Irving notoriety; *The Sketch Book of Geoffrey Crayon, Gent*, published eleven years later, gave him immortality. For in the pages of the latter were found a series of witty, satirical stories, two of which became national favorites: "Rip Van Winkle" and "The Legend of Sleepy Hollow."[3]

Irving's writings had a deep influence in New York, where through a literary periodical called *Salmagundi* he helped bestow the label "Gotham" to his hometown, and later through his pseudonym he helped affix the title "Knickerbocker" to all New Yorkers, though originally it carried a Dutch connotation that diminished as the city became less and less Dutch. Irving's influence on the Catskills was just as deep, though only the story of Rip Van Winkle touched the mountains themselves. Set in a fictive town at the foot of the mountains, "Rip Van Winkle" is the story of a likeable, ne'er-do-well farmer constantly chastised by his wife for idleness. To escape the henpecking, Rip retreats to the mountains with his loyal dog and his squirrel-hunting gun. After a long ramble, Rip finds himself on "one of the highest parts of the Kaatskill mountains," where he rests overlooking the "lordly Hudson." Just as he is about to come down from this perch, an approaching stranger calls out his name. Rip descends to help the man, who is carrying a full keg of liquor. As the two walk along, taking turns with the load, they come upon a number of mysterious figures in archaic clothing playing ninepin. The men drink together from the keg, with Rip famously taking multiple "flagons" of the liquor to quench his thirst, which apparently put him fast asleep. The point of the tale, of course, is that Rip awakens, twenty years later, to a much-changed world. As he stumbles confused into town, rusted gun in hand, he finds nothing familiar, save his view of the Hudson and the mountains he has just descended. He has slept through the American Revolution and the death of his wife, and so the twin tyrannies of the

King and Dame Van Winkle have both passed, much to his relief. Significantly, then, "Rip Van Winkle" is a story about dramatic change, where only the landscape remains the same.[4]

Although the story has little to do with the Catskills, they serve an important function in Rip's tale, for Irving easily cast them as "fairy mountains," where mysterious gentlemen might walk with kegs of liquor upon their backs, and where idle men might sleep for twenty years. Readers learn that the "Kaatskill mountains had always been haunted by strange beings," and that the oddly dressed men bowling on the mountain were probably ghosts of Hudson's *Half Moon* crew, with Henry himself keeping watch over his namesake river from the Catskills. Readers learn too that what sounds like thunder arising from the mountains might actually be the sounds of these men playing ninepin, and that the Kaaterskill Creek has some mystical origin in the breaking of a water-filled gourd. These details of the mountains became instant lore—a deep history created in the imagination of a fiction writer.[5]

Since Irving's geographical description of Rip's home remained rather vague, some debate about where the story actually took place ensued, with Irving himself having to answer queries concerning the true identity of Rip's hometown. While it may seem odd that readers would seek out the actual setting of a fictional story, it was all the more odd since, at its writing, Irving himself had never been to the Catskills. Like so many other New Yorkers, Irving had passed by the mountains while sailing up the Hudson, but not until the summer of 1832 did he actually climb into the Catskills. His earlier impressions of the mountains, as mysterious, deep blue, and changing "barometers" of shifting weather, had come from a distant perspective—the one from the river. Thus it makes sense that the only detailed description of the Catskills in "Rip Van Winkle" comes at the beginning of the story, where Irving writes poetically about varying light producing "some change in the magical hues and shapes in the mountains," and how in the evening, "when the rest of the landscape is cloudless, they will gather a hood of gray vapours about their summits." These were visions of the Catskills that Irving and thousands of other Hudson River travelers had experienced. He had no firsthand knowledge of the mountains themselves or the people who might live in and around them.[6]

Irving would later write a short essay on the Catskills that appeared in the *Home Book of the Picturesque* and *Littell's Living Age* in the early 1850s. He called this "mountain zone" the "great poetical region of our country" and "the fairy region of the Hudson," designations that, if true, clearly reflected the influence of Irving's earlier work. He also described his first vision of the Catskills, from a Hudson River sloop where he "lay on the deck throughout a long summer's day, gazing upon these mountains, the ever-changing shapes and hues of which appeared to realize the magical influences in question. Sometimes they seemed to approach, at others to recede; during the heat of the day they almost melted into a sultry haze; as the day declined they deepened in tone; their summits were brightened by the last rays of the sun, and later in the evening their whole outline was printed in deep purple against an amber sky." Clearly this was a place from which the mysterious tale of Rip Van Winkle and other legends might spring: a place well studied from afar, but nearly unknown up close.[7]

The Hudson River view Irving described was central to the early understanding of the mountains. For two centuries the Catskills were more seen than explored, as many travelers simply passed by on their way to other important destinations, like Albany, Saratoga, the Erie Canal, and Niagara Falls. For passengers aboard slow-moving sloops, the mountains followed the river for a distressingly long time, and in the passing of many hours, the changing daylight and shifting weather aided in the creation of an ever-various scene—the mysterious mountains that sometimes "seemed to approach, at others to recede."

By the late 1820s, however, more visitors decided to disembark in the village of Catskill and take a short carriage ride to the mountains themselves. Many of these tourists were inspired by published accounts of the mountains—both factual, like Dwight's, and fictional, like Irving's. After a steep and often harrowing trip up the precipitous mountainside, visitors could obtain a second view, one that quickly became as important as the one from the river. From the mountaintop, visitors looked back down on the Hudson and a vast region around. From there the importance of the Hudson became all the more clear, its traffic in sailing ships and steamboats providing the only motion (other than the clouds) in a panoramic view of hundreds of square miles. The Hudson had been and would long continue to be at the heart of New York's growth. Connecting the vibrant port city at its mouth with a rich hinterland, the Hudson's commerce helped propel the state from fifth largest in the Union in 1790 to first by 1820. Upon its completion in 1825, the Erie Canal assured New York's premier economic position in the United States, connecting New York's port with the nascent inland markets of upstate New York and beyond, via the Hudson River. Through it all, New York City's growth was astounding; a city of 60,000 in 1800 became one of 202,000 thirty years later, and it contained more than 800,000 persons by 1860. Even in 1918, long after the railroad had supplanted the river as the quickest route north, T. Morris Longstreth could look down from the mountaintop and pronounce the Hudson "the river of civilization." The still heavily trafficked Hudson so clearly contained commercial energy that as he watched over it, Longstreth "seemed to feel the presence of the unseen city at the end of the river." Through much of the nineteenth century, the river was indeed the highway by which the "unseen city" made its presence felt in the mountains.[8]

If Irving had poetically captured the vision of the mountains from the river, it was another New York writer who did the same for the opposite view. James Fenimore Cooper had grown up on the other side of the mountains, in Cooperstown, but had moved to Westchester County in 1817. There, at the encouragement of his wife, Cooper tried his hand at writing fiction. His first novel appeared in 1820 and a second, *The Spy*, a year later. When *The Spy* became a critical and financial success, Cooper dedicated himself fully to writing novels and in 1822 moved to New York City, where he became a darling among the city's growing literati. In 1823 Cooper published the first of what would become known as the Leatherstocking Tales. Called *The Pioneers*, the novel offered a fictionalized version of Cooperstown's settling, in which Cooper placed an unusual emphasis on the costs that accompanied the conquest of wilderness. Cooper's sense of loss came largely through the words and actions of the novel's hero, Natty Bumppo, also known as Leatherstocking, an aging pioneer who pined for the freedom of the frontier and chaffed at the arrival of civilization.[9]

While *The Pioneers* could not match the success of *The Spy*, the character of Leatherstocking soon became one of the most important in nineteenth-century American literature, appearing in several of Cooper's subsequent novels, including *The Deerslayer* and *The Last of the Mohicans*. In Leatherstocking, Cooper had captured the mythical frontier hero, a man more comfortable in wilderness than in town, a man fully capable of making his own way and determining his own fate with nothing more than his considerable skills and strong character. Throughout *The Pioneers*, Leatherstocking stands in opposition to the waste, avarice, and even cruelty of civilization. His pioneering ways are threatened by the arrival of so many settlers, who bring with them new rules and expectations—and their axes. Leatherstocking laments: "They say that there's new laws in the land, and I am sartain that there's new ways in the mountains. One hardly knows the lakes and streams, they've altered the country so much."[10]

Although *The Pioneers* is set in Cooperstown (called Templeton in the novel), one passage, spoken by Leatherstocking, refers to specific, recognizable spots in the Catskills. "When I first came into the woods to live," Leatherstocking confesses late in the novel, "I used to have weak spells when I felt lonesome; and then I would go into the Catskills and spend a few days on that hill to look at the ways of men." The Catskills, affording a commanding view of the Hudson and "the carryings on of the world," reminded Leatherstocking why he had chosen his life of solitude, and the grand vista gave him fortitude. In the midst of this confession, made to a curious young man named Oliver Edwards, Leatherstocking utters the most famous words ever written about the region while describing the Hudson overlook near an area called Pine Orchard:

> "You know the Catskills, lad; for you must have seen them on your left as you followed the river up from York, looking as blue as a piece of clear sky, and holding the clouds on their tops, as the smoke curls over the head of an Indian chief at the council fire. . . . the place I mean is next to the river, where one of the ridges juts out a little from the rest, and where the rocks fall, for the best part of a thousand feet, so much up and down, that a man standing on their edges is fool enough to think he can jump from top to bottom."
>
> "What see you when you get there?" asked Edwards.
>
> "Creation," said Natty, dropping the end of his rod into the water and sweeping one hand around him in a circle: "all creation lad."[11]

The words were more fitting than Cooper might have imagined. When he said "Creation," Leatherstocking meant the river, the Green Mountains, the Massachusetts hills, the Connecticut Valley, the Hudson Highlands, all of which can be seen from the spot—the Hudson alone visible (or so Cooper claimed, and others would repeat) for seventy miles. This was God's creation, surely, as Natty noted. But in this expansive view too was the heart of the new nation—the farms of New York and Connecticut, and, most important, the Hudson, the busiest river route in North America. Over the next century hundreds of thousands of travelers would do just as Leatherstocking had—stand at the precipice and over-look the Hudson, look down upon civilization, see "all creation." And, when they did, they would know Cooper's words, and perhaps even utter them, for that grand view and that short passage would be so intimately linked for generations.[12]

Although Cooper would eventually move back up to Cooperstown, and Irving would spend many years in Europe, they were among the most important authors in a growing literary scene in New York City. Indeed, by the 1820s New York's rapid growth had helped the city become the lit-erary center of the United States. Home to a growing number of publish-ing houses, newspapers, and magazines, New York also became home to a growing number of established and aspiring writers, some of whom would become known collectively as the "Knickerbockers." Among them was James K. Paulding, who had collaborated with William Irving, brother to Washington, in creating *Salmagundi*, and Nathaniel Parker Willis, who founded *The American Monthly* in 1829 and later merged it with the *New York Mirror*. Although largely forgotten today, Willis was a major literary figure in the mid-1800s, his many travel accounts gaining considerable attention. Another, later-arriving Knickerbocker, Bayard Tay-lor, moved to New York in 1848 and worked for the *Tribune*, though he too became well known as a travel writer. All of these authors and many others would contribute to a growing Catskills literature.[13]

In the mid-1820s, when Cooper was at the center of New York's thriv-ing literary world, another young author arrived in the city, coming from the Berkshires of Massachusetts. Already a published poet, William Cullen Bryant had worked as a lawyer for a few years but found it uninspiring. When he moved to New York, he had his sights set on making a living as a writer, and within a year of his arrival he gained a position at the *Evening Post*, a paper he would eventually control. Like the other Knicker-bockers, Bryant traveled widely, but by the 1830s he had become the most important figure in New York literature, and remained so until his death in 1878. Cooper and Bryant became friends, and Bryant joined the Bread and Cheese Club, a social organization for writers and artists Cooper had founded in 1822. With a membership of New York's best and brightest, the Bread and Cheese Club represented the growing success of New York arts, and fostered what would become a supportive literary community. The Bread and Cheese Club lasted only four years, gradually falling apart after Cooper left on an extended European trip, but in 1829 it was replaced by another social organization, the Sketch Club, which like its predecessor could boast of a remarkable membership of accomplished writers and artists.[14]

It was not through the Sketch Club but through his many writings, both prose and poetry, that Bryant gained renown as one of the young nation's most talented authors. He had penned his most famous work, "Thanatopis," as a teenager in Massachusetts, where as a child he had developed a great affinity for the beautiful Berkshire Hills. Although Bryant flourished in the city, particularly as a versatile journalist and editor, his poetry remained romantic, focused on nature, and, more than most of his generation, revealed an interest in the wild. Like Irving, Cooper, and many others in New York's literati, he found he could not thrive as a writer outside the city, but he could not live contentedly always inside it. Although New York was still a small city in 1825, Bryant found its urban air stifling, and he pined for the open spaces and freedom of the countryside. When he had the means, Bryant established a residence in Roslyn, on Long Island, where, like Irving in Westchester County, and Cooper in Otsego County, he could live as a country gentleman while remaining an urbane author. Like so many of his generation, Bryant's romantic notions of nature would only deepen in the city, and a suburban life could only partially quench his desire for more wild scenes.[15]

Even before settling into New York, however, Bryant revealed how deeply romanticism influenced his thinking about nature. His 1825 poem "A Forest Hymn" opened with the famed line, "The groves were God's first temples." According to Bryant, forests presented the opportunity of "continual worship" through tranquility, silence, and "calm shades," all of which presented a rather fanciful interpretation of woods, which for most Americans still represented work to be done, either in clearing fields or cutting firewood. Five years later, Bryant offered a shorter "Hymn of the City," which, while written "'Mongst the proud piles, the work of human kind," still featured natural imagery. And Bryant only grudgingly admitted that "Even here" he could find God, "amidst the crowd." For our purposes, Bryant's most important poem, "Catterskill Falls," appeared in 1836, and described "this wild stream and its rocky dell." By the time Bryant's Kaaterskill poem appeared, the falls had already become one of the most recognizable places in the East. Cooper's Leatherstocking had already declared the falls "the best piece of work that I've met with in the woods."[16] By the time Bryant approached the subject, the falls had long been a popular tourist destination and an oft-painted and litho-graphed scene. Bryant's contribution was unique, however—a romantic tale set "Midst greens and shades" and "verdant steps." Here, where the "Catterskill leaps," a "youth of dreamy mood, / A hundred winters ago," wandered up from the valley into a wilderness. At the falls, the boy gazed with "a throbbing heart," all the while a winter's night gathered, along with the danger of the encroaching "deadly slumber of frost." In his trance he saw "phantoms" pass before him: "bands of warriors in glittering mail, / And Herdsmen and hunters, huge of limb," and others, mothers and "youthful lovers." Fortunately for the dreamy youth, "Hard-featured woodmen" rescued him and laid him on a "couch of shaggy skins." Altogether, the poem represented the power of Bryant's romantic pen, creating a fantastic and yet somehow historical scene, not unlike those of Rip Van Winkle and Leatherstocking.[17]

In 1872, Bryant sang the nation's praises in *Picturesque America*, a beautiful two-volume collection of essays on the country's most valued natural places, including the Hudson Highlands and the Catskills. But the book had a national focus and included places much farther from New York, like Yosemite and Yellowstone, and lesser-known spots like Florida's St. John's River. Still, the weight of the New York bias becomes clear, not just in the selection of places, but in the prose that describes them. "Among our White Mountains, our Catskills, our Alleghanies, our Rocky Mountains, and our Sierra Nevada," wrote Bryant in the preface, "we have some of the wildest and most beautiful scenery in the world." The nationalist mission of the work is clear here, but only a New Yorker who had spent time in the Catskills could place those rather modest mountains alongside the country's more spectacular ranges. In just this way, New York's literary importance elevated the Catskills, granting them national significance.[18]

Some of the Knickerbocker writers had only brief adventures in the Catskills, and in portfolios of hundreds of pieces they dedicated little space to the mountains in their writings. But nearly all of them did write about the Catskills. The proximity of New York's literary circle to the mountains, the easy access afforded by the Hudson, and the inclination of authors to write from their personal experiences, particularly in an age when travel writing became very popular, essentially guaranteed that the Catskills would attract the talents of dozens of nineteenth-century writers.[19] And, although many of the authors preferred the society of talented writers in the city, most were deeply influenced by the scenery of the Hudson Valley. Perhaps most famously, Irving retreated from his city of birth to Sunnyside, a beautiful home overlooking the Tappan Zee in Westchester County. Willis, too, retreated up the Hudson, to an estate called Idlewild near Storm King in the Hudson Highlands.

Together the Knickerbocker writers created a body of Catskills literature, romantic in its intent and urbane in its tone. Most important, it was a literature written from without, by visitors to the mountains, and in the case of Irving's "Rip Van Winkle," by an author who had not even set foot in the mountains. It was a literature that emphasized wildness and stasis—two qualities New Yorkers could hardly expect to find in the city, except through literature and art. In a rapidly changing city, more than just population growth and increasing ethnic diversity gave residents a sense of instability. The physical city changed just as rapidly as the demographics, with buildings coming and going as property values soared and the city attempted to make room for its expanding population and economy. In 1856, for example, the Irving House, a prominent Manhattan hotel, was demolished after having occupied its Broadway lot for just a dozen years, causing *Harper's Monthly* to lament that a "man born in New York forty years ago finds nothing, absolutely nothing, of the New York he knew." In this ever-changing world, stasis gained significant psychological currency, as New Yorkers sought out anchors that connected them with a familiar past. At the same time, the growing turmoil of urban life, complete with growing dangers and discomforts, encouraged more residents to seek refuge from New York, especially through journeys into the surrounding countryside. Ironically, while away from home, New York's tourists could find the familiar. The countryside served as an important contrast with the city not just in its abundance of natural scenes but also in its comparative stability. As New York continued to grow, and its residents found themselves even more removed from natural and stable landscapes, they increasingly sought them out through travel.[20]

When economic affairs, social engagements, or inclement weather kept New Yorkers at home, they could turn to a growing body of travel accounts to provide some respite, especially in the rural imagery produced by tourists' pens. Importantly, urban romanticism encouraged a very limited portrait of rural life—one that diminished the role of hard work in making agricultural landscapes and in making a living from them. New York's writers were much more interested in an idealized countryside, one awash in a proper mix of sublime spaces to stir emotions and picturesque visions to calm the soul. For these writers, the countryside provided inspiration for sentiments that might sell in the city. The idealized Catskills, in particular, contained myths and fairytales in lieu of an actual past, and ghosts and symbolic heroes instead of real farmers and bark peelers.

One of the most powerful idealizing sentiments, or really a collection of them, was called "the sublime."[21] A variously defined set of feelings, ranging from awe to terror, the sublime usually played a central role in the journeys of nineteenth-century romantic writers. They sought out extreme landscapes, those in which witnesses might easily discern the hand of God. These scenes overwhelmed viewers, resulting in speechlessness and even tears. In capturing their own reactions to the Catskills scenery, especially Leatherstocking's view of "all creation," New York's authors, and many other visitors, encouraged subsequent travelers to experience the region in much the same way, sometimes through their example and other times through earnest exhortation. One lesser author, Philadelphian Willis Gaylord Clark, encouraged specific reactions to sublime scenes in his regular contributions to New York's premier literary magazine, *The Knickerbocker*, edited by his brother Lewis Gaylord Clark. Here Clark recorded his travels through the East in the 1830s, including two trips to the Catskills in the summers of 1836 and 1837. After the first, he instructed readers to witness the view, "whence you shall look down beneath the clouds on smiling counties, and towns and cities, spread forth as on a map, at your feet." After the second he was even more dramatic: "Good Reader!" he exclaimed, "expect me not to describe the indescribable. I feel now, while memory is busy in my brain, in the silence of my library, calling up that vision to my mind, much as I did when I leaned upon my staff before that omnipotent picture, and looked abroad upon its God-written magnitude." One might intuit that upon his second visit Clark should have been well prepared for the vista at the overlook, and therefore less likely to be so overcome. But the sublime had the opposite effect: the more you anticipated the sensations, the more you could feel them when the moment was right.[22]

Other urban writers were just as dramatic—and demanding—as Clark. In *The New World*, a magazine he edited, Park Benjamin described a trip he took to the Catskill Mountains in 1843. "It would seem that the Great Creator of the Universe, had built up this mighty eminence that man might know *His* power, and feeling his own insignificance, despise and shun the vanities and hollow-heartedness of life." He concluded by exhorting his fellow New Yorkers: "Come then ye multitude of uneducated mortals, and from this great book," he wrote, "store your minds with deep reflections, leading to wisdom and to happiness." These were emotions, lessons even, that could be garnered only in the mountains. Wiser, happier travelers could then return to the city, at least temporarily girded against urban life.[23]

Through the mid-1800s, most of the Catskills remained largely untraveled by urban tourists, and undescribed by urban authors. One of those undescribed places, Plattekill Clove, lay just a few miles from the well-trod reaches. In a fitting description of the lesser-known clove in 1856, travel writer Charles Lanman called it "a world of unwritten poetry," giving some sense of how it really differed from the more famous Catskills features. The Plattekill Clove had beauty, but as yet it had no poet.[24] On the other hand, the well-known features of the Catskills clustered around the high plateau called Pine Orchard, and included North and South lakes, Kaaterskill Falls, and Kaaterskill Clove, all of which attracted artists of pen and paint, who captured it annually in their works. By the 1840s, the Kaaterskill region was well-known territory to traveling New Yorkers, a much-storied land. Writers described the Catskills in newspapers, literary magazines, travel books, and in a new form—special collections of Catskills literature. This landscape had been so abundantly described, T. Addison Richards used a literary metaphor when he called the Kaaterskill Clove "the finest chapter of the Catskills scenery," inadvertently revealing how much the landscape and the literature had in common, and, just as important, how much the latter determined how visitors would experience the former.[25]

As early as 1843, publisher Daniel Fanshaw collected the Catskills writings of New York's great authors, and a few by lesser-known pens, and sold them under the title *The Scenery of the Catskill Mountains*. Marketed to the region's growing legions of tourists, the pamphlet guided visitors to the Catskill Mountain House, built on the spot from which Cooper's Leatherstocking had surveyed "all creation." It contained the expected snippets from Irving, Cooper, Bryant, Willis Gaylord Clark, N. P. Willis, Park Benjamin, and Thomas Cole. In 1864, a revised edition, with a lengthy piece from Bayard Taylor added, came from a printing house in the village of Catskill. Published again in 1872, *The Scenery of the Catskill Mountains* was more than just a marketing tool that made good use of respected authors. It was an instruction booklet, describing where visitors should go, what they should see, and how they should feel when they saw it. These pieces and others also appeared in Charles Rockwell's popular 1873 book, *The Catskill Mountains and the Region Around*.[26]

Taken together, in their original places of publication, reprints in tourist pamphlets, and in Rockwell's collection, the Catskills literature was remarkably accessible to New York readers, and was very well known, especially to those who would come to the mountains as tourists and those who would host them. The literature's repeated publication, both in the city and in the Catskills, does more than reveal how useful it had become in advertising the region, however. Although most pieces came from without, by midcentury locals had accepted the literature, had allowed it to help define the region, and it had become an important component of the Catskills' identity. Henceforth this literature would serve as a source of great pride among mountain residents, who over time would do much to keep it alive. Washington Irving may have been a Knickerbocker, a city man through and through, but Rip Van Winkle was a local, as native as anyone born in the Catskills.

One of the authors appearing in both *The Scenery of the Catskills Mountains* and Rockwell's book was not a well-known literary figure; although he did write several published essays, Thomas Cole was primarily a landscape painter. Indeed, at the printing of the first collection of Catskills literature, Cole was, and had long been, America's most important painter, the founder of what would become known as the Hudson River School, and the central figure in the creation of a new American landscape aesthetic. Clearly Catskills literature helped define the mountains for prospective New York travelers, but the landscape paintings of Cole and other artists who worked through the New York market were even more influential. Following the growth of New York's literary scene, by the mid-1830s the city had also become the center of American art, attracting many of the nation's finest painters and lithographers, who sought work as portraitists or illustrators for a growing list of publishing houses. Despite the economic downturn of the 1830s, New York remained the most important destination for American artists, and when the economy boomed in the 1840s, the cluster of entrepreneurs wealthy enough to amass great collections of art expanded rapidly.[27]

Beyond seeking portraits of themselves and loved ones, New York's fine arts patrons purchased European art, both works of the masters and much cheaper copies, but increasingly these collectors sought out American pieces, not just by American hands but of distinctly American landscapes. New York's artists worked to supply native art to fill the demand, and as a practical matter many of these men sought inspiration in the landscapes near at hand. Artists struggling to sell their works hoped to capture scenes that caught patrons' eyes, which often meant familiar places—places well known to New York's elite. At the same time, limited finances restricted most artists' travel, keeping them close to Manhattan.

Landscape painters captured American scenes on their sketching trips through the countryside, but they did so using European sensibilities. Cole and others would create American art, but they generally followed customs of landscape painting long since established on the Continent, especially by Claude Lorrain, the seventeenth-century French painter. Claude deeply influenced other European landscape painters and the Americans who learned from European masters. So complete was this influence that Americans, both artists and patrons, may have been viewing distinctly American landscapes, but, in the phrase of art historian Barbara Novak, they were "viewing them through European spectacles." Claudian conventions required artists to frame their scenes, most often with large trees or some other vegetation on either side of the canvas. In the middle, the view stretched from small figures in a generally pastoral foreground, past some form of water in the middle of the canvas, and out toward a mountain scene topped by dramatic skies. So common was this Claudian "stamp" that viewers expected landscapes to contain these components, and paintings that strayed too far from these expectations could be labeled flawed or even grotesque.[28]

For the Catskills the most important aspect of the Claudian "stamp" was the nearly universal appearance of mountains in the background. Obviously other topics drew artists' attention—sailing ships, stormy seas, et cetera—but mountains gained disproportionate interest. Revealing the centrality of mountains to successful landscapes, English author and landscapist John Ruskin dedicated one of the volumes of his guide to painting, *Modern Painters*, to "Mountain Beauty," in which he declared, "mountains are the beginning and the end of all natural scenery."[29] So, when landscape artists set out from the city, very often heading north on the Hudson, they were by custom drawn to rising landscapes, such as the Hudson Highlands and, of course, the Catskills. As transportation improved, artists would travel much farther, to the Adirondacks and White Mountains, most importantly, and eventually to the Rockies and Sierra Nevada after the opening of the transcontinental railroads. In the meantime, however, the Catskills often sufficed as the mountains that filled the backgrounds of American landscape paintings, so much so that the collection of midcentury painters would take the name Hudson River School, a designation that had more to do with the location of New York City at the river's mouth than with beautiful mountains along its banks. Had the nation's arts scene flourished in Hartford, for instance, no doubt the school would have become known as the Connecticut River School, as artists sought out highlands near that city.[30]

So many nineteenth-century artists headed up the Hudson to the Catskills that it became one of the most frequently painted regions in the Americas, and the mountains clearly influenced the young nation's landscape art. American paintings often featured the narrow cloves common in the Catskills, the misty atmospherics of its humid, shifting weather. Just as important, Hudson River art also shaped the mountains, creating nearly standard images of the Catskills that would so deeply influence American perceptions of that place even into the present. Just as wild, romantic scenes dominated Hudson River art, they would also determine how New York consumers would conceptualize the Catskills. Hudson River artists practiced a type of realism that captured the essence of natural scenes, what Asher B. Durand called "the simple truths of Nature." Rendering these truths required remarkably accurate and detailed vegetation and rock formations, and Hudson River artists were well known for their thorough sketches made firsthand in "the studio of Nature."[31]

Still, Hudson River realism did not require the accurate presentation of a real scene. In fact, the style encouraged otherwise. In the interest of capturing some larger truth, artists could transform reality, especially by adding or removing natural objects, not just to satisfy Claudian requirements, but also to heighten the desired effects. Mountains rose to meet artists' expectations; their features became more dramatic, more rugged. Trees aged to give a sense of time; they became hoary, often twisted, to reveal the landscape's ancient past. Although praised for the realism of his wild scenes, Cole took liberties with his compositions. "If the imagination is shackled, and nothing is described but what we see," he wrote to a patron in 1825, "seldom will anything truly great be produced either in Painting or Poetry." While Cole surely understood the importance of studying nature, he did not believe the artist should copy it directly; "on the contrary," he wrote, "the most lovely and perfect parts of nature may be brought together, and combined in a whole, that shall surpass in beauty and effect any picture painted from a single view." To accomplish this,

Cole made sketches of natural subjects, but let them sit for a while, allowing "time to draw a veil over the common details, the unessential parts."
In this way, Cole and other Hudson River painters created realistic landscapes that were deceivingly fantastic—more perfect, effective, and
essential than their subjects could ever be.[32]

From the 1820s through the 1870s, dozens of important landscape
painters headed up the Hudson on sketching trips, and then retreated
to their studios to produce beautiful, often sublime portraits of idealized American nature. In the process, they both reminded their customers
of a place and time they once knew, the familiar scenes along the well-
traveled Hudson, and created nearly new images of the region, shaping
viewers' ideas about how the city's hinterland actually appeared. Among
these painters, Cole was clearly the most important. As a young man in
Ohio and then Pennsylvania, Cole tried his hand at art, and after moving to New York City to rejoin his family in 1825, Cole began making the
short trip up the river to the Catskills. His first visit resulted in a series
of sketches, which he later used to create five wonderful landscape paintings, including one of South Lake and another of Kaaterskill Falls. William
Coleman hung three of Cole's paintings in his Manhattan shop, where
they gained the attention of prominent artist John Trumbull. After he
purchased Cole's painting of the falls, Trumbull notified two friends,
painter William Dunlap and the engraver Asher B. Durand, who in turn
purchased the remaining two Cole landscapes. The sales gave Cole a mod-
icum of financial success, but more important the paintings garnered
critical praise. Just months after Cole had shown his first paintings in
the city, the *New York Review and Atheneum Magazine* declared him
"among the most eminent landscape painters."[33]

This early success gave Cole the confidence and funding to take an
extended European trip, to see the works of the masters, learn the finer
techniques of their art, and survey the landscapes they had painted. Such
a European trip was the general practice for American painters, and would
remain so through the century, despite the growing interest in American scenes. After several years in Europe, Cole returned to the United
States in 1832, and over the next four years he moved back and forth
between New York and Catskill, spending the warmer months near the
mountains, and the winter months, the "studio season," in the thriving
art scene of Greenwich Village. In the city he enjoyed the company of
family, some of whom still lived in New York, and "other persons of taste
& refinement." But Cole did not enjoy the city's "fashionable parties,"

even though they brought him into contact with the types of people who would purchase his work. In November 1834, having returned to New York after summering in Catskill, he complained in his journal: "here is nothing but turmoil my mind is distracted with a thousand cares." Before long, the society of the city, the easy contact with artists and patrons, could no longer keep Cole away from the mountains. Preferring "the quietness of the country" to the "turmoil" of New York, Cole found he could hardly paint in New York, and despite the considerable time he spent in Gotham, he apparently never undertook a painting of the city itself. In April of 1835, after an unproductive winter, during which he didn't finish a single painting due to "so many interruptions," Cole determined "not to remove to the city next year," deciding to remain in the country and thereby remain productive and happy.[34]

In 1836 Cole moved into the Catskill home of his new wife—a home with a stunning view of the mountains. There he lived until his death, taking frequent "rambles" into the nearby Catskills. He entertained many of the artists of the Hudson River School in this home, and even went with some on sketching trips into the mountains. Although he took another trip to Europe and sketching trips to other scenic regions in the United States, Cole, more than most nineteenth-century landscape painters, was largely content to stay close to the comfort of his home and the beauty of his Catskills. His love of the mountains was clear not just in his paintings, a large number of which are Catskills scenes or draw upon Catskills scenery, but also in his writings. In one essay, "The Clove Valley," Cole wrote lovingly of the Kaaterskill region, which he found as picturesque as any he had seen in the world. "Nothing can exceed the beauty of the mountain forests," he wrote, "and this valley they have clothed in their richest and most varied garb. . . ." Cole's romantic sensibility allowed him to see a most perfect Catskills, in which even the "picturesque ruin of an old sawmill" in the heart of the clove "has a fine effect in that secluded situation." In the village of Palenville, at the foot of the clove, Cole found several mills and tanneries but declared the situation "romantic." As surely as the Claudian stamp shaped Cole's canvases, romanticism limited his perception of the mountains. To Cole, the Catskill region was not a collection of struggling rural towns, replete with farms, tanneries, and quarries; it was simply the home of the "richest" of "mountain forests."[35]

Even after Cole moved to Catskill, living in his ideal landscape, painting in his backyard studio, and periodically rambling in search of the sublime and picturesque, he maintained close connections to the city, via convenient Hudson River transportation. But river travel in New York had one dramatic flaw: the river froze. More than just the attractiveness of mountain summers had brought Cole to Catskill in the warm months, and more than the fear of winter's harshness had sent him back to New York in the late fall. Cole needed the city, even when he lived in Catskill, but each winter the frozen Hudson greatly impeded transportation between the two places for weeks or, more commonly, months.[36] Except during the worst snows, carriage travel remained viable, but the trip was arduous and uncomfortable in the cold. "I do not feel any great inclination to come to the city before the river opens," Cole wrote to his patron Luman Reed in January 1836, during the first winter Cole had spent away from the city since returning from Europe. At the time, Reed was anxious to see his friend and his current work, *The Course of Empire* series that Reed had commissioned, but the frozen river proved to be a critical divide. Three years later, Cole wrote Durand in December, anticipating the closing of the river and consequently feeling "as though my friends in N. York" would be "removed one thousand miles farther." Sensing the isolation that would come with the frozen river, Cole asked Durand to keep up their correspondence, "in the hope that through you I shall from time to time hear a little news from the world of art."[37]

Cole frequently begged his friend Durand to move out of New York, claiming the change would be good for his health, especially his mental health. "Nature is a sovereign remedy," Cole wrote to Durand in the fall of 1836. "Your depression is the result of debility and you require the pure air of heaven." Cole even suggested that should Durand move to Catskill, both would be benefited by their closer relationship. Still, Durand stayed in the city, content with the society of so many of the nation's landscape painters and the patrons who purchased their work. Although the distance from New York to Catskill usually separated the two painters, Cole and Durand traveled together on rambles, sketching trips "in search of the picturesque," most famously to Schroon Lake in the Adirondacks, an adventure that produced notable works from both painters. The two also shared a long correspondence in the 1830s, as both artists achieved considerable fame. Though he frequently urged Durand to move out of the city, Cole made good use of his friend's continued presence in New York. Cole regularly requested paints, varnish, and canvases, which Durand purchased in the city and then sent by steamer up the Hudson. Cole even sent canvases down to Durand to hang in the city. In sum,

Durand's continued presence in the city made Cole's absence that much easier.[38]

Many of Cole's best customers also lived in the city, including Reed, who lived in Greenwich Village. In 1815, Reed had moved to New York from Columbia County, along the Hudson River, and turned his success in grocery wholesaling into a large fortune. He then turned his fortune toward the encouragement of native art, especially through his patronage of Durand and Cole. As a native of the Hudson Valley, Reed particularly craved parochial landscapes, as did many other New York patrons. Although Cole's artistic interests took him in multiple directions, toward European landscapes and fanciful allegorical paintings, his Catskills landscapes always sold well. Historians have often assumed Cole had complete artistic control over his work, selecting the scene and the mood of his landscapes, but in actuality several of his works were more or less described by their purchasers before Cole began to paint. After seeing Cole's first painting of Kaaterskill Falls, for example, Hartford's Daniel Wadsworth commissioned another from Cole. And later, in 1835, W. Stuyvesant commissioned two works from Cole and "expressed a desire to have two pictures similar to W[illiam P.] Van Rensselaer's." Another patron, Robert Gilmore, urged Cole to be true to his subject, to paint the "desolate wilderness of American nature," for clearly those were the paintings that moved Gilmore most. And in 1840, A. N. Skinner commissioned a work from Cole but turned down one of his soon-to-be famous Schroon Lake landscapes. Skinner preferred a different, less wild tone, and a scene with "green meadows" like those he had seen in another Cole landscape, "In the Catskills," which Cole had painted for Jonathan Sturges in 1837. "Perhaps I expect too much in one painting," Skinner wrote Cole in describing his desires, "but unless my mind deceives me, all I wish is in the Catskill. . . ."[39]

If the market helped determine what he painted, and even sometimes the mood of his work, Cole retained predominant artistic control over his canvases. He painted several well-received pastoral landscapes, but more than most painters Cole tended toward wilder scenes. Though praised for their realism, Cole's paintings were not simply representations of actual places. They were constructions, for which Cole used painterly techniques to capture the beauty of a natural scene, even when in the process the actual scene became unrecognizable. Claudian custom required that Cole introduce some elements—framing trees at times, larger mountains at others. And commonly used symbolic features added meaning to natural scenes—tree stumps suggesting the coming change due to human settlement, and blasted vegetation representing the continuing power of nature. In all of his landscapes, Cole struggled to do more than capture a true, beautiful, natural scene. Cole's work was fundamentally religious in nature. He took his role as creator seriously. In 1842, Cole described art as "man's lowly imitation of the creative power of the Almighty."[40] He was, quite literally, recreating God's own work on his canvas. One surely did not want to cheat God of his powers, so Cole sought landscapes, created landscapes, that made clear God's presence in nature.

Cole's influence over the mountains was as significant as his influence over American art. Many of Cole's wilder images removed all evidence of culture. He strove to make the American landscape both ancient and timeless—the unchanged Eden. In doing so, he could boast for America a landscape richer in history than that of Europe's. This was natural history, of course, not cultural, which meant that often the actual human history of the places Cole painted had to be ignored. Although Cole famously spoke out against the destruction of America's great forests, he also had the ability to see only the forests, to ignore human intrusions. In July of 1835, Cole enjoyed one of his best outings to the Kaaterskill Clove, where he hiked and sketched in the familiar territory. In recounting the visit in his journal, Cole boasted that the "painter of American scenery has, indeed, privileges superior to any other. All nature here is new to art." Among America's "primeval forests, virgin lakes and waterfalls," Cole felt he had the opportunity to paint something new, simply by the fact that so little of the American landscape had been captured on canvas. What's more, Cole believed much of the American landscape was not only new to art, but also virgin altogether—untouched by human hands. Cole traipsed through the Catskills thinking that the American artist might fill "his portfolio with their features of beauty and magnificence and hallowed to his soul because they had been preserved untouched from the time of creation for his favored pencil." And yet the clove was hardly "virgin altogether," as his comments about a romantic ruined sawmill make clear. Farmers' fields, sheep pastures, cleared forests, quarries, and the many roads and paths that connected them together gave ample evidence of the region's history as a place other than wilderness. On that same trip in 1835, Cole and a friend launched a boat on the "virgin waters" of South Lake, around which "fine dead trees" stood "like specters on the shores." The trees, the subject of one of Cole's first Catskills paintings, were "a striking feature in the scenery of this lake, and exceedingly picturesque." Since dead trees symbolized the power of nature in the vernacular of landscape painting, Cole intended his 1825 canvas to represent the wildness of the region. Just below these "virgin waters," however, Silas Scribner had built a milldam in 1823 on South Lake's outlet, the boulder-filled stream that led to Kaaterskill Falls. Cole neither commented upon the Scribner mill nor portrayed it in his many paintings of the Kaaterskill area.[41]

Cole's work influenced dozens of important American painters, some of whom knew him well, like Durand, and others who never met him. Cole's work inspired these landscape artists, and no doubt so did the critical acclaim and commissions Cole garnered. Over the five decades after Cole's first sales, New York's artists created hundreds of important paintings of Catskills scenes, and thousands of lesser works. Historians have attributed the growing market for native landscapes to a surging nationalism following the War of 1812, as Americans sought to further distance themselves from European culture, a process that would require the strengthening of fine arts in the United States. Nationalism also encouraged painters and patrons to prize noticeably American scenes—especially wild scenes—for nothing distinguished America from Europe more than its abundance of wilderness. So, while European masters had filled their paintings with pastoral scenes, with ruins that evidenced the long-domesticated nature of the landscape, American painters increasingly created canvases nearly devoid of culture, a trend begun in earnest by Cole and his *Lake with Dead Trees* in 1825. Clearly some wealthy New Yorkers patronized local artists and purchased native landscapes as part of this nationalist effort, and some may have favored the wilder scenery created by New York landscapists because they could recognize the scene as clearly American.[42] Still, wilderness scenes were not the only native landscapes that drew attention and praise in New York, as painters continued to capture traditional pastoral scenes. Indeed, the variety of landscapes created by the Hudson River School from the 1820s through the 1860s suggests a continuing appreciation for the great variations within the American countryside—from the pastoral to the wild. Perhaps more than nationalism, a growing pining for the countryside increased demand for native landscapes, paintings that reminded urban residents of beautiful, peaceful, and wild landscapes increasingly unavailable to them in the city. Not surprisingly, the most popular landscapes were those that tended to be familiar to wealthier New Yorkers, especially sites along the

Hudson and tourist destinations in the East. Just as significant, they also tended to be images that minimized the role of work in rural society, and represented an urban idealized portrait of a country life. Along with the growing body of romantic literature, Hudson River landscapes created idealized images of nature, and as they became ever more commonplace, they narrowed urban conceptions of the countryside.[43]

Even after Cole's death, the Catskills remained a popular stop for artists during the sketching season, with the region around Kaaterskill Clove attracting the most attention. Artists frequented the Mountain House, as Cole had done, but those who stayed for longer visits usually sought out quieter spots, farther from the tourist crowds. In 1848, while conceptualizing his painting to commemorate Cole's life, Durand traveled to the Catskills, and, with fellow artists John Casilear and John Kensett, he stayed at Pine Orchard for two weeks. They then moved down to a boardinghouse in Palenville, where they remained an additional two weeks, sketching and socializing with the many other artists who passed through. By 1857 *Appleton's Illustrated Hand-Book of American Travel* could identify Palenville as "the humble village" preferred by artists, probably because of the cheap rents and the limited number of tourists, who preferred to stay up in the mountains themselves. Palenville provided easy access to the Kaaterskill Clove and apparently to sufficient wilderness inspiration, despite the continuing operation of a tannery in town. Also in the 1850s, John Rusk's boardinghouse in Tannersville became a popular spot for artists, including Durand, Kensett, Jervis McEntee, and T. Addison Richards. At the same time, Sanford Gifford made Scribner's boardinghouse near South Lake his favorite spot, at least until the increasing number of boarders from the city spoiled its attraction. He and others also utilized Brocket's boardinghouse in the Clove itself.[44]

By the mid-1850s, then, the Catskills had become a well-known sketching ground for both accomplished and aspiring artists. In his 1854 travel narrative, *American Scenery*, T. Addison Richards repeated an amusing play on words concerning the abundance of artists, noting that he had been told the Catskills were "infested with 'painters'," a vulgarism for "panther." In actuality, of course, the Catskills teamed with real painters. Ironically, the Catskills canvases would seem no less wild despite the absence of big cats in the mountains. Richards described a landscape so full of artists that he finds "an enraptured student" around every turn, or "an unfinished canvas, carefully secreted in the cavities of the rocks," symbolic, perhaps, of the way the actual landscape became conflated with the abundant landscape art.[45]

In part because of Cole, the Kaaterskill Clove had accrued historical value; its landscape held special cultural currency. Nowhere else could landscape artists find so many scenes worthy of attention, not just because of their beauty and cultural significance, but also because changing weather and light offered seemingly endless variety. "Short distances in our Catskill country often bring us to changed landscapes," wrote Worthington Whittridge, the Ohio-born painter who had moved to New York City in the 1850s. Whittridge had arrived in New York hoping to produce something new in the way of landscapes. He turned to nature and, thus, to the Catskills, for inspiration. "I hid myself for months in the recesses of the Catskills," he wrote in his autobiography.

Most artists only spent a few days or perhaps a week in the Catskills on their sketching trips, but others, following Cole, began to summer in or near the mountains, often taking trips into the mountains for weeks at a time. Most sought out the companionship of like-minded painters, including Whittridge, who traveled and sketched with Jervis McEntee, whose home in Kingston overlooked both the Hudson and the Catskills, and who frequently traveled with friends on long trips into the mountains.[46]

If the Catskills became critical to Whittridge's success, they were more so to his good friend Sanford Gifford, of whom Whittredge wrote: "We were told that he was born in Saratoga County. As an artist, he was born in the Catskill Mountains." From the mid-1840s through the late 1850s, Gifford spent his studio seasons in New York City, where artists clustered in social organizations, like the Century Club, formed in 1846 by some former members of the Sketch Club. Gifford also worked at the 10th Street Studio Building, where Frederic Church and many other well-known landscape painters rented space during studio seasons. Through this era, the landscape art of these men and others dominated the annual showings at the National Academy of Design, which had featured native art since 1826. In the summer and autumn months, however, Gifford, who had a home in Hudson, across the river, took long trips into the mountains, both sketching and fishing. Over his lengthy career, Gifford created a considerable portfolio of Catskills landscapes, some of which are among the best of the Hudson River School. As Whittridge wrote, Gifford sought out the "fleeting effects of nature" produced by changing weather and light, and which became so important to the atmospherics of Gifford's emerging luminist style. In this way, the atmospherics of the Catskills encouraged the development of a new painting technique.[47]

While dozens of prominent painters followed Cole into the Catskills, only one painter entered a formal student-teacher relationship with him: Frederic Church. Born into a wealthy Hartford, Connecticut, family, Church decided he wanted to become a painter at a young age. He sought out the best landscape artist, Cole, and in 1844 he moved to Catskill, where he studied with the master for three years. He then moved downriver to New York, where his talents were easily recognized. By 1851, Church was among the leading American landscape artists, and, unlike his teacher, he still had a very long career ahead of him.[48] In 1860, Church married and purchased a farm overlooking the Hudson, Cole's old home in Catskill, and, of course, the Catskill Mountains. Using his considerable wealth and talents, Church designed and built a large home near the top of the hill, and, just as important, designed a new landscape for his extensive property, building a large pond and planting thousands of trees. Complete with winding carriage paths and walkways, the grounds reflected the romantic vision of rural landscapes encouraged by the Hudson River School, and indeed surely Church considered his estate, called Olana, one of his finest pieces of art—a landscape created by artifice as completely as any upon his canvases.[49]

Although he traveled widely and regularly painted far-off places, including South America, Church's return to the Hudson revealed the continuing importance of both Cole and the Catskills in his work. He had painted at the 10th Street Studio for a number of years, but later in his career Church returned to his place of training, to a region certain to inspire his work. As an 1878 *Art Journal* article on Church stated succinctly, "The Catskill region has been, since the days while Cole's pencil first drew attention to its picturesque beauty, Nature's great Academy of American landscape Art." For landscape artists, returning to the Catskills not only brought the opportunity to pay homage to Cole but also to tackle a popular subject, one freighted with meaning. And, as the article continued, the "primeval haunts" of the Catskills afforded "unrivalled" opportunity for "studies of our Northern skies, of atmosphere, phenomena of rugged mountain-forms, of the manifestations of Nature in the seasons, and for the accidental lights and shadows which give variety to a landscape."[50]

Hudson River paintings were so plentiful, especially in New York, that their influence over popular culture is hard to exaggerate. Certainly wealthier New Yorkers were much more likely to own an original oil painting, but nearly all residents of the city had ample opportunities to see the works. Artists supplied landscape paintings for shows at the American Academy of Fine Arts and the National Academy of Design, both of which held regular exhibitions as early as the 1820s. Later, the 10th Street Studio held shows to attract purchasers, and, of course, smaller galleries regularly featured Hudson River landscapes. Some patrons staged shows of their collections, either to establish their position within the arts community or to raise the value of the paintings. Other shows allowed interested citizens to pay some nominal amount to view assorted paintings, and even before museums built their collections, special circumstances also allowed public access to privately owned paintings. For instance, after Luman Reed's death, over one hundred of his paintings hung in a gallery for twenty years, accessible to the public for twenty-five cents. The death of Cole also resulted in the creation of a retrospective show at the American Art-Union, where eighty-three of his paintings, owned by many individuals, hung together in a display of Cole's great accomplishments.[51]

Despite the large number of Hudson River paintings and the many opportunities to see them, with rare exceptions most of the landscapes made only fleeting public appearances before hanging on the walls of private homes. Some works hung in public more permanently, however, including the Cole painting *Falls of the Kaaterskill,* which graced the stateroom of the steamboat *Albany,* giving passengers on their way up the Hudson an artistic vision of what they might find in person if they disembarked at Catskill.[52] More important, several landscape painters had their works replicated as lithographs, which publishers could then reproduce as stand-alone art pieces or as illustrations in larger works. Cole's own *View of the Catskill Mountain House, N.Y.,* for example, appeared in lithographic form in the 1832 book, *The History and Topography of the United States.* Thomas Doughty's *Catskill Falls* appeared in lithographic form in *The Atlantic Souvenir* in 1828 and again in Theodore Dwight's *The Northern Traveller* that same year. Even more commonly, engravers simply used the Hudson River School style to create their own art, selecting their topics in much the same way as the painters. In this way, Hudson River School art made its way into even modest homes, in books, magazines, and inexpensive wall hangings. According to historian Hans Huth, Cole's works even became favorite patterns for pottery. In sum, most New Yorkers were familiar with the Catskills landscape, if not through their own travels up the Hudson, then through the work of artists recreating the American landscape. All of this art taught urban Americans the beauty and value of the American rural landscape.[53]

Paintings are static representations, but Hudson River landscapes generally strove to create an impression of movement or change. The frequent appearance of sunsets, the arrival or clearing of storms, the inclusion of tree stumps, and many other indications or portents of change reflected the artists' interest in capturing narrative movement in a static image. These landscapes regularly gave the impression that something new was on the horizon (literally on the horizon in the case of dramatic sunsets), whether it be progress wrought by continued settlement, or a darker foreboding of wilderness lost. However much Hudson River artists sought to create a sense of movement, though, their works generally did the opposite—they stopped time, creating, in Emerson's words, a "concentrated eternity." In the short term, this meant capturing fleeting cloud formations or dramatic colorations; but the consequences for the long term were more important, for Hudson River art created an expectation about what the Catskills actually looked like, and, more important, how they should continue to appear. The art created an ideal expectation, particularly for urban viewers of art who hoped to find that the paintings were simply reality in miniature, and that ideal mountain landscapes did indeed exist just up the Hudson.[54]

By the 1860s, improved transportation, especially the opening of the transcontinental railroad, allowed greater mobility for landscape painters searching for worthy scenes. Albert Bierstadt famously traveled west, painting the grand and expansive landscapes of the Rockies and the Sierra Nevada. Frederic Church traveled widely, becoming all the more famous with his massive landscapes of the Andes in South America. Paintings of the Catskills looked quaint and especially tame in comparison to these more distant, wilder scenes. Even as Bierstadt and Church worked on more rugged, more distant mountains, however, the Hudson River School was under attack, its name, apparently affixed around 1870, intended to criticize the parochialism of New York's landscape painters. Still, the school's decline had less to do with improved transportation diminishing the focus on regional landscapes and more to do with decreasing appreciation for the school's style. After the Civil War, American arts became less nationalistic, and European art once again gained favor, especially the fresh style of the French Barbizon School. In comparison to Barbizon canvases, which portrayed more mundane landscapes using a more impressionistic approach, the Hudson River landscapes appeared much too literal, too heavily detailed. The romanticism of the Hudson River School looked old-fashioned. As early as 1867 the *New York Times* became highly critical of the National Academy of Design for showing essentially the same work year after year. A column accused McEntee of "wasting his brilliant powers upon works which he learned to do thoroughly years ago," and flatly stated, "Kensett repeats himself in almost every picture." Other prominent landscapists, including Gifford and George Inness, came in for the same criticism. It was time for innovation. Gifford died in 1880, followed by Durand in 1886, but both had lived long enough to see their own great works ravaged by critics eager for something new.[55]

Art critics and the art-purchasing public may have grown tired of the sameness of Hudson River art, but the criticism, in part shaped by the appreciation of the more impressionistic works appearing in Europe, helped obscure the accomplishments of the older landscapists. Accusing the Hudson River School of too much realism, too much detail and literal description of nature, at the expense of more interpretive, artistic work further concealed what the American painters actually did—create ideal landscapes, full of symbolism, emotion, and movement. The criticism pointed to a growing sense that the Hudson River canvases simply captured a moment in time in actual, familiar places, some within easy reach of the city. In this way, the decline of the Hudson River School helped solidify a common misperception of the mid-century landscapes—that they were really historical portraits of wild American scenes.

By the late 1800s, the Hudson River School had fallen out of favor, and even into disdain, but the accomplishments of that group of artists were many and significant. Together they established a uniquely American art tradition, one that elevated their native landscape's cultural significance. However, for our purposes, the images themselves, the wild scenes, the places made familiar by repeated paintings, constitute the most important legacy of the Hudson River artists. Along with the many writers from the city, artists created a new and surprisingly deep history for the Catskills—the ancient forests, the stories of lore. Irving, Cooper, Bryant, Cole, Gifford, Church, and dozens of others filled the Catskills with cultural value—the associations Sarah Hale had longed for in 1835. For New Yorkers, the mountains became much more than just a natural place, more than nondescript localities where farmers hoped to make enough money to raise their families. As art historian Barbara Novak wrote, "Cole tried to raise landscape to the level of history painting," and to the degree that he helped create a history of the Catskills, he surely succeeded. For in his paintings, and those of many other Hudson River painters, and in the stories of New York's writers, we find recorded moments in time, places held still in a condition of wilderness or semi-settlement.[56] Few sites in America have been so completely defined by artists—both writers and painters—as have the Catskills.[57]

Many great works can represent the accomplishments of the Hudson River School, but one deserves special attention: Asher B. Durand's *Kindred Spirits*, completed in 1849. Painted as a eulogy to Cole, who died the previous year, it is probably the most famous of the many Catskills paintings, and easily the most reprinted. In the painting, Bryant and Cole are perched overlooking a fictional Catskills clove. Here poet and artist stand in a landscape of Durand's making, derived from sketches from the Kaaterskill region. But the scene is really of Cole's creation, his idealized wilderness. Like much of the Hudson River art, Durand's realistic style hides the exaggeration—art has made this clove more beautiful, spectacular, more perfectly seen, than any the Catskills could actually offer. Proper perception and vision, after all, were everything. The clove reaches toward infinity, framed perfectly by the tree to the left. The falls in the center speak to the eternity represented in the landscape, the blasted vegetation in the foreground to the power of nature. All the symbolism of the genre is here. But there is more, for also in the center are Bryant and Cole, the latter with sketchbook in hand. The position of writer and painter, with Cole clearly acting as teacher, speaks to the power of the artist not just as the interpreter of the scene, but also as its creator. Durand includes his familiar detailed foreground, the exquisite vegetation, the rocks complete with lichen and moss, but beyond the figures, beyond Cole's sketchbook, inside the frame of tree and cliff, we see a familiar landscape painting—Cole's, not Durand's. It was, and is, a fine tribute to Cole's contribution to the creation of the ideal American landscape, the Edenic wilderness.

New York wholesaler Jonathan Sturges commissioned *Kindred Spirits* upon Cole's death, and when Durand completed it, Sturges gave the large painting to Bryant in recognition of the poet's own eulogy of Cole. The painting hung in Bryant's Roslyn home for decades, where the many writers and painters who regularly visited the famed author at his Long

Island retreat could see it. One of those visitors was Candace Wheeler, who visited frequently with her husband from their nearby home, Nestledown. Wheeler became so influenced by the work that she continued to see its forms, the spot where Cole and Bryant stood, even after she returned to the Catskills years later. "When I came to live in the mountains I was always recognizing that ledge, whether my steps led me east or west, north or south."[58]

Wheeler perfectly described the real power of the art. It encouraged New Yorkers to envision the mountains in a particular way, both while in the city and even while in the Catskills themselves. Any number of Catskills visitors would "recognize that ledge" and the many other famed images of the mountains, and, just as important, they would continue to visit the Catskills, eager to see these familiar scenes. For just over a century, the New York Public Library owned *Kindred Spirits*, and for most of that time it hung in that beautiful edifice on the corner of Fifth Avenue and 42nd Street, a little piece of Catskills wildness at the very heart of the city. In a recent appeal to keep the painting in the city, historian Thomas Bender noted that " 'Kindred Spirits' embodies the beginning of New York's metropolitan claims," meaning, I suppose, that in it two consummate New Yorkers stand above a world over which they held great control. Although Bender argued that the painting belonged *in* the city, it so clearly belongs *to* the Catskills as well, one of hundreds of paintings that helped make those mountains so famous around the nation, one of hundreds of images that over time have become naturalized pieces of Catskills heritage.[59]

Chapter 3

The Mountain Hotels

When city people come to the country they do not walk, because that would be
conceding too much to the country; beside, they would soil their shoes and would
lose the awe and respect which their imposing turn-outs inspire.

—John Burroughs, 1881

For none more than the Americans make it a principle to desert the city, and
none less than Americans know how to dispense with it. So we compromise by
taking the city with us, and the country gently laughs us to scorn.

—George William Curtis, 1852

O utsiders may have played a disproportionate role in creating popular nineteenth-century Catskills images, but locals did their best
to sell the culture created for the region—to market the mountains using
those writings and representations. This was especially true of Washington
Irving's "Rip Van Winkle." Though Irving had not set foot in the Catskills
before setting his famous story in "the highest parts" of the mountains,
his description of a Hudson River view and a "deep mountain glen" convinced many that the setting was real (if not the story itself), and that
Irving had indeed described the region around Kaaterskill Clove. As early
as 1828, a cabin along the road to the famed Mountain House became
known as Rip Van Winkle's shanty, where travelers on their way up to
see the view could stop for ale or other refreshment in the "very spot"
where Rip had overslept. Eventually the steep stretch of road approaching the shanty became known as "Rip Van Winkle Hollow," and then,
confusing Irving's best known stories, "Sleepy Hollow." By 1870, the small
shanty had been replaced by a larger building, the Rip Van Winkle House,
which prospered as a boarding business only as long as stagecoaches
passed along that route, and it would disappear altogether after railroads
provided much easier access to the mountaintop. Still, Richard DeLisser's
1894 work on Greene County included photographs not just of the Rip
Van Winkle House but also of Rip's Rock (labeled as such by paint applied
directly to the rock itself), on which the henpecked Rip had supposedly
sat, drunk from his flagon, and avoided his wife. By that time Rip's story

had helped animate the entire region with legend and folklore, and locally produced tourist guides eager to sell the mountains used Rip's name, including the Ulster and Delaware Railroad's annual guide, which carried the subtitle "The Haunts of Rip Van Winkle."[1]

More than just the name attached itself to Catskills locations, however, for the very story seeped into the landscape. Irving's characters peopled Palenville and the region around, as locals took ownership of the story, retelling its most fantastic parts; the sound of ninepin, the *Half Moon* crew, and Rip's slumber all cast mystery about the place. Irving's images of the Catskills affected more than just the tourists, for they had become naturalized, part of the local culture. Annie Searing, growing up in the Hudson Valley just below the mountains in the 1860s, recalled how her family celebrated "Rip Van Winkle Day" around Palenville, with her father retelling the story and encouraging the children to picture Henry Hudson's men bowling. Searing remembered entering an old house, identified as Rip's, and feeling his presence there. All of this was so real to Searing, and no doubt to her father too, since the tale—even if fictional—was an important story of that very spot, or so they believed. Indeed, it was *the* story of that spot, accepted as such by tourists and locals alike.[2]

Well beyond the story of "Rip Van Winkle," nineteenth-century artists and authors reconstructed the mountains in their work, creating powerful images of the mountains, developing expectations for Catskills visitors and encouraging pride among the region's residents. Still, the real work of remaking the Catskills would come through the tourist industry, as locals attempted to meet visitors' growing demands for amenities and activities in the mountains. Beginning in the mid-nineteenth century, American tourism grew rapidly, as the urban middle class expanded, allowing more people the wealth and time needed for travel, and as cultural proscriptions against leisure waned. Although the growing tourist industry transformed dozens of places, it changed few regions as completely as the Catskills. In easy reach of the thriving, wealthy metropolises of New York and Philadelphia, as well as dozens of smaller cities, the Catskills became one of the most popular tourist destinations in the nation. Since tourists' experiences helped drive changing conceptions of rural landscapes, the evolving ideas of Catskills tourists reflected urban America's changing ideas about nature, and, in fact, helped precipitate those changing ideas.[3]

Recreational travel predated the 1800s, especially for Americans of means who sought edifying European trips, taking the "Grand Tour" through the great capital cities of the Continent. As transportation afforded better access to the American interior and as nationalism grew in the United States, an "American Grand Tour" developed in the East, giving tourists the option to explore their own country and revel in its natural beauty. By the 1830s, the typical tour began in New York Harbor on a Hudson River sloop that traveled up to the outlet of the Erie Canal, on which the tour continued by slow-moving barge to Niagara Falls. Along the way, tours generally included stops in the Hudson Valley, especially the Catskills, and in Saratoga, north of Albany. Additional detours took tourists to some of the most spectacular scenery in the East—New Hampshire's White Mountains.[4]

The American grand tour attracted mostly literate and wealthy travelers, and by the 1830s a raft of new travel books described the grand tour and all it had to offer. This literature did more than promote the growing tourist trade; it recorded the experiences of dozens of authors, some already famous, and some who would become well known through their travelogs. The "summer books" of wealthy tourists became quite popular through the 1840s and 1850s, a trend that historian Hans Huth claimed served "as ample evidence of the enormous increase of interest in the outdoors," but one must wonder how urban tourists could have more interest in the outdoors than farmers always had. Both the travel books and Huth's comments upon their meaning reflected an emphatically urban bias. Indeed, the midcentury witnessed an "enormous increase of interest in the outdoors," but only among urbanites who increasingly found their daily lives devoid of natural scenery. Not surprisingly, as urban tourists set out of the city in search of pleasing rural landscapes, they saw them very differently than did country residents. As Huth's conclusion suggests, in a rapidly urbanizing culture, the nation's conceptions of rural America were increasingly generated in the city, far from the farms, woodlots, and quarries of the mountains.[5]

A remarkable gender balance in the genre reflected the high participation of educated women in early travel. These women sought cultural attainment as much as recreational relief, and their books provided behavioral guidance to tourists hoping to replicate the experiences of those in their class. As the literature makes clear, these early tours could be extraordinarily predictable, with tourists finding what they expected at the many "points of interest" that quickly dotted the landscape. This approach to American tourism became particularly evident at Niagara Falls, where named locations filled the map, and tourists consumed the site "bit by bit," as historian John Sears has described.[6]

Although early tourism often reflected a desire to achieve or display middle-class status, health concerns also influenced nineteenth-century vacations. Spas were particularly popular, as Saratoga, Richfield Springs, and other locations with sulfur springs promised healthful tonics and baths, as well as peaceful, relaxing surroundings. Health was a very real issue for urbanites, who even in the early 1800s were subject to crowd diseases, including seasonal diseases like yellow fever, periodic epidemics of cholera, and the endemic tuberculosis, then an incurable lung disease, the only real treatment for which was rest and pure air. Indeed, through the mid-nineteenth century, as cities grew in size and density, health concerns and the desire to be out of the city during the hot summer months eventually eclipsed social status as the central motivation for travel. Over time, a much greater proportion of the urban population would travel, reflecting not just an expansion of means, but also the role of the changing city in the development of tourism in the United States.[7]

American vacations changed through the nineteenth century, but one theme remained rather constant. Urbanites dominated tourism in the East, and city dwellers consistently brought the city with them when they vacationed, even when they took self-described wilderness excursions. As tourist author George Curtis described, "none more than the Americans make it a principle to desert the city," but "none less than Americans know how to dispense with it." Consequently, Curtis noted, he and other urban tourists "compromise by taking the city with us."[8] Hotels sprung up along the grand tour route, offering urban-style accommodations, cuisine, and entertainment, creating what historian Dona Brown has called an "urban social network," which strung through rural New York and New England. In becoming a favorite destination for tourists on this grand tour, then, the Catskills took on a number of qualities we would more likely associate with the city from which those tourists came. In a very real sense, by catering to urban tourists, the Catskills became a remarkably urbanized landscape.[9]

Although travelers had come through the Catskills for decades, the region's tourist history properly begins with the opening of the Catskill Mountain House in 1824. At first just a small hotel, with about ten rooms, the structure stood at the most prominent spot above the Hudson River, the very spot described by Cooper's Leatherstocking in *The Pioneers*, which had appeared just the year before. Local carpenter Wells Finch and his former apprentice Samuel Chichester built this original building, which held out so much promise that the very next year the Catskill Mountain Association, a stock company formed to purchase land around the escarpment and build a fine hotel, contracted for a fifty-room addition.[10] As an important stop along the grand tour, the Mountain House became a destination for tourists from around the nation and Europe, many of whom would contribute to the growing fame of the Catskills by writing of their mountaintop experiences. By the mid-1830s, the Mountain House had already achieved considerable notoriety, and more travelers made certain their tours made stops at Pine Orchard, the name given to the grove surrounding the hotel. Steamships docked at the village of Catskill, where tourists climbed into a carriage for the 12-mile ride up a rough road, a trip that took the popular Irish actor Tyrone Power nearly five hours to complete. The destination was more than just the Mountain House, for although the long drive deposited guests at the rear of the hotel, they invariably walked immediately to the very precipice of the great cliff. The view was indeed the main event. As Bayard Taylor described in the *New York Tribune* in 1860: "Landing in the rear of the Mountain House, the huge white mass of which completely shuts out the view, thirty paces bring you to the brink of the rock, and you hang suspended, as if by magic, over the world."[11]

Here at the brink guests could have their requisite sublime experience. At the precipice, looking out over "all creation," tourists felt small, nature felt endless, and the power of God overwhelmed. Tears were not uncommon among tourists seeing the view for the first time. In 1891, John Burroughs visited the Mountain House while staying with a friend in the nearby Onteora Park. "The scene here is a great surprise," he wrote in his journal. "You drive swiftly along a good road up an easy grade till you alight in the rear of a great Hotel. You walk straight through the hall and there lies the world below you as if seen from a balloon. A young lady walked by my side, and, after a moment I turn to her to make some remark and found her in tears. The grandeur and unexpectedness of the scene had overcome her. She wept like a child." Even the well-traveled and eminently sensible Burroughs emoted at the scene. "I could hardly keep my own tears back," he concluded, though it is unclear whether the view or the young woman's reaction most affected Burroughs.[12]

Mid-nineteenth century tourists traveled up the mountain mostly to turn around and look back over the Hudson Valley. They stared out at the river, the most important commercial waterway in the United States, and watched the boat traffic. As Robert Vandewater wrote in his 1836 Hudson River tour guide, the view over the Hudson Valley featured a "seemingly endless succession of woods and waters, farms and villages." Towns and cities, he noted, were "spread out as upon a boundless map."[13] On clear days, they could see the Green Mountains of Vermont, the Berkshires of Massachusetts, the Adirondacks to the north, and the Hudson Highlands to the south, a truly "commanding view" of the thousands of square miles in what was then the heart of the north.[14] This view made the Mountain House world-renowned. Its growing number of guests came to take in the vista from many different locations, including the appropriately titled Artist's Rock, and Bear's Den, the spot from which Cole and other painters had gained perspective on the Mountain House and, at least on the canvases, the wilderness around. Although in the paintings the scene appeared timeless, in person the view was ever changing, altered by cloud movements and shifting light. After watching a fog recede from the valley, New York diarist George Templeton Strong called the view "the grandest sight I ever beheld."[15]

While the vista was potentially spectacular at any time of day, tourists paid particular attention to sunrise. Catching a midsummer sunrise required waking extremely early, but most guests made the effort. Strong awoke early on the second day of his visit to the Mountain House in 1843 to watch the sunrise, and when the morning light refracted in changing colors off the tops of the clouds below, he declared the sight "inexpressible altogether." The famed English writer Harriet Martineau, whose popular *Retrospect of Western Travel* detailed her American travels, described the sunrise in similar, though more poetic terms. Fearing her words could not capture the spectacle of her third sunrise on the mountaintop, she alleged that she "shall give no description, for I would not weary others with what is most sacred to me." She went on, however, claiming the sunrise gave her "a vivid idea of the process of creation, from the moment when all was without form and void to that when light was commanded, and there was light." For Martineau, then, the Mountain House overlook provided not just a vision of "all creation" laid out below, but a demonstration of the creative act itself. Another European visitor offered a more typical description, calling the scene "as indescribable as it was splendid and sublime, and we dwelt upon it with an intensity of admiration which almost made the head ache with the pleasure of the sight." Dozens of descriptions of the view were available to middle-class tourists, and they stoked the fires of expectation. If so many visitors wept at the precipice, they did so because on some level they thought they should.[16]

Since grand tour vacations of the 1830s featured quick stops at a number of locations, most guests stayed at the Mountain House just a night or two. Through the next few decades, however, extended visits would become common, as more than the view and sunrise attracted guests. Increasingly tourists traveled not just to see the sights, but also to flee the city, to find in the country something that the city could no longer offer. As Park Benjamin wrote in his weekly journal, *The New World*, in 1843,

> 'Tis pleasant, for a while to leave the heated pavements and the garbaged atmosphere of our ever bustling noisy city; to bid adieu to the continued rumbling and ratling [sic] of all the various vehicles that the worried horses are destined to drag in merciless labor to and fro the city's length; to shun the charcoal vender's unearthly guttural—the cries of the newspaper urchins, more varied in tone than the gamut's self . . . and perch one's self upon some mountainous elevation, where Nature's calmness changes the current of our thoughts. . . .[17]

Benjamin's remarks reveal how quickly the city had changed, how rapidly it grew, how densely it settled, and all the noise, heat, and dirt that came with it. His remarks also reveal how readily urbanites would think of the mountains, and the nature they found there, as the opposite of the city in which they lived.

As tourists began to treat the mountains as a refuge from the city, they would require more activities, beyond simply taking in views and strolling on paths to a few points of interest. As early as 1835, Thomas Cole lamented the increasing diversions sought out by tourists at the Mountain House. After taking breakfast in the hotel's dining room, Cole and his companion "loitered" at the precipice gazing out over the valley. However, Cole's journal entry for the day reflected less his appreciation of the scene than disgust for the bowling that occupied the men, the hobby horses on which the women played, and the dancing which kept everyone's attention focused on the veranda rather than on spectacular nature. "What a desecration of the place where nature offered a feast of higher holier enjoyment—alas that men should thrust their frivolities into the very face of the sublimest regions of the world—we turned away disgusted and sought pleasure where we were sure to find it pure healthful and unalloyed," he wrote.[18]

While sitting and dancing on the veranda remained favorite vacation pastimes, Cole was hardly the only visitor to set out on walks to take in the splendid natural scenes nearby. By the late 1830s, trails led to numerous popular destinations, including Kaaterskill Falls. By 1854, T. Addison Richards could describe a number of walks he and his companions took around the Mountain House, including up North Mountain and then around North Lake, which he called the "next pilgrimage which the tourist is expected to make." Clearly visitors anticipated experiencing some type of strong emotion at the end of each walk—often as strong as religious awe—hence the popularity of the term "pilgrimage."[19] Richards's description also suggests how regularized the walks around the mountaintop had already become. Nine years later the *Guide to Rambles from the Catskill Mountain House* described in detail the walks guests should take to maximize their romantic experience.[20]

By this time, guests had trouble securing rooms at the Mountain House, which in high season overflowed with visitors eager to experience the famed sunrise and the other sights around the hotel. Especially before the telegraph, poor communication between the city and the mountain meant that on some weekends dozens of tourists could arrive to find no room at the hotel, and, given the length of the trip off the mountain, many would become desperate for shelter nearby. As Charles Rockwell noted in 1867, "Very genteel-looking people may at times be seen coming from hay-lofts, at large hotels; and steamers, loaded with passengers, have had to accommodate them or carry them away, because there was no room on the mountain." Other tourists, including Henry David Thoreau, arrived on the mountaintop with no intention of staying at the pricey Mountain House. Unenthusiastic about staying at a resort hotel, Thoreau opted to lodge with Ira and Mary Scribner, who operated a sawmill on the stream between South Lake and the Kaaterskill Falls, not far from the Mountain House. During his 1844 visit, the Scribners were in the process of expanding their home, probably in an effort to make room for more visitors such as Thoreau. With so many tourists turned away or seeking less expensive alternatives, other hotels and boardinghouses flourished in the area, including the Laurel House, constructed at the top of Kaaterskill Falls, which, when it opened in the late 1840s, offered much cheaper lodging than the Mountain House. In addition, farmers in and around Haines Falls had long since begun taking in boarders as they presented themselves during the height of the season.[21]

Although the overflowing Mountain House encouraged the development of other accommodations in the area, its first real competition for the fashionable tourists derived from a dinner dispute. When George Harding, a wealthy Philadelphia lawyer who frequented the Mountain House, demanded fried chicken for his daughter, he was told the kitchen would only prepare meals that appeared on the menu. The conflict led to heated words between Harding and the proprietor of the Mountain House, Charles Beach, during which Beach apparently suggested that Harding open his own hotel, at which he could serve himself whatever he fancied. Harding did just that, acquiring property just two miles from the Mountain House on South Mountain and building the larger, more elegant Hotel Kaaterskill, which opened in the summer of 1881. The massive hotel could accommodate 800 guests by 1883, and after expansions just four years later, it could sleep 1,200. At that point it claimed to be the largest mountain hotel in the world.[22]

The Hotel Kaaterskill, perched on a South Mountain ridge, appeared equally elegant inside and out. During his 1881 visit, New York lithographer Henry Schile described the Kaaterskill "looking as charming in the mist of the verdant foliage as any of the most beautiful castles of Europe."[23] The hotel's own advertising promised "there is no hotel situated in the heart of New York or Paris where taste and wealth have more liberally contributed to secure to their guests comfort and luxury in highest attainable degree." The hotel offered the finest amenities, "perfect ventilation" and pure, sweet water, and the latest technology, too, with gas lighting inside and electric lighting outside. In its second year, the hotel published its own newspaper for guests, reprinting articles concerning the mountains, bits of weather information, guest lists, and even a few stock prices. The newspaper was just one more way in which the hotel hoped to combine the "beauties of nature" in its surroundings with "the comforts and luxuries of a city home."[24]

Despite the competition between the Hotel Kaaterskill and the Mountain House, as well as the nearby Laurel House, which had also expanded greatly by 1884, all the mountaintop hotels continued to flourish. Indeed, the additional accommodations seemed to only increase the popularity of the region, now known by two names, Pine Orchard and Kaaterskill Park. While the older name reflected the location's already deep tourist history, the latter reflected the ongoing effort to improve the region around the grand hotels, to make the entire region a great scenic park, complete with pleasure drives and a network of paths leading to points of interest, including spots intended for quiet contemplation. Indeed, excepting the spectacular nature of some of the destinations—the view over the Hudson and the Kaaterskill Falls, for example—the design of the Kaaterskill Park could not more closely resemble that of New York's own Central Park, developed in the 1850s. Constructed in an era when Kaaterskill Park continued to gain in popularity, Central Park's esthetic qualities echoed those of the mountain retreat. In fact, one of the architects of the city park, Calvert Vaux, had been a frequent visitor to the Catskills in the early 1850s, when he took excursions from the Newburgh office where he worked with famed landscape designer Andrew Jackson Downing. Even after leaving Newburgh for the city, Vaux continued to tour the Catskills, making many trips with his brother-in-law, the landscape painter Jervis McEntee. Vaux's interpretation of the picturesque was clearly shaped by Downing, but no doubt also by his visits to the Catskills, especially around the Mountain House.[25]

In constructing Central Park, Vaux and his partner, Frederick Law Olmsted, attempted to introduce the many positive aspects of country landscapes to what would become the heart of the city. As Olmsted wrote, one of the purposes of the park was "to supply hundreds of thousands of tired workers, who have no opportunity to spend their summers in the country, a specimen of God's handiwork that shall be to them, inexpensively, what a month or two in the White Mountains or the Adirondacks is, at great cost, to those in easier circumstances." The park, then, was a tourist spot for urbanites, a place to experience a bit of the countryside recreated in the city. Olmsted and Vaux's plan included the expansive "greensward," an open lawn that gave the greatest possible sense of space, and meandering footpaths, which created ever-changing vistas for walkers. A lengthy bridle path and winding carriage roads also gave urbanites the opportunity to take what amounted to a country drive without leaving Manhattan. Central Park even inspired its own tourist literature, to ensure that visitors took full advantage of its various offerings. Julian Larke's 1866 *Davega's Handbook of Central Park* described the rustic "Summer House on the Rock" situated to allow "a very fine view" of the Mall and great lawn, one of many spots created specifically for quiet contemplation. In addition, the fully constructed "Ramble" contained "little arbors, summer-houses, seats and snug retreats," and could take hours to negotiate, not unlike the walks around Kaaterskill Park. The Ramble even included a constructed mountain stream complete with a small falls and a number of seemingly natural pools.[26]

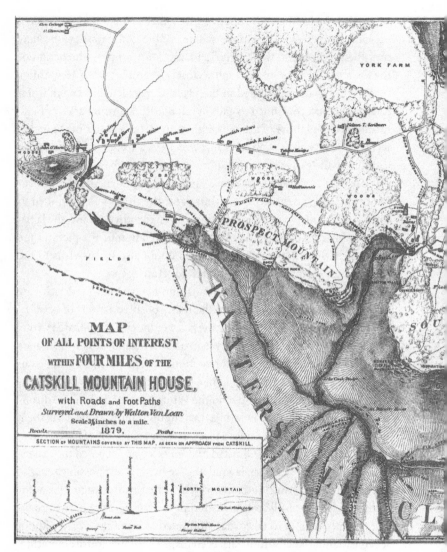

Map 2 Walton Van Loan's 1879 tourist map of Kaaterskill Park, the region around
the Mountain House, reveals a remarkably mixed landscape. Tourist paths are marked
by points of interest, such as Artist's Rock, Bear's Den, and Eagle Rock. Farms and
fields break up the forests admired by Hudson River School artists, while "old tannery ruins" and a number of quarries and "wood roads" reveal an extractive past.

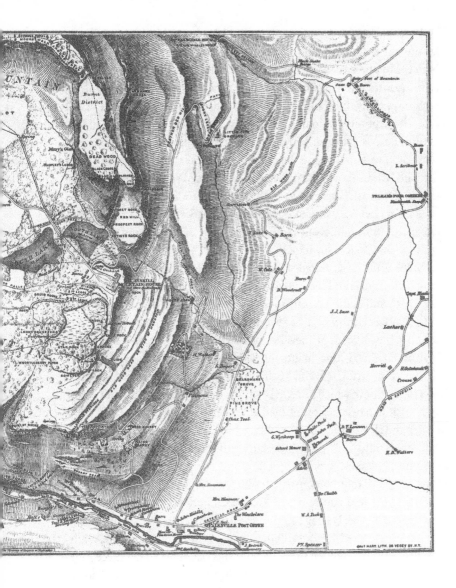

Both parks clearly reflected middle-class sensibilities concerning leisure, quiet contemplation, and the need for retreat from the stresses inflicted by the city. Both Central Park and Kaaterskill Park attempted to provide a variety of experiences for urbanites confined by Manhattan's monotony; both offered "various charms" and "diversified beauties," descriptions found in a guide to the mountain park but which just as easily could have described the city park. Both parks reflected an urban sense of nature's value and the proper role of the rural landscape in civilized life. Clearly both parks reflected a blending of rural and urban attributes in the construction of ideal recreational landscapes. Perhaps most important, Central Park, and the dozens of urban parks that followed using the same philosophy, reinforced expectations about what the country should actually look like.

In his usual exaggerated style, Henry Schile described how transformative the hotels and their guests had been on the landscape surrounding North and South lakes by the early 1880s. He concluded, "inasmuch as the whole country here has become a modern roaming ground, even the once magnificent primeval wood has lost all its glory and charms. A beautiful pathway now divides the two lakes, and no remains of the former wilderness can be found." Schile was at once outraged at the destruction of the forest, which he called a sin against nature, but also impressed with what had been accomplished at Kaaterskill Park. "This evinces the power and skill of human ingenuity, which changes an unapproachable wilderness into a beautiful pleasure ground." Indeed, the area had become a "pleasure ground," picturesque, romantic, and in important ways quite urban in its construction. It was anything but wild.[27]

The structured nature of the Kaaterskill Park suggests how regularized visits could be. During a stopover in August of 1884, President Chester Arthur experienced the Catskills the way many other guests would. While staying at the Hotel Kaaterskill, Arthur, his daughter, and a niece took the requisite drives to Kaaterskill Falls, Haines Falls, and a few other "noted points." Like other guests at the grand hotels, the president had not come to the mountains to partake of rural cuisine, and although the hotel's own dairy did provide fresh milk, cream, and butter, the menu had an urban, Continental focus. Their evening meal included an elaborate French dinner, complete with little-neck clams and fillet of sole—not local trout. Orchestras composed of accomplished musicians provided the evening music—not the resident crickets. Altogether, Arthur's visit, perhaps less physical than some, reflected the fundamentally urban feel to the Kaaterskill Park. As Charles Rockwell summarized a decade earlier, the hundreds of mountain hotel guests were treated to "all the comforts and luxuries of the best hotels in our large cities," for which they paid "about the same price." In sum, Kaaterskill Park represented a remarkably complete blending of city and country, of urban amenities and rural scenery, of French cuisine and fresh milk.[28]

The same year the Hotel Kaaterskill opened another massive retreat began operations up the mountain from the small village of Pine Hill, along the Ulster and Delaware Railroad. Simply called the Grand Hotel, this new facility's considerable distance from Pine Orchard reflected a dramatically altered tourist landscape in the mountains, as new rail lines gave travelers easy access to much more of the mountain range. These railroads spurred the development of new accommodations in Ulster, Delaware, and Sullivan counties. Just six years after its debut, the Grand Hotel reopened greatly enlarged. The hotel's publicity for the occasion, a pamphlet called *The New Grand Hotel, Catskill Mountains,* highlighted the convenient travel from New York City. The Grand Hotel had its own station on the Ulster and Delaware, and the pamphlet bragged that parlor cars arrived on the front lawn, which was only a slight exaggeration. Lest prospective visitors fear the mountain location would prove too distant for guests who needed to remain connected to the city, the hotel also boasted its own telegraph and post office, and a "news-stand supplied with all the daily papers and periodicals." The Grand's other amenities included a "resident physician and pharmacy," at 2,500 feet the highest elevation of the large hotels, pure spring water, and an atmosphere free of "malarial influences" and mosquitoes. All of these advertised amenities spoke to the tourist industry's emphasis on selling the healthfulness of a mountain visit. The same pamphlet concluded with a list of the "three most important points in which all tourists are now interested: the purity of the drinking water, the dryness of the atmosphere, and perfect drainage"—not exactly a romantic description of a wilderness retreat.[29]

Of course, the hotel had attractions, too: an orchestra, billiards, a bowling alley, croquet, tennis courts, archery, a shooting gallery, all on the grounds, and superior trout fishing nearby. Meandering walks traversed the expansive property, and long-term guests were expected to take several drives through the mountains during their visits. By 1902, the Grand Hotel, like the Mountain House and Hotel Kaaterskill, could boast of its own golf course. Baseball also became a popular sport, with hotels organizing teams and playing each other, an especially popular pastime in Fleischmanns, down the mountain from the Grand Hotel.[30]

Despite the mountain locations of the grand hotels, guests generally did not expect to strike out on wilderness adventures. Nearly everything about the typical vacation smacked of urbanity—the cuisine, the entertainment, and, of course, the guest lists. As an 1887 tourist guide gushed: "Esthetic furnishings, luxurious tables, seductive music, charming companions, well-graded drives, shaded walks, a bracing air and glorious views, offer everything to be desired in the way of eating, drinking, dancing, flirting, making merry, and enjoying life to the utmost."[31] The title page of the 1905 Catskill Mountain House advertising circular contained two boxed facts: "Elevation 2,250" and "Four hours from New York City." Nowhere could New Yorkers get so high so quickly, and yet remain so attached to the city. Even Tanner House in distant Stamford boasted of "two New York mails per day." This was the simple arithmetic of the Catskills' success—elevation plus accessibility. The mountains would supply cool, healthful summer months to city residents who could not hope for them back home.[32]

This formula grew all the more successful as railroads continued to improve access. The Grand Hotel was just the largest of dozens of newer hotels opening along the Ulster and Delaware line, begun in 1866 in an effort to connect the Hudson River at Rondout to Oneonta over the Catskill Mountains. The construction went slowly, but the line reached Stamford in 1873, having found financing from stock-purchasing locals eager to have the railroad connect them with urban markets. After enduring financial troubles, the railroad reorganized and took the name Ulster and Delaware, for the two counties through which it ran. By 1875 the company was in better financial shape, and business picked up along the line, especially during tourist season. Tourism played such an important part of the road's business that it published its first guide, "A Catskill Souvenir" in 1879. In 1880 the U&D carried 111,000 passengers, the vast majority of them summer tourists. In 1883 business further improved with the completion of the West Shore Railroad, running north from Jersey City, connecting to the Ulster and Delaware at Kingston, and giving the U&D an even more reliable stream of summer passengers.[33]

The railroads helped redefine the Catskills, not just by increasing the number of visitors to the mountains, but also by giving New Yorkers better access to locations far from Kaaterskill Park. In the 1830s, the term "Catskills" had generally referred to the cluster of peaks close to the village of Catskill itself, the region surrounding the Mountain House. In this regard, tourist knowledge of the mountains remained superficial. For decades, nearly exclusive attention to this part of the range allowed visitors to retain a miscalculation concerning the tallest peak in the Catskills—long thought to be either Round Top or High Peak, both of which are visible from the Hudson River and Kaaterskill Park. In the 1880s, tourists' knowledge of the range expanded right along with the rail lines that pushed through the mountains. More travelers came to realize that Slide, more than 500 feet taller than High Peak, was the highest mountain in the region.[34] At the same time, the Catskills name spread too, as towns well distant from Pine Orchard garnered for themselves the good reputation of that resort region. By 1902, Richard Barrett's *Eagle Guide to the Catskills* could describe the recently expanded range, claiming that the "Catskills occupy that portion of the great Appalachian Highland embraced in Greene, Ulster and Delaware Counties, with spurs extending into Albany and Schoharie."[35]

Two villages in particular benefited from the expanded railroads: Pine Hill, just down the hill from the Grand Hotel, and Stamford, which for many years served as the terminus of the Ulster and Delaware Railroad. In the 1880s, Pine Hill grew rapidly, turning into a bustling tourist town with dozens of new buildings, including hotels, boardinghouses, and summer cottages. Stamford, at seventy-two miles from Kingston and more distant than Pine Hill, seemed an unlikely vacation spot until the arrival of the railroad. Located near the source of the East Branch of the Delaware River, Stamford lay at the head of a broad agricultural valley, the one containing the Roxbury farm of the Burroughs family. By the early 1900s, Stamford claimed the title "Queen of the Catskills," even though just decades earlier the little Delaware County town would have been well west of the Catskills as defined by most tourists. Though still far from the most fashionable hotels, Stamford could accommodate 2,000 guests in dozens of establishments and participate in the good fortune of the Catskills tourist industry.[36]

Beyond providing quicker, cheaper access, the railroads also encouraged tourism through advertising. All the major railroads into the region offered annual summer guides, including the Ulster and Delaware, the West Shore, and the New York, Ontario and Western Railway. These free booklets provided lists of hotels along the rail lines and short descriptions of the scenery and attractions of the region. The Hudson River Day Line provided a similar guide, *Summer Tours*, hoping to encourage tourist travel by Hudson steamer. But transportation companies provided just a few of the dozens of tourists guides that appeared in anticipation of the summer seasons. Some of the guides came from locals, such as Walton Van Loan, of Catskill, who published his *Catskill Mountain Guide* from the 1870s into the 1910s. Others came from downstate, including those issued from new authors and publishers who specialized in tourist guides, such as Rand McNally, and Charles Taintor, who published twelve guidebooks on tourist regions within easy reach of New York City.[37]

The material within these guides overlapped considerably, with advertising from hotels and boardinghouses generally predominating. Most did much more than provide bare information concerning lodging and transportation, though. The guides generally contained rich cultural material, too, giving readers a sense of the place and its storied past. Most contained liberal quotations from James Fenimore Cooper, Washington Irving, and some other literary figures. Even the guides published by the larger hotels promoted not just themselves but the region as well. The Hotel Kaaterskill even republished Washington Irving's "Rip Van Winkle" and "Sleepy Hollow," as an introduction to the "Sketch of the House," which advertised the hotel itself. In this way, Irving's writing set the mood in the mountains, supplying a fantastic history for the region. The tourist literature provided not just physical guidance—on where to stay and how to travel—but also continued to offer cultural guidance, too—on what to experience and how to react.[38]

Taken together, the guides' contents provide excellent insight into the motivations behind typical turn-of-the-century mountain vacations. Health issues lace the guidebooks, making clear that tourists retreated to the mountains expecting to reap significant health benefits. The Ulster and Delaware guides encouraged New Yorkers to seek a "breath of Nature, uncontaminated by the dregs of city civilization." The guide continued with fairly typical assertions about the healing qualities of a mountain vacation, noting "flabby muscles and pale cheeks, the feeble respiration and the exhausted brain, all these beckon us away to the green hills and valleys." The U&D went farther than most, however, in relating health claims to human genetics, which the guide asserted favored a life of movement and change—one that replicated a hunting and gathering lifestyle. For those living in port cities, like New York, the most effective change in environment offered the greatest contrasts, including higher altitude and dryer air, or so the guide claimed. This simultaneously scientific and mystical argument helped the U&D sell mountain vacations by making a case against the popular seaside resorts. "The cool air of the inland hills is a far different article from that found at the sea shore," the guide continued. "Instead of the saturated product of moisture and condensation, the air is dry and strong from the rarefying processes peculiar to the laboratories of the skies." Since the sea air was moist, "those afflicted with rheumatism, consumptive or bronchial tendencies, asthma, malaria, nervous disorders, or anything akin to these maladies, will be wise in seeking the mountains."[39]

Despite these common themes, the guides' contents did differ significantly. Obviously the transportation companies advertised the regions they served, giving some explanation why vacations to their regions would be most satisfying. Not surprisingly, guides published in the Catskills themselves were especially gushing in their praise for the "Switzerland of America." Unlike those offered by the railroads and some individual hotels, the guides published downstate were not free, but they could be more helpful to their readers, particularly by offering more objective appraisals. Sylvanus Lyon expressed great sympathy for his fellow New Yorkers, when he dedicated his *Outing in the Catskills* to "the many weary, careworn workers; to the laborers and delvers toiling for sustenance, and dwelling amid the turmoil and strife of city life; to the poor shop girls compelled to stand and work in factories. . . . ." Clearly Lyon hoped to provide useful information to travelers; his guide provided practical tips, including clothing suggestions. The Rand McNally guide, too, attempted to provide useful, accurate information, using less poetic license. It went so far in its attempt to correct false images of the Catskills that it actually called them "only big hills," which didn't compare with the White Mountains of New Hampshire, let alone the Rockies or the Alps. Still, the Rand McNally guide offered more than forty pages of information on the Catskills, plenty of publicity for the region.[40]

As the guides made clear, tourists had a wide variety of accommodations to choose from in the mountains. "Scattered all over the Catskills mountains, in every valley, near every stream, are hundreds of hotels and boarding houses," boasted the short-lived seasonal tourist newspaper, *The Catskill Mountain Breeze*, in 1885.[41] Five years later, the New York Central's guide claimed that "the Catskills may be said to literally teem" with boardinghouses. "They are on every side—in front of you, behind you, to the right of you, to the left of you, above you, on the mountain tops, below you in the valley."[42] Three years later, Richard DeLisser called Tannersville "one immense boarding-house." The town had stores of all kinds, and a particular breed of hucksters dedicated to the tourist trade. "Here you will find the tin-type man, the cane man, the try-your-weight man and the souvenir-of-the-Catskill man, and others, not forgetting that silent, but voracious monopoly, 'drop-a-nickel-in-the-slot-and' -." On hot summer evenings, guests out for promenades crowded the planks of the wooden sidewalks. Mail time was a major event in the town, and as tourists from Tannersville and the many nearby hotels and boarding-houses congregated around the post office in anticipation, the success of the region's tourist industry became clear.[43] By the turn of the century, railroad company statistics revealed that altogether nearly 500,000 people visited the Catskills each summer.[44]

Although the many grand hotels gained a disproportionate amount of the media's attention and became the topics of traveling authors who stayed at the finer resorts, most visitors to the Catskills stayed in much more modest accommodations. Indeed, the region was well known for its boardinghouses, most of which were nominally adapted farmhouses, where guests paid room and board and essentially lived with the local family for a week or more. Boardinghouses became extremely popular in the late 1800s and early 1900s, as farmers opened their homes to tourists in an effort to gain desperately needed cash income, and lower-middle-class New Yorkers sought inexpensive vacations away from the sweltering city. By 1908 the Ulster and Delaware guide to the Catskills reached 170 pages and contained a list of over 1,000 hotels, farmhouses, and board-inghouses accepting summer guests.[45]

One of the listed boardinghouses was the Bishop Falls House, opened by brothers Frank and DeForest Bishop in 1895. Just two miles from the Ulster and Delaware's Brodhead's Bridge station, and thus just over 100 miles from New York, the Bishop farm was ideally located for the operation of a summer boarding business. The 106-acre Bishop farm bordered the Esopus Creek, the fast-flowing mountain stream well known for its trout fishing and lovely scenery. The stone farmhouse, built in 1796 by the first Bishops to move to the Catskills, was less than a half-mile from Bishop Falls, one of the better-known spots on the creek.[46] In part because of its advantageous location, the Bishops' business grew, so much so that in 1900 the brothers expanded the ten-room house, adding twenty-five rooms in two wood-frame wings, built with their own hands.

In 1905, the expanded Bishop Falls House entertained a total of 135 guests during the short season, many of them staying for an extended period. The business took in $3,000 that summer, having long since become the most important source of income for the Bishops.[47]

Although much lower in altitude than the mountain hotels, farmhouses offered certain advantages over the larger establishments, including the guests' ability to feel at home while on vacation. Many of the Bishops' guests came year after year, no doubt in part because of the location and amenities, but also because of the Bishops themselves, who worked as a family to operate the business. DeForest's wife prepared the meals, and Frank's wife did the pastry cooking. The owner of the property, the brothers' mother Anna, helped out as much as she could. The men worked the farm and the livery, supplying the table with fresh fruits and vegetables and giving guests rides through the countryside and to and from the train station. When business was good, the brothers hired neighborhood girls to help their wives in the house, their own children being too young to be of much assistance.

Guests at the Bishop Falls House undoubtedly spent much of their time in and out of the Esopus, swimming in the stream's pools, basking in the sun on the larger rocks in the bed, and perhaps retreating to the shade of the large maples around the house during the heat of the afternoon. They could take walks through the farm's thirty-acre woods or down the road to the falls, where the natural beauty seemed little marred by the presence of mills on either side of the water. On Sunday, guests could walk to the church in Olive Bridge, near the falls, and on other days to the post office in the same hamlet. Throughout the day, guests enjoyed spring water (the farm had several active springs), and at mealtimes the table featured products of the farm. There were fruits in their seasons, including cherries, pears, peaches, plums, grapes, raspberries, and apples; and there were vegetables, such as tomatoes, potatoes, cucumbers, radishes, beets, lettuce, string beans, peas, and, of course, sweet corn— all of them grown by the Bishops themselves. The farm supplied milk and cream, and some of its own meat, but the brothers also purchased some food from neighboring farms, including supplemental roasting chickens and eggs, when they were busy.[48]

Although the Bishop Falls House had special advantages, guests in similar establishments around the Catskills enjoyed comparable days of respite from the summer in the city, with cool temperatures, pure air, pure water, and ample fresh food leading the list of attractions. Of course, for boardinghouses as much as for the grand hotels, easy access was most important to making the Catskills the vacation spot for tens of thousands of New Yorkers each summer. The inexpensive prices of boardinghouses made that vacation attainable for a larger portion of the city's population.

Although some families traveled together, especially for short visits, with better connections between city and mountains it became more common for men to come up on weekends, taking a Friday evening train and returning either on a Sunday night or early Monday morning train. Women and children, then, could stay for weeks at a time at their favorite retreats while husbands continued to work in the city, a trend that was particularly strong among the wealthier classes. As a result of this arrangement, much longer stays in the mountains became the norm, with some families choosing to remain a month or more. This only further solidified the connections between city and county, as tourists came to think of the Catskills as their summer home. In addition, the removal of so many men back to the city during the week meant that the resort culture primarily centered on women and children, and so by the late 1800s, at least in the summer, the Catskills resort region had become a predominantly feminine world. Not surprisingly, then, the mountains became particularly liberating space for women, a place where strict Victorian gender norms were somewhat relaxed. Mountain hotels became famous for flirtatious behavior among young men and women, but, just as important, women could feel a freedom of movement and a freedom from household work that differed dramatically from their lives in the city.[49] Novelist Lucy C. Lillie summarized activities at the Mountain House in 1883 as "dressing, dining, and flirting," and listed "tennis, croquet, the delicious racquet of evenings, and reading the newest novels and magazines" as the most prominent amusements. At the large hotels, then, women's activities centered on the veranda, where they could engage in conversation, take refreshments, and, mostly, relax—all symbolic leisure activities that spoke to the class status and refinement of the women.[50]

Women did not stay on the veranda, of course, and many engaged in more active endeavors, including bowling and tennis, both of which gained in popularity late in the century, by which time most of the large hotels provided facilities for these games. Still, the most important physical activity engaged in by women was hiking. Almost all women would have taken some lengthy walks while in the mountains, especially to seek specific views or to meet trains, retrieve the mail, or achieve some other objective. But some women engaged in even more rigorous hikes, including Julia Olin, who in 1863 recounted a tramp up Overlook Mountain. That particular outing included several women, some of whom rode in a wagon up the steeper grades. Two of the women decided to climb on foot with the men, however, and all of the women slept in a tent, or at least would have had they not been so excited by their assent.[51] Many years after Olin's tramp, Samuel Rusk reported that on the summit of the oft-climbed High Peak, a tree had been supplied with a ladder to allow hikers to gain an unobstructed view. Rusk reported that "one most estimable young lady of a party assured the writer that she had looked out upon the world from among its upper branches." Although Rusk found many women who, like Olin, sought out physical adventure, in describing the popular Hunter Mountain hike he warned, "Probably ladies will not care to make the attempt." Ten years later, Sylvanus Lyon assumed women would be active in the mountains, making recommendations concerning dress, and although at points his prose appears rather mocking, he did write, "for those loving freedom and health, with the luxury of a good walk, there is beauty and use in a true bloomer costume—short skirts, pantlets, stout shoes, tasty hat, jaunty parasol."[52]

Considerable evidence points to good relations between Catskills natives and city tourists, especially in the long relationships they often shared. Many tourists became so taken with the mountains that they fled to them more permanently, either through complete relocation or the building of a second home. Similarly, many mountain residents relocated to the city in search of a new start, especially through better employment. Still, while the relationships between tourists and the many Catskills natives who relied on the industry may have been good, at times the relationship between urbanites and farmers especially could be strained. Some Catskills natives complained about tourist behavior, particularly concerning activities on Sunday, so much so that the *New York Tribune* carried an article entitled "City Folk Corrupt Country People," in which an Ulster County minister complained about visitors failing to observe the Sabbath. Reverend Wilson claimed the tourists "play games of various kinds, both indoors and out on the athletic fields. And some of the indoor games are further away from the church and more unsanctified than those of the open air." The *Tribune* article only hinted at the urban impression that "country people" were old-fashioned, but the tourist magazine

The Catskill Mountain Breeze contained more direct evidence of urban disdain for rural folk. The *Breeze* regularly reprinted material from other publications, including its periodic cartoons. In 1884, three cartoons presented unflattering caricatures of farmers, and though the cartoons were just as likely to be critical of urbanites, the portraits contained unmistakable urban stereotypes about rural people; they appear stupid, dirty, impoverished, and unsophisticated.[53]

As historian Dona Brown has noted, tourism "complicates the questions of ownership and control" in places that become dependent on the industry. Certainly tourists returning year after year developed strong attachments to their favored places, and they generally expressed a desire to exert some control over them, especially in an attempt to keep them the same. For some tourists, the purchase of land or cottages afforded a fuller sense of ownership and, of course, gave them control over at least their own property. But for many tourists, simply a momentary occupation of a memorable place could inspire thoughts of possession. Note Julia Olin's prose concerning her climb of Overlook Mountain: "We had an ownership in all that wondrous landscape—its splendor and its glory were ours! We could exult and triumph in this heritage." While locals might easily accept momentary feelings of possession, the ability of outsiders to control the mountains' future, especially through outright purchase, portended conflicts that would only grow over time.[54]

Still, in the nineteenth century conflict was not the major theme in the relationship between Catskills locals and city tourists. The long relationship between the Butler family of Brooklyn and the Haynes family from Highmount gives a hint of how many city and country lives must have come together in lasting friendships. What's more, although city tourists clearly drove the mountain economy, everywhere one looks locals participated too—buying stock in the railroads, building hotels, expanding farmhouses to suit boarders, publicizing their region's many attractions. Building the infrastructure of tourism in the mountains was clearly a collaborative process, one that blended city and country interests, capital, and labor. By the 1880s, the tourist industry had substantially remade the mountains, recreating the landscape to meet tourists' expectations but also to suit local economic interests. Tens of thousands of summer visitors strolled through Catskills towns, took pleasure drives along mountain roads, and scrambled up nearby peaks, all of them swarming over the various tourist landscapes. These landscapes did more than provide services like lodging, food, and transportation, and they offered more than winding carriage roads and well-marked trails to points of interest. Local entrepreneurs filled the region with enterprises designed to keep as much urban money in the mountains as possible, through the sale of items as various as fresh produce and cheap souvenirs. On his 1893 tour of the Catskills, the author Richard DeLisser found a souvenir shop at Barton's Mill, near Palenville, selling handcrafted wooden items—mountain sticks, inkstands, little pails, and "a host of other articles of every conceivable suggestion and embodiment of an active imagination, stimulated by that manna in the wilderness, the dollar of the 'summer people.'"[55]

Through the late 1800s, the primary object of consumption remained the mountains' sublime scenery. Educated by the work of Irving, Cooper, Cole, and the like, tourists sought out the sublime views found in Hudson River art and the romantic spots of the region's literature. As Paul Shepard argued in *Man in the Landscape*, "Modern scenery-tourism has been the attempt to apply the esthetic learned from art to the landscape as a whole."[56] That application did more than shape tourists' perceptions; it literally encouraged the landscape to change to meet expectations. Although the mountains would gradually fill with examples of this reshaping to match the image created by art, the most remarkable recreation occurred very early in the development of Catskills tourism—at Kaaterskill Falls. Recall that as early as 1823, Cooper, through the words of Leatherstocking, had declared the falls "the best piece of work that I've met with in the woods," and a clear example of the "hand of God." In the following decades dozens of artists produced major works featuring the falls, including Thomas Cole, who sketched and painted them repeatedly, and William Cullen Bryant, whose poem on the falls glorified "this wild stream and its rocky dell."[57]

The popular, exaggerated images of the falls in Hudson River art and in romantic literature helped make the falls a major tourist attraction, but also determined what the attraction was—the falls at spring flow— for rarely did images reveal the flow as anything other than a torrent. Unfortunately, in midsummer, when tourists were most likely to see the falls, the stream could be quite dry, making the falls little more than trickles over mostly dry rocks. Adding to "the hand of God," then, a local miller, Silas Scribner, who had built a dam on the stream as it passed between South Lake and the falls, would let loose the water for a fee as early as the mid-1820s. The idea, of course, was to reproduce the falls for viewers not in the way that God (or nature) intended, but in the way the artists had decreed and the tourists expected. In describing the process by which Hudson River artists created their ideal landscapes, historian Barbara Novak claimed that the "artist made the necessary changes on the canvas. Nature remained intact." At Kaaterskill Falls, at least, this was not entirely the case.[58]

Scribner's milldam was just the first of many alterations to the falls site. Upon his visit to the falls in 1843, George Templeton Strong claimed, "the pictures one sees of those falls don't give one the remotest idea of their effect," and he wrote nothing of paying Scribner for the privilege of a spring flow. However, Strong did praise the "little shanty that hangs over" the falls, from which observers could gain a better perspective on the scene. A decade later, Calvert Vaux was less enthusiastic about the "clumsy boarded structure that has been erected just on the brink of the descent." In true romantic fashion, however, Vaux did not criticize the mere presence of this intrusion on a wild scene. Rather, he suggested improvements, with "a rough stone wall" built in an "irregular manner" to replace the platform that had clearly been constructed in a "rural way." Vaux thus suggested how an urbane landscape architect like himself could improve not just upon the "clumsy" rural work, but upon nature itself, providing a platform from which the falls might be seen as artists saw them. Of course, Vaux would spend his career designing just such improvements on nature, though no one commissioned him to improve Kaaterskill Falls.[59]

By the mid-1850s Peter Schutt operated the Laurel House just above the falls and the falls themselves, having built a dam closer to the falls than the Scribners' mill. In 1879, Samuel Rusk described what had become the well-established procedure for viewing Kaaterskill Falls. After a stroll from one of the surrounding hotels, tourists could purchase refreshments at the Spray House, where one could gain access to a platform over the "awful chasm." Those interested in seeing the falls from below—and most were—could also pay twenty-five cents per season to use the stairs down to the base of the falls. "While parties are down here," Rusk noted, "the gate of a dam immediately above the falls is opened, thus augmenting the usual flow of water and the scene is then truly marvelous."[60]

Many visitors complained about the dam, if not the fee to let the waters go. George Curtis called the process "ludicrous" in his 1852 "summer book." "But," he went on, "most of us are really only shop-keepers, and natural spectacles are but shop-windows on a great scale." Moving beyond the idea that tourists are merely consumers in a natural setting, he concluded, "People love the country theoretically, as they do poetry." In other words, unembellished nature could not so effectively capture urban imaginations. In 1884, Annie Searing, in a fictionalized account of travel through the mountains, was less forgiving than Curtis, even if the purchase of falling water fulfilled some poetic need. "It is a humiliating thought that this beautiful mountain stream should be dammed up and turned on at twenty-five cents a piece for the lovers of nature," she wrote. But even Searing had a practical and positive conclusion about the arrangement, since "we should have only a little thread of water all summer otherwise, whereas now for a consideration we get all the majesty of the spring floods let on."[61] One wonders how awe-inspiring nature could be when turned on by human hand to perform for a fee. Surely this process muted the feelings of sublimity encouraged by Cole, Bryant, and others. Still, the performances reached well into the twentieth century, with the Laurel House continuing to operate the dam purely for the purpose of putting on a sublime show of nature.[62]

Despite their artificiality, the falls had their effect. Writing in 1881, Henry Schile failed to mention the artifice of the falls he saw, even though the dam and the platform were then present. Instead, he claimed, "Not only can art not create a picture more beautiful than the one we see here, but it cannot even approach it." In actuality, the many artists who did attempt to recreate the falls overachieved, and the expectations created by the artists did lead to the creation of the falls as Schile saw them.[63] At the falls, the "natural" experience couldn't have been more controlled. T. Addison Richards, writing for *Appleton's Illustrated* travel guide, noted the twenty-five-cent fee, calling it simply "a disagreeable bit of prose in the poem of the Catskill Falls," perhaps inadvertently confirming how completely the cultural and natural had mixed in the tourist landscape. The remade falls also revealed how completely the mountain landscape could change to suit evolving urban perceptions of nature.[64]

Although the region continued to sell its romantic image, by the early 1900s the sublime had lost much of its currency as the result of a cultural shift that included the decline of Hudson River School art. But the most important shifts in tourist expectations resulted from changes in the city itself. New York's explosive growth continued through the late 1800s, driven largely by increasing immigration. Newly arriving Germans, Jews, Italians, and, in smaller numbers, Chinese helped make New York's the most culturally diverse population in the world. New York teemed with people, Manhattan surpassing a million inhabitants by 1880, and Brooklyn doing the same by 1900. By then, Brooklyn and Manhattan had joined with Staten Island, Queens, and the Bronx, to create a city of nearly three and one half million people, the majority of whom lived in and around the dense, industrial neighborhoods of lower Manhattan and waterfront Brooklyn. While continued economic and demographic growth brought some positive changes, including increasing prosperity for more New Yorkers, ethnic and class conflict meant escalating tension in the city, resulting in greater segregation by wealth and ethnicity. Most famously, wealth congregated in the Upper East Side, especially along Fifth Avenue, while poverty congregated in the immigrant neighborhoods of the Lower East Side.

Crowded Manhattan provided limited opportunity for geographical separation, but in the mountains segregation could be more complete. Of course, the poorest New Yorkers could not even make the trip, but even among those who could, class segregation increased over time. In the late 1800s, reflecting a national trend, a host of new private parks sprang up in the Catskills, including Onteora Park (1887), Elka Park (1889), Santa Cruz Park (1889), and, finally, Sunset Park (1902). These exclusive retreats allowed members to enjoy the benefits of the mountains while controlling the type of person with whom they would have to socialize.[65]

Begun in 1888 by Charles Wingate, Twilight Park was among the most successful in the Catskills. In July of 1887 Wingate visited the Hotel Kaaterskill for a convention. A sanitary engineer from Manhattan, Wingate was impressed enough with the region around Kaaterskill Clove that he purchased a 160-acre sheep pasture owned by Charles Haines, the proprietor of the Haines Falls House. Named for Manhattan's Twilight Club, of which Wingate was a founding member, the community hoped to attract members of "mental and personal worth."[66] The park's publicity described its raison d'être: "Sensible people are no longer content to spend their vacation lounging and gossiping on boarding-house piazzas or promenading hotel corridors. The taste for outdoor sports has led to an interest in more healthful forms of exercise than dancing in heated parlors." Predicting a trend away from the large and fashionable hotels, the park's promotional literature claimed, "People now seek for seclusion and privacy." It estimated that a thousand cottages could be built in the Kaaterskill and neighboring Plattekill cloves.[67]

By 1891, Wingate had created a cottage community with a summer population of 300, with new cottages offered at $1,500. Like the other private communities, Twilight did not allow nonmembers to enter park grounds, except as guests of members. The regulations written in 1895 noted: "No peddlers, beggars, itinerant musicians or persons of a similar class will be allowed to pass the gates." The mountains crawled with traveling salesmen and performers, and the gates prevented the commercialism that characterized urban culture from intruding on relaxing summer retreats. Although essentially a gated community, Twilight was not simply a refuge for the extremely wealthy. With a membership comprised of educated and artistic New Yorkers, Twilight was exclusive, but not necessarily rich. Wingate hoped to create a community of thinking people in the mountains, where healthful rest was the major attraction. The community centered on the clubhouse, which had a family atmosphere (and no alcohol, by mandate of Charles Haines, the seller). Early plans included solely communal dining, in part to spare women cooking duties during vacation. Accordingly, the cottages were not to have their own kitchens, though this arrangement did not persist. However, this conception of communal dinning may have provided a special attraction for women, as early resident lists included the names of thirteen women out of forty-eight cottage owners. One of those women, Josephine Redding, praised the clubhouse restaurant plan as a boon to both professional women and housewives.[68]

Although the exclusive nature of the clubs clearly had a class component, the Onteora and Twilight clubs both claimed to be more interested in excluding the boorish and the boring rather than simply the lower classes. Though founded by a very wealthy New York businessman, Francis B. Thurber, Onteora became famous for its "parties of well-known artists, litterateurs, and musicians." It also became well known for its talented women, including Thurber's sister, the designer Candace Wheeler, and Candace's daughter, the artist Dora Wheeler. Other, nonresident writers and artists frequented these cottages in the summer months, with Mark Twain in residence in 1890, and John Burroughs and Robert Underwood Johnson visiting in 1891.[69]

In one instance the private park movement overlapped with a growing ethnic segregation in the mountains. Elka Park, not far from Onteora, took its membership largely from the Liederkranz Society, a German-American choral group based in New York. But even outside exclusive private clubs, hotels and boardinghouses catered to specific ethnic groups, especially by offering menus to suit ethnic tastes. In addition, some ethnic boardinghouses clustered near sectarian churches, and included such information in their advertising. As early as 1879, the La Dew Farm near Mount Tremper bluntly advertised itself as "A Favorite Resort for Germans." In the early twentieth century, as working-class New York immigrants gained the means to take family vacations, Irish, Russian, Ukrainian, and Polish resorts flourished in the Catskills. By the 1920s, advertisements regularly included some reference to the ethnicity of the cuisine, whether German, Hungarian, or Italian-American.[70]

The most important segregation in resort hotels was not voluntary; it resulted from the discrimination against Jews. Openly begun in the famous case of Judge Henry Hilton denying a room to Joseph Seligman at his Grand Union Hotel in Saratoga in June 1877, overt discrimination quickly spread in resort areas. Clearly a product of urban anti-Semitism (both Seligman and Hilton lived in New York City), discrimination at rural resorts spoke to the power of cities to reorganize cultural space in the countryside. As the Jewish population of the city grew and some Jews gained considerable wealth, as had Seligman, all Jews faced growing anti-Semitism. Hilton defended his decision to deny Seligman and his family a room by claiming that Christian guests preferred not to vacation with Jews. Hilton's position led to outrage in the city papers and in the national press, but the practice spread, seemingly confirming Hilton's assertion that many Christian vacationers preferred not to mix with Jews.[71]

Saratoga catered to a wealthier clientele than did most Catskills resorts when Hilton announced his anti-Semitic policy, and so the exclusive nature of that resort town lent itself to overt discrimination. Still, the practice spread even to unassuming locations. Soon after the Hilton-Seligman controversy, on August 2, 1877, the *Windham Journal* reported under "Hunter Items": "Mr. Everdell of the Breeze Lawn House, recently cast adrift a family of Jews that were boarding at his house. He says no more Jews can be accommodated by him. He agrees to the letter with Judge Hilton regarding Jews." The *Rondout Courier* reported two years later in its "Mountain Notes": "One of our summer resorts recently cast adrift a party of Jews. Of course the proprietor does not believe a Jew is as good as a Gentile."[72] After a series of cases such as these, the northern Catskills became well known for discrimination against Jews. Interestingly enough, anti-Semitism seems to have been strongest where Jews were most likely to frequent—in the towns of Tannersville and Hunter, both of which accommodated large numbers of Jews. As in the city, conflict arose where ethnicities bumped together. By 1887, in an attack against anti-Semitic hotel policies in *The Forum*, Alice Hyneman Rhine singled out the Catskills for its "race prejudice." "In the Catskills, especially," she wrote, "this proscription has increased year by year, until at the present time more than half the Jewish applicants for board are refused accommodations." The practice gained such acceptance, particularly among the smaller hotels and boardinghouses, that a rumor apparently held that the entire Catskills region would not accept Jews during the 1889 season, sparking a New York City petition campaign in protest. Even the Bishop Falls House, operating at some distance from the popular Jewish resorts, included a bold "No Hebrews Taken" in its advertising pamphlet published in the early 1900s.[73]

Despite the rumors, Jews were never completely cast out of the Catskills. The Tannersville area continued to cater to Jews, as did the Fleischmanns-Highmount area, where even the Grand Hotel continued to accommodate Jews. Still, anti-Semitism kept tensions high, perhaps especially in areas where Jews remained welcome. Certainly coincidence cannot explain why private cottage parks flourished around the towns that continued to accommodate Jews. In 1893, while touring the region in preparation for writing his book *Picturesque Catskills*, Richard DeLisser commented on a common scene. On his way up Kaaterskill Clove, the author found "two descendants of the great Abraham" eating a "simple repast." The two Jews were traveling salesmen, which DeLisser noted could be found "on every by-path along every highway." He also offered praise for "these thrifty, hardworking sons of Israel," who made their living selling to both tourists and locals, Jews and Gentiles (although not to the residents in gated communities that barred them). While DeLisser's comments revealed great sympathy for Jews, his own book, published in 1894, contained references to discriminating establishments, including the Central House in Hunter, which charged $10 to $18 per week and promised "No Hebrews Taken."[74] Some establishments would eventually use code words or phrases, like "Catholic and Protestant churches nearby," or "Christian Management," to indicate that Jews need not apply for a room, but in the 1890s it was not uncommon for advertisements to simply state "No Hebrews," as had the Central House. The 1900 Ulster and Delaware guide included an advertisement for the Meadow Lawn House in Tannersville, which explained, "People familiar with the Catskills, know that the Jews and Gentiles will generally not board at the same house, but being a fact the proprietor begs to say he accommodates Gentiles only." By this time, the Catskills had long been known as both the most important rural place to Jews in America and home to some of its most obvious anti-Semitic policies.[75]

Anti-Semitism gained influence in the northern Catskills at a time when the number of middle-class Jews in New York expanded quickly. Indeed, the discrimination in the north helped fuel the growth of Jewish-friendly resorts in Sullivan County, especially along the New York, Ontario and Western Railway. With its tracks completed from Jersey City to Oswego in 1873, the O&W gave the southern Catskills much-improved access to the city. Initiated as a freight line, primarily serving the region's many dairy farmers, by the 1880s the O&W had become yet another tourist road, with boardinghouses and hotels clustering near stations in Mountaindale, Fallsburg, Liberty, and in a dozen other small towns. Additional accommodations opened along the region's larger streams and its many lakes. Like other railroads, the O&W published a tourist guide, entitled *Summer Homes*, an annual pamphlet issued from 1878 through the 1940s. The guides advertised the many accommodations along the line and sold the region to New Yorkers looking for an inexpensive, healthful vacation. Since the O&W changed *Summer Homes* to match the evolving urban market, the guides marked changes in the mountains and, just as important, revealed the evolving relationship between the city and the country.[76]

In 1879 the guide's title gave no doubt as to its purpose, listing *Summer Homes of the Midland for New York Business Men* in a brief, thirty-eight-page pamphlet. It conceded that the region served by the railway, within four to ten hours of the city, was not fashionable like Saratoga, Newport, Lake George, or even the Catskill Mountain House. Instead, the guide attempted to attract "persons of moderate means and quiet tastes—who have no relish for the gayeties and frivolities of the great resorts." The guide listed several reasons for selecting the region, elevation (between 1,000 and 1,500 feet) being foremost among them. The guide also promised "a pleasant region with fine landscapes, and pleasant walks, good roads, and fine drives, homelike, neat, and well-ventilated rooms." Guests could expect "good bread, sweet butter, new and rich milk, fresh eggs, poultry," and excellent fishing and hunting.[77] These mountains provided a retreat, but they held no spectacles like those in Greene County. This was no "American Switzerland." Most of the "summer homes" were literally homes, mostly of farmers seeking to augment incomes by boarding a small number of summer guests. Most of those listed could handle fewer than ten people.

At eighty-four pages, the 1881 *Summer Homes* was a more substantial pamphlet. On its cover were two rural scenes. The larger of the two drawings featured men duck hunting from a small boat, and the smaller pictured a couple docking a rowboat on the bank of a stream. Both drawings were framed with fishing gear and strings of fish. The pamphlet's prose articulated the change already evident in the document's growing size: "summer homes" were "multiplying all along the route." The previous year, by the railroad's accounting, 110 hotels, farmhouses, and boardinghouses had offered accommodations for up to 4,000 people. Over the course of the season, nearly 10,000 had come.[78]

The Sullivan County tourist areas had two selling points: excellent fishing (and, to a lesser degree, hunting) and healthful air and water. In 1894, *Summer Homes* contained a section entitled "What Medical Experts Say," which included testimonials from physicians. The section opened with tuberculosis mortality statistics, comparing death rates in New York counties. New York County (Manhattan) led with 3.5 per 1,000 residents, followed by Brooklyn with 2.9, while at the bottom of the list were Sullivan and Delaware counties, with 1.0 and 1.2 respectively. One of the testimonials, from Dr. John Young of Brooklyn, claimed that vacationing in Monticello was "unsurpassed." "The air is dry and bracing, cool and exhilarating; the water is pure, wholesome and plentiful." He went so far as to conclude, "for invalids, and particularly those suffering from pulmonary troubles, no more health restoring and fitting spot could be found than Sullivan County."[79] Claiming there were no mosquitoes, a common assertion for the mountains generally, nor danger of malarial diseases or hay fever, the pamphlet also boasted of the region's beauty, though this was of secondary importance. Instead, the region was "gaining in popularity each year" because "many a tired city merchant and wearied belle" could "find rest and recreation among its many quiet and peaceful homes." Clearly the O&W hoped to attract residents with pulmonary disease, and indeed Liberty became an important retreat for tuberculars, especially after the opening of the Loomis Sanitarium in 1896.[80]

Changes in *Summer Homes* illustrations over its seventy years of publication mark some of the transformations underway in the southern Catskills. Early guides showed many rural scenes, including depictions of farmers at work. For many years the guide's cover highlighted the region's milk production, showing a milkmaid with pail and sometimes a cow. But in 1909 the milkmaid disappeared, replaced by a summer home. Increasingly, the photos within pictured dirt roads leading through the woods. By 1911, the cover showed only trees and a forest stream. Inside the cover, a William Cullen Bryant quote created a different mood than the milkmaid of earlier years:

> Enter this wild wood
> And view the haunts of nature, the calm shade
> Shall bring a kindred calm, and the sweet breeze,
> That makes the green leaves dance.

Nearly all of the agricultural scenes were gone, replaced by streams and waterfalls, and photos of country roads leading through uninhabited woods. The people pictured in the guide were tourists, not locals, and certainly not farmers.[81]

The evolving *Summer Homes* pamphlet could not capture all the trends in Catskills tourism. Over the course of nearly a century, Catskills residents had changed the landscape to meet tourists' expectations, from expanding their homes into boardinghouses to building structures around Kaaterskill Falls for enhancing tourists' experiences. If urbanites exerted exceptional control over the Catskills in some instances—such as the creation of gated communities like Twilight Park—many locals participated fully in the tourist industry, growing wealthy and satisfied. They marketed their sublime spaces and their cultural associations, and in collaboration with the tourists themselves they made the Catskills world famous. Sullivan County's tourist industry had grown too late to capitalize on the era of grand hotels; it never catered to the mid-nineteenth-century market for sophisticated, urbane vacations, and even though tourism had spread to the region before the power of the sublime had fully receded, Sullivan County had too little to offer. Still, *Summer Homes* revealed an important late-century shift, as fewer city residents sought out agricultural retreats, rich in wholesome foods and pure milk. Increasingly, they demanded something wilder. As the city grew—in size, density, and energy—so too did its antidote. No longer would the pastoral sooth the urban soul; only wilderness could provide sufficient retreat. As the city leapt into its crowded future, the country would withdraw to its wild past, and in the process erase much of its history from the landscape.

Chapter 4

Making Wilderness

A few nights ago I ascended a mountain to see the world by moonlight, and when near the summit the hermit [thrush] commenced his evening hymn a few rods from me. Listening to this strain on the lone mountain, with the full moon just rounded from the horizon, the pomp of your cities and the pride of your civilization seemed trivial and cheap.

—John Burroughs, 1871

In the wilderness all men are equal, whatever they be in cities.

—Theodore Gordon, 1912

At the turn of the twentieth century, most urbanites who headed into the mountains made good use of hotel facilities, relaxed, and ate well. They enjoyed the views, the cool temperatures, and the pure air. Other visitors did more, experiencing the mountains through longer hikes, climbing expeditions, and even overnight camping. This more rigorous experience gained in popularity in the late 1800s, as increasingly physical vacations replaced sedentary days on hotel verandas. More city residents hoped to experience something wild in the forests surrounding their lodgings. Beyond taking the many brief day hikes advertised by the grand hotels, adventurous tourists set out on "tramps," longer trips, sometimes covering several days and reaching a series of destinations. Tramping regularly included stops at farmhouses along the way, where milk, food, directions, or even lodging might be acquired. In this way, tramping experiences mixed the natural and cultural offerings of the mountains and gave tourists a much more interactive and truly rural vacation.

Tramping was part of a gradual movement toward a new type of mountain vacation, one that sought to leave the city behind more completely. Though tramping had deep roots, by the early 1900s it was part of what historian Roderick Nash called "the wilderness cult." Repulsed by growing cities, their pollution, crime, corruption, and stress, more and more Americans sought total respites from urbanity. Encouraged by the naturalistic art of the Hudson River School and by romantic literature, many middle-class and wealthy urbanites came to see wild nature as the necessary antidote to the poisons of cities, and wilderness became more important to urban conceptions of rural American and natural landscapes. This cultural trend would have dramatic implications for the Catskills, as more New Yorkers came to see the mountains as a place where wilderness might be found and used. From the late nineteenth century through the entire twentieth, the Catskills landscape would change to meet this new urban demand, especially as the state of New York sought to build a usable wilderness in the mountains.[1]

Although the term "wilderness" has had a variety of definitions over time, historians often point to the language of the 1964 Wilderness Act for some concrete grounding. That act identified wilderness as "an area where the earth and its community of life are untrammeled by man, where man himself is a visitor who does not remain," a phrase that has sufficed as a more or less accurate description of wilderness for all time, regardless of the connotations of a particular era or population. This is an anachronistic approach, of course, one that can obscure the historical diversity of definitions, and, just as important, removes too much of the American landscape from the discussion of wilderness. Few who wandered into the Catskills could expect to find much left "untrammeled by man"—though even in the late nineteenth century the mountains still contained broad swaths of first-growth forest. Even though most rugged tourists fully expected to find the Catskills well occupied, they also thought the mountains capable of sustaining a wilderness adventure. As used by most urban visitors to the Catskills, "wilderness" defined an experience more than a place. A wilderness experience required some lengthy and sustained contact with a recognizably natural landscape, but the length of that contact could vary tremendously depending on the expectations of the individual. Just as with the sublime experience, the wilderness experience came largely from within, and it varied from person to person.[2]

Among the earliest to tramp extensively in the Catskills was Thomas Cole, whose search for the sublime and picturesque in the mountains also meant a search for the wild. Even as early as the mid-1830s, however, Cole grew concerned about the fate of his beloved mountains and their wild forests. In his well known "Essay on American Scenery," delivered before the National Academy of Design in 1835, Cole favorably compared the American landscape with that of Europe, making special reference to the Catskills, which he claimed possessed "an unbounded capacity for improvement by art," a phrase that neatly summarized what Cole had been up to in his own work. However, Cole also included what would become a familiar American lament: "I cannot but express my sorrow that the beauty of such landscapes is quickly passing away—the ravages of the axe are daily increasing—the most noble scenes are made desolate." American wilderness was in jeopardy, and Cole sought its protection, if not through legal restriction then through the spread of cultural appreciation for the nation's distinctive wildness. "We are still in Eden; the wall that shuts us out of the garden is our own ignorance and folly," he concluded. Just months later, in the spring of 1836, the cutting down of "all the trees in the beautiful valley" that ran between his new home in Catskill and the mountains, the valley that would grace his canvas *In the Catskills* a year later, threw "quite a gloom" over Cole. Though he recovered, perhaps remembering the necessity of cutting timber in his town, Cole continued to express concern about the passing wilderness the rest of his life. "If I live to be old enough," he wrote to his friend and patron Luman Reed, "I may sit down under some bush, the last left in the utilitarian world, and feel thankful that intellect in its march has spared one vestige of the ancient forest for me to die by."[3]

Cole thought wilderness held special value as an inspirational landscape, where one might experience deeper emotions, contemplate God and "eternal things." This romantic notion of nature's power deeply influenced New York's literate culture, as witnessed by the experiences of others tramping in the mountains. Travel writer and artist Charles Lanman included a long description of his tramp through the Catskills region in *Adventures in the Wilds of the United States*, published in 1856. Lanman first stopped at the Catskill Mountain House, the most famous of the many available lodgings, and then explored the region around it, finding hospitality at the farmhouses he came upon, where he secured meals and conversation. On one fishing and sketching tramp along the Schoharie Creek, Lanman stopped at a farmhouse where he received a dinner "seasoned by many questions, and some information concerning trout." Like most Catskills tourists, Lanman had been steeped in the literature and lore of the region. He sought out particular spots during his tramps, and, while he claimed that the area around the Mountain House was "a wild and uncultivated wilderness," his hikes were punctuated by named and storied places, including "Hunter's Hole," "Bear Bank," "Eagle's Nest," and "Rattlesnake Ledge." Each location's name clearly spoke to the nature of the place, but each also came with a human story, no doubt nearly all of them apocryphal. In this way, the wilderness was indeed broken by the many stories of human habitation, true or not, and the many trails that strung these storied places together. Lanman's knowledge of all these places, his recounting of all these tales, also indicated the importance of human culture to the Catskills experience, even deep in the woods, at its most wild and scenic spots.[4]

Like Cole, Lanman described his Catskills experience to a national audience, but he was far from the most famous literary figure to tramp in the mountains. Naturalist John Burroughs was the consummate tramper, and his best Catskills essays contain all the ingredients of great tramping adventure: sleeping on beds of hemlock boughs, drinking fresh milk on a farmer's stoop, eating abundant trout and berries, the sources of which—the mountain streams and forest clearings—often served as destinations for his wanderings. Dozens of famed nineteenth-century writers described the Catskills, but most, like Lanman, did so as tourists, offering an outsider's view, and usually an urban perspective, on landscapes they knew only briefly and incompletely. This was not the case for Burroughs, born into a Catskills farming family. In some ways Burroughs provides the ultimate local voice in his many descriptions of the mountains and life in the Catskills, published over a long career that began in the 1860s and ended with his death in 1921. He reflected on his home with the deepest of affection, viewed it with the keenest eye. But his tone, his sentiment, was shaped not just by his fond memories of life in the mountains but also by the fact that he had moved away from home when he sought to make his living as a young man. His Catskills writings reveal a pining for his beloved landscape, to which he became a frequent visitor, but only a visitor, through most of his life. In this way, Burroughs also became an outsider. But then again, since so many sons and daughters of the mountains would experience the Catskills as a home they had to leave in order to make a living, Burroughs's yearning for home is a common part of a Catskills native's perspective. Thus, Burroughs's voice—both native and popular—deserves special attention, for, as much as he loved the Catskills, he provided a remarkably honest appraisal of the place in an era when romanticism encouraged writers to reflect on landscapes in a most unrealistic way. Significantly, though, Burroughs's conception of the Catskills would differ dramatically from the vision that guided the twentieth-century remaking of the mountains.[5]

Burroughs clearly enjoyed his agricultural childhood, late in life writing lovingly of the farm and his large family in *My Boyhood*, completed and published by his son the year after Burroughs died. But upon marrying in the late 1850s, the young Burroughs left in search of work, traveling to New York City in a failed attempt to find a position in some business, and eventually working outside Newark, New Jersey, as a teacher for two years. While in New Jersey, Burroughs made frequent trips into New York City, in search of work and of the many books he hoped to read as he pursued his own interests in writing. In 1863, Burroughs headed to Washington, DC, seeking work in the wartime capital. He found employment in the Treasury Department, where he worked until 1872. While in Washington, Burroughs wrote extensively and took frequent excursions into the countryside around the small city, but most importantly he befriended another wartime employee of the federal government—Walt Whitman. The young poet had already published *Leaves of Grass*, and Burroughs became deeply influenced by Whitman's style and determination. Indeed, Burroughs's first book, *Notes on Walt Whitman as Poet and Person*, published in 1867, revealed a real devotion to his new friend.[6]

While working in Washington, Burroughs made frequent trips to the Catskills, and his summer tramps became the basis of some of his best-known essays, including "Birch Browsings" and "In the Hemlocks," both of which appeared in his first book of essays, *Wake-Robin*, published in 1871. Two years after this book appeared, Burroughs left Washington for a new home on the Hudson, a farm he purchased and called Riverby, where he hoped to grow fruit and write. Riverby's location seemed ideal for Burroughs, giving him easy access to the Catskills, the eastern edge of which provided a backdrop to his farm, and equally easy access to New York City, which he visited frequently via train as he pursued his writing career. At Riverby, Burroughs attempted to create that perfect space, somewhere wild and full of inspiration, but connected to the urbane world of literature in which he now moved. He would later write in his journal: "The intellect, the judgment, are sharpened in the city; the heart, the emotions, the intuitions, the religious sense are fostered in the country." From Riverby he could balance the two, living in one and frequenting the other.[7]

When the fine home he built at Riverby became too crowded—or too domesticated—Burroughs sought greater solitude at a secluded study he built on his property, which he called Slabsides. Here he thought, wrote, and watched the birds that passed up and down the Hudson Valley. These birds became important topics in his writings, both in his published essays and in his diary. Indeed, later in his career Burroughs would gain the nickname John o' Birds, which contrasted him with the other famed naturalist of his era, John Muir, sometimes known as John o' Mountains. From Riverby, Burroughs made frequent visits to Roxbury, where he kept in touch with his aging parents, who continued to work the family farm. But Burroughs more frequently visited the city, where he kept in touch with publishers, other writers, and admirers of his work.

By the late 1870s, Burroughs's writing sustained his fruit farming, rather than vice versa.[8] Despite his improving fortune as a writer, Burroughs remained melancholic, and his melancholy deepened the further he traveled from his Roxbury home. Upon visiting "strange towns and cities," as he frequently did, he regularly took walks out into the country, where he had "sad, yearning thoughts." "What do I want, what does my heart crave?" he asked in his journal. "I don't know. But I know I leave myself all along the road and I know I send out messages that never return." It was this sentiment, that one left oneself "all along the road," in whatever landscape one visited, that is so powerful in Burroughs's writing, what most clearly separates him from other nature writers of his era. "The lover of solitude sows himself wherever he walks—the woods and fields and hills and lanes where he strolls come to reflect himself," he wrote. "There is a deposit of himself all over the landscape where he has lived and he likes to go the same route each time because he meets himself at every turn."[9]

Home, family, the past, and nature all mingled in Burroughs's mind. Burroughs's ideal landscape was the one in which he lived and left himself, and, though he was no longer home, his ideal landscape was clearly where his parents had lived, too. "When father and mother are gone," he lamented, "I know I shall have a sad pleasure in the look of the hills where they lived and died."[10] In 1893 he wrote in a letter to a friend: "I went out to the Old Home after you were here. I get thirsty for those fountains of youth, but I find it is an unquenchable thirst. 'Gone, gone!' is written upon every field and object there. . . ." In 1908, Burroughs attempted to return home, at least for part of the year, when he turned an abandoned farmhouse near his birthplace into Woodchuck Lodge, where he spent many summer months until his death.[11]

Clearly, Burroughs's connection to the landscape was an intimate one, filled with personal memory. His writings almost never included the estranged awe that became so central to the writings of the romantic authors, those who peddled in the sublime. Writers like William Wordsworth, Henry David Thoreau, and John Muir, all of whom Burroughs read and admired, described encounters in nature as religious events, moments at times filled with terror, or ecstasy, and regularly filled with intense emotion of some kind. Burroughs surely shared in this romantic vision, for he clearly gained inspiration from its many authors, especially Ralph Waldo Emerson. But Burroughs could be critical of the awe that some romantics experienced in nature, and especially the rapture in their writings. He asked in his journal, "Who has seen or heard in nature what Wordsworth did? She is a book printed full of his own thoughts. Nothing is hers but the paper." "You find in nature," Burroughs wrote, "only what you bring to her." Unlike most romantics, Burroughs regularly found the comfort of home, and he seldom found himself overcome.[12]

Although drawn into the urban world of literature, Burroughs never lost his rural voice. Particularly in his Catskills essays, Burroughs was just as likely to reflect positively on a well-cultivated farm as a wild stream. He never wrote disparagingly of human artifacts left deep in the woods. Cultural intrusions on the natural landscape did not distract him. Forest clearings did not portend that distant time when nature might be completely subsumed by culture, the wild entirely cultivated by humanity. He had witnessed too much agricultural decline in the Catskills, and seen and felt the disappointment of failed family farms, to fear the same advance of civilization that had haunted Cole decades earlier. In "Pepacton," his telling of an 1879 rafting trip down the East Branch of the Delaware, he stops occasionally at farms for fresh milk and comments about the relationship between good land and good buildings—richer lands making richer farmers. In "In the Heart of the Southern Catskills" and "Speckled Trout," he recounts tramps deep into mountain woods, where the landscape reveals its human history. He offers no complaint about the bark roads, the clearings, the ruins he finds high in the mountains. He is as enthralled with the pasture as the deep woods, the millpond as the fast-running stream. He finds blessings throughout the region, in nature's handiwork, and in man's. The landscape Burroughs loved and described was clearly the product of collaboration—of nature and culture—and, like his own life, it just as clearly revealed the blended influence of city and country.[13]

Late in life Burroughs became somewhat of a cult figure, a literary superstar. His admirers sought him out at Riverby and exhausted him with letters. The famous wanted to tramp the woods with him, including Henry Ford, Thomas Edison, and Harvey Firestone. Perhaps they thought he could more completely connect them to nature—a connection their own romanticism encouraged them to seek. Burroughs hiked with John Muir and Theodore Roosevelt, and traveled on the famed Harriman expedition to Alaska in 1899. Capping his long literary career, Houghton Mifflin published a beautiful fifteen-volume collection of his natural history essays in the 1910s and special collector's editions from its Riverside Press. By then Burroughs had become a central figure in the nature-study movement: an effort to teach about nature in elementary and secondary schools. Burroughs's essays, especially those on birds, became favorites in the movement, with several of the most suitable essays collected together by Chicago schoolteacher Mary Burt for a children's textbook in 1887.[14] As his popularity grew, Burroughs received invitations to speak before students and teachers. Although the nature-study movement must have pleased him, at one point Burroughs expressed skepticism about the trend: "I cannot tell them how to teach Nature in the schools. Nature cannot be taught, and I cannot bring the country with me to give you all a whiff of it."[15]

Despite his popularity, Burroughs's star would begin to fade soon after his death. While late-twentieth-century environmentalists would find Muir, read him, and turn him into their philosophical guide, Burroughs would be all but forgotten. Even in the Catskills, where his writings remained popular, other visions of his home region would become more powerful—those that envisioned a wilderness reborn. Cole's wilderness paintings and prose would serve as a better guide than Burroughs's mixed landscape of fields and forests. This much more romantic vision—with less room for the farming, fresh milk, and pastures that inhabited Burroughs's Catskills memories—would guide the making of wilderness in the mountains. Increasingly, visitors hoped to find wildness in their nearby mountains—a wildness that suggested not just the tourist's own status as brief visitor but also suggested that all people were only visitors in the mountains. In the process, Catskills residents, both present and past, would seem all the more out of place. Making wilderness would require, as historian William Cronon has written, "a flight from history"; it would also require a redevelopment of the present.[16]

Nineteenth-century romanticism expressed in the prose of authors such as Cole and Lanman heightened appreciation for wild places and encouraged a fear that those places might someday disappear from the American landscape. Though literary romanticism would fade in the twentieth century, its influence over land-use policies in New York (and around the country) would persist. However, the initial protection of wilderness in New York actually had a cause far removed from the romantics' notions of nature. In 1885, a more scientific, pragmatic movement to conserve natural resources for future use convinced the state to create the nation's first state forest preserve, one that protected scattered state lands in the Adirondack and Catskill mountain ranges.[17] As the state debated the preservation of forestlands in the 1870s and 1880s, arguments focused on the Adirondacks, where many claimed that the rapidly diminishing forests must be protected to save the headwaters of the Hudson River and other critical watersheds in the state. Derived from the landmark 1864 work of George Perkins Marsh, *Man and Nature*, the argument that the state needed to preserve its forests to protect its waters gained substantial political backing, particularly from downstate economic interests, which argued that despite the growing importance of railroads, New York City's commercial status still relied upon the easy and inexpensive access to interior markets afforded by the Hudson River and the Erie Canal, both of which required the consistent flow of water out of the Adirondacks.[18]

After an 1883 drought left the Hudson and other rivers much diminished, the state legislature finally heeded calls for action, with special influence coming from the New York Chamber of Commerce and other downstate organizations. In 1884, the state created a temporary Forestry Commission to investigate the situation in the Adirondacks and recommend action. Led by well-known Harvard forester Charles S. Sargent, the commission included D. Willis James, a businessman from New York City, William A. Poucher, a lawyer from Oswego, a Lake Ontario port city near the western edge of the Adirondacks, and Edward M. Shepard, a lawyer from Brooklyn. The commission directed most of its efforts toward the Adirondacks, but its members did tour the forested region of Ulster and Delaware counties. In its report to the state assembly, issued in early 1885, the commission recommended the creation of a forest preserve in the Adirondacks and proposed a bill that stipulated they be "forever kept as wild forest lands." However, the commission concluded that the protection of Catskills forests was "of less general importance," in part because the region's potential to supply merchantable timber had been greatly diminished through previous cutting and because the forests guarded "no streams of more than local influence"—a remarkable miscalculation, given the use of Catskills water for New York's municipal supply just twenty years later.[19]

In quick response to the report, the state legislature created the Forest Preserve later that year, declaring that state-owned forestlands within certain enumerated counties would remain part of the public domain, never to be sold or leased. A new three-person State Forest Commission, appointed by the governor, would oversee the management of the preserve. Few people seemed to notice that the final bill contained three Catskills counties—Greene, Ulster, and Sullivan—in addition to the Adirondack counties, despite the fact that Sargent's report had recommended against the inclusion of the Catskills. Ulster County representatives, led by Cornelius A. J. Hardenbergh, who found Ulster's obligation to pay state taxes on county-owned lands to be especially odious, had added the three Catskills counties so that they could take advantage of tax provisions. Henceforth, tax-delinquent lands in failing mountain townships might be acquired by the state and included in the Forest Preserve, eliminating any question about the county's obligation to pay state taxes and, just as important, securing state payments of county taxes on those same lands. In this rather roundabout way, the Catskill Preserve, at first just shy of 34,000 acres, joined the real object of concern, the Adirondack Preserve, which began at over 681,000 acres.[20]

All praise for the 1885 legislation focused on the state taking historic action to protect the Adirondack forests. Concern for the northern mountains far outshone interest in preservation closer to the city, both during the debate in the 1880s and in the effort to make the preservation permanent through its inclusion in the 1894 state constitution, which prohibited the cutting of all timber within state forest preserves. This tendency to focus on the Adirondacks to the exclusion of the Catskills has continued in the work of historians, with several books on the creation of the Forest Preserve failing to mention that state lands in the Catskills gained the same protection at the same time.[21] That historians have largely overlooked the fact that the Catskill and Adirondack preserves date to the same legislation is not particularly surprising. Even the State Forest Commission gave little consideration to the smaller preserve. The only significant attention paid to the Catskills in the Forest Commission's annual reports came in 1887, when the state published the report of Charles F. Carpenter, who had made "a thorough examination of the Catskill Preserve." Carpenter's report was nearly entirely descriptive, giving few recommendations regarding the management of the Catskill forests, and it failed to increase the profile of the smaller preserve in subsequent years. The 1891 Forest Commission report included maps and tables concerning the Adirondacks but none of the Catskills, an omission repeated in the 1892 report. The 1893 report failed to mention the Catskills at all, let alone provide a map of state holdings there.[22]

The relative neglect of the Catskills Preserve was reflected in state land purchases as well. In the decades after the preserve's creation, the legislature passed a series of laws allowing the purchase of forest lands, in part encouraged by the continuous agitation of the Association for the Protection of the Adirondacks, an interest group of concerned citizens, including many of New York City's wealthy elite. No similar organization lobbied for state purchases in the Catskills. An act passed in 1900 provided funding for the purchase of nearly 48,000 acres in the Adirondacks and Catskills, more than 42,000 of which would be added in the northern preserve. By 1904 the state owned 1,415,775 acres in the Adirondacks, but only 104,524 acres in the Catskills. In both preserves, the largest state holdings protected the highest elevations, where forests covered the headwaters of significant streams.[23]

As the state focused its purchases in the Adirondacks, supported by considerable downstate lobbying, those who sought increased purchasing in the Catskills devised a separate justification for expanded state ownership in that region. As early as 1894, the Forest Commission itself argued that the Catskills Preserve should add 100,000 acres (which at that point would have tripled the size of state holdings there), because "thousands in our cities" lacked the means "to reach the more remote and expensive resorts" of the Adirondacks. Indeed, according to the Forest Commission, the Catskills continued to attract nearly 100,000 tourists each summer, more than twice as many as the Adirondacks. "The great middle class that forms the population of New York City and vicinity are unable to bear the expense of a trip to our North Woods," the state Forest Preserve Board argued in 1898. Thus, the Catskills remained "the summer home of the masses." One state senator went so far as to claim in 1904 that the "Adirondack preserve is largely for the benefit of the millionaires who own large estates in that section, while the Catskill preserve is of benefit to the common people." In all these references, and many others, the theory held that the state should make purchases in the Catskills to protect land *for* the people of New York City, not *from* them. The Catskills forests, forever wild, would provide a permanent retreat for the city's masses.[24]

The Association for the Protection of the Adirondacks made an even more remarkable argument as it lobbied for the expansion of state ownership of forestlands. Although its major concern lay in the Adirondacks, at one point the group did argue specifically for purchases in the Catskills because "they have become invested with a wealth of legendary and historical association which gives them a peculiar and exclusive charm." In other words, the state should purchase lands to protect a historical landscape, the one that inspired Cole, Durand, Church, and Gifford. The topic of numerous authors and home to Rip Van Winkle and Natty Bumppo, the Catskills forests, the association claimed, "may be said to have given the State a Literature." In sum, the region's "romantic traditions and legendary lore," the association argued, gave the Catskills wilderness a "peculiar claim upon the community." And, since the Catskills of art and literature appear wild, so too should the Catskills in reality. The result of a selective reading of the past, one that favored the layers of fiction and art laid upon the landscape, this argument ignored much of the region's actual history. This romantic vision of the Catskills left little room for agriculture; it left little room for the mixed landscapes of Burroughs's essays.[25]

Efforts to expand the Catskills Preserve included outright purchase of desirable lands, especially those that would create larger contiguous state holdings. But the preserve expanded primarily through continued tax sales, including one in 1900 and another in 1910. In both cases, the state purchased lands sold to pay back taxes and then inspected the acquired properties to ensure that they were unoccupied by squatters at the time of purchase. The 1910 tax sale brought 2,542 acres into the Forest Preserve in Denning, Hardenburg, and Shandaken, the three most mountainous townships in Ulster County, and the region where state properties already clustered. In total, fifteen properties entered the Forest Preserve in these towns, averaging nearly 170 acres, and state inspectors found no squatters on any of them, just as they had failed to find squatters ten years earlier on tax-sale lands in the mountains. Clearly, squatting in an effort to make a living in the harsh Catskills highlands was a thing of the past.[26]

Acquisition by tax sale indicated more than just the state's desire to expand the public domain in the Catskills. Along with the absence of squatters, it also indicated the continuing failure of agriculture in the region. As more farm families left their lands through the early twentieth century, they also ceased supplemental economic activities, such as logging, sugaring, and quarrying. By 1930, Harry Haring noted that "fifty or sixty years of new growth of timber has obliterated all the scars laid upon the mountainsides by lumberman and quarryman." At the same time, with an agricultural depression already well under way, Haring claimed that general farming had disappeared from the region, and that "much of the land is, for farming purposes, 'abandoned.'" In a few short years, unused farmland could take on the appearance of a young forest. Some of these abandoned lands became tax delinquent and were taken by the county, through which they could be acquired by the state and added to the Forest Preserve. Through this process, the preserve expanded rapidly in the 1930s.[27]

The creation and expansion of the Forest Preserve had multiple significant implications for the Catskills. The 1885 law creating the preserve required that state lands within the listed counties "shall be forever kept as wild forest lands." Although that stipulation seems straightforward enough, the simple language hides how much work would be required in subsequent decades. As historian Karl Jacoby has argued, one of the central myths surrounding the conservation movement posits that preservation efforts involved protecting places that were still wild. Jacoby points out in his study of the Adirondack Forest Preserve that the legislation creating these reservations required that they be "kept" as wild forest lands, suggesting an a priori wilderness status. In reality, however, much of the land protected by the state was hardly wild, especially since tax-sale lands had generally passed to the state after owners had extracted as much of value as they could. What the state actually set out to do was designate that certain places *become* wild, mostly through the prohibition of disruptive activities, but also through intervention. In the Catskills, as in the Adirondacks, making wilderness would require considerable construction—some in the mountains themselves, but mostly in new regulations, laws, and government institutions. If the legislation requiring that the preserves be "kept" as "wild forest lands" posed significant problems for the state, it was largely the consequence of the idea that this protection should be "forever." Indeed, the permanence of wilderness posed the most serious problem for those who would work for its creation. As historian Mark David Spence discovered in his study of western national parks, the preservation of wilderness "required a great deal of management and manipulation." In the Catskills, the state would have to manage its preserve to keep the woods from being destroyed, the game from being overhunted, and the streams from being overfished, all of which became critical issues for resource management in the first decades after the creation of the Catskills Preserve, and would remain so "forever."[28]

Making wilderness in the Catskills required the creation of extensive social and legal structures, because protected wilderness is more than simply a natural place lacking evidence of human occupation. When New York State stipulated that the Forest Preserve remain "forever wild," it clearly intended certain human uses. The preserve would be a place with wild qualities, where people could experience certain feelings and engage in certain activities. The creation of this wild state in a long-inhabited and exploited landscape would require every bit as much human effort as any development the mountains had thus far experienced. The result—highly protected expanses of forests and free-flowing streams—would hide much of this hard work. Even with its invisibility, however, the effort to make a wilderness in the mountains, and to make that wilderness accessible to tourists, was a concrete endeavor to shape the Catskills landscape to suit urban needs. Even as a protected place—a natural, wild space—the Catskills were shaped by urban visions. The wilderness would still be productive—of resources urbanites now desired: long, well-marked trails through thick woods, campsites in scenic spots, and abundant trout and game for gentlemanly sport. The expanding and evolving Catskills wilderness reflected a developing conception of nature in the twentieth century, a conception predicated on the distance between people and natural places created by the nation's continuing urbanization.

In recognition that these state lands should be more than just preserved forests, the legislature established the Catskill Park in 1904, twelve years after the creation of the Adirondack Park. This law set a new boundary to define the mountains, the "blue line" that enclosed much, but not all, of the mountainous regions of Greene, Ulster, Delaware, and Sullivan counties, totaling 576,120 acres. As in the Adirondacks, this park would include both public and private lands, and held out the possibility that the state might institute new regulations for residents and property owners inside the blue line. More important, at least in the short term, park status gave the state greater flexibility in managing the lands. Forests would be preserved, but the park would also be "maintained and cared for as ground open for the free use of all the people for their health and pleasure." This included the laying out of new roads and paths for improved access to wilderness resources.[29] The region was already laced with trails and old wood roads, but the state improved some existing routes, built new ones, and made maps of them all. As early as 1891, the state improved the trail to the summit of Slide Mountain, the tallest of the Catskills. Trail construction proceeded as the state acquired more land, especially in the 1920s and 1930s. The Civilian Conservation Corps provided considerable labor in the mid-1930s, constructing and repairing trails through the woods.[30]

As hiking increased in popularity through the second half of the twentieth century, the construction of well-marked and -maintained trails would help minimize the damage to the environments through which the foot traffic traveled. In the same manner, the state's provision of campgrounds, with marked and regulated campsites, helped minimize the impact of campers. In 1926, the state opened a campground at Devil's Tombstone in Stony Clove and a second in Woodland Valley. In 1931 the state opened a third campground at North Lake, on an expanse of property it purchased a year earlier from the Catskill Mountain House. Eventually the state would build more campgrounds along paved roads and a series of "open camps" along trails, where shelters provided hikers with convenient campsites. Other improvements, such as the construction of a beach on North Lake in 1936, enhanced recreation for camping families.[31] All told, expansion of the public domain within the Catskills brought much more than "preservation" to the mountains; the state initiated a series of programs designed to create an altered landscape, one that invited the use of the mountains as an urban wilderness retreat.

The central attraction of this vacationland remained the forests. The 1885 legislation gave specific instructions regarding the regulation of timber on Forest Preserve lands, and a three-member forest commission had the power to "prescribe rules or regulations" designed to protect state lands. The commission could hire wardens, inspectors, and "forest guards" to monitor the forests and make arrests. State employees had two major tasks regarding the forests: preventing timber theft and forests fires. Theft was less of an issue in the Catskills than in the Adirondacks, undoubtedly because the state owned such a small percentage of the land, and that which it did own was least accessible to locals who might desire firewood. Still, Catskills residents were subject to Forest Preserve regulations designed primarily to protect the Adirondack forests. For example, a 1904 Forest Commission pamphlet, "Fire! Fire! Fire! An Appeal to the Citizens of the Adirondack and Catskill Regions," listed several regulations that restricted behavior in the mountains, including the prohibition of fires intended to clear agricultural lands in the spring and fall.[32]

Fire prevention left permanent changes on the landscape, in part by limiting fire damage, but also through the construction of a series of fire towers on mountain summits. Some towers had already been erected in the mountains in an effort to obtain better views from tree-covered summits. As early as 1879, *The Windham Journal* reported the completion of a sixty-foot "look-out" tower on the summit of Tower Mountain, easily reached by tourists from Lexington and Jewett.[33] Although these tourist towers popped up on several summits, including Slide Mountain, the fire towers have been a more lasting addition to the landscape. After terrible fire seasons in the early 1900s, the state constructed the towers on eight mountains throughout the region, including Belleayre, Hunter, Overlook, and Slide. In building the towers, the state constructed new, wider trails—truck roads—that allowed better access and enabled the placement of a telephone line up the mountains. Occupied during the dry months by fire spotters, the towers became equally important as destinations for hikers, who began to treat the summit of the towers as the actual apex of the mountains.[34]

In addition to protecting standing forests from fires and logging, the state initiated a reforestation program, first in the Adirondacks and then in the Catskills. The Adirondack effort began in 1898, with the opening of a tree nursery in Axton. Four years later a nursery opened near Brown's Station in the Catskills, but it would be short-lived, closing in 1906 as New York City finalized plans for the Ashokan Reservoir. Although that particular effort ended quickly, as did two efforts to reforest fire-damaged acreage on Mount Tremper and Terrace Mountain in 1900, systematic tree planting did continue in the Catskills, particularly in the 1920s and 1930s, when stands of Norway spruce, white spruce, white pine, and other evergreens replaced mountainside pastures as the state stepped up the acquisition of failed farmland and the Civilian Conservation Corps provided ample labor.[35]

To enhance wilderness resources, the state also managed wildlife, both fish and game. By the time the state created the Forest Preserve, the Catskills were no longer a valued hunting ground. During the midcentury, as farming in the valleys and logging on the hillsides opened up the forests and created better forage for deer and other mammals, the fauna of the Catskills may have increased in diversity and number. But by the late nineteenth century, hunting pressure had removed most game species and prized predators. Gone were wolves, foxes, and panthers. People still reported seeing bear and the occasional lynx, but generally hunting was limited to chance encounters with animals or to the least desirable animals, such as woodchucks, raccoons, and porcupines. Thus, by the 1880s, the Catskills provided limited opportunities for hunters from the city.[36]

At this time, however, the popularity of sport hunting was expanding rapidly, particularly among wealthy, urban men. Sport hunters preferred specific species, to be taken through particular, "ethical" means. They especially prized white-tailed deer and waterfowl, both of which flourished in the Adirondacks when the state created the Forest Preserve.[37] Unlike in the Catskills, which had only a handful of small lakes, the Adirondacks were full of large lakes, perfect habitat for migrating waterfowl. And deer populations rose in the northern mountains, as they replaced the native moose, which fared poorly in the patchwork of forests created by logging and agriculture. The large deer herds offered an important meat source for local populations and wonderful sporting opportunities for tourists. Thus, protecting deer as a game animal became one of the state's primary interests after 1885, as state foresters sought poachers who illegally hunted on state land.[38] Unlike the Adirondacks, the Catskills contained very few deer in the 1880s, and they were "rarely killed," as Carpenter's report to the Forest Commission noted. Carpenter blamed the absence of deer on a very heavy snow in the early 1870s and on Pennsylvania "pot hunters," who, according to Carpenter and belying their derogatory nickname, killed deer for their hides and left their carcasses to rot. More likely, of course, Catskills deer suffered the same fate as deer throughout most of the state and around the Northeast; continuous hunting pressure dramatically decreased numbers to the point of scarcity.[39]

In 1887 the state initiated efforts to return deer to the Catskills. The Forest Commission set up a 100-acre pen near Slide Mountain, enclosed by a ten-foot fence. There foresters placed animals captured from the Adirondacks, and by 1894 the "deer park" had fifty-three deer, watched over by a deer keeper who lived in a lodge nearby. Just a year later, the state set free the deer, which by that point numbered ninety-five. The deer park continued to operate after this first release, even growing in size, and by the early 1900s it had become a tourist destination. The stocking of deer was part of the state's effort to improve hunting in the Catskills, which the New York Times hoped could be made "a hunters' paradise" through the addition of deer, pheasants, hares, and other game. At the same time, improved hunting would require increased regulation, to prevent "pot hunters" from taking too much game, or taking it unfairly, as in steel traps. A critical part of this regulation was a five-year ban on deer hunting in the region passed in 1892, designed to allow the introduced deer an opportunity to establish themselves in sustainable numbers.[40]

If some observers believed state efforts could turn the Catskills into prime hunting territory, many more believed that state action would be required to protect its already famed sporting asset: trout fisheries. Throughout the nineteenth century the popularity of sport fishing grew dramatically, as evidenced by an explosion of sporting literature, equipment sales, and, most important, in the numbers of men streaming out of cities in search of good fishing. While numerous prime destinations became well known to sportsmen, trout fishing near New York City gained special status. In the same way that the New York art market helped elevate the Catskills as landscape painters migrated up the Hudson in search of scenery, the growth of a large cohort of sport fishermen in the city helped develop a remarkable reputation for Catskills streams. New York fishers were a particularly literate bunch, and taken together their articles and books created a vast literature on Catskills fly-fishing.[41] Their writings found publication in a number of periodicals, the most important being the popular sportsmen's journal, *Forest and Stream*, founded in New York in 1873. *Forest and Stream*'s editorial staff and many of its regular contributors wrote extensively about the region around the metropolis. In the early 1900s another leading outdoors magazine, *Field and Stream*, moved to New York after having begun publication in the Midwest. Like its competitor, it had a national audience and national content, but the places near the city received inordinate attention, including Catskills rivers.

Together, New York City and the Catskills became home to an extraordinary number of articulate fly fishermen who publicized their favorite streams. Among the most famous was Theodore Gordon, who by the turn of the century had become a living legend among fly fishers. His fame derived in part from his practical innovations, such as his perfection of dry fly techniques and the development of several new artificial flies, one of which took his name, the Quill Gordon, but he was also well known to the many sportsmen who read his regular contributions to England's *Fishing Gazette* and New York's *Forest and Stream*, where his column appeared from 1903 until his death in 1915. Born into a wealthy family in Pittsburgh, Gordon retreated to the Neversink River in the 1890s due to poor health. He clearly loved his sport and was eager to exchange ideas regarding flies and techniques, but he regularly fished alone. He enjoyed the mountain setting around the Neversink, and he wrote about the joys that came after a few good fish were already in the creel: "we can take more interest in the beauty of our surroundings, the clear rushing water of the rifts and deep pools, the tender verdure of young June and the wooded hills about us." Gordon's revelry in the Neversink, published in *Forest and Stream*, undoubtedly helped attract even more sportsmen to the region.[42]

Unlike Gordon, most of the well-known fly-fishing authors lived in the city, including Emilyn Gill, author of *Practical Dry-Fly Fishing*, published by Charles Scribner's Sons in 1913, and George M. LaBranche, whose *The Dry Fly and Fast Water*, appeared on Scribner's list the next year.[43] Several of the prominent, published fly-fishermen of New York, including Gill and LaBranche, were members of the first New York City club dedicated solely to fishing, the Anglers' Club of New York. Created in late 1905 through the efforts of Perry D. Fraser and Edward Cave, both of whom worked for *Field and Stream* in Manhattan, the Anglers' Club promoted the gentlemanly sport, offering an institution through which its members could exchange tales of their adventures and accumulated knowledge about angling. The organization grew quickly, reaching nearly seventy members in its first full year. The club worked primarily through nonpolitical means to promote sport fishing and served largely as a social club. Members met for annual dinners and for casting competitions, held in Central Park. By the early 1920s, the membership had grown to over 250, most of whom lived in Manhattan, with significant numbers coming from the various city suburbs. Although the Anglers' Club had a general interest in fishing, its members clearly focused on the Catskills trout region. The club's bulletin featured regular reports on the Beaver Kill, Neversink, and Willowemoc, and beginning in 1921 the club organized annual outings, where members could enter a contest and enjoy the camaraderie of the sport. With very few exceptions, the club's outings took them to the Catskills, to the Esopus, where members stayed at the Phoenicia Hotel, or the Beaver Kill, at the Trout Valley Farm, or on the Willowemoc at the DeBruce Club Inn.[44]

Urban gentlemen, like those who joined the Anglers' Club, developed and promoted sporting ethics that praised catch-and-release fishing and chastised "market" fishing. They lobbied for greater state regulation of fisheries, including abbreviated seasons, sport licensing, and catch limits to protect fish stocks. The support of state regulation often brought urban fishers in conflict with locals, who regularly fished for family consumption, as a supplement to their meager rural incomes.[45] In the Catskills, conflict between locals and vacationers generally involved access to streams, as urbanites leased or purchased lands and then posted the waters to protect their fish stocks. Despite these conflicts, a remarkable overlap in interest and experience among trout enthusiasts developed in the Catskills, as some of the most famous trout fishermen lived in both the city and the mountains, and some of the most revered fishers, like Gordon, were indeed locals, not visitors.[46]

The fame of the Catskills' best streams, the Beaver Kill and the Neversink, reached back into the 1850s, when growing numbers of city anglers began to shift their attention from nearby Long Island streams.[47] The Erie Railroad offered better access to the region beginning in 1848, with the line passing through the Delaware River Valley and past the Beaver Kill's mouth. Catskills trout streams grew in popularity through the 1850s and more rapidly after the 1871 opening of the even more convenient New York, Oswego and Midland Railroad. Eventually known as the Ontario and Western, the new line connected the heart of the trout region with the city, and the tourist industry blossomed along the rails. Among the tourists who began their seasonal migrations were sportsmen eager to try the renowned trout streams now within just hours of the city. In 1874, *Forest and Stream* even announced the preferred train schedule for quick visits to the trout region, recommending the "6 o'clock morning train," which would have a New Yorker fishing by 10:30, enabling a fresh trout breakfast even for "gentlemen who have no opportunity for long vacations."[48]

Not surprisingly, the stream sections closest to rail stations, especially near Livingston Manor on the Willowemoc and Rockland on the Beaver Kill, soon revealed the consequences of increased fishing. In 1862, well-known New York City figure and avid fisherman Robert Barnwell Roosevelt reminisced about the region before the railroads. "When the railroad was first opened," he wrote, "the country was literally overrun, and Bashe's Kill, Pine Kill, the Sandberg, the Mon Gaup and Callicoon, and even the Beaver Kill, which we thought were inexhaustible, were fished out."[49] Roosevelt clearly overstated the problem, but fishing pressure did lead to many complaints about wasted trips with nary a strike, diminished fish size, and a pining for more abundant days long since past—though it might be noted that fishers of every generation have longed for "the good old days" of abundance. Despite fears of declining fish stocks, Catskills streams continued to gain in popularity and notoriety through the late 1800s and early 1900s. In 1901, the *New York Times* announced the coming of trout season in the mountains, noting that each train brought scores of men who make the annual "pilgrimage," hoping "to be among the first to whip the streams." The *Times* noted that the typical Neversink fisherman "may fish for an hour or two, or he may fish all day, but when he returns he carries, slung over his shoulder, a basket of the finest fish in the world."[50]

Clearly the streams had not been fished out. Still, the number and size of trout in Catskills streams diminished, and sportsmen took action to save their pastime. One of the earliest and most important strategies involved creating fishing clubs and securing property rights to critical trout habitat. This practice began in the Catskills in 1869, when a few men from Poughkeepsie, a small city on the Hudson River not far from the trout region, purchased land on the Willowemoc Creek, including the stream's source, Sand Pond, which they renamed Lake Willowemoc and where the new organization, the Willowemoc Club, established its clubhouse. As the first president of the club, Cornelius Van Brunt, explained in *Forest and Stream*, the club was formed, "not only to have a pleasant place of resort, but for the protection of the fish." This "protection" came largely through the simple prohibition of fishing save by club members. But the club did more than protect fish. It improved the trout habitat at Lake Willowemoc, by building a race for spawning fish and through the improvement of the one small tributary stream. These improvements, combined with the raising of water levels in the pond, allowed the trout to spawn in sheltered areas, where eggs and fry could more readily survive.[51]

The Willowemoc Club's driving force was James Spencer Van Cleef, a Poughkeepsie lawyer, who made the original land purchase around Sand Pond and then continued to add to his holdings and those of the club. By 1883, Van Cleef had accumulated land on the upper Beaver Kill too, and he had become a founding member of the Balsam Lake Club, where a new clubhouse eventually replaced the one at Lake Willowemoc.[52] This new club included members from New York City, such as George W. Van Siclen, who had five years earlier obtained the leases for several long stretches of the Beaver Kill. At that point, Van Siclen made a public announcement through the pages of *Forest and Stream*: "No more trout fishing in the upper Beaverkill." Van Siclen had grown tired of seeing fishers who trudged out of the woods carrying all the trout they could, including tiny fish that ought to have remained in the stream. Van Siclen knew his announced posting of the upper reaches of the Beaver Kill, land that would become the heart of the Balsam Lake Club's property, would "undoubtedly cause great disappointment to many, especially to sportsmen of Ulster, Delaware, and Sullivan Counties," but he hoped his property rights would be respected. Van Siclen concluded his plea by noting that "forest and streams near the great cities are almost stripped of fin and feather. Those who cannot take time to go far have but one resource— to preserve the game by restricting the privilege."[53]

Urban authors often blamed local fishermen for the declining numbers of trout in the region, both because they tended to fish with bait rather than flies, which gentlemen found less sporting, and because they consumed their entire catch rather than releasing the smaller fish. But Van Siclen's comments spoke the obvious truth: the diminishment came largely at the hands of the thousands of touring sportsmen from the city, many of whom had limited skills and undeveloped sportsmen's ethics. Indeed, some city fishermen went so far as to hire locals to do their fishing for them, so that they might come back to the hotel or clubhouse fully stocked with trout.[54] Others clearly tagged along on fishing trips for the camaraderie, the opportunity to be out of the city, and perhaps even to secure business. In this regard, the clubs sought to police the behavior of city tourists as much as that of mountain residents. The privilege of fishing would be restricted based on gentlemanly behavior, and in some places on the ability to join a club, not on the residence of the sportsman.[55]

Private ownership of streams created conflict in the mountains, not just as locals demanded access to waters that they had long fished but also as proponents of fishing tourism demanded equal access to the finest fishing spots. In early 1885, the *New York Times* reported on an effort in Sullivan and Ulster counties to counter the posting of club properties, which by that point had already affected "some of the most famous streams." "As it is now," the *Times* complained, "a few men control the great trout region and alone enjoy it to its best advantage." Although this conflict was in part regional, with many of the clubs that purchased property or secured leases having their base in the city, it was just as clearly a conflict along class lines. Still, the opponents to posted streams were not entirely impoverished fishers looking for inexpensive meals. Indeed, the railroads, including the Erie and the O&W, had a direct financial incentive to keep the rivers open, as did many hotel and resort owners who themselves controlled little or no access to the streams. A proliferation of posted streams could only mean the diminishment of the region's tourism, a consequence that had greater ramifications for the Catskills economy than simply the decreasing availability of fish for locals.[56]

The increased private posting of streams sparked conflict in the mountains, but the response revealed considerable confluence of interests among urban anglers and Catskills residents who relied on the streams. The effort to maintain open, productive streams crossed regional and class boundaries. Even the highly respected Theodore Gordon expressed concern about the growth of private clubs and their practice of posting streams. While Gordon himself was generally welcome on all the Catskills streams due to his fame, Gordon questioned the ethics of the privileged keeping the masses from using such prized resources. Still, Gordon well understood the need to regulate fishing in some way. "If everyone is to have equal opportunities, the rank and file will have to exercise some self-restraint, which they are little inclined to do," he wrote.[57]

Of course, posting was not the only way to protect fisheries. As early as 1849, Sullivan County had attempted to protect fisheries with a law that prohibited the use of poison for fishing and protected fish during spawning season. In addition to such local initiatives, the state legislature expanded its regulation of fisheries in 1857, prohibiting all types of fishing other than those using a hook and line. By 1888 the state had created a Fish Commission to monitor New York's fish stocks and suggest legislation to ensure their protection.[58] In addition to governmental regulations, private clubs also restricted fishing on streams they controlled. Beyond simply keeping undesirable fishers away from their waters, the clubs also established rules of conduct among their members. The Neversink Club, for example, which by the late 1870s controlled parts of the West Branch of the Neversink River, limited club members to twenty-five fish a day. Those fish had to be at least eight inches long and had to be caught with a fly. Such rules not only ensured that members and their guests conform to the standards of their gentlemanly sport, but also that enough fish might be left in the club's waters to sustain the sport through the season, and leave the population healthy enough to sustain the next season as well.[59]

In addition to self-imposed regulations, the Neversink Club purchased thousands of yearling trout for their stream. Indeed, stocking of young trout was undoubtedly the most effective action club members took to protect their sport. Most clubs took it upon themselves to stock their waters, including the Orchard Lake Club, a group of fifty wealthy New Yorkers who purchased 500 acres around their club's namesake in 1911. The club created its own hatchery for brook trout near its clubhouse, making certain that each season would bring its reward.[60] Some young trout came from private hatcheries, but beginning in 1870, the state Fish Commission operated its own hatchery in Caledonia. Although it was some distance from the Catskills, the new facility had easy access to rail connections and would soon send stocking fry all over the state. Operated by Seth Green, a central figure in the nation's developing pisciculture, the state hatchery began sending brook trout fry into the Catskills by 1876. Most of the state-raised fish entered streams through private hands, as interested parties could order fry to place in their own waters. Through this process fishing clubs, hotels, and private individuals placed thousands of young fish in the state's streams every year. In 1896, for example, individuals placed 331,000 fry in Catskills waters, most of them brook trout, in addition to the 15,000 trout that the Fisheries Commission itself placed in the Beaver Kill.[61] Some local governments also initiated stocking programs to ensure the success of sport-related tourism. As early as the mid-1870s, Greene County had begun its own stocking efforts, having established a hatchery for trout in Palenville. Samuel Rusk reported that 60,000 brook and lake trout "were procured and put in the creeks and ponds of the towns of Catskill and Cairo in 1876–7."[62]

In the southern Catskills, the O&W Railroad engaged in fish stocking, acquiring fish from the state hatcheries and releasing them into the streams along its line. The company boasted that it had released over 2.5 million brook trout, and "a large number of lake and California trout" between 1878 and 1887. For the railroad, fish stocking became an important tool in maintaining the attractiveness of this tourist region and a marketing coup in itself. By the late 1880s, the O&W's summer guides included figures on how many fish it had stocked, including 900,000 brook trout in 1886, "put in the trout streams from Walton to Mountaindale." In 1894, the O&W announced that it had stocked over nine million brook trout over the previous fifteen years.[63]

In 1892, the New York Times noted that the "effect of restocking the streams throughout the Catskills was unmistakably visible," meaning that the mountains had experienced the return of "such fishing as had not been known in several previous seasons." By the late 1800s, then, stocking had become an essential management tool in "keeping" the Catskills wild, ensuring that the mountains would forever contain the attributes

Glentworth Butler Haynes, behind, shares a ride with Jimmy Butler, son of Glen's namesake, behind the Butler's Highmount summer cottage in the early 1920s. Jimmy lived in Brooklyn for most the year, but spent enough time in the Catskills to become one of Glen's closest childhood friends.

(*above*) Fleischmanns, New York, ca. 1902. Though nestled in a tourist region, Fleischmanns still possessed an agricultural landscape, with pastures on the hillsides above town and plowed fields in the distance. In the foreground a lumberyard holds unmilled logs. By the late 1800s, agriculture and various extractive industries had stripped the Catskills of much of the region's forests. Library of Congress, Prints & Photographs Division, Detroit Publishing Company Collection, LC-D4–10667C.

In this lithograph, Harry Fenn greatly exaggerates the ruggedness of the Catkills, just as many authors had done for decades. Here diminutive tourists look out over the Hudson, not far from the Catskill Mountain House. This lithograph, "The Catskills: Sunrise from South Mountain," appeared in William Cullen Bryant's *Picturesque America* in 1874.

(*opposite*) A wide variety of mills filled the Catskills, including these two at Bishop Falls—one a gristmill, and the other a sawmill. The mills remained in service long after they appeared to be in disrepair, as they are here in a late-nineteenth-century photograph. The presence of the mills apparently did not diminish the area's reputation as a tourist destination along the Esopus Creek. Courtesy of the Town of Olive Archives, West Shokan, NY.

Rip Van Winkle House in "Sleepy Hollow" on the road up to the Mountain House. Local residents marketed the region and specific businesses through the use of Washington Irving's fictional character. By 1900, at about the time of this photograph, the vast majority of tourists bypassed "Sleepy Hollow," preferring to take the railroad up into the mountains, which explains the dilapidated appearance of the Rip Van Winkle House. Library of Congress, Prints & Photographs Division, Detroit Publishing Company Collection, LC-D4–14529.

Laurel House sits above Kaaterskill Falls, ca. 1900. The original hotel, the typical small country inn on the right, sits next to the much larger and finer addition, finished in 1884. The "shanty" sits perched at the top of the falls, supplying a platform for proper viewing of the falls. The dam used to hold back water for spectacular releases is just upstream from the falls. Library of Congress, Prints & Photographs Division, Detroit Publishing Company Collection, LC-D4–14506.

The New Grand Hotel, Highmount, ca. 1900. Advertised as the "highest mountain hotel in the world," the Grand Hotel offered both urban and wilderness attractions. Library of Congress, Prints & Photographs Division, Detroit Publishing Company Collection, LC-D4–10665.

Railroads redefined the mountains. In this turn-of-the-century photograph of the Haines Corners Station near Kaaterskill Park, the word "Prompt" suggests the intrusion of urban ideals along with urban tourists. Library of Congress, Prints & Photographs Division, Detroit Publishing Company Collection, LC-D4–14510.

Many farm families took in boarders to earn supplemental income. In many instances, catering to tourists soon became more lucrative than farming, as was the case for the Bishop family, which opened Bishop Falls House in 1895. Here lodgers sit in front of the ancestral Bishop stone house, with the 1900 frame additions for guests visible in the rear. Courtesy of the Town of Olive Archives, West Shokan, NY.

DeForest Bishop, shown here holding the reigns, took guests at Bishop Falls House for wagon rides through the countryside, a common pastime for urban tourists around the turn of the century. Courtesy of the Town of Olive Archives, West Shokan, NY.

THE ASCENT TO KAATERSKILL FALLS.

By the mid-1800s, the area around Kaaterskill Falls had been significantly altered to allow tourists to experience spectacular nature fully. This 1886 *Harper's New Monthly Magazine* illustration shows the stairs that allowed tourists to see the falls from both the top (near the hotels where many of them stayed) and the bottom. The seated woman records her thoughts on the spectacle, indicative of how tourists expected to experience the falls and other examples of sublime nature. Courtesy of Cornell University Library, Making of America Digital Collection. *Harper's New Monthly Magazine* 72 (May 1886), 896.

SUMMER HOMES

AMONG THE MOUNTAINS
ON THE NEW YORK ONTARIO & WESTERN R.Y.

J. E. CHILDS,
GENERAL MANAGER.

J. C. ANDERSON,
GENERAL PASSENGER AGENT.

56 Beaver Street, N. Y.

These *Summer Homes* covers reveal the changing nature of the Ontario and Western's marketing of the region along its line. In 1894 a milkmaid graced the cover, as she had for years, indicating the attractiveness of agricultural landscapes to urban tourists and the draw of fresh produce and milk. By 1911 the cover featured a wild scene—a trout stream running through a forest—reflecting the popularity of wilderness vacations.

SUMMER HOMES

1911

AMONG THE
MOUNTAINS
ON THE
NEW YORK
ONTARIO &
WESTERN
RAILWAY

J. E. CHILDS,
 Vice-President and General Manager
J. C. ANDERSON, Traffic Manager
J. R. DUNBAR, General Passenger Agent

GENERAL OFFICES
56 Beaver Street, New York

Trout fishing in the Catskills, ca. 1900. Catskills streams became world famous for trout fishing, largely because of their popularity among New York City's sportsmen, who publicized the streams in magazines and books. Library of Congress, Prints & Photographs Division, Detroit Publishing Company Collection, LC-D4–32836.

West Shokan was one of the nine communities removed to make way for the Ashokan Reservoir. Courtesy of the Town of Olive Archives, West Shokan, NY.

Many of the laborers who built the Ashokan Dam and cleared the basin came from outside of the Catskills, including African Americans, who lived in segregated housing and worked in segregated crews. Courtesy of the Town of Olive Archives, West Shokan, NY.

(*opposite top*) Construction of the Ashokan Dam. The Bishop Falls House was one of the first properties taken by the city so that construction towers, such as those in the background here, could be built. Courtesy of the Town of Olive Archives, West Shokan, NY.

(*opposite bottom*) The Ashokan Reservoir quickly became a tourist destination, as did the aeration plant that shot city-bound water into the air before it entered the aqueduct. This postcard features the water aeration plant, completed in 1915.

WATER AERATION PLANT, ASHOKAN RESERVOIR, CATSKILL MTS., N. Y. NEW YORK CITY WATER SUPPLY 55

By the 1970s, the Concord Hotel had become a city unto itself. Although guests continued to recreate outdoors, especially around the large pool and the two golf courses, the hotel also offered plenty of indoor recreation, including swimming and (shown in this postcard) tennis.

Thomas Cole, *Lake with Dead Trees (Catskill)*, 1825. Cole painted *Lake with Dead Trees* and two other landscapes after his first trip to the Catskills. The success of those paintings catapulted both Cole and the Catskills to the center of the New York art scene. Courtesy of Allen Memorial Art Museum, Oberlin College, Ohio.

Frederic E. Church, *Morning, Looking East over the Hudson Valley from the Catskill Mountains*, 1848. Oil on canvas, 18 ¼ × 24 inches. Church was Cole's only formal student. Although Church's long and successful career took him far from the Catskills, his home remained along the Hudson, overlooking both Cole's home and the mountains. Courtesy of Albany Institute of History & Art. Gift of Catherine Gansevoort (Mrs. Abraham) Lansing.

(opposite) Asher B. Durand, *Kindred Spirits*, 1849. Oil on canvas, 44 × 36 inches. Durand painted *Kindred Spirits* in remembrance of his friend Cole, who had died the previous year. The painting, perhaps the most famous of all Hudson River art, hung for many years at the home of William Cullen Bryant, who appears with Cole overlooking a fictional Catskill clove. Courtesy of Walton Family Foundation.

Sanford Gifford, *October in the Catskills*, 1880. Gifford became one of the finest landscape artists in New York, developing a luminist style inspired by the Catskills. *October in the Catskills* captures a twilight glow over Kaaterskill Clove, the heart of perhaps the most-painted region in nineteenth-century America. M.77.141. Courtesy of Los Angeles County Museum of Art. Gift of Mr. and Mrs. J. Douglas Pardee, Mr. and Mrs. John McGreevey, and Mr. and Mrs. Charles C. Shoemaker. Photograph © 2006 Museum Associates/LACMA.

of a proper wilderness and that the streams would not come to resemble those nearer the city, where combinations of pollution and overfishing had created barren waters.[64]

Stocking may have been part of the effort to keep the Catskills wilderness productive, but it changed the varieties of fish, not just their numbers. Sport fishermen prized the native brook trout, but the fish fared poorly in the warming waters of midsummer and flourished only in the smaller brooks that remained well shaded by thick forests and were fed by cold, clean mountain springs. In an effort to expand the fishing season deeper into the summer and farther downstream into the state's larger rivers, the state hatchery at Cold Spring Harbor began receiving brown trout eggs from Germany in 1882. Despite concerns that the larger, more aggressive browns might outcompete the native brook trout, the state made browns available for stocking, and in 1887 several thousand fry entered the waters of the southern Catskills. By the early 1890s, the brown trout had become so well established in the warmer waters that fishermen sought them out in the slower-moving, wider sections of the Beaver Kill, especially around Roscoe and Rockland, where the stocking had taken place.[65]

Another species entered Catskills waters as early as 1878, when A. S. Hopkins of Catskill introduced over 1,000 rainbow trout, also known as California mountain trout, to waters in Greene County. By 1880, fishing enthusiasts had introduced rainbows to the famed streams of Sullivan County. Like the browns, rainbows could survive in warmer waters and grow larger, both valued attributes at a time when the number and size of brook trout continued to diminish. Rainbows did not fair as well as browns in the Sullivan County streams, but after the construction of the Ashokan Reservoir on the Esopus in the 1910s, the rainbow flourished in that stream, as they migrated in and out of the massive artificial lake.[66]

Some controversy surrounded the introduction of nonnative species, particularly the brown trout, which many claimed preyed voraciously upon smaller brook trout. Some fishermen simply praised the superiority of the native trout—"speckled beauties" as many called them—claiming that they tasted better than the European imports, even though the brook trout were smaller. Others went so far as to disparage the immigrant fish, echoing the era's nativist sentiment, particularly during World War I, when trout of German origins faced discrimination similar to that faced by their human counterparts. Despite the debate, the stocking of nonnative trout had its intended effect, giving sportsmen a better chance of success in the region's larger streams and prolonging the high season.[67]

As the popularity of their sport grew through the late nineteenth and early twentieth centuries, fishers, from both the city and the mountains, became powerful conservationists, coming together to protect and preserve the streams of the Catskills. They fought battles against a range of threats, including deforestation. Sportsmen sought the preservation of forests, both through their own purchases of land and through lobbying efforts to encourage increased state purchases. Fishers also fought stream pollution that threatened prime trout waters, particularly by fighting the acid factories that developed in the southern Catskills in the late 1800s. In the fall of 1900, *Forest and Stream* publicized the problem of acid pollution, which leaked from small riverside factories making wood alcohol. Complainants included Ed Hewitt, a New York chemist, who noted acid pollution's devastating effects on trout near Fallsburgh. Although publicity concerning water pollution may have limited the negative consequences of the industry, the acid factories did remain in the area until changes in the chemical industry brought their closure in the 1940s.[68] Sportsmen met with some successes in their conservation efforts, as the state increased purchases of land to protect critical headwaters and improve public access to the streams. Still, one dramatic loss came in the mid-1960s with the building of Route 17 through the Beaver Kill Valley. The construction brought considerable temporary disturbance to the stream and, more importantly, a permanent disruption of the wilderness values of fishing along the lower Beaver Kill.[69]

The development of Catskills fisheries was a significant part of the building of a wilderness infrastructure in the mountains, closely akin to developing trails and campgrounds. Throughout the twentieth century, sportsmen, especially from the metropolitan region, were particularly active in lobbying for the creation and protection of a usable wilderness in the Catskills. By 1931, Harry Haring could describe a much-altered environment that resulted from this effort to create wilderness, which served as "a glorified playground for the city." The highly prized brook trout still spawned in the region's streams, but fishermen were more likely to find increasingly successful and continually stocked browns and rainbows. A 1935 New York State Conservation Department report on the Delaware Watershed went so far as to announce that the Beaver Kill, Willowemoc, and Neversink were "famous for brown trout fishing," apparently forgetting that the fame had come from brook trout fishing.

However forgetful, the state's language appropriately symbolized the naturalization of brown trout, for although debate persisted about whether browns harmed the still-preferred brook trout, browns had become an important part of the region's fishing culture. Indeed, from 1925 to 1934, the Conservation Department had overseen the stocking of 1.2 million browns in the three famed rivers, while placing just over 770,000 brook trout in those same waters. In a clear indication of the difficulty in preserving the Catskills natural resources "forever," the Conservation Department's 1935 report included a twenty-five-page discussion of "stocking policy" and "fish management policies." Obviously, an intensely used wilderness resource required careful, continuous management if it were to continue serving the needs of its urban visitors.[70]

The wilderness cult of the early 1900s only grew in its influence throughout the remainder of the century, and by the 1960s, with the Wilderness Act passed, environmental activists turned their attention toward the protection of specific places under new rules, both on federal and state lands, where new protections could borrow from the national legislation's language and intent. In New York, wilderness enthusiasts focused first on the Adirondacks, where regulations already greatly restricted development but did not prohibit it, even on state lands. In response to public pressure, in the early 1970s the Department of Environmental Conservation created new management classifications for state lands inside the Adirondack Park, including "Wilderness Areas," in which the state would take no action to improve access or use. These new management categories also affected the Catskills, where eventually the D.E.C. would create four wilderness areas totaling 118,000 acres, most of them around Slide and Big Indian mountains. The wilderness designations encompassed primarily first-growth forests, mostly at higher elevations, and their boundaries skirted long-settled land, such as that along Haynes Hollow, where members of the Haynes family had lived for generations and which is now nearly enveloped by the Big Indian Wilderness.[71]

Although many adherents would seek their wilderness experiences in much grander, more open spaces in the American West, smaller patches of forests in the East, such as Big Indian and Slide, could suffice, as could less wild, second-growth forests. In 1959, Jean Craighead George published a children's novel, *My Side of the Mountain*, which captured the common childhood fantasy of running away from the city to live in the wilderness. The story neatly links city and country, as the young Sam

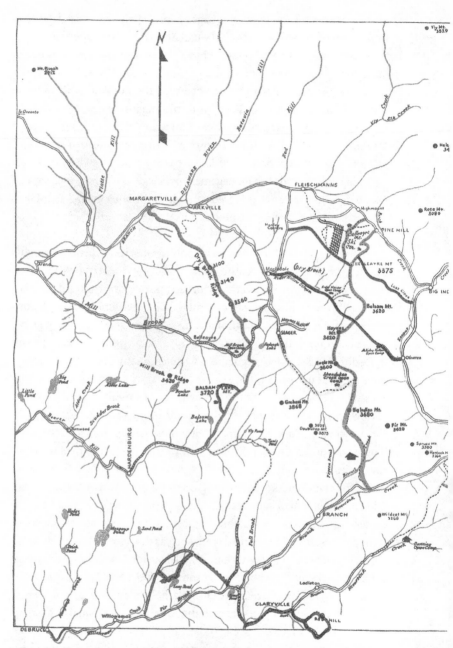

Map 3 Making a usable wilderness required the building of trails, campgrounds, and open camps. This 1965 New York State Conservation Department map features trails through the areas that eventually became the Big Indian and Slide Mountain wildernesses.

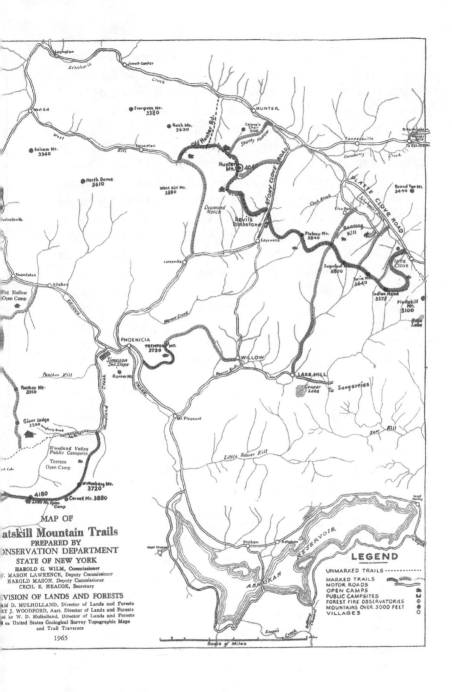

Gribley flees his family's Third Avenue apartment in New York, taking a train and then hitching rides as he sought out his great-grandfather's farm near Delhi in Delaware County. Sam arrives at a hemlock grove, which he declares is "just the kind of forest I have always dreamed I would run to." Soon Sam finds a tree with the name "Gribley" carved into it, marking his failed ancestral farm, and he finds himself at home, in a countryside he has never known. Here Sam expects to live off the land, not as a re-created farm, but as a miraculously provident wilderness. Though just a boy, Sam thrives in the Catskills forest, living in a hollow tree, training a falcon as a companion and aide, hunting, fishing, and gathering the food he needs, and even tanning deer hides to make his own clothing. Using little but his own imagination and determination, Sam survives the long, hard Catskills winter. Fittingly enough, a college English teacher lost in the woods stumbles upon Sam's campground, where he falls asleep. When stirred by the rather primitive-looking Sam, the teacher declares he has awakened "in the middle of the eighteenth century." Then, getting his centuries wrong, he takes to calling Sam "Thoreau," though he might just as accurately have called the boy "Leatherstocking," after James Fenimore Cooper's hero of the receding New York State wilderness.[72]

My Side of the Mountain tells us much about the continuing power of the wilderness ideal in the second half of the twentieth century, especially in regard to the Catskills. The book became a classic in children's literature, no doubt because it so brilliantly captured a common fantasy. This was not just a fantasy among children, either, for many adults believed fervently that the solutions to their city-born troubles lay in the mountains. Like Rip Van Winkle, whose twenty-year snooze was only slightly more fantastic than this boy's one-year survival, Sam Gribley inspired readers to seek the actual place of his fictional story, heading off to Delhi in search of the hollow tree in which he lived. Wilderness, even in the postagricultural landscape of the western Catskills, held remarkable power over many New Yorkers—and others in urban and suburban America. It held out the possibility of escape back into a simpler time. At the end of *My Side of the Mountain*, Sam's family joins him in the forest in a chapter entitled "The City Comes to Me." The father announces a plan to build a proper house, there in the wilderness. Sam expresses a bit of disappointment that the tree house and hammocks will no longer suffice, but in the end he is resigned to this new, seemingly permanent life living off the land.[73]

The Gribley family, two generations removed from farming in the Catskills, had returned to the mountains, a movement that might symbolize the broader return to the country of individuals whose ancestors had lived on farms, not in the deep woods. Thus, the Gribley story captures an important shift in the evolving urban conception of rural landscapes. No longer did "the national imagination" consider "the most beautiful country to be that composed of beautiful farms," as John Stilgoe concluded about the early 1800s. The antithesis of urbanity was no longer the well-tended agricultural landscape; rather, it was the deep woods, the wilderness, which suited the needs of urban tourists and second-home buyers.[74]

If *My Side of the Mountain* symbolized the growing importance of this conception of nature, it also represented the actual return of wilderness to parts of the postagricultural mountains. Local residents bemoaned the decline in agriculture that made the spread of forests possible, but in other ways locals and urban residents expressed very similar hopes for the Catskills' future, hopes that centered on the persistence of a rural life in the mountains and stability in landscape and economy. Both local and urban hunters, fishers, hikers, and other admirers and users of the Catskills' many natural resources revealed a remarkable confluence of interests that increasingly focused on preservation, of both mountainous wilderness areas and the valleys of rural culture that ran between them.

—ων— *Chapter 5* —ων—

Mountain Water

Indeed, the water of all this Catskill region is the best in the world.
>   —John Burroughs, 1894

New York says it has the best water in the world. But it's our water.
>   —Andrew Dresser, 2001

Although many tourists headed into the Catskills expecting a wilderness experience, at the turn of the twentieth century so many arrived in the mountains every summer that parts of the mountains simply felt crowded. In 1892, the authors of the Ulster and Delaware guide even felt compelled to counter charges that the mountains were "in danger of becoming a suburb of New York City." Apparently some tourists who preferred a more complete escape from the city began to feel that the railroads brought too many guests to the Catskills. In the heat of the summer, the crowds of the city became the crowds of the mountains, diminishing the prospect that anyone would experience wilderness during their vacations. The U&D pamphlet declared, however, "The romantic Catskills will never be annexed to New York City." Given the city's acquisition of thousands of acres in the Catskills for building reservoirs, beginning just thirteen years after the pamphlet's publication, the irony is rich. Still, the statement is accurate. The romantic Catskills—the imagined mountains of art and literature—would not be annexed. Instead, civic engineers and city boosters would create a new vision of the Catskills, one that featured a wild landscape—pure and healthful as before—but now nearly vacant and available for the city's acquisition. The pure air of the mountains would stay put, but the pure water would be held back and channeled to the city via huge aqueducts. The wilderness of the mountains would be put to yet another urban use.[1]

Tourists came to the mountains for elevation, for the grand views, for the exhilaration of climbing, and for the scenery of steep cloves. But, as the work of poets and painters and the words of the tourists themselves make clear, water was also central to the Catskills experience. A land rich in waterfalls, laced with fast-moving streams and pure-running springs, the Catskills gained nearly as much attention for the quality of its water as it did for its alpine scenery and atmosphere. As early as 1820, before the tourist industry developed in the mountains, Henry Dwight praised the "sweetness and purity" of Catskills waters, noting their "soft luster and transparency" and claiming that "these fountains cannot escape the observation of the spectator."[2] Over time, as more tourists visited the region, the mountain waters became all the more famous. Fly fishermen were especially enthusiastic about the clear, cold waters of the Catskills, and, as we have seen, Theodore Gordon and other fishermen/authors helped make the Neversink, Beaver Kill, and Esopus world famous.

John Burroughs's wide-ranging natural history essays frequently described Catskills streams. In one moving passage in "Speckled Trout," published in 1879, Burroughs depicted a trout fisherman's approach to a stream:

> I am sure I run no risk of overpraising the charm and attractiveness of a well-fed trout stream, every drop of water in it as bright and pure as if the nymphs had brought it all the way from its source in crystal goblets, and as cool as if it had been hatched beneath a glacier. When the heated and soiled and jaded refugee from the city first sees one, he feels as if he would like to turn it into his bosom and let it flow through him a few hours, it suggests such healing freshness and newness. How his roily thoughts would run clear; how the sediment would go downstream! Could he ever have an impure or an unwholesome wish afterward? The next best thing he can do is to tramp along its banks and surrender himself to its influence.[3]

Burroughs may have been right about the healing powers of mountain waters, but he underestimated the ability of city folk to capture the streams. Catskills water proved so attractive that the city eventually demanded more than visitation rights, more than bottles of spring water sent down by the case, or even tanker-car loads sent down for bottling in the city. Eventually, the city would enter the mountains, build great structures, hold back the spring floods, and send them through aqueducts to the metropolis. In the process, rural communities would be sacrificed to the needs of the great city, and the Catskill Mountains would take on a new definition as the Catskill Watershed.

Historians have long commented on the importance of water in the arid American West. San Francisco's turn-of-the-century taking of the

Hetch Hetchy Valley inside Yosemite National Park and Los Angeles's acquisition of Owens Valley waters have become icons of imperial cities' power over their hinterlands, their ability to use wealth and political influence to quash opponents.[4] Of course, water is no less important to residents in the East. And, although more precipitation falls in most of the East and surface water is abundant there, no large coastal city with the expectation of long-term economic growth could long rely on a truly local source of water. The great Eastern cities have behaved just as the metropolises of the West in exercising power over nearby rural communities in an effort to secure suitable sources of potable water.[5]

By 1905, it had become clear that New York would have to expand its water supply greatly, almost ensuring that some rural communities would be forever changed. Through the long debate about the water supply's expansion, the urban conception of the mountains—and of wild nature more generally—played a central role, revealing both the flexibility of urban conceptions of the Catskills and the power that wilderness values had gained in urban culture. At first a private company held water rights in the Catskills, and opponents decried the mountains as crowded and deforested, far from ideal as a source of healthful waters. When the threat of private ownership ended, however, the city regained interest in the Catskills, and the mountain slopes became wild once again, the waters once again pure. Natural springs, feeding mountain steams, promised not just an ample source of water but a healthful source, far superior to the "city water" supplied by the Croton system. Through it all, the Hudson River, a more accessible and cheaper potential source, gained no significant support as the city's supply, since it was simply too impure, too unnatural, too much like the city itself.

In the long history connecting New York City and the Catskills, the construction of the water supply most directly suggests an imperial relationship, for the reservoirs most clearly represent the ability of the city to control space in the mountains. The story of their creation is one of conflict and, in the mountains alone, loss. On the other hand, although the impetus and planning for the reservoirs clearly came from outside the mountains, much of the labor that made them came from within. In addition to this labor, the great number of sacrifices—in giving up homesteads, businesses, even entire communities—would bind local residents to the reservoirs, give them a sense of ownership. Not unlike Rip Van Winkle and brown trout, the reservoirs would become naturalized, accepted by locals as part of the Catskills identity, integral to the landscape. Almost immediately upon their completion, the reservoirs could elicit both resentment and pride among Catskills residents, conflicting sentiments that represented the complicated nature of the collaboration that made them.

New York City's nineteenth-century boosters well understood that economic factors delimited the city's growth, but they also knew that physical realities posed equally important, if not more fundamental limits. None of these physical realities was more evident than the need for a water supply that expanded to meet the demand of a growing population and industrial base. Throughout the nineteenth century, foul water, either tarnished by human pollution or natural putrefaction, remained a critical health concern, especially in large cities. During the 1832 cholera epidemic, more than 3,500 New Yorkers died, and although residents were just as likely to blame the mostly impoverished victims for impure morals and unclean habits, people believed that somehow the spread of the disease was related to miasmas, the odorous gasses released by foul water. Even beyond epidemic diseases, New Yorkers had come to assume that their impure waters, drawn from tainted wells and for decades from a polluted pond unpoetically referred to as "the Collect," contributed to poor health in the city. Even in the early 1800s, those with means paid for bottled water, carted in from a safe distance from the city. Those with means sought healthful restoration outside the city for many reasons, and pure country water was among the most important.[6]

Immediately after the devastating 1832 epidemic, the city and the state began taking the steps necessary to secure a healthful and plentiful water supply for the booming commercial port. In 1833, the state granted New York City the power to create a water commission, and over the next few years debate focused on just where the city should acquire its water, though by 1835 most thought Westchester County's Croton River the best source. Just as opposition to the city's acquisition of the Croton Valley grew in Westchester, a fire ravaged Manhattan, a tragedy made worse by the city's poor water supply. Firefighters simply had no access to water under enough pressure to operate hoses for a substantial period. Subsequently, Westchester, then a predominantly rural county, could not gain support in the state legislature to block the city's use of the Croton. In 1842—after weathering an economic downturn, stiff opposition in Westchester, legal battles concerning eminent domain, and complaints about the poor behavior of the Irish immigrants who actually did the work of building the dam and the impressive Croton Aqueduct—country water flowed into the York Hill Reservoir, just north of the city on the island of Manhattan. Although the continuous growth of the city would require concomitant expansions of the Croton system, by the mid-1840s New Yorkers began to boast that their water system was among the best in the world: a great water supply for a great city.[7]

Though the city's water supply had improved considerably, in the late 1800s mountain hotels still marketed their pure water as a major attraction. The Hotel Kaaterskill claimed it served "the purest, sweetest water from a limpid mountain lake." And it reassured guests that its large facility was "perfectly drained," so as to avoid the sewage problems that plagued the city. The Grand Hotel went even further, making health claims and publishing a chemical analysis of its "elegant spring water." Its 1887 pamphlet boasted: "We feel assured that a free use of this water will produce beneficial results, as its purity affords medicinal qualities of great value, and especially in affections of the kidneys, digestive organs, etc." In an affirmation that pure water should be more liberally consumed than that supplied in the city, guests received a glass of spring water in their rooms each morning before breakfast. Apparently, any water brought into the city—even from the Croton—became tarnished by the process. Truly pure waters remained in the country.[8]

Even after the construction of the Croton Aqueduct, discussion concerning the adequacy of the water supply never really ceased. To meet the demand of the growing city, the Croton system added new reservoirs in 1873, 1878, 1892, 1895, and 1897, and the largest, the New Croton Reservoir, was completed in 1905, even as the city sought out more distant sources. By the time the city completed the Cross River Reservoir in 1908, the Croton system contained ten separate reservoirs in Westchester and Putnam counties, and yet this was not enough.[9] Just as important, the long string of battles over new reservoirs in Westchester and Putnam counties pointed to the permanent problem of finding a reliable water supply that could grow as fast as the city. The piecemeal approach in the Croton watershed would only suffice for so long—soon the city would capture *all* the water from that source and would have to look elsewhere. Some New Yorkers with grand dreams considered the Adirondacks as a logical next source, given the purity of the waters in those distant mountains. Lake Champlain received some attention, along with smaller bodies of water, such as Lake George. Others suggested the Great Lakes—the only truly inexhaustible fresh water source on the map. No water source promised to support endless economic and demographic growth for New York City like the Great Lakes. Some even dared suggest the Hudson itself, though its heavily populated and industrial watershed made this among the least desirable of potential sources.[10]

In 1886, as the city constructed a new, larger aqueduct from the Croton watershed to handle the increased flow from Westchester, *Scientific American* published a three-page article proposing the use of the Esopus and Schoharie creeks for New York's supply. In what was primarily a critique of New York's continued reliance on the Croton watershed, R. D. A. Parrott noted that the city, then growing at about 800 persons per week, would naturally expand northward, and that the watersheds in Westchester and Putnam would inevitably be compromised by pollution from the growing suburbs or, just as unfortunate, population growth would be thwarted to protect the supply. Instead, Parrott recommended a dam on the Esopus near Olive Bridge and a tunnel connecting the Schoharie to the Esopus. The only significant way in which Parrott's plan deviated from that which was eventually built was his addition of another tunnel connecting the Schoharie to the Batavia Kill, farther to the north. Parrott praised the quality of the water, the high elevations from which it would be gathered, and the region's suitable geology. He said nothing of the people in the Catskills, which, according to his prose, might even be devoid of population. "High up on these mountains," he concluded, "aside from the paths of development, and remote from the influences of thickly settled districts, is a park which the city may preserve as a collecting region for unpolluted water."[11]

Part of the object of the 1898 consolidation of Manhattan, Brooklyn, Queens, Staten Island, and the Bronx was the equalization of services across the metropolis. This was particularly true of water, a resource that Brooklyn had been finding more and more difficult to secure. With consolidation looming, the Brooklyn Manufacturers' Association issued a report concerning water supply, indicating the importance of finding some reliable source if the city were to continue its remarkable growth—as indeed it would. In 1900 the recently consolidated city contained 3.4 million persons, and just ten years later it counted 4.7 million, meaning that the city added on average 130,000 people to its total every year. Although the growth rate slowed somewhat, by 1920 the city held 5.6 million persons, and a decade later 6.9 million. The city's growth did not end until 1950, when it peaked at nearly 7.9 million. This era of dramatic growth, from the moment of consolidation through 1950, during which the city more than doubled in size, is not coincidently the era in which the metropolis reached out to the mountains to secure a larger water supply.[12]

As the metropolis consolidated, a private contractor, the Ramapo Water Company, pledged that it could supply ample water for all five boroughs in just a few years. Ramapo had incorporated in 1887, when the company proposed supplying the city with water from Orange and Rockland counties, taking its name from the Ramapo River.[13] In an era of machine politics, with some actual corruption and even more assumed malfeasance, any project as large as revamping the water supply was bound to run into problems, and the Ramapo plan was quickly denounced as an insiders' scheme to defraud the citizens of New York. Eventually, legal problems ended this first water supply scheme in the 1880s, but the company returned, aided by an 1895 state law that granted Ramapo remarkably broad powers to create a water supply system. By 1899 Ramapo had hired Brooklyn civil engineer Peter Nostrand to scour the Catskills, make surveys of potential reservoir sites, and draw up contracts with property owners. In this way, Nostrand concluded deals with dozens of Catskills residents, giving them modest signing bonuses up front and promising to actually purchase the land after Ramapo secured a contract with the city. As required by the state law, Nostrand then filed maps with the Ulster County Clerk's office that declared Ramapo's intention to build a reservoir along Esopus Creek. Ramapo then offered a contract to the city to supply up to 200 million gallons of water daily, charging $70 per million gallons. Over the course of the forty-year contract, the city could pay Ramapo the enormous sum of $140 million, and in the end it would not have control of its supply, since Ramapo would still own the delivery system. Thus, the city could be forced to sign another, similarly expensive contract. The suddenness of the Ramapo proposal, combined with its magnitude, was enough to convince the New York Times that "monstrous corruption" was behind the scheme. Unfortunately for the Times, finding the source of the corruption was quite difficult, since the company originated among Republicans, and its new plan now sat before the city's Democratic municipal government. At times editors blamed connected Republicans for the scheme; at others it leveled accusations at the familiar foe of good government, the Democratic machine that operated out of Tammany Hall in Manhattan. Regardless of who was responsible for the plan, or more accurately, the assumed corruption, Ramapo came under intense attack, with opponents (led by the Merchants' Association of New York) pointing to the bad economics of the scheme, and the probability that the company could not deliver on its promises, even at the extreme price demanded.[14]

Reacting to the Ramapo scheme in late 1899, Bird Coler, the city's comptroller, hired respected civil engineer John R. Freeman to produce a report on the water supply. Freeman had an extensive background in hydraulic engineering, including a stint with the Massachusetts commission charged with solving Boston's supply problem. Coler hired Freeman to calculate the city's actual need for additional water, weigh the relative benefits of potential sources, and determine the advantages and disadvantages of the Ramapo proposal. Freeman concluded that the city would need a new supply, and soon, since the Croton watershed could only reliably supply the city for five more years if the current rapid growth continued. Freeman advised that saving water through the reduction of waste would be necessary, but it could not long delay the need for a larger supply. Just as important, Freeman found "the price proposed by the Ramapo Company exorbitant," and thus the city should no longer pursue the plan. With the publication of the report, it became clear that both Freeman and Comptroller Coler hoped to convince the city to keep the water supply in public hands, and a *Times* headline labeled the report a "Blow at Ramapo Scheme."[15]

Freeman also listed potential additional sources of water, determining that the Ten Mile and Housatonic rivers, north of the Croton watershed on the eastern side of the Hudson, would provide an ample supply at an economical price. Indeed, Freeman concluded these rivers were the "cheapest and most available source, by far."[16] After examining the Esopus Creek, the heart of the Ramapo plan, Freeman concluded that the river could supply only 100 million gallons per day—less than half what the city would require, even in the short term. When he visited the area, Freeman found no favorable sites for a high dam, adding that a large dam on the Esopus would flood "the thriving village of Shokan" and the Ulster and Delaware Railroad, causing "great disturbance of population and the flooding of a large proportion of all the good land in the valley." Even at this great cost in disturbance, Freeman thought the Esopus could only reliably supply 200 million gallons per day if supplemented by the Schoharie Creek, as Parrott had suggested fourteen years earlier.[17]

At 587 pages, Freeman's report was nothing if not thorough. Still, it was not the only major report on the water supply to appear in 1900. Just a few months later, the Merchants' Association issued its own compre-

hensive report, 627 pages in length. Working with Freeman's coopera-
tion, and toward the same goal, the Merchants' Association inquiry,
headed by another well-known water supply engineer, James Fuertes, concluded that the Ramapo proposition would be much too expensive.
Indeed, as the report pointed out, since the city actually made money
supplying water, why would it want to contract out this service to a private company? Like Freeman, Fuertes recommended conservation, particularly through the use of meters—then only required of large
commercial customers—but also agreed that a new source would have
to be found in the short term, with new waters supplied by 1910. By the
time the Fuertes report appeared, however, the interstate nature of the
Housatonic watershed (which flows through Connecticut) had made that
option politically infeasible. The Merchants' Association recommended
instead the Hudson itself, with an intake at Poughkeepsie, above the salt
line, and a filtration system to purify the water. Although the Hudson
seemed a rather tainted source, cities did use it, including Albany and
Poughkeepsie. And, as the Merchants' Association went to pains to
explain, other large cities, including London and Hamburg, also purified
tainted rivers to obtain their water. In addition, while the water itself was
unattractive, clearly the Hudson would be large enough to supply the
needs of the growing city for quite some time, perhaps permanently.[18]

The Hudson River project would require building reservoirs in the
Adirondacks to ensure a steady flow down the river, but the system would
not require a lengthy new aqueduct. Thus, the Hudson supply would be
considerably cheaper than any attempt to acquire water from the
Catskills. Like Freeman, Fuertes went beyond a simple economic explanation for rejecting the Ramapo plan. The report claimed that a "serious element of danger in the use of the natural waters from the streams
in the Catskill Mountains lies in the possibility of pollution from isolated houses and hotels, in which probably over a hundred thousand
tourists and summer boarders reside during the summer months. Many
of these are present on account of their suffering from disease." The reference here is to tubercular patients who regularly sought relief in
mountain regions, often staying year-round. The report also noted,
"These watersheds have not, as a rule, a very large amount of timbered
land, as often supposed. Much of the land is cleared for farming purposes." Thus, according to both Freeman and Fuertes, Catskills waters
were not nearly as attractive as the Ramapo Company would have the
city believe.[19]

Clearly both of the 1900 reports hoped to find flaws in the Ramapo plan. They did so easily, each identifying more desirable alternatives. In 1901, however, the state legislature repealed the act that had empowered the Ramapo Company, and all its Catskills planning came to naught, its water rights contracts voided. Instantly, the city regained interest in the Esopus. With the Housatonic idea quashed due to objections from Connecticut, and the filtered Hudson idea gaining no enthusiastic support, the city began to study the Catskills anew. As early as August 1901, the city's chief engineer claimed, "The supply of water in this Catskill region is practically inexhaustible. There will be more water there than the City of New York will ever need." And, "There is no doubt but that the finest water in the country can be found in that section."[20] Obviously, the removal of the Ramapo threat had greatly improved both water quality and quantity in the Catskills.

In late 1903, yet another massive engineering study of the city's water supply appeared, this one conducted by the city's recently created Commission on Water Supply. At 980 pages, the report included lengthy discussions of existing sources, the issues of filtration and waste, and all realistic potential sources, though the Corporation Council instructed the commission not to consider out-of-state supplies, a stipulation that excluded the Housatonic and Ten Mile rivers. William Burr led the three-man commission, which included John Freeman, who three years earlier had dismissed the Catskills as offering too little water and containing no great dam sites, and another prominent civil engineer, Rudolph Hering. With the Ramapo threat now cleared from the mountains, the Catskills gained disproportionate attention. In praising the Esopus, the report redefined the region, which it declared extensively forested, in direct contrast with the Merchant's Association report. While the commission determined that an estimated 5,200 persons lived in the watershed above the proposed reservoirs, and that during the summer perhaps another 4,300 visitors inhabited the area per week, these human obstacles were minor compared to the value of the slopes, deemed "practically a wilderness." Above Prattsville, the Schoharie watershed contained more than 6,000 residents and doubled in population during the summer tourist season, posing a greater threat to water quality. In both valleys, villages would require sewage systems and scattered hotels would need better septic systems, but the commission found none of the serious pollution concerns that laced earlier reports about the Catskills.

Beyond redefining the region, the report redefined the water itself, which now gained lengthy praise for its softness, a quality bestowed upon it by favorable geology. The water's softness had real urban value, the report argued, in extending the life of bar soap and tea kettles, etc. Potatoes even boil better in soft water, the report concluded. Should all of this sound insignificant, the commissioners included a calculation, granting a savings of a quarter pound of soap per resident per year due to the softer water afforded by the Esopus, and arriving at a total savings to the city, in hand soap alone, of $455,000, a figure that included "capitalization," as if the savings in soap would somehow earn interest. As the accounting contortions indicated, softness had suddenly become the city's critical water quality concern, apparently greater even than biological contamination—perhaps because this was the one criterion by which the Esopus bested all other competitors.[21]

The Commission on Water Supply's report may have indicated a growing consensus among engineers that the city required a new source and that the Catskills would best suit the city's needs, but some opposition to the Catskills plan did develop in the city. Undoubtedly this opposition inherited some momentum from extant resistance to the Ramapo plan, which had loomed so large in the discussions concerning expanding the city's supply that some observers took the entire issue to be a product of corruption. To combat the notion that New York urgently required a greatly expanded water supply, opponents charged that the city wasted a large percentage of the water it already possessed. In its long campaign, first against Ramapo and then against the rush into a new watershed project, the *New York Times* clung to Freeman's very lose estimate that the city wasted perhaps 50 to 67 percent of its supply, and repeatedly asserted that the city could in effect double its supply if it just better managed what it had.[22] In another argument made against the Catskills project, the *Times* asserted that engineers were reluctant to recommend fighting leaks rather than building a new system because the process would entail considerable hard work but would result in none of the glory that comes with massive engineering works. "We are foolishly proud of our big dams and our long tunnels," the *Times* editorialized in 1909, "and only here and there does a man try to make us ashamed of the necessity for them." But even the *Times'* own coverage revealed a strong bias favoring large projects. One lengthy article on the "World's Biggest Water System" proudly declared the Ashokan the "greatest reservoir in the world," an accomplishment comparable to the Egyptian pyramids. Later, the *Times* labeled the aqueduct's Hudson River tunnel "one of the greatest engineering feats in the history of the world," second only to the Panama Canal. After New York's mayor ceremoniously fired the last blast to open the tunnel, the *Times* made the most apt comparison yet—linking New York City with Rome, the famed imperial city with a penchant for building monumental waterworks. Fittingly, J. Edward Simmons, the president of the Board of Water Supply, made the same comparison at the opening ceremony for the construction of the Catskill Aqueduct in 1907, confirming that the Catskill Aqueduct revealed New York's status as a great imperial city.[23]

Even if the new system brought Catskills water "to the gates of a wasteful city," as the *Times* had editorialized, and even if the Catskills project represented the hubris of civil engineers, by the time construction began in 1907, the system's necessity was clear. New York's rapid growth continued, and the city would surely need more water, and soon. If in the aggregate the city wasted water, the "'great unwashed' of the east side should at any rate be encouraged to consume more," the *Times* concluded, giving up the notion that the city should put off bringing more water to the city while it got its leaks under control.[24] In addition, even as the city debated how best to secure ample potable water, Croton waters actually diminished in quality. Once the pride of the city, the Croton system became suspect, muddied after heavy rains and distasteful during low water. In the spring of 1901, a Harlem resident complained that his water was "as brown as strong coffee." In 1904, one New Yorker expressed wonderment that the city would permit its water "to be brown with sediment," and a year later a *Times* editorial noted that since most people could not afford bottled water, they had to "take their chances by drinking the unfiltered city water, now thick with the impurities of a short supply, of typhoid and other dangerous diseases." In 1907, a typhoid outbreak among Italian laborers working on the Cross River Reservoir led to calls for a new filtration plant at Jerome Park to purify Croton waters. The city's Department of Water Supply, Gas, and Electricity went so far as to conclude, "the necessity of filtration is no longer open to doubt."[25]

With the growing concern about the quality of Croton water—now tellingly called "city water"—Catskills waters gained considerable press. Some entrepreneurs took advantage of the free publicity, setting up bottling and exporting establishments in the mountains, and in the process helping to solidify the conception of Catskills water as especially pure and healthful. In Pine Hill, the Crystal Spring Water Company gained the right to tap a popular spring near the Grand Hotel, and in 1901 distributed a twenty-four-page pamphlet in the city, marketing its product as a healthful alternative to "the liquid nastiness" of the "Croton abomination." Sounding somewhat like Burroughs or Cole, the pamphlet rhapsodized: "Sparkling in the sunlight; distilling in the dew; gushing from the hillside, an infinite wisdom has provided one drink for man—pure water." The company appears to have established itself with the sole intention of selling its water in the city, where the water's wilderness birth held the most value. Business was so good that in 1905 the company built a new bottling facility along the Ulster and Delaware tracks. A year later, the Sunset Park Inn, in Haines Falls, advertised its own spring water, using a quotation from a Fifth Avenue doctor who claimed the water was "of excellent quality, very soft, uncontaminated," the very qualities that the city used to describe the water from all the Catskills watersheds.[26]

With the Burr-Hering-Freeman Report, the Catskills had garnered the experts' stamp of approval. In addition, as city engineers focused on the Catskills, other locations became off-limits, including Dutchess County, protected by a 1904 state law supported by Assemblyman John T. Smith.[27] Still, if the city wanted Catskills water, it would require state approval. In 1905, the state legislature passed the McClellan Act, named for New York Mayor George McClellan, which allowed the city to create a Board of Water Supply, which in turn would develop and implement the final expansion plan, with the approval of a new state water commission. So, with Albany willing to empower the city and eager to encourage continued urban economic growth, the Catskills region now found itself at the mercy of the city's engineers, who would continue their work in the mountains over the coming decades, identifying appropriate streams to capture and locating ideal dam sites. After 1905, Catskills residents could really only hope for fair treatment from the city and the state in the form of just compensation for what would be lost.[28]

As the city moved toward its final plan, it looked exclusively at the Catskills, all other serious options having been removed from the table through political maneuvering. Hoping to move quickly, the Board of Water Supply issued a report to the city in October of 1905, proposing the creation of the Catskill Aqueduct and the Ashokan Reservoir. After hearings in Kingston a month later, the State Water Supply Commission weighed all the information before it, including the three massive engineering studies, and determined that the city did indeed require Catskills water. The state commission did amend the plan, most importantly by requiring that the enabling law force the city to pay indirect damages it caused to property and business owners outside the takings line, an important addition to existing eminent domain law. Of course, the city also had to compensate owners for property it did take, though a poorly conceived clause required that the city pay only half of the property's assessed value at the time of the actual taking, unless a mutual agreement had been reached before the transaction. Owners who had not reached an agreement with the city, representing the vast majority, would only see fairer compensation after hearings to determine what the city owed, a process that could take months or even years.[29]

In and around the mountains, the consequences of the coming aqueduct regularly made the press. Not surprisingly, a diversity of opinions regarding the city's plan developed, since some residents around the mountains would clearly lose if the city came to the Catskills, while others stood to benefit. In early 1905, for example, the president of the National Ulster Bank expressed support for the idea, noting that millions of New York City dollars would be spent in the mountains—some of which would no doubt pass through Ulster County banks. In Kingston, just about twelve miles from the proposed Ashokan Reservoir, some feared that the project would prove a menace to their city, with a catastrophic dam failure promising to sweep the city into the Hudson. Kingston's Board of Trade debated the plan in February, with some members noting that depressed land values in the mountains meant that many would probably gladly sell to the city, assuming they got a good price. The board's president, James H. Everett, took a larger view, claiming that Ulster County had an obligation to supply water to the city—with the "greatest good to the greatest number" supplying his logic. In the end, the Board of Trade tabled a resolution opposing the city reservoirs, despite some members' claims that if the plan depopulated nearby mountain townships, Kingston would be gravely injured, since so many Esopus Valley residents traveled into their city for business and shopping.[30]

Kingston's newspaper was aghast at the Board of Trade's decision. "The merchants of Kingston apparently have no adequate comprehension of what is involved in the taking of the watersheds," the *Daily Freeman* editorialized the day after the board's meeting. The *Freeman* claimed that 6,000 would be forced from the mountains, and that another 30,000 would be prevented from vacationing there. "And what do we get in return for this?" the paper asked. "A vast horde of foreign laborers would be quartered in contractors' shanties while the great dams were being built, and such supplies as they used would come from New York in carloads." The editors asked that Ulster look to Westchester to see what economic benefits accrued from the Croton supply. A day later, the *Freeman* used much-exaggerated figures to denounce the proposed takings. "Once condemned to meet the needs of New York all this property will be forever wiped off the map so far as any availability to the people of Ulster County," the paper concluded, and though the assertions about how much land would be taken were way off, this much was true. When the McClellan Bill appeared in Albany, the *Freeman* remained adamantly opposed, a position that appeared to be gathering support. A new meeting called by the Board of Trade brought a new result—with those in attendance voting to exempt Ulster County from the city's scheme, though obviously the group had no such authority. One concerned resident chastised those who still favored the plan by paraphrasing the parable of Esau: "You are throwing away your birthright for a mess of pottage."[31]

As the state legislature debated the McClellan Bill, a public hearing allowed Ulster County to express its concerns. A well-regarded and well-connected Kingston lawyer, Alfonso Clearwater (a wonderfully poetic name given the situation), made a stirring speech in the senate chamber. Clearwater described Ulster as a well-populated, economically diverse and significant county, a county bound to be devastated by the McClellan Bill, where thousands of people would be displaced, where millions of dollars would be lost every year due to diminished economic activity. In an effort to gather support from other counties, Clearwater pointed to the city's voracious demand for water. "I wish to say to the county of Orange that after New York has sucked Ulster dry she will turn to the Neversink and the Lackawaxen. When she has finished with Orange, she will take the East Branch and the Beaver Kill from the county of Delaware. When Delaware has been exhausted, she will take the Plattekill and Schoharie Kill from Schoharie." While the city claimed to be content with the Esopus at the moment,[32] Clearwater understood that the ever-growing city would eventually tap more and more rivers nearby, and his list proved at least partly prophetic. Unfortunately for Ulster, the effort to create a unified front against the city on the west side of the Hudson proved futile, with the arguments of the city's Corporation Counsel John Delaney ultimately taking the day. The *Freeman* paraphrased Delaney as declaring that in the "march of events" it is "essential that rural communities should to some extent be sacrificed to the needs of a great city."[33]

Clearwater may have spoken the thoughts of many average Ulster County residents, but he worked in the employ of some of the county's largest economic interests, including the Ulster and Delaware Railroad. The U&D ran up the Esopus Valley and figured to be among the big losers should the city build the Ashokan, not just because the company would have to relocate several miles of track, but also because the valley itself would be so diminished in population and economic activity. Samuel Coykendall, the Ulster and Delaware's principal owner, had joined Clearwater in speaking before the legislature regarding the McClellan Bill, and when their efforts failed, the two returned to Albany two weeks later in support of a bill that would expressly exclude Ulster County from the city's water supply plans. Modeled after the bill that had protected Dutchess County, the Ulster bill failed to gain much support, despite the pleading of Coykendall. "If our mountain sides and valleys are ever taken by New York city," Coykendall declared, "it will not be with the consent of our people, but because it is forced upon us by the representatives of the other counties in the state." When asked if no one in Kingston supported the building of reservoirs in Ulster, Clearwater responded that he knew of perhaps half a dozen lawyers who did, only because they hoped to sue the city for damages after construction began.[34]

In late 1905, the Board of Water Supply presented its plan to the State Water Supply Commission, which heard evidence from both sides of the issue. The city put forward the testimony of experts—Chief Engineer J. Waldo Smith, William Burr, and John R. Freeman. They all claimed that their professional wisdom had led them to conclude that more water was needed and that the Catskills provided the best choice. As the Board of Water Supply would report to the mayor in early 1906, "the whole problem of New York's water supply is mainly an engineering undertaking," and so the testimony of leading engineers seemed sufficient.[35] Of course, claiming that this was an engineering decision was misleading. Political maneuvering had spared Dutchess and Suffolk counties, and interstate concerns placed other waters out of reach. Though technically taking water from the Hudson was possible, city politicians had no interest in selling filtered river water to city voters. Indeed, though Catskill waters were suitable for urban consumption, the political weakness of the region, combined with its saleable wilderness qualities, made the waters particularly attractive, even to engineers. The State Water Supply Commission, aware of the importance of New York City's growth to the entire state, approved the Catskills plan, and the Board of Water Supply moved forward—into the mountains.

Metropolitan residents have never been accused of being too acutely aware of upstate concerns, of adequately accounting for the needs of those who lived outside the city. Although urbanites often use the adjective "parochial" to describe the outlooks of their country cousins, suggesting an inability to see beyond the local to gain a more cosmopolitan outlook, in some instances that term accurately describes Gotham itself. So self-absorbed was the city as it sought out a new source of water that the press consistently misrepresented rural concerns about self-determination in the Catskills and elsewhere. As Assemblyman Smith introduced his bill protecting Dutchess County from city intrusions, the *New York Times* warned of "Ramapo's Ghost" and a year later went so far as to claim that "powerful private interests" had secured the bill's passage, hoping to force the city into a contract with Ramapo. The editors were apparently unwilling to accept that the Ramapo Company had been disabled by state law, which it had; that the company's Catskills options had expired, which they had; or that Dutchess residents might have their own reasons to oppose New York's use of their streams, which they did. In 1905, as Ulster County attempted to block the McClellan Bill, the New York City papers apparently uncritically accepted the notion that county representatives were in league with Ramapo, attempting to block the city's plan to build a municipally owned system. And again, in 1906, as Catskills representatives attempted one last time to deflect the city's use of mountain water through state legislation, the *Times* claimed that the Ulster County assemblyman was working in Ramapo's interests, even though the company had disappeared five years earlier. The city newspapers, especially the *Times*, were so consumed with big-city corruption that they failed to take seriously the concerns of rural residents about the city's water supply plan.[36]

If the city papers did a poor job of representing rural concerns, the Kingston press was not exactly the voice of the Catskills either. Though the small city's economic and political elite was clearly concerned with the fate of the county as a whole, Kingston's interests differed somewhat from those of people living in the mountains. One newspaper at the head of the Esopus Valley, the *Pine Hill Sentinel*, initially expressed a wait-and-see attitude, noting that if the city paid well for the land, most county residents would support the project. Just a week later, however, the *Sentinel* assumed a less positive tone, noting that the town of Shandaken "as an inhabited region is doomed to be wiped off the map." The *Sentinel* expressed the grave concern not just about the Ashokan, but also about what the construction of the city's aqueduct would mean for the watershed in the long-term. "One or many reservoirs does not alter the fact that sooner or later they will condemn and take everything to the Grand Hotel Station," the paper prophesied.[37] The *Sentinel*, which rarely published anything of length regarding local news, ran a full article in May 1905 under the equally uncharacteristical dramatic headline "Shandaken Valley Doomed." The article, reprinted from the *Walton Chronicle* published in neighboring Delaware County, predicted that the state would soon give the city permission to build "an immense dam near Shokan." What's more, the *Chronicle* article reported, "it is expected the entire watershed from there to Grand Hotel will eventually be utilized and all the buildings removed. There seems but little doubt that the picturesque Shandaken valley is doomed and that the villages of Boiceville, Cold Spring, Mt. Pleasant, Phoenicia, Shandaken, and Big Indian will disappear."[38]

Of course, this was not the actual plan, but the description here spoke to both the poor understanding of New York's intentions in the mountains and a very good understanding of what had happened in Westchester and Putnam counties, where time and again the city added to its Croton system, eventually even drowning its original Croton dam under a larger reservoir. Indeed, the city's own water-supply report, printed in 1904, listed no fewer than twenty-two potential dam sites on four different rivers in the Catskills. Along the Esopus, the list included the Ashokan, the only one that would actually be built, the "Shandaken Reservoir," which would drown 260 acres, and the "Big Indian Reservoir," with a water surface of 193 acres. While much smaller than the proposed Ashokan, listed at nearly 6,000 acres, the other reservoirs, named for the communities they would flood, would have brought the city's supply system deep into the mountains. No wonder opposition to New York's intrusion grew along with the certainty that the city would look to the mountains for its water. "The attitude of the people of Ulster County is as bitterly hostile as ever toward the measure," reported the *Chronicle*, "and it is said they will oppose it before the governor in event the legislature passes it."[39]

Catskills residents had good reason for concern. The examples of

Westchester and Putnam counties provided some unfortunate evidence regarding New York's treatment of its upstate neighbors. Since acquiring Westchester lands in 1837 for the first Croton reservoir, the city had come back over and over again, taking new lands and building more reservoirs. In other words, once the city began acquiring Croton waters, no one upstream could feel secure on their property. Even as the city cast its reach northward, Westchester continued to lose ground—literally— to the city. In July of 1905, three more Westchester towns—Croton Falls, Cross River, and Somers—faced "obliteration" during the construction of the Cross River Dam.[40] The *Freeman* pointed to Putnam County's experience, where farmers were disappointed by low payments for their lands and the much-delayed process by which they received them. Just as important, those whose lands were not taken also suffered, according to the editors. "The depredations of the hordes of Italians imported as laborers and living along the line of work, so annoyed and alarmed such boarders as still frequented the resorts and farm houses," the paper continued, that the region had been deserted by tourists.[41]

Of course, all the debate and consternation in the mountains would have no real effect on the "march of events." As the city proceeded in making its plans, the relationship between the city and the region around the proposed Ashokan Reservoir only deteriorated. Surveyors had traipsed through private property as early as 1901, making the maps that would inform the Burr-Hering-Freeman report, though they did little more than raise concerns among local residents. After 1903, as the city prepared its actual plan, engineers became more invasive. For example, New York employees drilled test holes along lands they projected to become the Ashokan Dam, which at the time still belonged to Mary Winchell, who had given no permission for the trespassing. In 1905, the Board of Water Supply even felled trees, cut wire fences, and moved stone walls as they dug a series of holes and trenches, some of which ran through pastures and potato fields. All of this occurred, apparently, with no advance warning to the residents, and before the state had approved the Catskills project. These trespasses invited the ill will of Catskills residents, but they were fleeting and no doubt of less general concern than the consequences of the long delay between the announcement of Ramapo's Catskill plan in 1899, the city's initial claim on the Esopus, made in 1903, and the beginning of actual takings in 1907. All the while, the Kingston attorney Amos Van Etten noted, "there was a projected taking of this entire section, and it has been hanging over this entire section like a cloud." Van Etten pleaded that the first takings commission consider the effects of this cloud in determining the value of the property. "If you or I or any other person owned property there during the ten years we would not have expended one dollar for improvements; we would say 'why should we expend any money here when the city is to acquire the property?'" According to Van Etten, this explained much of the deterioration in the takings area, and the fact that so few properties had changed hands and so little money had been invested in the region. This, of course, was good reason for ill will, even before the takings began.[42]

Ironically, the construction of an urban water supply in the mountains first required building a small city. In September 1907, as workers arrived from downstate, especially from the Cross River project in Westchester County, then nearing completion, the first order of business was building a railroad spur to the dam site. Shortly thereafter, workers began building the temporary city that would house the hundreds of laborers who would soon arrive. Up on Winchell Hill, overlooking the new camp, workers built two large storage reservoirs to capture pure spring waters, to provide the instant city with clean water—reservoirs for reservoir workers. All manner of town infrastructure followed: a grid of streets named mostly for the great engineers of the project (Burr, Freeman, and Stearns) and another named for the mayor (McClellan Avenue); a bank, so workers could deposit savings; and three churches, one Catholic, one Union Protestant, and a third for "Coloreds." Though the town was only temporary, it would be modern, even more so than the villages the reservoir would displace. It had electric lights, telephones, and a hospital. It had its own police force and fire protection, a post office, and, for uplift, a YMCA. Sanitation was up-to-date, with a sewage plant, regular garbage pickups, and even fumigation "to prevent the arising of any epidemic." Eventually the workforce at the Ashokan site peeked at 3,000 men, some of them locals, but most of them imported by the contractors and the Board of Water Supply in the city. Counting family members, the camp reached a population of 4,500, making it the largest village in the Catskills at the time. To ensure proper social segregation, the workers' village was, as the Board of Water Supply reported, "divided into Italian and Negro sections, while white Americans lived separately." Many of the whites, especially the engineers and foremen, lived outside the camp in homes taken from nearby residents. In sum, the instant city was the urban ideal of its age—clean, safe, healthful, and segregated. To keep the mountains pristine, to keep the waters pure, the Board of Water Supply had to guard against defilement; New York City could not actually come to the mountains.[43]

The instant village at Ashokan was not the only encampment created to house workers. The aqueduct also required considerable labor, housed at the mouths of access tunnels. The camp near High Falls, just on the edge of the Catskills, gained a reputation as the toughest, especially after the *New York Times* ran a lengthy description in its Sunday Magazine in early 1910. "Frontier Camps Close to the City's Border," the headline read, as the reporter blamed "the greed for gold of our pious up-country neighbors" for the outlaw conditions at the camp, where prostitution, cocaine, and drinking ran rampant, especially at casual businesses that popped up outside the encampments.[44] Catskills residents were much more likely to blame outsiders than profit-hungry locals for the bad behavior of the laborers. Ulster County residents frequently expressed racist attitudes concerning Italians and African Americans, even to the point of declaring that their presence in the mountains decreased property values. Crime, prostitution, and drugs all followed the workers out of the city, as did the need for a large police force, supplied by the Board of Water Supply. In a good indication of where the Board of Water Supply thought its problems might develop, the city's police force did not monitor behavior inside the camps, but patrolled around them to protect local residents from misbehaving laborers, especially since carrying concealed weapons was "a strong habit with both Negroes and Italians."[45]

In this regard, then, the vice of the city had come to the country, but this was only temporary. The Board of Water Supply boasted that after the work was completed, "these camps were so thoroughly obliterated that scarce a trace can now be found." The choice of this phrase was unfortunate, for the camps were not the only places "thoroughly obliterated." Much of the work of reservoir building involved the removal of the basin's contents—homes, businesses, and churches—indeed, all structures. Graves were disinterred, fences pulled down, barns burned to the ground. Trees were cut, with the good wood sold for lumber and other purposes, and the waste piled and burned. Along the waterline, stumps and roots were pulled, to facilitate the making of a beach and improve the sanitation of the reservoir. In sum, by the time the waters rose, the Esopus Valley would be cleansed of its past, nearly all evidence of habitation gone, and its buildings, its orchards, its woodlots all removed.[46]

Some property owners made deals with the city to sell their lands, perhaps content with the final offers or simply too wary of the legal process that provided the only alternative. Most property owners took this other route, however, hiring a lawyer and filing a claim against the city. State law dictated how the eminent domain process would take place, with hearings scheduled before a series of three-person commissions, with one representative from Ulster County, another from the city, and a third from some other New York county, usually in the Albany area. All proceedings took place at the courthouse in Kingston, where from 1907 through 1914 lawyers debated the value of certain properties before these commissions, though some of the cases dragged on for years afterward, due to appeals. In the meantime, however, the city took property for half the assessed value, which for most claimants was an extremely low figure, one that made moving to new, permanent residences difficult, at least until their cases were settled.

One might anticipate that this process would favor the city, with talented New York lawyers taking advantage of local claimants and their lawyers. This was not the case. Almost universally the Ashokan claimants hired excellent lawyers, with a great deal of the work going to Clearwater, Ulster's best lawyer, and even more going to Harrison Slosson and his partner Arthur Brown, two downstate lawyers who had made their careers trying eminent domain cases against New York City in Westchester County, especially during the expansion of the Croton Reservoir. Altogether, the claimants' lawyers conducted excellent cases, and regularly outshone city attorneys, some of whom were actually Kingston residents who frequently found themselves outmaneuvered. The claimants had another advantage, too, in that the commissions were universally lenient in their determinations on what constituted proper testimony. Commissioners gave claimants considerable leeway to make their cases.[47]

The city needed to control the costs of the Catskills project in any way possible, especially by defending itself against excessive claims for property and damages. In addition to lawyers, the city also employed "expert" witnesses, who could testify on a range of local issues, including quarrying, farming, and the boarding business. Drawn from communities around the Ashokan, these witnesses generally had a good sense of the value of property and businesses in the valley. While most of the testimony was straightforward and civil, at times the city's lawyers became exasperated by the testimony of claimant's witnesses, who tended to have backgrounds similar to those who worked for the city and who also generally worked dozens of cases. Not surprisingly, city witnesses always offered considerably lower estimated values than those who worked for the claimants, leaving lawyers feeling compelled to impeach each opposing testimony. In several instances, city lawyers found themselves making some rather untenable arguments in an effort to lower the value of taken lands. For example, John I. Boice, who owned the Bishop Falls dam and surrounding land, argued that his property was worth at least $325,000—an extremely high sum—because he might have constructed a larger dam on his property to provide electricity to Kingston or some other nearby customers. His lawyers argued that Boice should be compensated for this lost opportunity to build a generating facility like others that already existed in the region. In an attempt to show that the Esopus was not a good stream for power generation, the city's lawyer, John Linson, a Kingston native, noted without a hint of irony, "If there is anything I want to have you show, it is the utter unreliability of this stream." In another case, a city witness, Charles Shufelt, attempted to explain why potential mill sites had no real value in the region, noting that up to 75 percent of the mills had shut down in the area in the previous fifteen years. The city's lawyer, Augustus Van Buren, asked what had become of the lumber business in the region. "Gone," Shufelt responded, "the forests have been destroyed and the lumber sawed up." According to city lawyers and witnesses, then, the unreliable Esopus ran through a denuded landscape—not exactly the ideal location for a massive reservoir, and not the portrait of the region engineers had painted while selling the Catskills' wilderness qualities.[48]

If the pressure of formal hearings forced city attorneys to make occasional outlandish statements, claimants and their witnesses were no less likely to make incredible arguments in their attempts to secure the greatest possible compensation for their property. The largest, and least reasonable, claims centered on a variety of potential uses for the property. Almost all significant properties held bluestone quarries, though most had been lightly worked for a decade or more. Claimants' expert witnesses estimated the value of all the stone in the ground anyway. Many properties had excellent views of the mountains, or a pretty stream nearby, suggesting a potential value as a boardinghouse. Many properties had water running through them, with potential mill sites, several of which had actually contained mills at some point in the past. In a tactic that did not work, some claimants pegged the value of their land by assuming the construction of a gargantuan reservoir that would provide water to some unspecified large city. Though clearly all the taken lands really did have value as a reservoir, eminent domain law prohibited this argumentation, since the determination of the property's value referred to the moment of the taking, not after the city had added the dam and aqueduct. Indeed, much of the testimony in these cases addressed what these properties might have become in the future—their potential values. Although this line of argumentation was not legally correct, the commissions allowed the testimony anyway, perhaps because, taken together, these efforts spoke to the larger truth of the matter, to the greatest consequence of the city's takings: that these places would never be any of these things in the future—not boardinghouses nor quarries nor mill sites. These places had just one future—as a city reservoir.

If claimants' lawyers frequently pressed potential uses to inflate land values, city lawyers hoped to stick to the accepted theory that the market best determined value. In this approach, previous sales of similar properties provided the clearest guide. While this theory might function well in cities, where many properties might have similar characteristics, in the country every property had a unique combination of qualities— in numbers of acres under plow, in pasturage, the quantity and quality of timber on the land, the number of springs, the presence of streams and quarries, not to mention the size and quality of the home, the barn, and other buildings. Then there was the distance to train stations and post offices, views from the home, the size of shade trees, and the quality of fruit trees. The number of variables was staggering, and assured that no similar properties could be offered as comparative evidence. In addition, since so many of the properties had been passed down through families, and therefore had not been sold for generations, their own histories often provided little clue as to what the market might bring. As a result, at times the hearings devolved into piecemeal discussions of what the properties contained. In some cases, witnesses literally enumerated the number of trees that could provide lumber, the number that might be sold as telephone poles, and the remaining number that might be used in some other, less valuable way, perhaps as cordwood or pulp. Witnesses for claimants frequently enumerated the parts of structures—the amount of lumber, roofing, flagging, windows, etc.—to give an estimate of what the whole house might be worth.[49]

In this way, the lawyers for both sides frequently helped create a fictive value for these properties, based on the sum of the pieces they held. For the claimants this could prove advantageous, since, as city lawyers pointed out, farmers regularly constructed homes that cost more to build than they would have earned if sold, even under better circumstances. But the city could also benefit from this additive theory, since focusing on the parts ignored the value of the whole. This latter value, of course, was much more difficult to ascertain, since it included so many intangibles. In very moving testimony in the business damage case brought by the Bishop brothers, hoping to earn compensation for the destruction of their boarding business, the Bishop Falls House, John McGrath, who owned the Globe Hotel in Phoenicia, demanded that the commission look at the larger picture. McGrath noted the value that came through the family arrangement, with the brothers living in their mother's home and their wives providing the critical labor. The commissioners pressed McGrath for his reasons for declaring the business worth $15,000, completely separate from the value of the property, for which Anna Bishop had already been paid. Why couldn't the Bishop "boys," as they were called at trial, start over someplace else? McGrath's emotional response focused on the name of the place—the Bishop Falls House. There was value in this, surely, that the falls, the boarding business, the brothers, the mother all shared the same name, one known throughout the region. "There is sentiment, for instance," McGrath concluded, "that was of benefit to these boys, that they could not derive any place else. They have grown up there. I knew their father and I remember their grandfather. They all lived on this place and those boys came up there." How could anyone affix a value to that? How could the Bishops start another Bishop Falls House without the soon-to-be-submerged Bishop Falls?[50]

McGrath's outburst notwithstanding, the testimony in these cases could be plodding and dull, especially when issues of potential waterpower or the quality of bluestone appeared. Only rarely did claimants give a real hint of the pain their removal must have caused, perhaps because of a stoicism developed in defense of an agricultural life's vagaries, or perhaps because of the proceeding's formality. The case of Nathan H. Gordon included some of the typical testimony, including one expert witness who claimed that the fifty-nine-acre farm was worth $81,000, since it might be used as part of a reservoir, which of course it would. In reality, Gordon had filed a claim for just $6,407, in compensation for the Brown's Station farm he had purchased in 1893. Most of the land remained pasture, though fifteen acres held good timber. Gordon had built the small house himself. Part of Gordon's claim involved damages before the actual taking, when city employees had cut trees and bored holes. Gordon claimed that in 1906 the city had ruined his potato crop, which constituted his only substantial planting. Gordon and his lawyer, Slosson, clearly hoped to increase the sympathy of the commissioners as they proceeded through the trespassing stories, and in the end the panel determined his property to be worth $3,502, about ten times its assessed value. Before this determination, however, Gordon testified as to the uses to which he put his land. Apparently not a very energetic farmer, Gordon only tilled two acres for potatoes and rented out the pastures, as he only owned one cow himself (Gordon mostly made his living as a carpenter). When asked what else he raised on his land, Gordon claimed to have "pastured about 2000 rabbits," though he then admitted they were wild. He also noted his fields had supported "woodcock, lots of them." Perhaps tiring of these answers, city attorney Linson asked again, "what other use, if any, did you ever put that property to?" Gordon replied: "I raised my family there, I have eight children."[51]

Gordon's candid reply reminded everyone what was really happening in that courtroom and in the mountains. The Ashokan's construction would do more than determine the future of the region; it would also literally submerge its past. The Bishop and Gordon families had real attachments to their lands, built over generations or through the raising of children. The physical evidence of this real past would be lost, in the most dramatic example of urbanity's demands on rural America. More directly, Gordon's reply illustrated how difficult the task of determining the value of these lands really was, for mixed with the pastures, orchards, outbuildings, and homes, were the experiences of families, sometimes going back generations. Though eminent domain law left no room for sentimental value—the market alone should set the price—sometimes in the country, where the land gave so little, much of the value lay in sentiment. Why would the Bishops move away from Bishop Falls? Why would Gordon sell the land on which he had raised his eight children? The attachments of home and history, more than the value of boarders and potatoes, kept them along the Esopus.

However, since the commissions could not compensate for this value in the land, the eminent domain process forced these rural lands into what from the city's perspective might be called a more rational, modern system of real estate. In a process already underway elsewhere in the mountains, as farms became second homes and cottage communities, a formal market replaced tradition. Homesteads, once passed through generations, broken up and shared among relatives and with neighbors through agreements concerning quarry rights or taking hay or timber, had long moved through the informal, mixed, rural economy, sometimes without so much as a dollar figure attached. Eminent domain required that dollar figure. It also required a rational means for determining that figure.

By the end of 1932, when most but not all of the cases had been settled, the commissions had heard 755 cases, with a total of over $10 million in claims.[52] They had awarded a little more than $1.4 million to claimants.[53] New York's real cost of acquiring the land was considerably more, however, since claimants received just about two-thirds of what New York City spent on land acquisition, the remainder going to pay commissioners, lawyers, and the city's many expert witnesses.[54] The process had been so lengthy, so regularly delayed and prolonged by commissions, lawyers, and witnesses, many of whom were paid per diem, and the hearings had been so full of spurious and inflated claims, that even the *Kingston Daily Freeman* had long since referred to the takings area as "Plumland."[55] Even if lawyers made out well, most of those evicted would not consider their compensation "plums," though generally the city appears to have paid well over actual market value for the properties, some of which truly were failing farms, even if they were ancestral homes. Witnesses for claimants regularly placed value of land at $100 per acre, though $50 would have been closer to market value even for fine farmland, and most land within the takings line would not have fetched that price in the years before New York's plan became public. In the comparatively few cases settled before hearings, the city probably paid a premium in an effort to speed the process and reduce the costs of the process. For example, Frank W. Brooks received a very reasonable $7,500 for his seventy-seven-acre farm and home.[56]

Construction did not await legal resolutions concerning damages, of course, and in spring 1908, the city began the process of removing people from their homes, beginning with those whose property lay along the dam site. Among the first to receive notification of their removal were Anna Bishop and her extended family. By May 8, even before the family had left, workers had torn down one wing of the Bishop Falls House; engineers were eager to make way for construction equipment. As the *Kingston Daily Freeman* reported the next day, "The carriage house had already been demolished and on Wednesday afternoon the torch was applied to the large barn on the farm," burned, apparently, to make room for the construction derricks that would move heavy stones. "The massive frame of oak timbers made a very hot fire," the *Freeman* continued, "and was a sight that brought sorrow to the hearts of many to see this old land mark destroyed." At the time the family left the home, Anna Bishop had received just $900. Her son, Frank, his wife, and his nine-month-old son moved to Shokan, near the reservoir site; her other son, DeForest, and his family eventually settled in Stone Ridge, ten miles south of Bishop Falls.[57]

Over time, the city took additional properties, though sometimes it acquired buildings to house its own employees rather than to make way for construction. It even took some properties and then rented them back to their previous owners, an arrangement that gave the contractors greater flexibility. By the end of 1910, the city was earning more than $1,200 per month renting out properties acquired through eminent domain, with most of the rent paid by workers rather than former owners. By this time, the city was also cutting hay on acquired properties, used principally to feed police mounts and workhorses. The city sold apples from the orchards it acquired, and also sold off timber as it cleared the valley. In what must have been the most painful part of the process for local residents, the city cleansed the landscape. In total, when workers completed the process in 1914, the city had cleared more than 12,000 acres, and nearly all traces of the villages and farms had been removed. In total, more than 500 homes had been destroyed, along with thirty-five stores, ten churches, and eight active mills.[58]

The Ashokan would displace more than 2,000 living persons, but even more dead. By late spring, 1912, the city had removed 2,637 bodies from graves within the reservoir line. The city had identified forty separate grave sites, ranging from well-marked church cemeteries to individual family plots on farms, some containing only a single body. The Board of Water Supply commented on the haphazard nature of these country internments, noting that even in larger cemeteries "little or no attention had been paid to order or arrangement." The city awarded residents $15 to cover the expense of removing any body, and an additional $3 to move any headstone, and very briefly in 1909 and 1910 a small industry in removing the dead developed around the reservoir. In hearings concerning one cemetery property, the city denied it had any obligation to pay more than the local rate for individual plots, to which Harrison Slosson objected. Since many people from the Ashokan region were moving to Kingston,

Slosson argued, "they have a right to bring their dead with them and have the right to be paid the reasonable price of a lot there." After a specified date, unclaimed bodies were disinterred by the city and reburied in a cemetery outside the fill line. The Board of Water Supply noted that, in marked contrast to the chaotic country plots, the city's cemetery presented "the appearance of a military burial ground, with graves arranged in orderly rows, each marked by a bluestone marker 12 inches wide and 12 inches in height above the surface," a marshalling of the dead that symbolized the city's reordering of the landscape. Just as eminent domain brought a rationalization of land valuation, disinterment brought its own regimentation.[59]

For some mountain residents the reservoir and aqueduct construction brought mostly good news. Employment boomed as contractors and the Board of Water Supply found locals to fill a multitude of jobs. Most skilled positions went to city residents, or professionals who traveled the country working on large civil works. Ulster County residents were much more likely to gain common laborer positions. Albert Roosa of Olive Bridge, for example, gained a $2 per diem position in 1905, despite the fact that he would make a claim against the city for his property. Roosa was not alone. The Board of Water Supply hired a total of 15 men the day it hired Roosa, all of them from West Shokan, Olive Bridge, or Brown's Station.[60] The Bishop brothers found work on the reservoir, too, even as they prepared their case against the city. Frank worked as a foreman for the city, leading a crew of men clearing brush. At $3.50 per day, this was the best job Frank had ever had, and he earned more than $1,000 in 1910. DeForest worked for the contractor, McArthur Brothers, Winston & Company, and though he made less than Frank, he also had a steady income, probably higher wages than any in his life—at least while the work lasted.[61] Even beyond the takings region, the arrival of the Ashokan project brought employment, as the Board of Water Supply hired residents scattered around the watershed to measure rain. These "gage keepers" noted rainfall and sent the data to Brown's Station. In the Esopus watershed, thirteen gage keepers tallied rain for the city, one of whom was Clarence Haynes of Highmount, who took over the position after the passing of his father-in-law, John Olmstead, in early 1913.[62]

On September 9, 1913, the Board of Water Supply halted the flow of the Esopus Creek at the Ashokan Dam. Just five days later, rising waters completely submerged Bishop Falls. Within three weeks, the reservoir held more than 1.6 billion gallons of water.[63] Although the project had destroyed communities, a beautiful artificial lake rose in their place. In short order, the reservoir, its dam, and its aerator became attractions in themselves, no doubt seen by many times the number of visitors who had stopped to see the now-gone Bishop Falls. The people from the takings area had been scattered, to be sure, and while some traveled far from their taken homes, a study of migrations revealed that 75 percent of them stayed within ten miles of the new reservoir. Some even moved to reconstituted villages just outside the takings line, and many others settled in nearby Kingston.[64]

The completion of the Catskills system brought great relief to New York City, and not a little joy. Just as the city had marked the completion of the first Croton Aqueduct with a parade and commemorations, the arrival of Catskills water in the fall of 1917 provided the city with cause for celebration.[65] The festivities included the publication of pamphlets describing the great engineering feats just completed. The mayor's Catskill Aqueduct Celebration Committee also published a brief history of New York City's water supply, Edward Hagaman Hall's *The Catskill Aqueduct*, which declared the arrival of mountain water "an occasion for unreserved pride in American genius."[66] Fittingly, given the significant role of Italian laborers in the system's construction, the city merged its "water fete" with the Columbus Day celebrations planned by numerous Italian societies. After the arrival of mountain water at the new Central Park reservoir, politicians and engineers would continue their celebrations at the Waldorf Astoria Hotel. Interestingly, both the Museum of Natural History and the New York Public Library timed exhibitions of Hudson River art to coincide with the celebration, as if to remind New Yorkers of the beautiful region from which their new waters originated, confirming through art the wilderness birth of the city's supply.[67]

In its gushing editorial concerning the celebrations, the *New York Times* briefly described the new supply and the Catskills, noting "the whole region, comprising 257 square miles, has been beautifully transformed."[68] Though this would seem a gross exaggeration, the editorial could hardly have been more accurate, for the celebrations ushered in a permanently revised relationship between the city and the mountains. Henceforth the city would wield considerable legal power over the Esopus watershed and the many others it would come to acquire. Through its takings, the city became a major taxpayer in the mountains—in some towns the largest taxpayer. From the very beginning this awkward arrangement posed serious problems. The city consistently fought assessments of its property, demanding that it be taxed at a rate comparable to other lands in the county, not at a rate that reflected its massive investment in the region. Even before Catskills water reached the city, New York had gained the reputation as a "tax dodger," as it initiated certiorari proceedings to challenge assessments along the aqueduct, and as it repeatedly attempted to pass state legislation that would limit its tax liabilities. The issue of property taxes would be a perpetual problem.[69]

The city's ownership of property in the mountains meant other permanent changes as well. Not all of the city's lands lay under the Ashokan waters, with thousands of acres held as a forest buffer around the reservoir. The Board of Water Supply intensely managed these forests, in most instances actually planting the trees, using saplings from its own tree farm, and in other instances simply engaging in "forest sanitation." As the Board of Water Supply concluded, "These woods have been improved by removing dead trees and undesirable undergrowth, and under-planting where the forest was thin." Engineers preferred evergreens as buffers, as they produced fewer leaves that might decompose and foul the water, and since they provided a year-round screen between the reservoir and roadways. The city planted scotch, red, and white pines, along with Norway spruce, and in the process transformed the valley's forests. In total, from 1914 through 1917, the city planted over three million trees on its Ashokan property.[70]

Due to New York's continued growth, in short order even the great Ashokan Reservoir would require help in quenching the city. In the early 1910s, the city gained on average more than 150,000 persons a year. The state census of 1915 revealed that with a population of over 5 million, the city was now more populous than the remainder of the state, a fact not overlooked by those who would request permission to expand the Catskills system. Even as the Ashokan became fully operational, discussion turned to augmenting city waters using the Schoharie Creek. Part of the original plan approved by the city and the state, this second reservoir would send water from the Schoharie through a lengthy tunnel to the Esopus Creek, where it would help fill the Ashokan. In early 1916, the city finalized the Schoharie plan, moving the dam from the Prattsville area down to Gilboa, a village that would have to be destroyed to make way for the reservoir. The most spectacular aspect of the plan was the Shandaken tunnel, which ran just over eighteen miles under mountains to deliver

Schoharie water to the Esopus at the hamlet of Allaben. When completed, this tunnel was the longest in the world, as the Board of Water Supply never failed to mention, and it forever altered the Esopus Creek from the discharge point down to the Ashokan Reservoir. By the time it completed the Schoharie project in 1928, the city had acquired over twenty-seven square miles of land in the mountains.[71]

Of course, the Schoharie was not the last reservoir constructed in the Catskills. From 1937 to 1965, New York built the Delaware System, with four new reservoirs in the mountains and a new aqueduct into Westchester County, where Delaware waters mixed with those from the Catskill System behind the Kensico dam. Altogether, New York City would acquire nearly 43,000 acres to build the Delaware System, most of it good bottomland along the East and West Branches of the Delaware. The new reservoirs displaced nearly 3,500 Catskills residents, more than a thousand of whom lived along the Rondout Creek.

Though the Rondout Reservoir displaced more people, the Pepacton Reservoir gained more attention, perhaps because the valley itself was so remarkably beautiful and had a long history, which included the famed essay by John Burroughs detailing his rafting trip down the East Branch in 1879. Since 1906, when the Delaware and Eastern Railroad completed its line through the Pepacton Valley, the communities along the river had gained better access to outside markets, and the economy had turned toward dairy farming, though sawmills still produced lumber. Some farmers sent vegetable crops to the city via rail. But the 1927 Delaware Watershed plan from the Board of Water Supply cast a shadow over the valley, cutting short its prosperity. Approved in 1928 by the city and state, the Delaware River plan faced a challenge from the State of New Jersey, since New York proposed taking water that would otherwise flow past the Garden State. In a 1931 ruling, the United States Supreme Court allowed New York to take the interstate waters. Slowed by the Depression and then by World War II, the city completed little of the Delaware System until the early 1950s. In the meantime, the Pepacton communities suffered. Dave Williams, a Union Grove real estate broker complained to a *New York Times* reporter in 1949 that his business had suffered since the plan had been first announced twenty years earlier. "The entire valley seems to have withered and died," he said, adding, "people were afraid to come in and invest because they did not know what they'd get when and if the city took over and others wanted to locate permanently." The Pepacton Valley and the West Branch Valley, where the city built the Cannonsville Reservoir, were no longer places one could hope to settle permanently.[72]

Alice Jacobson grew up on a farm a mile down the East Branch from Shavertown, one of four communities removed to make way for the Pepacton, the largest of New York City's reservoirs. Years later Jacobson remembered the valley fondly, the great beauty of the river, the peacefulness of the setting. She remembered the productivity of the people, and with evident anger she recounted how people felt trapped in their situation. The city evacuated the valley piecemeal, taking sections only as required by the contractors. Intended as a merciful arrangement, allowing people to live on their properties as long as possible, it actually only added stress to an already difficult situation. Residents had little idea when they might be forced to leave and felt all the more at the mercy of the city. To make matters worse, if residents wanted to fight for more money for their properties, they had to make due with only half the assessed value, which by law the city had to pay upon taking land. As in the case of the Ashokan takings, additional monies would have to wait until a commission had ruled on the proper value of the property and any challenges worked through the courts, a process that could take years. By early 1954, however, essentially everyone had left, with only workers remaining, many of them living in the houses of those forced to leave. Communities like Shavertown had been scattered, though most stayed relatively close to their former homes. Those moving to villages tended to select Margaretville, just upstream from the new reservoir, or Walton, a larger village on the other branch of the Delaware. Some went farther afield, to Delhi or Cooperstown or even New York City, though some found places much closer to home, such as up the Tremperskill Valley. As much as anything—the loss of property, the destruction of villages, the removal of graves—it was this scattering of people that brought real sorrow to those affected. "The city has no sentiment," complained Inez Atkins, the Shavertown postmistress and longtime resident of the valley. "This has been my home for thirty-seven years. I have friends and know my community. When they transplant me it will be difficult."[73]

The power of the Delaware and Catskill systems to redefine the mountains is evident, in a symbolic way, in Department of Environmental Protection maps of New York City's water supply system, where the Catskills have taken on new boundaries and even new names. In these maps the Catskills appear not as mountains but as watersheds, inverted mountains.

What matters to the D.E.P. are the valleys, the catch basins, the rivers that give watersheds their names. Lands upstream from the various dams define the watersheds, and so the Catskills have taken on a new shape since the 1950s, one defined by the engineers' placements of the reservoirs. Since watersheds generally take the names of the rivers that drain them, the Delaware watershed is somewhat accurately named, although Neverskink and Rondout waters also flow through this system. However, the Catskill Watershed is fictive, a new name cast from the aqueduct onto the valleys that feed it. Catskill Creek skirts the mountains to the north in Greene County, and thus there is an actual Catskill Watershed, one that does not send water to New York City.

Another common map, issued by the Board of Water Supply, also pointedly revealed the relationship between the city and the mountains. It appeared in the board's annual report in 1939 and has been reprinted in modified form repeatedly since. Covering the area from Manhattan up to the northern Catskills, the map identified the major city reservoirs and included the three aqueducts that brought the water to the city. As was common, the shaded watersheds clearly illustrated the water's origins. In addition, however, concentric circles radiated out from Manhattan, marking distances from the city—25 miles, 50 miles, 75 miles, 100 miles, and finally 125 miles—as if to reveal the true extent of the city's command. Appropriately, at the epicenter of the circles lay City Hall—the city's seat of power.[74]

Of course, the city controlled more than the maps; in many ways it now controlled the watersheds themselves. At the city's behest, the state would issue new land-use regulations, limits to development that pertained to all lands within their watersheds. As early as 1905, the city understood how invasive the reservoir system would be. The city, or a state agency, would henceforth regulate the watershed, monitor sanitation, and make changes as the law mandated, all to protect the purity of the city's water. Before the State Water Supply Commission in 1905, George Sterling, testifying for New York City's Corporation Counsel's office, revealed his contempt for the people in the watershed in dismissing the implications of this intrusion. "If some of them are compelled to live in a little more cleanly manner than they have been accustomed to do, and not to pollute the streams unnecessarily, they will have been taught a useful lesson in decency, cleanliness and healthfulness." By 1915, the city had formalized its watershed rules, having cleared them through the state's Department of Health. The "rules and regulations" covered a range of concerns, such as sewage control, house slops, garbage, manure, dead animals, stables, slaughterhouses, factories, and even swimming. The rules were so broadly conceived, in fact, affecting not just the reservoirs themselves but also all "watercourses" leading into them, that should the city feel it necessary, it could concern itself in every aspect of life in the mountains—domestic, agricultural, industrial, and even recreational.[75] In sum, henceforth the city would exert remarkable control over the mountains, regulating sanitation, maintaining the roads it had built, policing its lands, and employing dozens of people in the mountains. Most of all, the city controlled the water. It controlled the flow of the Esopus below the dam, and its flow above the reservoir as it sent water from the Schoharie into the Ashokan. Interstate rules limited the city's control of Delaware waters, but altogether the city made its decisions regarding water management to suit the needs of its consumers.

At one point, unsatisfied with its ability to manage Catskill surface waters, the city attempted to expand its authority to include the moisture in clouds above the mountains. After a severe drought in the summer of 1949, reservoirs failed to fill during the winter months. With the Delaware System not yet ready for use, the city urged voluntary conservation measures early in 1950, hoping to prevent a disaster during the hot summer months. Further, the city sought advice from a meteorologist, Wallace E. Howell, director of New Hampshire's Mount Washington Observatory, who claimed he could make it rain over the mountains. Cloud seeding had gained attention recently, with many believing that impregnating moist skies with dry ice and silver iodide could spark and prolong rains. With reservoirs at just over 50 percent capacity at a time of year when they should have been full, the city was desperate to avoid a crisis. So, the city's Board of Estimate approved $50,000 to fund Howell's rainmaking efforts in the Catskills. After preparations, including gathering equipment and securing the use of airplanes, Howell awaited the proper weather conditions to begin seeding. Ironically, as a fast-moving cold front approached the mountains, a pouring rain and fog grounded Howell's plane on a Brooklyn tarmac. After the fog lifted, the plane soared through blue skies over the mountains, nary a cloud to seed. The first effort to make rain had been rained out. The project continued, however, and just a little over a week later so much rain had fallen over the Catskills that the city halted its cloud seeding, as the Schoharie Reservoir filled to overflowing. With the other reservoirs still low, the rainmaking began again, and on April 30, the *New York Times* reported that cloud seeding had prolonged a three-hour rain in the Catskills. Through the summer, both the rains and the rainmaking persisted, and reservoir levels climbed back toward normal.[76]

Not everyone was pleased with the results, or even with the idea that the city should tinker with the weather in the Catskills. Ben Slutsky and his partners in the Nevele Country Club in Sullivan County sued the city, seeking an injunction against rainmaking, which they claimed had had an ill effect on their business. But in a case heard in the Supreme Court of New York, in Manhattan, Judge Ferdinand Pecora determined that regardless of potential damages the Nevele might sustain, the injunction would be "opposed to the general welfare and public good." In other words, Pecora's May 11, 1950, ruling declared that New York City had a right to make it rain in the mountains. The ruling could have only added wonderment, if not animus, to discussions in the Catskills regarding the city's control of mountain weather. George Yaeger, editor of the *Liberty Register*, asked if perhaps "the rain-making activities of New York City are not, in fact, inflicting a public injury upon one community, the Catskills, by another community, New York City." Resort owners and farmers alike, both now soaked by a summer of unusually heavy rains, wondered how it was that the city could have the legal right to make it rain outside the city itself. The city controlled the watersheds and the skies above them too?[77]

After a particularly heavy storm in late November 1950, mountain residents saw an opportunity to seek compensation for the city's interference in their weather. Herman Gottfried, an attorney from Margaretville, collected lawsuits against the city for flood damage due to the storm, with some of the suits coming from residents along the soon-to-be-submerged Pepacton Valley. The city admitted seeding the clouds that issued the damaging rains, sparking even more suits. In the end, the cases never came to trial, with a technical flaw in the filings preventing even a discussion of the cases' merits. By the time the court dismissed the cases, however, the city had abandoned its rainmaking efforts, most likely because reservoir levels had recovered, but perhaps also because city officials recognized that although they had the power to do so, making rain in the mountains may not have been a good idea. Perhaps city officials could see other storm clouds gathering in the mountains and knew they too were of their own making.[78]

Like making rain in the mountains, making reservoirs had created a great deal of anger in the Catskills, along with disappointment and sorrow, revealing the limits to the concert of interests that sometimes animated the collaboration between city and country. For many Catskills residents, in constructing its water supply, "the city" had become the quintessential distant, faceless power, always meddling in local affairs and more often than not getting its way. Throughout the twentieth century, periodic conflicts (over property taxes and watershed regulations) prevented the wounds caused by the initial takings from healing. Still, the reservoirs themselves quickly became naturalized, great lakes in a landscape that had held so few large bodies of water. As part of the *Kingston Daily Freeman*'s coverage of the fiftieth anniversary of the arrival of Ashokan water in New York City, reporter Tobie Geertsema noted, "The reservoir today is so much part and parcel of Ulster County that one is inclined to think it dates back to time immemorial." Seen from highways and mountaintops, the reservoirs became as integral to the mountain landscape as they were to its history. They became tourist destinations themselves and, as the shorelines ringed with rowboats attested, important sites for local recreation. By the late twentieth century, Catskills tourist literature usually featured at least one dramatic photograph of the Ashokan's expanse, often with its smooth surface reflecting Slide Mountain and other peaks beyond.[79]

Recently strolling through his hometown of Prattsville, just upstream from the Schoharie Reservoir, Andrew Dresser remarked on the city's acquisition of Catskills water. Not hiding his disdain for urban arrogance, he noted, "New York says it has the best water in the world. But it's our water." Dresser's comments, and tone, reflected a common mixture of anger and pride among locals: anger at what the city had forced upon them, and pride at what the mountains had accomplished as a result. A few years earlier, Town of Olive Clerk Sylvia Rozzelle expressed a similar mixture of emotions as she reflected back on the suffering endured by the "strong, resilient people" of Olive, whose sacrifices were as "monumental" as the reservoir itself. As Rozzelle correctly concluded, the Ashokan has given special meaning to these sacrifices, since it "created the foundation for New York City to develop into one of the greatest cities in the world." Clearly the importance of the city and the Catskills grew together, as the mountains became home of what the *New York Times* had called the "greatest reservoir in the world," the source of the pure waters that slaked the nation's thirstiest city.[80]

—ᴡ— *Chapter 6* —ᴡ—

Moving Mountains

A fresh stream of humanity is always setting from the country into the city; a stream not so fresh flows back again into the country, a stream for the most part of jaded and pale humanity.

—John Burroughs, 1886

The big hotels are air-conditioned, have at least two and sometimes three dance bands, and often indoor as well as outdoor swimming pools. A vacation spent at one of them is likely to be an intensification of city life. Exhaustion, not repose, is the goal. . . .

—David Boroff, 1958

In 1917 Abraham Cahan, then a famous Jewish author and activist, published the archetypal story of a Russian Jew making it in the garment industry of New York. *The Rise of David Levinsky* tracks the life of a poor immigrant who arrived in 1885, fleeing the murderous anti-Semitism of his homeland. Through the kindness of other Jews and his own hard work, Levinsky saves money, attends City College, and then starts what becomes a successful cloak factory. Americanization provides the central tension in Cahan's novel, as Levinsky struggles to find the right balance in preserving his traditional Jewish culture and accepting the changes that allow him to prosper in New York.[1]

While most of the novel takes place in Manhattan's Lower East Side, it includes a relatively brief trip to the Catskills. Levinsky takes a train to the mountains, where he expects to meet his fiancée and her family for a respite from the city. But since it is Saturday—the Sabbath, when Orthodoxy would prohibit such travel—he stops short of his destination so as not to offend his future in-laws. Levinsky steps off the train in a town modeled after Hunter, where he finds a throng of women and children greeting their husbands and fathers arriving from the city. In addition to the crowd, the mountain air strikes Levinsky. He inhales it "in deep, intoxicating gulps," finding it "so full of ozone" and unlike the air he had left "in the sweltering city." The village itself contains many resorts, clustered around the all-important rail station, and seemingly all of them cater to Jews. The town is full of Jewish nouveaux riches, whom Levinsky describes as "families of cloak-manufacturers, shirt-manufacturers, ladies'-waist-manufacturers, cigar-manufacturers, clothiers, furriers, jewelers, leather-goods men, real-estate men, physicians, dentists, lawyers— in most cases people who had blossomed out into nabobs in the course of the last few years." Most of these families are seeking status in the mountains and good marriages for their children as much as the pure air that so thrilled Levinsky.[2]

In effect, the annual migration of Jewish tourists into the mountains, rather faithfully depicted by Cahan, represented the successful completion of the initial migration to America.[3] Jewish participation in tourism and the consumption that accompanied vacation travel represented a real arrival in American society. Not surprisingly, the distinctive urban experience of Jewish Americans led to a distinctive relationship with nature, one intimately connected to tourist experiences in the mountains. In the Catskills, immigrant Jews developed their own ideas of nature's proper role in an urban life. In the process, they would remake themselves, as Americans, and they would remake the mountains. Once again the transformed mountains would reflect changes in the city.

Although most of Levinsky's brief stay in the mountains is consumed with the era's typical resort activities—eating, flirting, and socializing on the veranda—Cahan added multiple references to the mountain environment. Taken by the beauty of the sky, Levinsky declares, "This is just the kind of place for God to live in." He decides that heaven lay above the mountains, whereas "overhanging the city was a 'mere sky.'" One guest even compares the next night's sunset to "the work of a well-known landscape painter," who goes unnamed, but Cahan most likely had Frederic Church in mind. In another scene Levinsky describes a coming storm, a torrential rain that, like the fantastic sunset described earlier, is a reminder that here in the mountains nature holds different powers. Cahan even takes a cue from Washington Irving, casting the Catskills as a mysterious place. As Levinsky sits captivated by the evening sky, he stares out at the mountains before him—at some "enchanted spot"—where the changing light encourages him to see ghosts "fleeing to the woods near by." Not unlike Rip Van Winkle's Catskills, described a century earlier, Levinsky's mountains are "charged with peace and soothing mystery."[4]

David Levinsky's Catskills are filled with meanings, then, both new and old. Cahan references Hudson River art and looks backward to the mythology of Irving, making certain that the mountain scene is familiar—

the Catskills New Yorkers had learned to expect. But in Levinsky's story too are new meanings, associated specifically with Jewish tourists, who in the early 1900s began to predominate in some parts of the mountains. Indeed, at the time Cahan wrote, the Catskills were rapidly becoming the second quintessentially Jewish place in America—set in partial opposition to the first, the city's Lower East Side. Over the remainder of the twentieth century, American Jews would look to the latter as a representation of their immigrant origins, as the place where Jews established themselves and their culture in the city. In contrast, the Catskills would come to represent the long Americanization process, the place where Jews participated in rituals of the broader culture, in leisure and consumption. Together, these two places provided physical representation of the duality of American Jewish existence.[5]

Levinsky's experience marks just the beginning of this story. Through the first half of the twentieth century, the Catskills would become ever more important to New York Jews, and vice versa. Eventually Jewish Catskills culture, mostly developed in Sullivan Country rather than the Greene County resorts Levinsky described, would become integral to the New York Jewish experience, so much a part of the lives of those who vacationed there that most developed a remarkable sense of ownership over their "summer world" and a great deal of pride in their distinctive "Catskill culture."[6] As with the grand hotel region along the northern Catskills rail lines, the landscape of the Jewish resort region thoroughly blended country experiences—especially the blessings of nature—with city residents' cultural expectations, leaving physical evidence of the collaboration between the local and city residents who participated in the tourist industry. Although significant segregation in the mountains separated most vacationing Jews from most resident gentiles, Jews themselves, some of whom lived in the mountains year-round and others of whom ritually vacationed in them over the course of long lives, thoroughly mixed city and country in the resort region they created.

The most significant change in the Catskills wrought by the Jewish tourist industry involved the location of the mountains themselves. At the turn of the century, the Catskills occupied the northern half of Ulster County and much of Greene County. As indicated on tourist maps, the Catskills lay west of Kingston and Catskill, occupying not much more territory than the resort region that had developed in the preceding seventy years. These maps reflected a definition of the Catskills created and advertised by the resort industry, but they also reflected the common definition of the region. In the late 1870s, the French geographer Arnold Guyot produced a map titled "Catskill Mountains," the result of his effort to more accurately locate and measure the many mountains of the range. At the map's center lay Hunter Township, Greene County, where Levinsky would vacation forty years later, and at the map's southern end lay Denning Township, Ulster County, just south of Slide Mountain. Importantly, Sullivan County did not appear on this or other early Catskills maps. But as the Jewish resorts of Sullivan County gained renown and the northern Catskills fell into decline, the mountains began to move, or so it would seem. Over the course of the twentieth century, Jewish tourists referred to the Sullivan region as "the mountains," or "our Catskills," and since eventually comparatively few tourists visited the historical Catskills, that region gradually lost a secure claim to its own name. As Sullivan County hotelkeeper Cissie Blumberg noted in her 1996 autobiography, "When a New York Jew said he was going to 'the mountains,' there was no question as to his destination—there were no other mountains." By the late twentieth century, the Sullivan County Catskills had become nearly everyone's Catskills. In perhaps the most dramatic transformation wrought by the city's residents in the Catskills, New York tourists had moved the mountains.[7]

At the same time that annual migrations of Jews transformed the Catskills, Jewish immigration transformed New York City, where each decade of rapid growth gave way to another. Throughout the late nineteenth century and into the twentieth, immigrants streamed into America's largest port. New York's commerce and industry generated incredible wealth, which itself streamed up the avenues toward Central Park and into the region around the city, where country villas and suburban retreats reflected the grandeur of the metropolis that spawned them. The five boroughs grew together after their union in 1898, linked by new bridges and, most important, a new subway system that provided inexpensive access to sparsely populated sections of the Bronx and eventually Queens.[8] The city's millions thus dispersed, some moving beyond the municipal limits, to Long Island, Westchester, and New Jersey suburbs, and others into new neighborhoods within the boroughs themselves. Despite this geographical expansion, the city's core remained densely populated, especially the Manhattan neighborhoods that housed the working poor. Here immigrants settled into ethnic neighborhoods, Italians clustering with Italians, Russians with Russians, etc. Here too, Jews clustered, and though their national origins varied, together their numbers were remarkable. By 1910, when the city had a little more than 4.7 million residents, an estimated 1.2 million were Jews. Ten years later, the total number of Jews in New York surpassed 1.6 million, representing nearly 30 percent of the city's population. By that point, New York City had long contained the largest concentration of Jews in the world. Those Jews would deeply influence culture within the city and, in turn, the culture of New York's hinterland, especially in the Catskills.[9]

As Europe's anti-Semitism deepened in the late 1800s, leading to restrictive laws and a series of pogroms in Russia, hundreds of thousands of Jews fled to the United States. Most arrived impoverished, though many had marketable skills. The newly arrived Jews settled in several parts of the city, and would eventually move out to the suburbs in all directions, but in the first decades of the twentieth-century the Lower East Side of Manhattan housed more than 500,000 Jews in just 1.5 square miles. By then another large enclave had developed across the East River in Brooklyn's Brownsville neighborhood, but the East Side, centered on the commercial district along Hester Street, had become the quintessential American Jewish neighborhood. By 1900, it had become the most densely populated place on the globe, with families squeezed into small tenement apartments, basements, and garrets. The Lower East Side's crowds, its lack of open spaces—save the busy streets themselves—and its filthy air, combined to make the neighborhood a particularly unhealthy place. Despite job opportunities, especially in the garment industry, and the strength of the immigrant community as it cohered around synagogues and mutual benefit societies, the Lower East Side became a neighborhood most residents hoped to leave, by moving out permanently and, in the meantime, by escaping temporarily for lengthy summer trips to the country.[10]

Partly because so many Jews clustered in this one city, especially strong stereotypical images gathered around American Jewish life, some anti-Semitic, some not. The popular press cast Jews as dirty and untrustworthy, and political cartoons exaggerated physical attributes, especially noses. Although nearly all immigrant groups bore the burden of insulting images, Jews gained a particularly virulent and pervasive stereotype, one that cast them as urban, upwardly mobile, and, when expressed as part of an anti-Semitic portrait, ruthless and unscrupulous in business. Even less offensive portraits of New York Jews contained a remarkable uniformity, featuring the struggle for success in the Lower East Side, arduous work in the garment industry, a yearning for education, and an abiding loyalty to other Jews. Although upward mobility, a philosophy of self-help, and an emphasis on education would all seem appropriately American traits, Jews retained a distinctiveness that made others suspicious. Part of that distinctiveness was their strong connection to the city.[11]

As Cahan's novel reveals, the surge of anti-Semitism in the mountains in the last two decades of the 1800s had not cleared the Catskills of Jewish retreats. Indeed, the Tannersville-Hunter region only gained in popularity among New York Jews, though before 1900 most may have been first- and second-generation German Jews, thought by many native-born Americans to be more socially acceptable than recently arrived Eastern European Jews. Another hamlet in Ulster County, Griffin's Corners, also became a popular Jewish retreat in the 1880s, after a wealthy Cincinnati industrialist, Charles Fleischmann, built a summer mansion on an old farmstead not far from the Ulster and Delaware tracks. Born in Hungary, Fleischmann had been in the United States for twenty years, during which he had created an extremely successful yeast company—and married a New York City native. Other family members and friends too built summer mansions outside Griffin's Corners, creating a cottage colony populated by wealthy Jews. The Fleischmanns entertained frequently, often bringing in guests via private rail cars on the Ulster and Delaware, which built a station nearly at the gates of the colony. In short order, that picturesque region became a popular retreat for wealthy Jews from around the nation. Within a decade, Griffin's Corners would take the name Fleischmanns, in honor of the socially and politically active family, and perhaps to advertise the products that bore its name.[12]

Despite the success of the Jewish enclave in Fleischmanns, at the turn of the century the heart of the Jewish resort region still lay to the north in Tannersville and Hunter. In 1900, Rand, McNally's Catskills tourist guide remarked that Tannersville was "a great resort, in particular, of our Israelite brethren, who love to gather where they can be together." The guide's author, Ernest Ingersoll, also added a lengthy caveat regarding the Tannersville resorts: "If one goes to the mountains simply to join a rollicking, highly varied crowd, which is bent upon having a 'good time' without much expense or attention to conventionalities, the Tannersville district will suit him; but it is not the place for quiet folk, who seek in the hills something else than a cheap copy of the noise and amusement of the city they have left behind." One gets a sense from Ingersoll's tone that Jews themselves were part of the city's noise that gentile vacationers hoped to avoid. Years later, Cahan described this noise himself, when Levinsky calls the din of the boardinghouse dining room "unendurable." "The better to take in the effect of the turmoil," Levinsky tell us, "I shut my eyes for a moment, where upon the noise reminded me of the Stock Exchange." For Levinsky and other vacationing Jews a trip to the mountains was only a partial retreat from the city. As with gentile visitors to the grand hotels, in many ways Jews brought the city with them to the mountains.[13]

Ingersoll's description of Tannersville reveals important themes in Jewish mountain vacations, themes that persisted over the next sixty years. Clearly Jews frequented regions that catered to many Jews; they vacationed "where they can be together" so they could attend religious services and keep kosher while away from home. Just as important, Jews gathered together in search of romance, in the expectation that the next generation of Jews would marry inside the faith. Thus, Jews tended to seek socially active vacations, rich in entertainment and activities, the situations in which young men and women might mingle and flirt. By the turn of the century, as native-born, middle-class tourists sought increasingly active vacations that brought them in contact with nature, if not wilderness, typical Jewish mountain trips appear to have been somewhat lacking in natural experiences—Levinsky's sunset and thunderstorm notwithstanding. New York's Yiddish weekly, the *Forward*, noted that few Jewish tourists did much to take advantage of the fresh air: "They sit either on the porch or under a tree nearby." Clearly these early Jewish tourists engaged in some outdoor activities, including bathing in the region's rivers and lakes and taking hayrides through the region's farmland; and, in concluding his brief description of Jewish vacations in the Catskills, historian Irving Howe sarcastically added, "It cannot be excluded that some Jewish vacationers did take walks in the woods."[14] Still, as much as the fresh, cool air drew Jews to the mountains, wild nature was hardly the main attraction.

Although Jewish tourists came to predominate in some Catskills towns, such as Tannersville and Fleischmanns, much more famously they flocked to Sullivan County, especially in a region in and around Monticello and Liberty. Sullivan County's tourist industry had grown only slowly in the late 1800s, and it failed to develop enough traffic to warrant the construction of a great summer hotel comparable to the Hotel Kaaterskill or the Grand Hotel to the north. Still, tourism did expand, especially with the growing popularity of angling and hunting among urban New Yorkers. In the late 1870s, the New York, Ontario and Western Railroad stopped at a series of picturesque towns with equally attractive names—Mountaindale, Fallsburgh, Ferndale, and Liberty. The desire to attract more tourists encouraged some villages to change their names, as in 1903, when Hurleyville became Luzon, and in 1918, when Centerville became Woodridge.[15]

The Ontario and Western did its best to sell the resort opportunities along its lines, but early advertisements didn't mention the Catskills, except for contrast. The O&W's 1881 *Summer Homes* pamphlet mentioned several mountain ranges, for example, including the Shawangunk, Pine, Blue, and Delaware mountains, but not the Catskills, which had well-established attractions and nationally famous hotels.[16] As late as 1909, the Ellenville resort Mount Meenahga House made clear the distinction between the Catskills, to the north, and the mountains nearest that town, the Shawangunks. In its privately printed advertisement, the hotel, one of the finest in the region, even made the "variety and grandeur" of the Shawangunks a major selling point and a distinguishing feature.[17] Most Sullivan County resorts were too far from the Shawangunks to use them as a selling point, but the hilly country around Monticello and Liberty did have advantages over the older resort region to the north. In addition to its generally less expensive lodging, the region offered ample lakes and streams—indeed, even more than Greene County. Still, it held none of the spectacular mountain scenery that had drawn tourists to the Catskills for nearly a century. The region along the O&W had natural beauty, certainly, but no Kaaterskill Falls or Mountain House overlook—and no Mountain House, for that matter. It had none of the cultural associations that enriched the Catskills experience: no Rip Van Winkle or Leatherstocking, no Cole or Gifford. With no great elevations, save the distant Shawangunks east of Ellenville, the O&W tourist region would appear to have had little chance to outcompete the historical center of Catskills tourism. But over the first half of the twentieth century, Sullivan County blossomed into the Borscht Belt, one of the most active and influential tourist destinations in the nation.[18]

At the same time, the northern Catskills began to decline, a partial result of rising anti-Semitism among both resort owners and the gentile tourists they hoped to serve. Anti-Semitism among Greene County's hotel owners grew largely from a concern that the arrival of Jews would mean a decrease in gentile tourists, the region's traditional clientele, who in addition to being more familiar were also on average wealthier. These fears were not unfounded. As more Jews came to the Mountain Top, fewer gentiles made the trip. The great hotels of the late 1800s lost their luster as the "better sort" of vacationers set their sites higher, seeking their urban retreats at a greater distance from New York's Jews. Even before automobiles dramatically altered Catskills tourism, anti-Semitism began to reshape the region. Unable to attract "respectable" gentiles, some hotels and boardinghouses closed, while others sold their businesses to Jews who then opened their doors to the one customer base that continued to expand. By the early 1920s, Harry Tannebaum had purchased the stately Hotel Kaaterskill and welcomed a largely Jewish clientele. A devastating fire in the fall of 1924 destroyed the massive wooden structure, and business prospects did not warrant rebuilding, a clear signal that the region was in decline. The Laurel House could not attract enough gentile guests in the late 1910s, and became a Jewish resort under new owners in 1920. After years of financial problems, the Catskill Mountain House also became a Jewish hotel in the 1930s, complete with a kosher kitchen, and it opened for the last time in 1942. By then, the thriving tourism of Sullivan County had long since eclipsed the northern, historical Catskills.[19]

Since the new Catskills were so closely tied to the Jewish resorts, they earned some nicknames, used both affectionately and derogatorily. "Borscht Belt" was popular by the 1940s, and the "Sour Cream Sierras" by the 1950s. Both monikers referenced the kosher cuisine featured in the mountains, and both indicated a new cultural definition of the resort region. Henceforth, the Catskills would constitute a cultural typology, tied to the people who visited the resorts, and the term would be cut loose from the actual mountains. More and more frequently, New Yorkers would use the term "Catskills" to represent the special kind of resort found in the "Borscht Belt"—the most commonly used nickname for the Sullivan County region.[20] More than a reference to the traditional beet soup enjoyed by Eastern European Jews, "Borscht Belt" described a circuit of hotels toured by stage acts from the 1930s through the 1960s. Though centered in Sullivan County, the Borscht Belt could also include hotels in other regions that catered to Jews, including those in the Poconos to the south, the Adirondacks to the north, and the Berkshires to the east. In other words, this new cultural definition of the Catskills introduced a new flexibility and expansiveness.[21]

The growth of the Sullivan County Borscht Belt resulted from more than just the growth of Jewish tourism and the failure of the northern

Catskills to cater to the growing demand. While most immigrant Jews remained in the city, making only brief trips to the countryside, some acquired farms, especially in New Jersey and New York, and most importantly in Sullivan County, where they would be instrumental in the development of Borscht Belt tourism. By 1910, Sullivan County and southern Ulster County became the most important region for Jewish agriculture in the United States, counting more than 500 Jewish-owned farms. As with other immigrant groups, Jews entered agriculture for a number of reasons, including simply the desire to leave the city and return to the type of rural existence they had left behind in Europe. Most Eastern European Jews had come from small communities, shtetls, where they would have had at least some agricultural experience. The crowds and pollution of Manhattan and Brooklyn most likely convinced some immigrants to return to the country. Sullivan County, and the region around Ellenville in Ulster County, provided good opportunities for these immigrants, with relatively low land prices and relatively easy access to New York City. However, the land was cheap because of its middling quality, with most properties passing into Jewish hands from gentile farm families who no longer desired to make a meager living on the rocky soil.[22]

Jewish farmers did succeed in the region, though generally not because they raised better crops. Instead, the region prospered as it combined farming with the boarding business, following a long tradition in attractive, accessible agricultural regions around the city. Jewish farmers tapped into New York's growing and underserved market of Jews looking for community (and kosher kitchens) while on vacation. The first advertisement for a "Jewish Boarding House" appeared in the O&W's 1899 *Summer Homes*. John Gerson, whose family had been farming near Woodridge since 1892, now advertised a "new house, newly furnished." Much of the description would suit any boarding business—"scenery unsurpassed," "fine shade," "good road to station"—but other phrases spoke to Gerson's attempt to attract a Jewish clientele—such as "prepare our own meats," and, more pointedly, "Jewish faith and customs throughout." Other Jewish farmers followed suit, and soon as many establishments advertised "Strictly Kosher" as warned "No Hebrews." As early as 1905, the Jewish Agricultural and Industrial Aid Society, formed five years earlier to support the movement of Jews into farming, lamented that in Sullivan County the "raising of supplies for hotels and boarding houses is all that can be expected."[23]

By the 1920s, with the resort region booming, farmers found ready markets for their products. Boardinghouse operators could sell their milk, eggs, vegetables, and chickens to tourists for city retail prices, without paying to transport their produce. Other farmers, who didn't take boarders, also sold their products locally, especially eggs and chickens, at least during the summer. Actually, kosher chickens provided one of the few real agricultural exports from the region, as the city required the birds year-round. Many of the larger, mostly gentile farms still exported dairy products to the city, though these farms were scarce in the hillier resort region. Over time, the success of the resorts convinced many farmers to give up agriculture and develop their tourist businesses. At the same time, however, the expansion of tourism allowed other farmers to remain in a region that otherwise might have lost most of its farms. In at least one instance, involving the Yasgur family, participation in the boarding business proved shorter-lived than farming, the reverse of the most common trend. Max Yasgur had been born on his family's farm near Monticello in 1919, shortly after his parents had purchased the property and moved up from the city. When Max's father died in 1936, the young man took over the farm, but he was uninterested in the boarding business, which his mother still operated. Ten years later, Yasgur moved to a larger property in Bethel, where he found land good enough to raise alfalfa and corn and expand his dairy, and allowing the family to stop boarding tourists. By the 1960s, Yasgur's 600–acre property was one of the most prosperous Jewish dairy farms in the county.[24]

Not all of the resorts catering to Jews in the 1920s began as Jewish-owned farms, or even as Jewish establishments. The Flagler House in Fallsburgh dated back to the 1870s and took its name from Nicholas Flagler, who had made his money in the fleeting tanning business. Originally marketed to gentiles, the Flagler advertised in the 1881 *Summer Homes* using the polite but telling phrase "near church." For thirty years the Flagler accommodated "first-class" guests, who by the turn of the century could enjoy lawn tennis and croquet, and lazy days in and around the Neverskink River, which passed through the property. In 1909, however, the business had new owners, Asias Fleisher and Phillip Morgenstern, who opened the Flagler that summer as a "strictly kosher" hotel. A great success, the new Flagler more than doubled in size in 1920, when Fleisher and Morgenstern opened a large stucco building next to the original. The Flagler was the most visible example of a trend well underway in the first two decades of the century, both in Sullivan County and to the north, as older hotels that catered to gentiles ceased operations, sometimes to be purchased by Jews who operated them for a new clientele. However, the transition in Sullivan County would lead to much greater success than it would in Greene County.[25]

As the Flagler example also makes clear, not all of the famed resorts began as farms, but many did. In 1901, Charles Slutsky, a Jewish immigrant newly arrived from Russia, purchased a small farm in southern Ulster County, on which he operated a boarding business. Eventually, the Slutsky family split the property in two, both portions of which supported thriving resort businesses, the Nevele on one and the Fallsview on the other, and both retained at least the dairying aspect of the original farm until the 1930s.[26] As with the Slutsky's, the Levinson family's history is atypical only in the degree to which their business grew. Max and Dora Levinson, both from Russia, relocated to Greenfield Park in 1900, after having lived in New York City for fifteen years. Even after purchasing a farm, Max Levinson continued to work in the city, not an uncommon strategy for those families needing supplemental incomes. In 1903, however, the Levinsons decided to join the growing trend and open a boarding business, where the farm's fresh milk would become the major selling point for guests. The Levinsons' business grew from an original six-bedroom enterprise into the Tamarack Lodge, which after a massive expansion in 1926 became one of the region's greatest successes.[27]

The most famous farm to evolve into a large hotel belonged to Selig and Malke Grossinger, who immigrated to New York's Lower East Side from Galacia. After a number of years working in the garment industry, the couple opened a restaurant in the city, in which they worked with their daughter Jennie. According to the family, Selig suffered a breakdown brought on by overwork, and his doctor recommended that he seek health and rest in the country, whereupon the family purchased a farm near Liberty. In 1914, shortly after making the move, the family opened a boarding business to augment the modest income from the farm. The business benefited from the success of the region and from Malke's cooking, which kept boarders coming back. Five years later, the Grossingers purchased a larger, nearby property that included a hotel. Within a decade, Grossinger's Hotel had expanded to a capacity of 500 guests and initiated the building of a golf course—surely a sign of success.[28]

Of course only a small percentage of the tourist businesses developed into large hotels. Most remained small establishments, despite the region's growth in the 1920s. Diversity in mountain accommodations not only persisted, it actually increased. Some farmers built small summer cabins in their yards, called bungalows. The cabins were inexpensive to build, and represented a flexible use of capital, with owners adding a few new buildings each season as income and demand allowed. Most cabins contained just two or three rooms—a kitchen and one or two bedrooms. The tight quarters sufficed since most activities would take place outdoors in communal space. According to sociologist Phil Brown, the clustering of the small cabins into colonies replicated the communal living most Eastern European immigrants had experienced in shtetls. Here, friends from city neighborhoods, from work, or even *landsmanschaftn* from the old country could gather for pleasure and communal responsibility. The hundreds of bungalow colonies that sprouted in the Catskills over the next thirty years distinguished the region from all other American tourist areas, and represented just one way in which the interests of the tourists themselves shaped the landscape.[29]

Although the Sullivan County region would eventually bear the burden of strong stereotypes, derived largely from Jewish experiences at the larger hotels, the diversity of retreats was remarkable from the beginning. Reflecting the diversity of New York's Jews themselves, some resorts catered to particular groups, some based in religious practice or national background. Other groups simply created their own resorts, ensuring that they would find suitable vacation spots. Labor unions in particular established colonies in the mountains, providing members with an extra perk. As early as 1893, the Jewish Working Girls Vacation Society organized to give young women a break from their workaday lives. The society operated a number of retreats, including a house in Margaretville, where the girls stayed free, courtesy of the society's benefactors. Other organizations opened camps in the Catskills to give city youth opportunities for escape and edification, including teaching Yiddish or Hebrew or, in the case of the Workmen's Circle, which opened a camp in 1926, exposure to socialist philosophy.[30]

The Workmen's Circle, a fraternal organization created by Eastern European immigrants, had also created an earlier development in Sullivan County, which by 1900 had gained the reputation as a retreat for tubercular patients seeking pure, dry air for their diseased lungs. Countryside sanitariums had become popular in the 1890s, with the Adirondacks gaining special attention among New Yorkers with the construction of Edward Trudeau's sanitarium in Saranac Lake. Since Saranac Lake was literally out of reach for most New Yorkers, Dr. Alfred Loomis worked to create a more accessible retreat closer to the city. In 1896, charitable donations built one of the largest sanitariums in the country, named in honor of Loomis, who passed away during the planning phase. Initially, the sanitarium brought some positive publicity, as New Yorkers heard about the pleasant weather and cool, dry summer air. After the sanitarium's opening, several hotels in and around Liberty found that their most reliable clientele were those seeking relief from their incurable disease. And, in 1910, the Workmen's Circle opened its own sanitarium in Liberty. Since tubercular patients could seek relief at any time during the year, with crisp winter days proving especially therapeutic, catering to consumptives was potentially lucrative. On the downside, however, Sullivan County, especially Liberty, gained an unfortunate reputation, diminishing the region's attractiveness to those who did not have the disease and justifiably feared contracting it.[31]

The tubercular reputation notwithstanding, the Sullivan County resort region flourished after World War I. The booming 1920s economy and the expanding middle class's rising automobile ownership combined to provide great opportunity for Sullivan County, where entrepreneurs added thousands upon thousands of modest accommodations to lure New York's millions. Some boardinghouses became hotels; some hotels became country clubs. A 1923 article in the reform-minded magazine *The Survey*, entitled "East Siders in 'the Mountains,'" described the "broad path" that had been worn "by Jewish families who seek a refuge" from their immigrant neighborhoods. In the tradition of progressive journalism, N. B. Fagin declared that Jews, most of whom stayed with farmers "largely of their own race," had created conditions in the mountains as congested as "the tenements of Hester Street." According to Fagin, "It is fear of the white plague that impels these pale New Yorkers to come to the mountains." He described finding sick and frail women sent to the mountains by city doctors for improved diets and pure air. The women also claimed to have come for their children, who "hadn't been doing well" in the "stifling, dirty tenements of the overcongested East Side and Brownsville." However, poor conditions followed these refugees to the mountains, according to Fagin, making the retreat much less healthful than it ought to have been. Indeed, conditions had deteriorated so badly, largely because of the rapid increase in summer boarders in northern Sullivan County, that the Jewish Agricultural Society had begun a campaign to improve sanitation in the mountains in 1918. "They came into the mountains to rest and forget their sorry East Side," Fagin concludes, "but it came with them, with its crushing problems, its sordid environment, its influence, taunting, persecuting, molding them." Though Fagin's alarmism reflected his muckraking training more than the reality of the resort environment, he quite accurately described the growth of urban crowds in the Catskills, just one of many aspects of city life that would accompany tourists to the mountains.[32]

Most New York Jews did not rise the way Cahan's Levinsky did, and many never did gain the means to travel far from the Lower East Side and other immigrant neighborhoods. Still, working-class Jews placed a high priority on sending women and children to the country, especially during the midsummer slowdown in the garment industry. Much more than other ethnic groups, Jews, even those with very limited incomes, strove to spend at least some time out of the city. Though perhaps initially intended as a healthful reprieve from the stifling ghettos of August, very rapidly the summer vacation took on social significance, indicating the success of a family. The Borscht Belt grew largely because it could attract wealthy Jews even while providing for the poorest of tourists. As one writer describing the Lower East Side noted in 1903, "poverty or no poverty, plans are made for a vacation in the country." By 1928, *American Hebrew* could call the Catskills the "Playground of Jewish Masses." Given the variety of resorts, running from exclusive clubs "with lake and links" to small farms overcrowded with working-class families, the Catskills could "supply the summer playground for every type and description of metropolitan Jews." On a summer tour of the resort region to conduct research for the article, Isaac Landman found none of the poor sanitation the *Survey* complained of just a few years earlier. More important, he was impressed with the options available for average Jewish families, most of whom remained relatively poor. "I saw workers of every description from the big city," Landman wrote, "happy that their families, within their means, can have a long vacation in the Catskills."[33]

The success of the 1920s gave way to the Great Depression of the 1930s and with it a decline in the tourist industry. The modest prices in Sullivan County served the region well, however. Many tourists scaled back plans, making shorter visits to the mountains, but others undoubtedly returned to the economical Catskills instead of taking more expensive trips elsewhere. Catskills boardinghouses responded to weakening demand by offering more *kuchaleins*, or "cook alones," that allowed tourists to rent rooms and prepare their own food. Kuchaleins were actually the opposite of what their name suggests; guests all cooked together in a common kitchen, setting the stage for many a battle over refrigerator space, ovens, and stoves—even accusations of food pilfering. Initiated in the 1910s, kuchaleins allowed families with tight budgets to spend more time in the mountains. In the 1930s, this option became more common, as families made sacrifices in an effort to continue their traditional summer trips. The kuchalein arrangement also allowed farmers to continue their produce sales to tourists, even if it meant less revenue, and freed up farming women, who previously labored to supply tourist meals, who then could dedicate more time to raising crops, which became all the more important during tight times.[34]

Though many resort businesses failed in the 1930s, the Catskills fared better in the Depression than most regions built upon customers' discretionary spending. Part of the Catskills' resilience came from the ongoing shift toward automobiles and buses from the fading railroads. As early as 1930, the Ontario and Western warned the Sullivan County resorts that as the railroad's receipts fell, all businesses along its lines would suffer. Although the O&W cut fares in the late 1920s, passenger totals continued to decline, as did revenue. Even a bump in spending on *Summer Homes* could not bring back the numbers. Outcompeted by automobiles and buses, the O&W had no choice but to scale back its service. The line declared bankruptcy in 1937. For another twenty years the railroad remained alive but in its death throws, earning its nickname "Old and Weary." It finally ceased operations in 1957.[35]

Despite the O&W's warnings that its failure would bring disaster to the communities along its line, it didn't. Indeed, the Catskills continued to prosper well after the railroad became irrelevant, with road improvements making the trip even quicker by car or bus—barring traffic, of course, not an inconsiderable problem even in the 1920s. By 1917 a good state route connected Middletown to Monticello and would soon reach to Liberty. And roads closer to the city improved, too, especially with the opening of the Holland Tunnel in 1927, followed by the George Washington Bridge in late 1931.[36] Residents of Manhattan, Brooklyn, and the Bronx now had good access to the western shore of the Hudson, and thence the roads leading north to the Catskills. As roads improved and more and more New Yorkers owned their own cars, automobile transportation became all the more important to the region. On Saturday, August 13, 1932, a twelve-hour study of traffic on Route 17, the main road connecting downstate to Sullivan County, counted more than 88,000 cars.

Just as important, bus lines increasingly replaced trains as the favored means of mass transportation for New Yorkers headed to the Catskills. Unlike trains, which left only from the station—in Weehawken, New Jersey, no less—buses could pick up travelers at almost any location in the city. Buses left from Brooklyn, the Bronx, and Manhattan, saving time and trouble for tourists. Hacks were even more flexible, picking up customers directly from their houses, even if economizing required traveling through the city to pick up multiple passengers. Buses were especially important for working-class vacationers, which constituted a large percentage of Catskills tourists. The mountains even gained a disproportionate advantage over Long Island vacation regions, when the new parkways, designed by Robert Moses, intentionally featured bridges so low as to prevent bus traffic. Buses and the passengers they brought were welcomed in Sullivan County.[37]

With greatly enlarged tourist capacity in the region, created by the 1920s building boom, followed by the weakening demand in the 1930s, competition among the resorts intensified. Even before the Depression hit, the larger hotels began to add attractions and distinctiveness, to give their establishments an edge over competitors. More hotels also began to offer professional entertainment, beginning with a social director, called a tummler, a word derived from the Yiddish expression for "tumult-maker." Tummlers entertained guests in any number of ways, from organizing stage shows, staging gags at the swimming pool, or leading games of Simon Says. All day they mingled with the guests, telling jokes, playing tricks, and keeping people happy.[38] Perhaps the most famous Catskills tummler, David Kaminsky came up from Brooklyn in 1929 and performed over the course of several summers. Using a stage name—Danny Kaye— he revealed remarkably versatile talents as a dancer, singer, musician, actor, and comedian while entertaining guests at Livingston Manor's White Roe Hotel. Kaye parlayed his success in the mountains into a Broadway debut in the late 1930s, and then a movie career with MGM. Like others who would begin their careers in the Catskills, Kaye had used his varied experiences in the mountains to hone skills, develop skits, and, though it was more important for comedians less talented than Kaye, create a shtick that audiences could recognize instantly.[39]

The Catskill hotels took a vaudevillian approach to entertainment, and because they had small staffs, performers had to display remarkable versatility—at times clowning, at others crooning, and, like Kaye, even participating in dramatic scenes. However, some entertainers simply focused on clowning, including another great Catskills tummler, Joseph Levitch. He could not match Kaye's varied talents, but Levitch was extremely funny. Following in the footsteps of his father, who had also been a Catskills comedian, Levitch worked long hours developing acts with outrageous physical comedy, extreme facial expressions, and his trademark squeaky falsetto voice. Levitch performed his manic acts at a series of hotels, most famously Brown's, before leaping, with a stage name—Jerry Lewis—into a film career that made him one of the most important twentieth-century American entertainers. As the Dean Martin and Jerry Lewis duo launched its film debut in 1949, the *New York Times* called their act the "Borscht Belt's Latest Gift to the Movies."[40]

Through the 1930s and 1940s, Catskills stages flourished, attracting both young and established talent from the city. Summers were slow at city venues, and so entertainers seeking work made their way to the mountains, where guests increasingly expected professional shows at least every Friday and Saturday night. Dozens of famous entertainers launched their careers in the mountains, especially comedians, who borrowed extensively from each other as they struggled to come up with new material to perform before familiar audiences. The casual atmosphere in the mountains and the flexibility of the venues allowed entertainers to offer acts with singing and dancing, but comedy gained a special place on Catskills stages. Here Milton Berle, Sid Caesar, Henny Youngman, Alan King, Joey Adams, Red Buttons, Buddy Hackett, and Jackie Mason all perfected their skills and developed the acts that would make them and the Catskills famous. In later years, the Catskills would become less important to launching comedians' careers, but the larger resorts remained favorite venues for young talent seeking exposure and on-the-job training. Even as the Catskills declined, Billy Crystal, Jerry Seinfeld, and many others made seemingly obligatory appearances.

Hotels typically included all entertainment under their American plans, in which guests paid a flat fee for their room, all the food they could eat, the use of all the facilities, and admission to all shows. This meant that guests had access to entertainment that many could not afford while in the city—a special bonus for tourists. In the 1940s, the Catskills and other resort regions in the East had remarkable control over summertime entertainment, as hotels booked talent for the season, and then, more commonly, booked touring acts for individual evenings. Under both arrangements, guests at the hotels were much more likely to see quality entertainment while in the mountains than they would back home. In the 1950s, that began to change, however. In 1950, Catskills favorite Sid Caesar jumped to television, bringing his act to "Your Show of Shows." Caesar also brought to the show writer Mel Brooks, a talented young man who had absorbed the essence of Catskills acts, including Caesar's. Caesar was just part of a wave of New York City/Catskills talent that found broader audiences through television, a wave that also included Milton Berle and Henny Youngmann. Others, like Kaye and Lewis, influenced the broader culture through Hollywood films. Ironically, the more the influence of New York's Jewish comedians grew in the broader culture, the less the Catskills could capitalize on their talent. By the late 1950s, New Yorkers and other Americans had access to entertainment in their homes that they had formerly found only on stages.[41]

The exportation of Catskills entertainment signaled the growing cultural importance of the mountains, represented not just in films and on television, but also in literature. In 1955, Herman Wouk published *Marjorie Morningstar*, the first, and probably the best, of many novels that would be set in the Jewish Catskills.[42] By then, the Catskills had entered its golden moment, what Myrna and Harvey Frommer called "the era."[43] As the economy revived in the early 1940s and the soldiers returned after the war, the resort region once again brimmed with activity. Over the next decade, capacity expanded to meet revived demand, and by one estimate the Jewish Catskills had 500 hotels and 2,000 bungalow colonies in operation by the late 1950s. When full, these accommodations could house 450,000 people. By itself, Grossinger's could accommodate over 1,000 guests, and the largest hotel, the Concord, could accommodate 1,800. David Boroff's 1958 *Harper's* essay on the Catskills claimed that during the high season "the population density exceeds that of most American cities." Boroff made the comparison purposefully, noting further that a vacation spent at one of the big hotels "is likely to be an intensification of city life." With high-rise buildings, cavernous dining rooms, nightly entertainment, and several hundred guests, the largest hotels had indeed created an urban atmosphere in the mountains—an atmosphere of affluence indicative of "the era." Clearly the consumerism of postwar Jewish tourism did not center on the consumption of nature, let alone wilderness.[44]

Tourism in the Catskills reflected the conflicted relationship between immigrant Jews—and even native-born Jews—and American society. Jews were at once full participants in a culture of abundance but aloof from the mainstream, clustered in segregated, kosher institutions. Jews continued to face the perplexing problems related to Americanization that had troubled David Levinsky fifty years earlier. How much of their own cultures could they preserve in this new land? How much should they separate themselves from gentiles? Should the younger generations learn Yiddish as well as Hebrew? Changes in the Sullivan County resorts over the course of the twentieth century reflected the evolution of New York City's Jewish population, as each generation answered these questions in different ways. As historian Andrew Heinze has argued, Eastern European Jews adapted to American abundance through their own consumption, both in the city and on vacation.[45]

Restrictive immigration laws of the mid-1920s curtailed Jewish immigration to the United States through World War II and beyond, and without the infusion of new immigrants one would expect American Jews to follow other ethnic minorities in a cultural migration toward the American mainstream, a migration well underway in the 1930s. But as the enormity of the Holocaust became clear and as Zionism flowered with the birth of Israel in 1948, American Jews had good reasons to hold tight to their ethnic identity, to both secular Yiddishkeit and religious traditions. Suddenly, maintaining a strong Jewish community in the United States took on greater historical importance. With European Jewry all but destroyed and Russian Jews under siege in the Soviet Union, American Jews felt all the more responsible for the persistence of Judaism in the world and especially for the success of Israel. Even the mountain hotels engaged in fundraising for Israeli causes and encouraged remembrance of the Holocaust. Preserving Jewish identity and passing it on to the next generation took on political meaning.[46]

Still, the American Jewish population changed dramatically in the decades following World War II. As native speakers passed away, Yiddish became much less common in New York, though the Yiddish press persisted. Jews also continued their march toward secularism, with Reform temples attracting those who dropped the daily and even the weekly rituals of Judaism. Just as important, New York Jews grew increasingly wealthy and suburbanized, two trends that eventually decreased demand for the type of vacation the Borscht Belt provided. Given the trends of secularization and suburbanization, it is fair to conclude that the Jewish resorts might have collapsed much more quickly without the resurgent interest in preserving Jewish identity, one that now firmly affected all generations of American Jews, not just those who remembered distant homelands.[47]

In the early 1950s, a Catskills vacation was a significant part of New York Jewish identity. Although the hotels would set the image of "the era," bungalow colonies continued to thrive in the mountains, constituting the traditional vacation for a large number of Jewish families. Many colonies even expanded during the 1950s. According to the *New York Times*, in 1953 the region held approximately 2,000 colonies, averaging around twenty-five bungalows each. Offering an inexpensive alternative to the hotels, the colonies allowed families to spend long summers with friends and relatives. Many colonies attracted the same vacationers year after year, which allowed them to develop close relationships across generations—the types of relationships that would help draw families back. While bungalows developed a reputation as an option for those who could not afford the expensive hotels, some chose bungalows because they liked the lifestyle that separate accommodations and dining afforded. Life there was much less regimented than at the hotels, giving guests much more liberty.[48] Noting how committees addressed basic needs and solved disputes, Boroff astutely concluded in 1958, "Bungalow colonies are, in effect, basic training for city people in the techniques and organization of suburbia."[49] They also allowed Jews to divide by need or interest; Orthodox and Reform Jews frequented different colonies, as did those with families and those without.

The largest bungalow colonies did provide entertainment, though certainly not with the famous names that graced the stages of the largest hotels. Some colonies made arrangements for guests to attend shows at nearby hotels. Often smaller colonies made their own entertainment, putting on skits, plays, and, most famously, performing mock weddings in which men and women cross-dressed. Children, many of whom stayed up in the mountains the entire eight-week season, made their own fun, playing in the woods, which were never too far off, or in one of the local streams. The Neversink River ran through the heart of the resort region, and before the mid-1950s provided hours of fun for swimmers and splashers. Competitive sports were common among children, but less so among adults, who preferred playing cards and mah-jongg. All in all, days of leisure involved little consumption, and, other than children's rambles in nearby woods or berry-picking outings, rather limited exploration of the environment beyond the colonies.[50]

Though a real diversity of accommodations persisted in the mountains, the largest hotels, led by Grossinger's and the Concord, became emblematic of the Catskills. Continuing competition forced hotels to seek any advantage in publicity. For Grossinger's this included the publication of a full-length book in 1952, Harold Taub's *Waldorf in the Catskills*, the title of which clearly indicated the high style the large hotel hoped to achieve. Taub's book, and a longer biography of Jennie Grossinger that appeared nearly twenty years later, were part of the hotel's extremely successful efforts to gain positive press. Both books recounted how Grossinger's evolved, becoming a country club in 1931 when its eighteen-hole golf course opened, and the addition of an Olympic-sized swimming pool in 1948. But the hotel and its publicists also kept an eye toward tradition, placing the Grossinger family and the homey atmosphere at the center of the resort's story.[51]

The Concord did not have the rich familial lore that made Grossinger's such a saleable product, but it did have the financial backing of Arthur Winarick. A Russian immigrant who arrived in New York in 1911, Winarick gained control of the Concord when its owners defaulted on a mortgage he held in 1935. Winarick had begun his career as a barber, but made himself wealthy by selling hair tonic and other salon products. Through the 1940s and 1950s, Winarick pumped his money into the Concord, developing what would become the largest Catskills hotel. After 1943, the Concord became a year-round resort. A 1955 feature in *Fortune* called the Concord the "Pleasure Dome in the Catskills," listing all its recreational features, which included golf, tennis, and swimming. In 1962, the Concord completed its second eighteen-hole golf course, called "the Monster," further solidifying its reputation as the premiere Catskills country club. Still, as the *Fortune* piece made clear, despite all the available outdoor activities, the real attractions "lie within the main building," especially in the dining room and in three separate nightclubs. By the 1960s, its cluster of high-rise buildings helped the Concord become a city unto itself.[52]

Ostensibly mountain retreats, the large hotels had grown away from their natural settings. The Concord, for example, once featured swimming in Lake Kiamesha, but by the 1950s guests were much more likely to swim in the indoor swimming pool. Indeed, several of the large hotels became well known for their artificial character. Between the lengthy meals, guests could ice skate in indoor rinks, shop in in-house stores, and even play tennis indoors. Capped by an evening in the casino, a day at one of the major resorts could leave guests without any contact with the mountain environment at all, save the fresh air. By the 1970s, even the fresh air became less important, as glassed-in walkways allowed guests at some hotels, like Grossinger's and Kutsher's, to move from building to building without having to go outside in inclement weather. Tania Grossinger was moved to comment that guests "could now spend a whole week in the country without ever going out for a breath of fresh air!" As early as 1955, Boroff had gone so far as to list the Concord's "assaults on the natural order"—innovations that took guests farther from a natural vacation. In addition to the indoor pool and year-round ice-skating, the Concord had become the first in America to make snow for its ski hill, extending the winter season.[53]

The big hotels didn't just compete through the building of new attractions and finer rooms; they also brought up long lists of celebrities, enticing them with free stays. These stars—entertainers, politicians, and sports figures—sometimes addressed the guests, sang a song, or gave some type of demonstration, but often they just came and made themselves visible, adding excitement to the hotel's atmosphere. In addition to the stars hired for the weekend shows, guests might also run into Nelson Rockefeller, Lucille Ball, or, later, Muhammad Ali. But the real stars were the entertainers, some of whom faithfully returned to the hotels where they got their starts. By the 1940s, the famed actor Eddie Cantor had developed a long relationship with Grossinger's, where he frequently stayed, performed, and provided wonderful publicity. There, in a staged event, Cantor "discovered" Eddie Fisher, a good-looking young man with a fine voice. Fisher's discovery in 1949 became a central piece of Catskills lore—emblematic of "the era." Other key events in Fisher's life also occurred at Grossinger's, including his 1955 wedding to Debbie Reynolds and his subsequent affair with Elizabeth Taylor, which became public during a rendezvous at the hotel.[54]

Eventually sports figures became important guests due to the attention they brought the hotels, as when the great female golfer Babe Didrikson visited Grossinger's in 1947. As early as the 1930s, some of the larger hotels had begun bringing up famous athletes, giving them free room and board in exchange for some small services, like exhibition performances, or simply for the publicity their presence brought. For thirty years a parade of prizefighters, baseball players, and golf's biggest names moved through Grossinger's, Kutsher's, and the Concord. In 1951, near the peak of the resorts' glory, Grossinger's attracted both Jackie Robinson and Rocky Marciano. In addition to hiring well-known golf pros, tennis pros, and swimming instructors, several of the larger hotels even sponsored their own basketball teams, recruiting college athletes and high school stars who both worked at the hotels and played games against each other throughout the summer. Kutsher's brought up a young Wilt Chamberlain and the Tamarack Lodge sponsored a team that featured a young Bob Cousey. Unfortunately, the glory years of Catskills basketball came to a rapid close after a 1951 point-shaving scandal rocked New York City's most prominent college basketball programs. Relationships between bookies and players had incubated in the mountains during the summer of 1950, when as many as 500 basketball players were on the payrolls of various Catskills hotels. Gambling on the games between the hotels had become routine, and unfortunately the possibility of larger paydays afforded by big-time college hoops proved too attractive for many players to pass up. After the scandal broke in 1951, with City College, Long Island University, New York University, and Manhattan College all under investigation, basketball in both New York City and the Catskills suffered a remarkable, lasting loss.[55]

In addition to Grossinger's and the Concord, a handful of other hotels participated in the great activities build-up. Kutsher's added to its sports facilities and its sport celebrity guests. The Nevele had its own golf course and a fine tower of modern rooms. The Raleigh, Brown's, and Brickman's all still drew full houses to their large resorts. However, smaller hotels had trouble keeping up, and even as the large hotels peaked in size and excitement, the region took on an air of depression. By 1955, near the apex of the Catskills' fame, Boroff could conclude that the modest hotels, which still mostly sold relaxation and cool, clean air, "simply do not offer enough." More tourists came to expect nightly shows, performed by some of the era's most famous entertainers, and resorts without large nightclubs began to falter. Some even closed, unable to keep pace with the capital investments of their neighbors.[56]

These changes in the mountain resorts resulted from changes in the city. As a group, Jewish tourists gained wealth in the postwar era; they could afford more and demanded more. Just as important, by the 1950s a much larger percentage of Jewish tourists arrived in the Catskills not for a respite from the crowds and intense heat of the Lower East Side or the South Bronx or Brownsville but from much more spacious Queens, Westchester County, Long Island, and the leafy suburbs of New Jersey. By 1957, Nassau County held nearly as many Jews as Manhattan, and Queens held more.[57] In other words, Catskills tourists were much less likely to be repelled by conditions at home and more likely to be attracted to offerings in the mountains, explaining why hotels had to offer more and more attractions. Beyond competing with each other, they were now competing with the suburbs themselves, and they had to be much more than just cool and pleasant. They had to be exciting—nearly urban. Without the entertainment and extensive recreation facilities, the mountains held little that most suburbs didn't already offer. By the 1960s, the most prosperous suburban Jews began to ask themselves, why should we leave our suburban country club for a week at a Catskills resort that offered a similar experience?

If the Borscht Belt represented an "attempt to build a Jewish Eden" in the mountains, as author Stefan Kanfer has described it, the building blocks clearly came from the city. The growth of the resort industry was a boon to Sullivan County, providing a strong tax base and employment opportunities, even if most positions were seasonal and poorly paid. Still, the resort economy was only partially attached to the mountains, since so much came directly from the city. This was particularly true of food, much of it kosher and more of it imported directly from city markets. Commuting husbands brought up treats and staples from the city, including deli items from trusted markets and cakes from favorite neighborhood bakeries. Paul Grossinger recalled that his father traveled down to the city twice a week until his death in 1964, to purchase supplies for the hotel, including fruits and vegetables at Washington Market. Irwin Richman recalled that to supply his bungalow business and feed his own family, his father "would do the bulk of our weekly shopping in the city and arrive with the trunk full of fruit, vegetables, groceries, and meat in an ice chest." The importation of fruits and vegetables, particularly, spoke to the changing nature of the tourists' relationship to the region. As tourists' experiences became less focused on the natural attributes of the countryside, tourists could actually begin to think the produce from urban markets superior to the fruits and vegetables from Sullivan County farms.[58]

The hotels certainly provided critical jobs for locals, both directly and indirectly, but even as the largest hotels became year-round resorts, downstate residents generally provided labor during the seasonal surge in employment. As the businesses grew, so did their staffs. The hotels hired young men as waiters and bellhops, usually Jewish college students who might provide some romance for young guests while working. Even the best jobs generally went to seasonal residents of the mountains, people who would spend their summer earnings far from the Catskills, including New York City teachers who took positions as camp counselors or athletic instructors to augment their modest salaries and provide their own families with lengthy vacations in the mountains. Some workers migrated between winter resorts in Florida and the summer resorts of the Catskills. Even many of the owners lived in the city during the off-season, leaving their properties to the oversight of caretakers.[59]

Other aspects of the city came to the mountains as well. During Prohibition, the city briefly exported organized crime, with the Catskills gaining some repute as a place for the dumping of bodies from mob hits. In 1931, the *Literary Digest* reported on "Gang Guns in the Catskills," and reprinted a political cartoon from the *Baltimore Sun* that depicted a gun-toting gangster looming over mountains, complete with barrels of illicit alcohol. Despite the spike in imported crime, however, other urban dis-amenities were more likely to reach the mountains. Traffic jams were commonplace along Route 17, especially before it was widened to four lanes in the 1950s. Even beyond the roads, crowds too gathered in the mountains, especially at entertainment venues and in the larger towns. In Liberty, Monticello, and Fallsburg, evenings featured crowded sidewalks and lines for the movie theaters. Beyond the movies, the entertainment was especially urban, with bits of vaudeville and Broadway transported, if often in altered form, onto the mountain stages. One entertainer remembered the crowds of the 1950s, especially on Saturday nights, when "the roads were so jammed with cars running from one hotel to another to see shows." During slower moments, vacationers maintained another urban habit—reading the New York City papers, including the Yiddish *Forward* and the *New York Times*. The local Sullivan County papers inspired much less interest.[60]

So complete was the transference of urbanity to Sullivan County that Jewish tourists could remain largely separated from the predominantly gentile local community. This was particularly true of the large hotels, where meals and entertainment were provided on the grounds, and guests could avoid interaction with gentiles, even if they cleaned the rooms. In the bungalow colonies, too, life could be remarkably segregated, with Jewish tourists interacting with other Jews, most connected to the city, but having little contact with local gentiles. According to Irwin Richman, in the Woodbourne area even the milk supply was segregated, with Jews using the Kanowitz brothers, who delivered their products seasonally, while local non-Jews used a year-round milkman. In Woodbourne, non-

Jews tended to shop at the Victory Market, while Jews frequented one of two groceries owned by Jews. This daily separation, undoubtedly preferred by almost everyone, allowed strong stereotypes to develop and persist within both groups. While Sullivan County saw its share of anti-Semitism, whatever discrimination existed in the mountains was not enough to discourage Jews from coming. Much less discussed, though probably just as important, Jews themselves developed stereotypes about locals, casting them as backward rural folk, and, using the disparaging Yiddish term *goyim*, labeling them as "others"—to be avoided. One frequent Catskills guest reminisced about a childhood warning about getting caught by "the Mountain People" when they went berry picking in the woods. "Sure enough, just like in the picture *Deliverance*, regular mountain people lived up there. They all seemed so big, with long full beards, dressed in overalls." One lengthy reminiscence of Catskills life casts non-Jewish locals in rather stark terms, using phrases such as "a goy up the road," and "the goyim weren't easy to find."[61]

Given this purposeful separation of Jews and non-Jews, and the importation of so much from the city—from vegetables to vaudeville—it seems reasonable to conclude that the local, gentile Catskills culture had very little influence over the "Jewish Eden" built by and for New York tourists. Still, by the 1920s Jewish tourism had become critical to Sullivan County's economy, affecting not just those who worked directly in the industry but everyone in the southern Catskills. Essentially every aspect of the region's economy felt the influence of tourism, from the growing population and tax base to the steady work in construction, plumbing, landscaping, auto repair, pumping gasoline, et cetera. Even as tourist dollars drove the economy, the region's reputation as the Borscht Belt gave the Catskills a national profile. Just as the city's reservoirs elevated Catskills water to international fame, Jewish resorts—and the many celebrated personalities who worked their way through them—heightened the Catskills' national reputation as a trendsetting tourist region. Though much of that reputation involved urban imports, from the outset the distinctive Catskills culture was a collaborative effort of local and urban residents, and even the most urban of contributions became naturalized over time, integrated into the local self-conception of Sullivan County.

By the 1970s, the "Jewish Eden" was in steep decline. Increasing wealth and transportation improvements combined to give New Yorkers many more vacation options beyond the Catskills. Automobiles, which had initially given the Sullivan County resorts a distinct advantage over the northern Catskills, now proved equally devastating to the Borscht Belt. At the same time, air travel became more affordable and common, and distant attractions gained at the expense of the nearby mountains. But perhaps more than anything, the changing residential conditions of New Yorkers themselves adversely affected the Catskills tourist industry. Tourists increasingly sought excitement in their vacations, experiences that greatly differed from their suburban lives—Vermont ski trips, Caribbean cruises, or the warm beaches of Florida in the winter; Europe, Cape Cod, or perhaps a tour of the American West in the summer. Just as important, residential air conditioning, increasingly popular in the 1960s, made the urban summer more tolerable. By then, it had become increasingly rare for families to flee the city for weeks at a time.[62]

Even before the worst of the decline set in, the Catskills had become a recognizable brand, conjuring images of a distinct hotel style, forms of entertainment, and even stereotypical guests. Despite continuing diversity among the resorts and those who visited them, most New Yorkers (both Jews and gentiles) held popular images of the Catskills: the heavy kosher food—the blintzes, stuffed cabbage, and chicken paprika; the hotels' garish appointments; and the gauche clientele. There were overbearing parents seeking just the right match for their daughters. There were stand-up comics delivering punch lines in Yiddish to tough crowds who had heard them all before. Perhaps this last part of the Catskills image was most important, for the Borscht Belt had long since become the great incubator for Jewish comedians.[63] With so many comics building their routines in the mountains, the Catskills themselves inevitably became part of the joke. As comedians continuously poked fun at individual guests, the hotels' cuisine, and other aspects of Catskills culture, they helped build the stereotypes that would eventually play a role in the demise of the resorts. As Cissie Blumberg lamented, comedians helped cement a negative impression of the Catskills, as "exceptions became the rule and the exaggerated descriptions became accepted as fact."[64]

These powerful and remarkably static images retarded the region's efforts to keep pace with tourists' changing tastes, preventing older hotels from attracting younger guests. After 1960, the Catskills resorts found themselves catering to an older generation that found comfort in consistency. As that generation passed, however, so too did the resorts. Irvin Richman described the decline of his family's bungalow business with the simple phrase "eventually our clientele literally died away." The younger generations of Jews were more secular—less kosher—and much more likely to marry outside the faith. In addition, in the late twentieth century, more and more women worked, even after having children, essentially ending all possibility for summer-long vacations for families. In sum, New York's Jews shared a decreasing interest in the traditional vacations the Catskills offered. In response, the hotels attempted to diversify their clientele, especially by attracting conventions, even of groups dominated by gentiles. At the larger hotels, those with their own golf courses and other amenities, this did at least partially succeed, but by the 1970s few could fail to notice the region's decline.[65]

The large capital investments of the 1950s required year-round operations and decreased the largest hotels' flexibility. As hotels failed to draw, they quickly accumulated debt. Many closed, bankrupt. Some burned, perhaps for insurance money. Even bungalow colonies changed hands, as owners could no longer make them pay. By the 1980s, most of the small towns looked worn out, somewhat abandoned, although this was certainly not uncommon in upstate New York, or the rest of rural America, for that matter. Still, the Jewish Catskills culture—the Borscht Belt—slowly died. Last rites were read in 1998, the year the already much-diminished Grossinger's gave up altogether, along with the Pines and the 1,200–room Concord. The Concord's closing put its last 400 employees out of work and left many of them without homes, since they lived in the hotel itself. Ruins of the golden age now litter the region. Some of the old hotels are still standing, though barely; others are gone, evidenced only by foundations. Handball courts peek out from overgrown fields; hydrangeas and other perennials mark once-tended flowerbeds. Even to the least observant traveler, this region's ruins are apparent, evidence that urbanites have once again redefined the mountains—now as a place that use to be. As Phil Brown poetically concluded during a 1993 tour of the region, "Everywhere is the tale of dead resorts that once teemed with life."[66]

The death of the Borscht Belt has brought great lamentation and nostalgia among New York Jews, especially those who trace many of their fondest childhood memories back to the mountains. Publishers have issued a wave of memoirs. A number of novels, too, have appeared, describing lost moments and the struggle to make peace with the altered Catskills landscape. One of these novels, Eileen Pollack's *Paradise, New York*, opens in the 1970s amid the rapid decline around Monticello. A joke relates the prevalence of arson in the area, as owners attempt to recoup something from their lifelong investments in the hotel business. Later in the novel, the narrator tells her fellow New York University students that she was raised in the Catskills. "The Catskills?" they respond, "You mean they're still there?"[67] Of course, what these students really mean to ask is whether or not there are still people in the Catskills, for surely the mountains could not disappear. But, then again, New York tourists had moved the Catskills southward only decades before. Perhaps now, through their neglect, New York tourists could make them disappear altogether, removed from the nation's cultural map.

The nostalgia for the lost Catskills culture has grown in response to the end of the golden age—the era that most memoirs and remembrances recount. Many participants in that culture gather each year in the Catskills, at meetings organized by the Catskills Institute, created to "keep alive the Jewish Catskills legacy."[68] The sense of loss is personal for many, especially those who spent childhoods in the mountains—for whom the Catskills will be forever the place of adolescence. This golden age—both in the lives of those who stayed there and in the resort culture itself—thus provides a lasting definition of the mountains. For these observers, significant changes in the region can only represent diminishment. For this reason, the growth of Hasidic and ultra-Orthodox Jewish resorts in the Catskills gives few outside those communities much consolation. As the persistence of Sunday evening traffic headed back to the city on Route 17 ably attests, the resort region has hardly failed altogether. Thousands of ultra-Orthodox Jews and Hasidim have replaced the more secular Jews of the 1950s and 1960s. One culture has eroded, much to the lament of its participants, but it has been replaced. One scholar of Hasidic life in Brooklyn has gone so far as to claim that they have saved the "Jewish Mountains." Hasidim and other devoutly religious Jews were not part of the golden age, however, and their mere presence now diminishes the sense of ownership developed in the earlier generation. The spread of religious camps, *mikvahs, glatt* kosher shops, and other changes in the cultural landscape mark the ongoing redefinition of the "Jewish Mountains."[69]

Of course, conflicting definitions of the mountains have always coexisted. The secular Jews of the Borscht Belt's heyday saw the mountains differently than local gentiles, who always constituted the majority of the region's year-round population. In his 1975 novel, *Summer on a Mountain of Spices*, Harvey Jacobs pointed to the quintessential difference between year-round residents and the mostly city-connected Jews. "There was a rumor that Monticello existed all year round," Jacobs wrote while describing the Catskills as the novel's protagonist, Harry Craft, drove into the mountains.

> Believers could point to a school, a library, a fire department, a police department, the Broadway and Rialto theatres, D. Diamond's Market, two drugstores, a department store, the New York Deli, and Burton's Sweete Shoppe. There were citizens, four churches, two doctors, a hospital, a graveyard, a ball field, even a small shul. Still, if the place had a winter life Harry Craft never saw it.[70]

Here lay the greatest division within the community. Some knew the Catskills only as a summer playground, a home away from home. For others, of course, it was their only home, one that "had a winter life" and, indeed, had a "life" before the rise of the Borscht Belt. That life has persisted beyond its fall, though clearly in altered form.

The rise and fall of the Sullivan County resort region reveals much about Jewish New Yorkers' singular Americanization experience. New York Jews developed their own relationship to the mountains, reflecting the distinctiveness of their experiences in the city. Over time, as Jews became more secular and suburban, and their lives less distinctive, their relationship to the mountains became less distinctive too. Changing metropolitan culture, especially related to growing affluence and suburbanization, reshaped tourists' expectations and experiences in the mountains, which in turn reshaped conceptions of the countryside and the value of nature. In this way, the once-crowded hotels of the Borscht Belt have much in common with the now-crowded beaches of Boca Raton.

—ᴧᴧ— *Chapter 7* —ᴧᴧ—

A Suburb of New York

Truly, man made the city, and after he became sufficiently civilized, not afraid of solitude, and knew on what terms to live with nature, God promoted him to life in the country.

—John Burroughs, 1886

I'm going on down to Yasgur's farm
I'm going to join in a rock 'n' roll band
I'm going to camp out on the land
And try and get my soul free

—Joni Mitchell, 1970

E vidence of decline in the Borscht Belt began to accumulate by the late 1950s, but it had become apparent in the northern Catskills resort region as early as 1918. In reporting on his tour through the mountains that year, T. Morris Longstreth observed that increasing mobility allowed New Yorkers to choose vacation destinations much further than the nearby mountain range, meaning "the Catskills are passed by." With decreasing activity in the mountains, Longstreth concluded, "They are actually getting wilder."[1] Despite this growing wildness, to Longstreth the old, sublime vision of the Catskills was quite dead. The Catskills were no longer superlative; the city no longer required that they be so. "If one visits [the Catskills] as one may visit the Canadian Rockies, in the expectation of having all of one's big emotions drawn out and played upon, there will be hideous disappointment," Longstreth wrote. "There is nothing big about the Catskills. They are as comfortable as home. They were created, not for observation cars, but for bungalow porches."[2] Longstreth's use of the passive voice allows us to misinterpret this quote. No doubt he meant that God, or perhaps Nature, had created the mountains, but we might just as easily substitute New York City as the unidentified creator, since urban tourists *had* created the mountains for observation cars, in the era of railroad vacations and grand hotels, and when that moment had passed, other tourists created mountains more suitable for bungalow porches. And, of course, the demands of city tourists had created the porches, too. As Longstreth's commentary made clear, even as the mountains shrank along with New Yorkers' expectations, rapidly retreating from their apex as the American Switzerland, urbanites would still make use of the Catskills. And those new uses would bring a series of new changes to the mountains.

Over the first half of the twentieth century, road building at the county and state levels allowed travelers to choose cars and buses instead of railroads as they made their vacation plans. Indeed, by 1950 ten different bus companies offered service to and through the Catskills, creating what one tour guide called a "comprehensive network of bus lines." On the other hand, the Ulster and Delaware, still in operation in the 1950s, no longer made the tourist maps, since by then it carried only freight, and not enough of that to keep it alive much longer. Like all the region's rail lines, the Ulster and Delaware suffered a long, slow death.[3] In replacing rail transportation, automobiles would reorganize the nation as thoroughly as had the railroads. Under the new regime, some places would prosper—those along the highways—and others would decline. The massive road building of the early twentieth century would permanently alter the relationship between city and country, redrawing the economic map. It also changed the experiences of tourists, who would now view the countryside in a new way, for automobiles would be much more flexible and liberating than the railroad. Altogether, the roads and the cars (and the passengers they served) would recreate the nation's landscape, with changes as evident in the Catskills as anywhere in the country. First the automobile would allow vacationers to reshape the Catskills tourist industry, especially by encouraging different types of visits. Then automobiles, and the many roads government built to make them more valuable, allowed New Yorkers to alter the state's residential landscape, even in the mountains.

Together these two trends—the rapid reorganization of the region's tourism and the spread of suburban-style residential patterns—placed new stresses on the Catskills economy and landscape. Both trends also altered the calculus of collaboration between city folk and local residents, even as the lines between those categories continued to blur. Still, if many locals simultaneously lamented the decline in tourism and the rise of second-home construction—and thus criticized the power of city residents over the mountains—they also found eager allies among these "outsiders" in their efforts to slow changes taking place in the Catskills. The dual threats of economic decline and suburban-style development fed a fear that the Catskills would lose their distinctiveness, their authenticity, built over the previous 150 years. Suburban sameness loomed in the countryside; urban blight crept through the faltering tourist towns. By the late twentieth century, a movement for both historic preservation and environmental conservation had become the most apparent component of the collaboration between city and country residents. Both local residents and urbanites expressed an interest in maintaining the Catskills as the home of a distinct culture and a treasured landscape.

The modern environmental movement that evolved in the second half of the twentieth century owed much to this gathering confluence of interest among those who would protect the countryside, this conservative movement to protect the virtues of country living by protecting the country landscape. Roads and automobiles allowed tourists and second-home owners to experience nature in new ways, but, as historian Paul Sutter has made clear, this new form of transportation also posed serious threats to the countryside. The most serious threat was not the cars themselves nor the ribbons of asphalt laid through rural regions but the development that always seemed to follow. As the metropolis exploded outward, into new suburbs and exurbs, leery observers could stand along a beautiful mountain roadway and anticipate the arrival of new homes, new residents, and the old, familiar problems of urban living.[4]

Although a number of causal factors worked changes on the mountains in the twentieth century, the growing importance of the automobile led the list, especially as the nature of tourism adjusted to this new mode of travel. A 1939 advertising campaign, created by the Barlow Advertising Agency for New York's Department of Environmental Conservation, gave a hint of the changes auto travel would bring. Designed to sell the state's tourist attractions to Midwesterners planning a drive to the World's Fair in New York City, the Barlow campaign invited travelers to pass through New York State rather than Pennsylvania. Print ads, to appear in the larger Midwestern newspapers and some national magazines, featured in turn Niagara Falls, the Finger Lakes, the Adirondacks, Thousand Islands, the historic Hudson Valley, the historic Mohawk Valley, and the Catskills. The Catskills advertisement hit familiar themes in the region's tourism, selling historical associations, wilderness appreciation, and even the beauty of the city's largest reservoir. Altogether, the campaign served as a primer in Catskills history. One Barlow advertisement, appearing in *Time* magazine, read in part:

> See the Catskill Mountains. Quaint 'Land in the Sky' where Rip Van
> Winkle used to hunt. . . . See the world of ancient fantasy, history and
> beauty that lies in the shadows of the Catskill Mountains. . . . Cross
> the bridge where Ichabod Crane fled the Headless Horseman. Sit on
> the hollowed stone where Rip van Winkle made his bed.

A radio ad that ran in six Midwestern cities featured William G. Howard,
Director of the State Division of Land and Forests, who touted the state's
wilderness resources. After starting with the Adirondacks, he described
the Catskills, where "you will find many a rocky gorge and glen whose
silence is broken only by rushing cascades." Howard encouraged visitors to camp in the mountains, which was then permitted anywhere on
state lands for up to three nights. Another radio ad, featuring only the
Catskills, connected the "romance, beauty, grandeur" of the mountains
with "a superb motor highway along the rim of the mountains," constructed "for your pleasure and enjoyment." The motor highway connected visitors with the past as it wound "among the gorges, glens and
waterfalls where Rip Van Winkle once lay down to sleep." It passed through
a "region famed in song and story, evoking memories of Hendrik Hudson and his crew," a region "enriched by Washington Irving's tales." If
this were not enough, the advertisement added, "You can park your car
beside the spurting geysers of Ashokan—the great reservoir that supplies
the water you'll-drink-and-bathe-in-when-you-reach-New-York."[5]

Although the Barlow campaign relied heavily on historical associations, attempting to sell the Catskills along familiar lines, the World's Fair
advertising reveals a remarkable change in tourist industry marketing.
The Barlow Agency had divided the state into saleable parts, each with
some marketable identity. In addition to the recognizable geographical
features, such as the Catskills, Adirondacks, and the Finger Lakes, some
regions clustered around cultural attributes, including the Capital District,
composed of a number of small cities around Albany. The Leatherstocking Region rightly included Cooperstown, home of the Leatherstocking novelist James Fenimore Cooper, but also the rolling farm
country of central New York, which otherwise lacked a marketable identity. With tourists traveling by automobile, advertisers could no longer
sell the points of interest—like Niagara Falls or the Mountain House—
that had sufficed in the era of railroad travel. Rather, the campaign bun-
dled together entire regions, creating some out of whole cloth, and then
gave each a theme or identity, attempting to satisfy auto tourists who

could make more frequent stops on meandering excursions. This might be among the most dramatic reconceptualizations of space encouraged by the adoption of automobile travel. Of course, the Catskills had long existed as a region, one at first defined by the resorts that grew among its peaks and the railroads that ran through its valleys. Henceforth, however, the Catskill Region would be just one of many in the state, and no place would be without its separate regional identity.

The Barlow ads revealed in the broadest stroke tourism's reorganization, but they did not address the reorganization of residence that automobiles and roads permitted. Over the twentieth century, and especially after the prosperity of the 1950s and 1960s, parts of the Catskills gradually became a suburb of rapidly expanding metropolitan New York. Obviously most late-century mountain residents did not commute into Manhattan for work, but by that point the Catskills had become a residential retreat from the metropolis, especially through the construction of second homes. More than seasonally utilized vacation homes, which were common by the late 1800s, these new houses held more permanent residents, who could afford long and perhaps irregular commutes to the city. Over the course of the century, more New Yorkers retreated from the city even more completely, including Bob Dylan and a host of other musicians and artists. With unplanned growth, subdivisions of low-density housing, increasing traffic, and even parking problems, parts of the Catskills began to look less rural and more suburban—though thick woods could hide much of the development. By the early 1990s, however, the trend was unmistakable. *National Geographic* author Cathy Newman might have exaggerated somewhat when she claimed, "Nearly everywhere you look, fields once flecked with Holsteins now sprout houses," but sprawl had clearly reached the Catskills. Suburbanization led to physical changes in the mountains, but the cultural changes may have been even more evident, for in a variety of ways the metropolis had made a more permanent home in the mountains, sparking fears that the Catskills landscape might succumb to suburban monotony.[6]

The cultural turn toward cars and highways that altered both recreational habits and residential choices occurred through a very long process, beginning even before the explosion in auto ownership in the 1920s. As early as 1907, New York State already counted 45,000 registered vehicles. A year later, the state committed to building thirty-seven highways, and set aside $50 million for the task. Even beyond this significant investment, the construction of an automobile infrastructure would require massive investments from the state, which had begun providing funds for road building in 1899, and from the individual counties and towns that were responsible for most construction. Roads fair enough for carriage travel could not support automobiles, especially as technology advanced, allowing automobiles to reach higher speeds when road conditions permitted. Seeing road improvement as a potential economic boon, governments undertook the task eagerly.[7]

Ostensibly the purpose of heavy state investment in road improvement was to connect farmers to markets. The new roads, generally made of macadam, a compacted crushed stone that resisted rutting and erosion, did indeed hold out the promise of improving rural lives by providing access to more distant cities. As important as this transformation was to rural New York, it could hardly match the influence of the reverse connection—the improved access granted urbanites seeking rural retreats. Indeed, even before significant road improvements, auto touring became a national rage, as auto-owning tourists set out to explore the American countryside. Most famously, tourists headed south to Florida and to the open spaces of the West. Many came east, as well. Unfortunately for Catskills business owners, however, their small region held little special value for extraregional tourists, who were more likely to seek out picturesque New England and the higher mountain ranges of the East.[8] Certainly many tourists did arrive from distant places, including an "automobile party" from Cleveland that spent several days in Haines Falls in 1905, though its arrival at this early date was unusual enough to merit media attention.[9]

Although auto tourists would eventually have access to nearly every place in the East, in the early 1900s they tended to seek out a balance between good roads and interesting destinations. Early on, the Catskills competed well. Even before the passage of the 1908 bond, the state had built a new road out of Saugerties and into the Catskills, connecting to Woodstock, Bearsville, and Mink Hollow, and providing a third major auto route into the mountains. One of the other routes into the Catskills, out of Kingston, still bore the scars of its bluestone origins, with the heavily rutted flagstone "making all kinds of pleasure traffic decidedly uncomfortable," according to the *New York Times*. Through the mountains themselves, however, above the region from which bluestone traveled by cart, a macadam road provided smoother travel from Mount Pleasant through Phoenicia and on to Fleischmanns. When New York City built the Ashokan Reservoir, it also rebuilt the state roads through part of the Esopus Valley, making the auto route from Kingston all the more attractive in the 1910s. By the early 1920s, the New York State Conservation Commission, charged with maintaining the Forest Reserve, published a "Catskills Highways" map that identified all the state roads in the region, along with other "improved" roads. The map revealed a region laced with acceptable auto roads.[10]

Tourists' growing reliance on auto roads rather than railroads would change much in the mountains, but one fact remained unchanged: the Catskills economy would thrive only if the mountains attracted large numbers of tourists from New York and other cities in the region. At first, they seemed to do so. In 1907, the New York Times listed the members of several "automobile parties" touring the Catskills, including two from Brooklyn and a third from Manhattan. A 1910 story in the Times described an "Attractive Trip, Covering Seven Days," passing "Through the Heart of the Catskills." The Times described the fine state roads through Woodstock, Phoenicia, Pine Hill, and north through Stamford. Although the article no doubt provided wonderful publicity for a region hoping to cater to the new type of tourist, it also included evidence of a growing problem. The trip proceeded through the southern Adirondacks, into Vermont's Green Mountains, and back to the city through the Berkshires. All this territory was to be covered in a week, meaning that tourists had little time to stop anywhere to sightsee, or, more important to those dependent on the tourist industry, to spend money. The macadam roads that brought automobilists into the mountains would as quickly lead them out.[11]

Just as increasing automobile travel gradually reshaped the region's tourist industry, it also reshaped individual experiences. Even before large numbers of automobiles began streaming over the countryside, their arrival brought some consternation to those who feared the contraption's intrusion—its noise, smoke, and its oft-terrifying effect on horses, with which it had to share the road. Cars probably had a greater impact on those who drove them, however. In 1918, Frank Hill, a Californian who tramped with his wife through the Shandaken Catskills for several days, reported on his successful journey in Outing magazine. After setting out on foot from Catskill Landing, on the Hudson, the couple initially feared they would not get away from the crowds in the mountains. But after passing by the resorts of Palenville, Haines Falls, Tannersville, and

Hunter, they found deep woods, ample trout, and the famed berries of the Catskills. Hill noted that the summer boarders they saw were "lazy, never adventuring past the town soda fountains." When the tourists did leave "their front porches," they did so in automobiles, and Hill assumed they stuck close to the roads. In any case, Hill concluded that he and his wife, tramping as had Burroughs and Cole, "had far more intimacy with [the Catskills'] beauty than the invading automobilist, who could not leave the roads for the quiet of the hills themselves."[12]

This last assertion was inaccurate, of course. Automobilists were just as capable of leaving the roadside and taking to forest trails as those who had taken carriage rides in previous years. Indeed, just three years after Hill's article appeared, *Outing* ran a lengthy essay from roadway tourists—motorcyclists—who "Buzzed and Bumped Along the Catskill Highways." Traveling along Route 2, heading north out of Phoenicia through Stony Clove, Roy Lewis received his "first hint" of the "intimacy and personality of these famous hills." Lewis found the rough macadam road distracting, but his reports on the scenery indicate how much he saw. In advising those who would drive to Kaaterskill, Lewis recommended turning onto a "wood road." "Follow it and stop where you will," he wrote. Here was the real advantage of automobile travel. Compared to carriage rides, much more ground could be covered each day, and compared to railroads, the travel was much more flexible, allowing travelers greater liberty in designing and improvising trips that suited their interests.[13]

In recounting his trip, Lewis also pointed out the challenge hotel operators would face in the automobile age. In traveling from Phoenicia to Kaaterskill, Lewis passed through Tannersville and Haines Falls, which he determined "doubtless have reasons for being so famous," but, he concluded, "the motorist is likely to pass on quickly." Early auto tourists were unlikely to find the great hotels attractive. The dress was too formal, the dining room hours too restricted. Some hotels even required the purchase of multiple meals under the American plan, an arrangement that greatly limited flexibility in travel. As historian Warren Belasco has argued, those who took to the open roads in the first decades of automobiling generally desired the greater liberty afforded by camping out. Others probably chose less formal boardinghouses and small country inns.[14] As early as 1909, the *New York Times* observed, "the multiplication of motor cars of moderate cost has undoubtedly injured to some extent the business of the Summer resorts." Owners of the larger resorts, the reporter claimed, would have to adapt to attract automobilists—"to arrange automobile meetings and mild road contests for prizes, try to cater as politely as possible to the week-end parties in motor cars, to provide garage facilities for them, and attract them by 'special rates.'" Eventually, hotels around the nation would seek the approval of the American Automobile Association, which recognized accommodations that provided proper facilities for automobilists and their cars.[15]

While encouraging restraint among critics of automobiles, some of whom were at the time attacking the technology as the bane to civilization, the *Times* accurately predicted that cars would spell the demise of summer resorts that catered to season-long guests. As early as 1912, the *Times* described the transition underway: "Where in past years, families spent June, July, and August at some resort, today these families spend their vacations touring the country, enjoying the scenery, stopping wherever their fancy desires, spending a day here, three days there, or a week at some place whence trips may be made through interesting country."[16] While some tourists would stick with the older habit of long stays in the mountains, the new tourist culture threatened to devastate Catskills tourism.

If the flexibility of automobile travel allowed the "fancy" of drivers to determine where to pull off the road, early cars also required frequent stops. This was especially true when autos' passenger compartments were open—when the noise of the car and dirt from unpaved or poorly paved roads could rapidly wear down drivers and passengers. The weather too could force stops, as auto tourists sought shelter from rain. Even as cars improved, and as most passenger compartments became enclosed, touring autos still required frequent attention—stops to refill gas tanks, check oil, or to tinker with famously fickle engines. In 1912, by one estimate, the 110–mile trip from New York to Catskill could be "easily made in six hours," meaning motorists averaged less than twenty miles per hour.[17] This mode of transportation, then, led to a re-creation of roadside environments, as popular routes gathered filling stations, restaurants, and eventually motels, where tourists could purchase needed services. In addition, country routes filled with turnouts and scenic overlooks, where auto tourists might simply take a break from the road.[18]

By the 1920s, New York State had laced the Catskills with fine roads, and auto touring only gained in popularity as both automobiles and roads improved.[19] Auto tourists could create their own "circuit tour" through the mountains, traversing much of the region in just two days. If the quick trip allowed only "glimpses of Catskill scenery," as the *New York Times* inadvertently suggested, it also allowed tourists to take in many sights quickly. Side trips could lead tourists up Mount Utsayantha, near Stamford, where a "good road" reached the summit, or perhaps through historic Kingston, which contained a remarkable number of eighteenth-century structures, including the old Senate House, built in 1776. Unlike their railroad-bound counterparts, auto tourists could also easily combine a trip to the mountains with several stops in the lower Hudson Valley, including West Point and Storm King, as well as the Palisades Interstate Park, opened in 1900 and greatly expanded thereafter. By 1919, the Palisades Park included a fifteen-mile parkway, which would continue to grow, and free campsites near Bear Mountain, on a large tract of land donated to the state by the Harriman family.[20]

In 1920, the Page Company published *A Wonderland of the East*, its latest edition in the "See America First" series. A travelogue of several auto tours taken by the author, William Copeman Kitchin, the book included rich descriptions of the lakes and mountains of New England and eastern New York. On his New York tours, Kitchin departed from his Schenectady home, describing numerous interesting stops along his routes, and so in the process created a series of chapters that presaged the Barlow advertising campaign that featured the various regions of New York nearly twenty years later. First Kitchin traveled through the Mohawk Valley, a region rich in historical associations, especially relating to the Revolutionary War. In a separate chapter, Kitchin covered Cooperstown and the region around, where he provided some background on Cooper's novels and the cultural value of these literary associations.[21]

Kitchin's chapter on the Catskills included descriptions of "Lake Ashokan" and the "Susquehanna and Delaware Valleys," but, not surprisingly given his interest in cultural and historical associations, Kitchin began this tour at the Mountain House. To describe the site, he borrowed the words of Bayard Taylor, who had visited the region eighty years earlier. In this way, Kitchin's guide to the region opened just as so many others had since the appearance of tour guides in the mid-1800s. Thereafter, however, Kitchin's work dramatically diverged from those that came before. He described the famed view from Pine Orchard, but said almost nothing of the equally famed hotel. Indeed, he wrote almost nothing about any hotel, for Kitchin was on a motor camping trip, one of several he had taken through the region, beginning as early as 1916. During some of his previous trips, Kitchin and his wife had toured "in a more conventional way," attempting to stay at the region's hotels. But given the vagaries of road conditions and weather, not to mention the unpredictability of personal touring interests, the Kitchins found hotel reservations too restrictive. Kitchin also complained, "it was sometimes impossible to have . . . breakfast served early enough" at the hotels to allow them to get underway "at the desired hour." Thus, by 1919 the Kitchins had taken to auto camping exclusively, seeking out roadside property on which they might assemble their "water-proofed auto-tent" and fire up their "simple cooking outfit."[22]

Finding "there is no lack of good camping sites along rivers and lakes in shady groves," the Kitchins drove through the mountains unencumbered by lodging concerns, or, for that matter, expenses. With their own camping equipment and provisions packed in their automobile, the Kitchins enjoyed the freedom of the road and minimal costs. Their favorite Catskills campsite was nothing more than a private field along Esopus Creek with an open gate, which the Kitchins called "Camp Esopus." Here the Kitchins camped for free, starting a cooking fire in the shelter of an ash grove. On a Saturday in July 1919, the Kitchins were joined at Camp Esopus by a family from Oneonta and a party from near Newark, New Jersey, which had "made the run" up to the Catskills that afternoon. In the informal campground, like so many others springing up around the nation, the tourists made themselves at home as best they could, some sleeping on fold-out cots, others on their car seats, and the Kitchins, already quite skilled at motor camping, on a mattress they laid out under their tent. The Kitchins even drove nails into the trees around their camp, on which they might "hang towels and cooking utensils." Upon leaving the camp, Kitchin noted to his wife, "We shall never again find a place like this." But, of course, the couple would continue their search, as was the habit of auto tourists.[23]

Kitchin's description of auto camping, with minimal equipment and limited expectations, illustrated the development of a new relationship between tourists and natural landscapes. As Paul Sutter argues, "Auto-campers turned to the open road to escape from the ease of modern living and to recreate older domestic routines lost to modernization." For these tourists, "Nature was a place where one cooked over an open fire rather than a stove, where one had to find water from its source rather than turning on a tap." In "roughing it" even while living out of the most modern of technologies, the automobile, early auto campers, and the many campers who would follow in subsequent generations, helped strengthen the urban conception of the countryside as a place where one might step back in time, experience the past through rituals long since lost to urban life.[24]

That the Kitchins and other auto tourists could pass through the mountains spending so little money did not bode well for the Catskills business owners. Neither did the rapid pace of their journey. Having seen Cairo and East Windham on their first day touring the mountains, the Kitchins spent the second driving around the Ashokan Reservoir, which they claimed was beginning to be called "Lake Ashokan"—part of the process by which the reservoir had been naturalized into the Catskills landscape. Kitchin himself noted that the dam and the circumnavigating road were "so completely in harmony with the setting of the green-sloped mountains," and that the artificial lake and the aerating fountains had already joined the list of natural attractions in the mountains. As beautiful as the Ashokan was, however, it didn't cause the Kitchins to delay their tour long. Following Kitchin's dictum that ideal auto camping allowed one to "see a maximum amount of country in a given length of time," the couple spent their second night outside the Catskills, along the Delaware River near Hancock. Here again they camped on private property, having received permission from the owners. In the end, the Kitchins had successfully toured the Catskills, appreciated its great scenic beauty, and seen several of its famed locations. In sum, they had spent just two days in the mountains, and, more important to the tourist industry, they had spent very little money in the process. Here was good evidence of how auto tourism would begin to transform the mountains.[25]

Other auto tourists did stay longer, of course, and spend more money, a trend the region very much hoped to cultivate, especially through the building and advertising of good roads. State routes through the mountains gained attractive names, including the Mohican Trail, which followed the Esopus to Pine Hill, then climbed over the mountain to Margaretville. It then circled back to the north through Roxbury, Grand Gorge, Prattsville, and Windham. The Mohican Trail, really three different state routes, thus provided a fine road through the mountains, allowing for pleasant drives through some of the most scenic parts of the region. It also provided good access to the villages of Windham, Acra, and Cairo, which had never had good rail service and so benefited greatly from the improved roads. Another named route, the Rip Van Winkle Trail, wound up Kaaterskill Clove and then along the Schoharie Creek through Hunter and on to Prattsville. The route names connected this new means of touring to the region's past—both real and imagined—confirming the sense that traveling out of the city meant traveling back in time.[26]

In addition to labeling the major route through the Greene County Catskills, Rip Van Winkle's name graced the Hudson River bridge between Catskill and Hudson, completed in 1935. Part of the heavy investment in new roadways in the 1930s, the Rip Van Winkle Bridge promised to bring more tourists to the region, connecting the Catskills with the Albany Post Road, which had taken on the U.S. Highway designation of Route 9. Just as surely, however, it gave those on the western side of the river greater access to the Berkshires and beyond. The bridge became yet another piece in a great new infrastructure that allowed tourists to scramble about the East on weekend jaunts or longer "runs" through the countryside.[27]

Clearly, and tellingly, the Catskills connection to Rip Van Winkle did not fade over the twentieth century, revealing just how naturalized Irving's work had become, how central it remained to local residents' thoughts about their mountains. In the early 1950s, *New York Times* correspondent Bernard Kalb authored two lengthy pieces on the "Vacationland Rip Van Winkle Built." "If you are anywhere in Ulster or Greene for the summer," Kalb wrote, "you become a van Winkle expert as casually as you acquire a suntan." Palenville had even erected a sign claiming to be "Home of Rip van Winkle." Unfortunately for the northern Catskills, Rip's powers had faded, as had those of many of the region's other historical associations. "Seen through an automobile window," Kalb wrote, "the Catskill towns don't qualify as sleepy; they seem to be voiceless, in fact, as though they had been suddenly emptied of people." For Kalb, the northern Catskills, still eager to market itself through its distinctive history, had seemingly faded into the past altogether.[28]

Tourism in the north did persist, of course, even in its diminished form, and the region did develop some new attractions. Like other rural entrepreneurs around the nation, some Catskills residents attempted to create roadside attractions that might capture dollars from passing tourists. Like motels and service stations, these attractions were also part of the new American roadside landscape. The most important such attraction in the Catskills began in 1933, when Roland Lindemann, owner of a farm outside Palenville, enclosed part of his property, filling it with white-tailed deer. He then charged tourists to stop, pet his domesticated animals (including donkeys and sheep), and watch the deer as they browsed on the farm. Lindemann's attraction, the Catskill Game Farm, steadily grew, adding more and more species (especially exotic animals, such as llamas) and offering refreshments to customers. Despite these changes, the game farm continued to give tourists an opportunity to touch rural life, petting the animals, feeding the deer, and observing their care.[29]

In addition to the construction of roadside attractions, beginning in the 1930s Catskills residents added winter sports facilities to expand its tourist economy. The first Catskills ski center grew in Woodland Valley, near Phoenicia. Built on private and public lands, through the hard work of the Civilian Conservation Corps in 1934, the Jay H. Simpson Memorial Ski Slope (named for a member of the family over whose property the initial run passed) opened during the winter of 1935. The very next year, the New York Central, which had purchased the failing Ulster and Delaware, operated a Snow Train, delivering skiers and their equipment near the base of the mountain. Although the train undoubtedly increased the use of the slopes, it also made it possible for visitors to take a Sunday morning train to Phoenicia and return to the city that same evening. Another Snow Train brought passengers up on Friday evening and returned them Saturday. Either way, the mountains had gained a good number of new tourists, but locals would find it difficult to earn a living from them.[30]

The growth of winter sports in the 1930s, a national trend, did have the effect of making the Catskills a multiseason vacation region. Increased visitation in Phoenicia and Woodstock—which developed its own small ski slope, a large toboggan run, and a large skating rink—transformed those communities "into throbbing, colorful boom towns," at least according to the *Stamford Mirror-Record*. Seeking to expand the use of the state forest lands, the Conservation Department planned a series of investments in winter sports facilities, especially trails designed for telemark skiing, a sport imported from Scandinavia. Telemarking allowed a combination of downhill and cross-country skiing, ideal for the long, narrow trails that passed through the mountains.[31]

After the success of the Phoenicia development, the state sought even greater improvements, hoping to build larger facilities and serve a larger public. In 1949, the state opened Belleayre Ski Center on state land, a development that required an amendment to the state constitution, since the land had been designated "forever wild." The amendment limited how wide ski trails could be, but it did allow the state to remove swaths of forests. Despite the limitations, the greater elevation and the construction of the state's first ski lift gave the Belleayre Center advantages over other, smaller slopes. However, New York continued to lose tourist dollars as an increasingly demanding skiing public sought out the higher, snowier mountains of Vermont and New Hampshire, a trend that convinced the state legislature to allot $15,000 for a study of the problem. As a partial result of the study, and continued pressure from organizations such as the Rip Van Winkle Ski Association, organized in 1956 to gain support for new Greene County ski slopes, the state continued to invest in its public facilities, such as Belleayre in the Catskills and White Face and Gore in the Adirondacks. It also permitted private investment in new ski resorts in Hunter and Windham, developments that required an additional change in the state constitution, since they too lay within the state forest. By the early 1960s, the Windham and Hunter slopes began to reshape the northern Catskills, with new motels and lodges clustering near the facilities, catering to tourists arriving over busy, snowy weekends.[32] The ongoing evolution of the ski industry had a variety of effects in the Catskills. Enthusiasts developed better skills, purchased better equipment, and demanded more challenging slopes. By 1955, after the opening of Belleayre and other modern facilities in nearby mountains, the Phoenicia Ski Center had become outdated. It operated only on weekends and holidays, and one reporter called it "a homey type of set-up," a clear indication that it had fallen off the list of desirable destinations for urban skiers. Eventually it could no longer attract even enough of the local market and closed in 1978.[33]

Try as it might, the Catskills tourist industry could not innovate itself back to prosperity. In 1946, concerned businessmen created the Central Catskills Association to boost the economy from Shandaken to Margaretville, along Route 28. Toward this end, the association published an annual guide to the region in the 1950s. Along with the traditional flowery portraits of the individual towns, including Pine Hill and Phoenicia, the eighty-page pamphlet featured an essay on the Belleayre Ski Center in Highmount, which had already become an important attraction. The most interesting essay, however, came at the end of the guide, under the headline "Central Catskills is now a New York Suburb via the Thruway." Thruway construction had begun between Saugerties and Catskill, an eighteen-mile stretch completed in 1950 that reporter Karl Schriftgiesser claimed had "pacified the countryside." By the end of 1955, the state had opened the Thruway from Yonkers to Albany, with the Hudson River crossing at the Tappan Zee Bridge, giving New Yorkers yet another means of accessing the western side of the mid-Hudson region. As the state built the Thruway, locals purchased land near proposed interchanges, anticipating increasing property values. Still, no one really knew what the impact of the new highway would be. Would improved access bring more tourists to the Catskills, or, as Longstreth had articulated more than thirty years earlier, would it encourage more to pass them by, on their way to higher, more distant mountains?[34]

The Thruway was the grand finale in New York's completely reworked transportation system, and the Central Catskills Association clearly understood the importance of the new highway to the mountains. Auto-owning New Yorkers could now reach the Catskills in roughly two hours, and it took only slightly more time to reach them by bus. The association looked beyond just the impact on tourism, though, which members clearly hoped would see a boost from the improved access. "By radically reducing the traveling time from New York City, and other metropolitan areas, the Thruway also will bring more suburban residents to the Catskill mountain area," the guide suggested. "These people will discover that the Thruway will make it possible for them to commute from this area to their jobs in the heavily populated areas in the lower Hudson river valley and New York city." Remarkably, then, the association's use of the term "suburb" was not figurative. The expectation was, even in 1955, that the Thruway would allow New Yorkers to commute to work from the mountains.[35] The Central Catskills Association understood that New Yorkers and their automobiles—along with the roads that made cars so valuable—were in the process of remaking the Catskills, even beyond reshaping the tourist industry. No trend would prove as important to the mountains in the twentieth century as the growth of automobile ownership and use. Over the course of the century, much of the Catskills did indeed become a suburb of New York.

The positive use of the word "suburb" in the Central Catskills Association literature certainly did not reflect the opinions of all Catskills residents, nor all mountain tourists. Not everyone relished the idea of New Yorkers building homes in the mountains from which they could commute to their distant jobs. But the appearance of the article in this promotional brochure does suggest how much the Catskills economy had changed, following the changing interests of urbanites. For decades the Catskills' very success in attracting masses of New Yorkers had posed problems for its reputation as an upscale retreat. As early as 1892, an Ulster and Delaware advertising pamphlet reacted to growing concern about crowds in the mountains, as the company hoped "to remove the strange notion that the Catskills are in danger of becoming a suburb of New York City." At that point, the Ulster and Delaware still sold the Catskills as romantic and secluded, where one might fill "his soul with awe" while admiring the works of God. One could hardly have an effective retreat from the city if the crowds came to the mountains too—if the mountains were merely a "suburb."[36] By the 1950s, however, most tourists no longer sought lengthy retreats from the city. Now tourists were more likely to hale from suburban neighborhoods,[37] and their desires for vacations changed right along with their changing domestic situations.

The completion of the Thruway played a critical role in the shifting economy of the entire Hudson River Valley. Failed industries along city waterfronts from Yonkers to Kingston, from Saugerties to Troy, could now be replaced by new economic developments near the Thruway's exits. In 1955, IBM, then experiencing dramatic growth, opened a new facility in Ulster Township, just outside Kingston, and near the Thruway. IBM brought middle-class jobs to the region, spurring suburban growth, including in nearby Catskills townships. At the same time, a homegrown company, Rotron, founded in Hurley in 1949, grew rapidly in the 1950s in response to skyrocketing demand for its primary product, small blowers used to cool electronic equipment. By 1956, Rotron claimed 225 employees, all of whom worked in its Hurley facility just outside of Woodstock. Both Woodstock and Hurley were also near the IBM plant, and with the growth of high-wage jobs, the once-rural townships gained several new residential subdivisions, not unlike thousands of other American places in the 1950s. Cul-de-sacs of ranches and split-levels replaced farm fields and woodlots. This was the type of suburban growth predicted by the Central Catskills Association, though clearly most cul-de-sac workers did not commute all the way to the city.[38]

By the early 1960s, suburbanization in the mountain townships nearest Saugerties and Kingston had become cause for concern. Together Olive, Hurley, Woodstock, and Shandaken townships had grown nearly 64 percent during the 1950s, and in the 1960s would grow another 42 percent. After a century of rather stable populations, the Catskills region between the Kingston and Saugerties exits was suddenly growing, adding more than 10,000 permanent residents and many more part-timers. Some residents feared that the subdivision of the mountains would destroy the region's rural character. Not surprisingly, this concern was strongest where the building of tract homes had become most obvious—around the quaint village of Woodstock. The Town of Woodstock alone nearly tripled in size in the twenty years after the Thruway opened.[39]

Not all of the growth around Woodstock could be attributed to the arrival of IBM and Rotron's success. Indeed, other changes in the village were even more apparent. By the mid-1960s, Woodstock had become one of the country's premiere destinations for free-living youth intent on pursuing their dreams of personal liberation and enjoying music, drugs, and the company of like-minded people. Eventually known as "hippies," these young people, almost all of them white and most of them from middle-class families, sought out peaceful settings and places where the arts flourished. Woodstock became New York City's most important hippie retreat, and on summer afternoons hundreds of young people crowded onto Tinker Street and the village green. Woodstock became the East-Coast epicenter of the Age of Aquarius.[40]

By then Woodstock had had a long history as an arts community. In 1902 artist Ralph Whitehead and novelist Hervey White settled on Woodstock to found a new artist colony. They were drawn to the area's great beauty and its easy access to nearby cities. (The anti-Semitic Whitehead was also pleased by the paucity of Jews, the presence of whom in other parts of the Catskills had soured his impression of the entire region.) Under Whitehead's direction, the new colony, called Byrdcliffe, grew outside the village on former farmland on the side of Overlook Mountain. Following the guidance of British antimodernist John Ruskin, Whitehead and White sought the "simple life," participating fully in the Arts and Crafts movement then gathering momentum. They gathered talented artists and craftsmen and craftswomen to teach at the colony, which opened to students in 1903. Over the next few decades, the colony drew hundreds of individuals to Woodstock, many of whom were so inspired by the place that they found themselves returning repeatedly. Some even found a way to stay permanently, creating a dense local population of artists, some associated with Byrdcliffe and some not. In 1906, the Art Students' League of New York began offering its summer school in Woodstock, and shortly thereafter Hervey White left Byrdcliffe to start his own colony, Maverick, just south of town. By the 1910s, then, Woodstock summers had become famously cultural, replete with fine arts, crafts, and music. In 1914, the *New York Times* reported that around the village one "sees artists everywhere along the roads or in the fields busily engaged in painting outdoor life."[41]

Woodstock's qualities made it ideal for serving the antimodernist Arts and Crafts community of the early century. Its country setting promoted peace and healthfulness. Residents could play at farming during their breaks from artistic endeavors. And the mountains—an arts colony had to have mountains—inspired their real work, their art. Woodstock had an additional advantage, though: its proximity to New York City. While artists came from all over the country to live and learn in Woodstock, its connection to the city's arts scene was obvious. As Longstreth noted after his 1918 visit to Woodstock, "Truly there is virtue in a place where the twice lucky residents can pursue their professions in a veritable refuge of delight, and yet not lose touch with the great city at the other end of the river."[42] Thus, by this time Woodstock was not unlike the village of Catskill in an earlier era, providing artists easy access to both inspirational nature and the indispensable city. Unlike Catskill, however, Woodstock would attract artists of all types, not just landscape painters.

Woodstock's reputation as an artists' retreat only grew during subsequent decades. In 1931, Harry Haring noted that the liberality of artists had colored all aspects of village life, including the "disregard for conventional dress." All the while, the economy of Woodstock held strong, even as other parts of the region experienced decline. In the mid-1950s, Woodstock began to host arts festivals, which by 1960 took the name "The Woodstock Festival of Music and Art." The summer-long festival included concerts at the Maverick, operas performed at the Byrdcliffe Theatre, folk music concerts, and other theatrical and musical events. By 1964, folk music had become even more important to the still-diverse offerings, with the program listing ten "Folk Concerts," reflecting the growing popularity of the music, which by its nature served as a protest to a mass culture steeped in what folk artist Sam Eskin called "radio and television with scarifying talk of cold wars, ICBMs, fallout and total destruction." Together, folk music and Woodstock provided a peaceful retreat from this terrifying world.[43]

Woodstock's cultural connection to the city proved very profitable. In 1963 the *New York Times* went so far as to call Woodstock the "Greenwich Village of the Catskills," a fitting description given how many individuals moved back and forth between those two communities.[44] In 1967, Woodstock hosted a "Sound-Out"—a festival featuring folk, rock, and jazz music, some of it performed by artists who had fallen in love with the Woodstock scene. The Sound-Out attracted perhaps a thousand hippies, most of them having made the trip up from New York City to a field just outside town. Mary-Jo Mack, a reveler from Queens, captured the essence of Woodstock's advantages after waking at the festival site on Saturday morning: "You can't sleep out on the ground for the whole weekend in Central Park."[45]

Woodstock's arts and music tradition had much to do with its growing hippie community, although most of those who came to the village, just to "check out the scene" or to stay longer, did not themselves practice in the arts. However, it was the appearance of several other individuals that most dramatically increased Woodstock's visibility in the nation's youth culture. Most important was the arrival of Bob Dylan, who came to Woodstock on the advice of his manager Albert Grossman, a resident of nearby Bearsville since 1963. Dylan had come to New York City in 1961 to make it in Greenwich Village's thriving music scene, where he played traditional folk songs about coal miners and dirt farmers to college kids and tourists in a series of subterranean clubs and coffee houses.[46] When he started writing his own music, he became famous. Soon thereafter, he began to retreat to Grossman's property, staying in an apartment built in an old barn. Using the peaceful setting for writing, Dylan moved back and forth between the city, where he lived in a series of hotel apartments, and the country, where in 1965 he purchased his own Woodstock home, a large Arts and Crafts cottage on the Byrdcliffe property. A year later, while at the height of his fame, Dylan crashed his motorcycle near Grossman's property, initiating a long recuperation in the seclusion of Woodstock.[47]

Dylan stopped traveling for many months, but he did not stop working. He contacted his touring band, the Hawks, then languishing in the Chelsea Hotel, and he encouraged them to come to the mountains. They came immediately. In early 1967, three band members—Garth Hudson, Rick Danko, and Richard Manuel—rented a modest West Saugerties house just a few miles from Dylan's home. (The fourth band member, Robbie Robertson, lived in the village with his wife.) Nicknamed "Big Pink," the house was, as journalist Alfred Aronowitz wrote, "one of those middle-class ranch houses you would expect to find in suburbia." In this house, Dylan and the band wrote dozens of songs, recording many of them in the basement of the Big Pink and others at Dylan's home. In the evenings, the band members, less reclusive than Dylan, ate and drank in Woodstock, and not infrequently played impromptu sets. The daily basement sessions went so well that Danko invited another former band member, Levon Helm, an Arkansas-born drummer who had been at the heart of the group when it went by other names, including Levon and the Hawks. Helm arrived in time to play on several songs and to join his old friends in creating a new sound, developed in the relative isolation of West Saugerties, away from the radio and the clubs of the city—away from the music of the "Summer of Love." They called it "mountain music."[48]

When Dylan left Woodstock to record the album *John Wesley Harding,* news of the tapes recorded in the West Saugerties basement leaked out, as did a series of bootlegs. *The Basement Tapes,* as they were called, quickly became the white whale of Dylan fans. After years of bootlegging and speculation on what the entire collection might contain, Columbia Records released a portion of *The Basement Tapes* in 1975, long after the back-up musicians had made a name for themselves as The Band. By that time, the West Saugerties home had become famous, at least among music fans, as the location where The Band had written the songs that appeared on their first album, *Music from Big Pink,* released in 1968. The album cover featured a Dylan painting on the front, and on the reverse a photo of the humble pink bungalow, its basement "studio" clearly visible, and accessible, from the yard.[49]

Following Dylan's lead, and that of The Band and Paul Butterfield, another national recording artist who lived near Woodstock, congregating hippies made Woodstock famous within the youth culture. Although Dylan was rarely seen in the village, everyone knew he was around, as were some of his closest friends, including, at times, Joan Baez. Ardent fans hoping to catch a glimpse of the folk-singer-turned-rock-star paraded through Woodstock. Even if most hippies stayed only briefly, the movement of restless youth to Woodstock represented a new urban-to-rural migration. Part of the hippie inclination to seek a peaceful place in a violent time, Woodstock became a "beautiful" retreat, far from the racial conflicts boiling over in urban America and the brutal realities of the Vietnam War. Seeking to cash in on the movement, Leslie Tobin purchased commercial space along Tinker Street, the main street through the village, and moved up from the city. In the summer of 1969, Tobin basked in his good fortune. "I never knew what people meant when they said, 'Man, it's groovy in the country,'" he told the *New York Times.* "But, now I see what they mean. There are just good vibrations from the whole scene."[50]

Tobin was not the only New Yorker hoping to cash in on the "good vibrations" of Woodstock. In early 1969, Michael Lang, a Brooklyn native, began peddling the idea of founding a recording studio in Woodstock. To publicize the development, Lang and his partner, Artie Kornfeld, an executive at Capitol Records, would put on a rock festival, in the hopes of copying the success of the 1967 Monterey Pop Festival. With the backing of a young millionaire, John Roberts, Lang began organizing the Woodstock Music and Art Fair, though he quickly realized it could not actually take place in Woodstock, which had no suitable site—or local support for that matter. First Lang searched near Saugerties (or, more precisely, near Thruway exit 20), but eventually he found a farm in Wallkill, more than thirty miles south of Woodstock and similarly close to the highway. As the August date approached, publicity for the festival, which would feature many of rock's largest stars—though not Dylan—made it all the more certain that the festival would gather its promised masses of music fans. Wallkill Township officials grew wary of the event, and less than a month before it was to occur, denied permission, fearing an influx of restless, drug-addicted youth.[51]

Lang quickly found a replacement—the 600–acre farm of Max Yasgur in Sullivan County. As the crow flies, Yasgur's Bethel dairy farm was about fifty miles from Woodstock, and it could hardly be less like the artsy village. Ten miles outside Monticello, Yasgur's farm was at the edge of the Borscht Belt, through which most festival-goers would drive. After the festival, alternative weekly *Hard Times* contributor Andrew Kopkind wrote with rich irony that the approach to Bethel from New York City passed by "Esther Manor and Siegel's Motor Court and Elfenbaum's Grocery" rather than "crash communes or head shops." Even before the music began, however, the festival had become big news, as the cause of one of the nation's all-time great traffic jams. Thousands of cars littered the shoulders of approaching roads. Some property owners charged for parking spaces; others did not, but found cars parked on their property anyway. One dairy farmer, Clarence Townsend, complained that thousands of cars parked on his fields, though he was three miles from the Yasgur farm. "There were kids all over the place," he said. "They made a human cesspool of our property and drove through the cornfields." One observer called Sullivan County "a great big parking lot." Kopkind wrote that even by Thursday "the ambience had changed from splendor in the grass to explosive urban sprawl."[52]

Although the traffic jams weren't exactly a "beautiful scene," and the Sullivan County farmlands bore little resemblance to the arts center for which the festival was named, the festivalgoers, numbering perhaps 500,000, certainly brought their "peace and love" mentality to the fair, along with ample illicit drugs. Despite serious logistical problems, including shortages of nearly everything from food to toilets, insufficient staff to monitor gates (which were quickly abandoned) or provide security, and rainy weather that left the alfalfa field little more than a sea of mud, all observers agreed that the excessive crowd was remarkably calm and good natured. Having driven—and for a few miles walked—out to a country field for a weekend of peaceful coexistence, good music, and, for many, drugs, Woodstock revelers were simply not in the mood to cause trouble or even complain. After three days of music and essentially no mayhem, the festival unwound, and its organizers, who lost money and would later face lawsuits, declared victory simply because it could have been much, much worse. Thousands of young people went to the mountains in search of peace, and many returned claiming they had found it, largely because half a million young people stood in the rain for three days without hitting each other. Even before it was over, Woodstock had become the iconic event of the hippie movement, and whatever its meaning, whether it symbolized the era's tendency toward irresponsibility or personal and political liberation, one conclusion is certain: it was hardly a homegrown event. Once again the city had come to the country, as it is wont to do; it had made a mess, and then gone home.[53]

Back in the actual village of Woodstock, hippies also came and mostly went, many of them simply attempting to tap into the positive energy of the festival. Dylan had had no inclination to participate, even though the event bore the Woodstock label largely because he lived there. Dylan now found the energetic following of hippies much too oppressive. "Woodstock had turned into a nightmare," he later wrote, "a place of chaos." By late 1969, after the festival further encouraged pilgrimages to the arts village, Dylan could no longer stay in his rural retreat at all. Having already moved out of his Byrdcliffe home to a more secluded location farther up Overlook Mountain, Dylan had grown tired of defending his privacy in the country and, ironically, he moved back to the city, where he would continue his career while seeking urban anonymity. Now a quiet family man, Dylan no longer wanted to live at the center of the "Woodstock Nation." Three years later, with aspiring musicians and hippies-in-training still flocking to the village, *Harper's* declared the scene past-tense in a cynical piece run under the headline "Woodstock Was."

The drugs and the "street people" were still around, but apparently the "vibe" had been lost.[54]

Despite the concerns of older Woodstock residents, the hippie invasion had not hurt property values, nor would the gradual—and incomplete—hippie retreat from the village. Through it all, Woodstock remained a desirable place to live, and an ever-more-expensive one, too. While locals complained about open drug use, nude swimming in local streams, and the threats the hippie culture posed to their own children, a larger threat to Woodstock's identity continued to loom: suburban subdivision of rural properties and a population boom. By 1980, the town's permanent population had swollen to nearly 7,000, more than twice its total in 1950. Although the Woodstock area was among the most affected by this suburbanizing trend, alarm over the spread of subdivisions and second home-building echoed through the Catskills.[55]

Largely in response to this growing threat, in 1969 half a dozen men created the Catskill Center for Conservation and Development, a collaborative effort of permanent and part-time Catskills residents. Unlike many of the conservation-minded groups forming around the nation as the environmental movement reached its peak of political power in the late 1960s, the Catskill Center's organizers intentionally linked environmental protection with economic development as twin goals for their region. Essentially, the Catskill Center worked to create what would now be called a sustainable region, one in which natural resources could be protected right along with the rural culture. This would require more than simply purchasing land and conservation easements, though the Catskill Center made these tactics important parts of its approach.[56] Still, protecting the culture of the Catskills would require protecting the economy, too, for no one wanted healthy forests surrounding dilapidated, impoverished towns. As founding member Sherret Chase put it, the people of the Catskills "like it the way it is." This conservative tone ran through the work of the Catskill Center, too.[57]

Chase and other members of the Catskill Center argued that unregulated development, especially the subdivision of land for home building, threatened the very character of the Catskills. In 1974 the Catskills Center published a conservation plan that noted "the emergence of a new suburban pattern of land use in the region, geared entirely toward recreation and radically unlike the agricultural and woodland pattern it is replacing." The plan described a number of ecological threats posed by suburban development, but it also made a cultural argument for better planning, claiming that the subdivisions created "isolated colonies" of disinterested part-time residents whose arrival "may alter the style and feel of rural life." Thus, the Catskill Center recognized that the new investments in the mountains had done little to enrich what had become one of the state's poorer regions. For the members of the Center, these twin developments made the implementation of new land-use regulations critical. New York State granted local governments the authority to control land use, but most mountain townships and municipalities were remarkably lax in their regulations—with many having no zoning ordinances at all, no rules concerning the subdivision of properties. The Center worked to decrease local opposition to such rules, and to make the idea of regional planning more acceptable to landowners in the mountains.[58]

Although clearly sensitive to the welfare of the local communities, Chase and other members of the Center also understood that the Catskills were "of more than local interest." This acceptance of the Catskills' extraregional significance, combined with the prominence of nonnative members, convinced some Catskills residents that the Center had been created by outsiders to serve outside interests—those that would lock up the region's resources, stunting economic growth. The organizing force of the Center had been Chase, whose own history in the Catskills dated to 1921, when his father purchased an old farm near Winchell Hollow outside Woodstock, to which his family began retreating from its Wayne, Pennsylvania, home each summer. Over the next fifty years, Chase worked outside the Catskills, as a biology professor, but returned to them when he could. By the time he helped found the Catskill Center, Chase had essentially become a local, as so many others had over the previous 150 years.[59] Suspicious Catskills residents may have been more concerned about the prominent role of other founding members, whose wealth set them apart from typical mountain folk, including Armand Erpf, a New York financier with extensive property in Arkville, and Kingdon Gould, Jr., whose family had strong ties to both the Catskills and New York City.[60] Despite the concerns of wary Catskills residents, however, the Center continued to grow in membership, influence, and visibility, especially after occupying a fine old homestead in Arkville, donated by Armand Erpf and called Erpf House.[61]

In 1970, the Center used its influence to convince Governor Nelson Rockefeller to establish what a year later became the Temporary State Commission to Study the Catskills. Here the Catskills followed the Adirondacks by three years, as Rockefeller had created a similar temporary commission to study the north woods, where essentially the same pressures brought by automobiles and the prospects of massive subdivision of land threatened to alter the wilderness character of the larger park. The state completed work on the Northway (Interstate 87) in 1967, which dramatically improved automobile access to the high peaks of the Adirondacks and gave new urgency to conservation efforts. The Temporary Study Commission on the Future of the Adirondacks recommended state regulation of private lands within the park. Despite intense local opposition, this became reality with the implementation of the Private Land Plan in 1973.[62]

Some residents of the Catskills had reason for concern, then, when the state turned its attention to the Catskills. The state legislature charged the Catskill commission to report on both natural and cultural resources in the region, a mission that reflected that of the Catskill Center. Although the legislature was concerned with the "general well-being of the rural communities," the impetus for the commission was clearly the need for the Catskills to protect itself "from unplanned population growth." Most of the Catskills region had seen no population growth since the mid-1800s, but just ten years after the opening of the New York State Thruway, "the pressures of population" now ominously threatened the mountains with "unplanned development." If the threat of state regulation of private lands raised concerns inside the Catskill Park, the commission's membership could not have eased fears. Governor Rockefeller appointed Kirby Peake of Bronxville, a tony Westchester suburb, as chairman. Other members hailed from New York City, Newburgh, Cooperstown, and Kingston. Only four of the nine members came from the mountains themselves.[63]

In 1973, as the Temporary Commission conducted its research, the state Department of Environmental Conservation, the agency charged with overseeing state property in the Catskills, dedicated an entire issue of *The Conservationist*, its popular, glossy magazine, to the newly besieged mountains. The magazine offered historical features, including an essay by Catskills Center member Alf Evers, whose remarkably thorough history *The Catskills: From Wilderness to Woodstock* had appeared just the year before. The issue also included the requisite essays on the state forest, trout fishing, and Hudson River art, and altogether they created a primer in Catskills culture. The magazine opened with an editorial titled "While Rip Van Winkle Sleeps." After using Irving's story to remind readers of the Catskills' long, storied history, the editor posed a critical question: "shall there be action to protect the Catskills from the pressures of population, from unplanned development and undirected change?" The D.E.C. thus asked state residents to ponder the same question then before the Temporary Commission, the same question posed by the Catskill Center at its founding four years earlier.[64]

The Conservationist's Catskills issue also included an ominous piece entitled "The Catskills Today and Tomorrow." Noting that the mountains "appear to be the perfect retreat for prospective second home owners," who "seek to own their own piece of the Catskills," the essay included two charts tracking subdivision lot approvals. The first concerned only the Town of Shandaken, in the heart of the Catskills along Route 28, where in 1967 and 1968 no subdivisions had been approved. By 1971 and 1972, however, 40 and 53 subdivisions earned approval. The second chart showed an even greater explosion of approvals in Sullivan County, where in 1972, 1,953 subdivisions gained approval, up from 207 in 1969. These subdivisions announced the region's rapid slide toward suburbia, and the D.E.C. warned that government would have to take steps to "preserve the rural flavor of Catskill land."[65]

The Temporary Commission conducted its work under this cloud of concern and in 1975 published its conclusions in *The Future of the Catskills*. As dictated by the legislature, the report focused on changes underway in Greene, Ulster, Sullivan, Delaware, Schoharie, and Otsego counties, giving the Catskills their most expansive definition yet. Much of the concern here was for agricultural decline, then occurring mostly outside the actual mountains, especially in Delaware and Otsego counties, and in the Hudson Valley, where failing farms were ripe for redevelopment as tract home subdivisions. The report's conclusion revealed the conflicted nature of the changes afoot in the region—economic stagnation combined with undesirable development. "It is imperative that continued deterioration be prevented and future growth be managed in an orderly fashion," the commission argued, apparently without a sense of irony that managing growth should become the overriding concern in a region badly in need of development. Clearly the commission's primary interest lay in protecting the status quo in the countryside: the forests should remain forests, farms should remain farms, and small towns should remain small towns. This goal derived in part from the metropolitan conservationism that had grown in the postwar era, as both precipitous urban decline and rapid suburban development encouraged a longing for constancy in the countryside beyond the metropolis. In other words, dramatic change in the metropolis encouraged the development of a remarkably conservative vision of the countryside, of the appropriate future of natural landscapes and the mountains outside the city. They must stay the same.[66]

The Temporary Commission's primary recommendation was for the creation of a permanent regional land-management commission for the Catskills. According to the commission, regional planning, conducted by a commission with members from various stakeholders, including the city of New York, the state, and the various local governments, would bring order out of chaos. Taking up the work of the Temporary Commission, which disbanded in 1975, the Department of Environmental Conservation put together the Catskill Study Reports, published in fifteen volumes beginning in 1976. Report topics ranged from rare and endangered plants to flood hazards in the region. The most important reports cataloged public lands, including those controlled by the D.E.C. and New York City, and offered a summary of regional, county, and local planning in the Catskills. The first volume outlined the conclusions of the various studies and offered recommendations for future actions. In his foreword to the report, D.E.C. Commissioner Peter Berle laid bare the central conflict impeding the regional approach: "local citizens and public officials" had "deep feelings" concerning land use planning. They were especially fearful that such planning would be imposed upon them from the outside.[67]

The D.E.C. attempted to make the case that effective management of the Catskills concerned all state residents, but in its enumeration of reasons it became clear that New York City had the most at stake, apart from local residents themselves. The city's six Catskills reservoirs provided nearly 90 percent of the city's water, and the city owned 34,079 acres around the reservoirs (and an additional 23,540 acres in them). Watershed rules, developed by the state, regulated a total of 1,581 square miles of land—the majority of the mountainous region. Given this presence in the mountains, the city had long been deeply involved in local politics; it operated five municipal sewage treatment plants and paid over $10 million in local taxes every year. Of course other resource issues affected citizens more generally, including the wonderful recreational opportunities in and around the 241,000 acres of state-owned lands, protected as "forever wild." Still, the Catskills Study made clear that the most compelling reason why the state should create a permanent Catskill

Regional Land Resources Management Commission was the importance of the region to New York City, especially as its water source.[68]

In 1977, Sherret Chase, president of the Catskills Center, offered his support for the regional commission when he spoke before a special meeting of the New York State Assembly's Committee on Environmental Conservation held in Leeds, as it considered the D.E.C. plan. Chase brought forth the then familiar arguments for its creation. He clearly had his work cut out for him as he faced local opposition to the creation of a regional board, whose members under the most popular plan would not necessarily hail from the Catskills. Locals feared losing control of their communities, feared having the Catskills managed to suit the needs of outsiders. Under any plan adopted by the state, a significant voice would be given to those outsiders, including the state and the city of New York, since both were large landholders in the region. Chase understood the necessity of such an arrangement, and further claimed that the plan "assures that local interests will be represented and balanced against county, regional and state interests." Chase argued, in vain it turned out, that "our history has shown that when outside interests have been in direct conflict with local interests, the local interests have been sacrificed."[69]

Skeptical local residents might wonder, however, why in the Catskills local interests had to be balanced against any others. After all, Catskills residents had no hand in shaping land-use policy in New York City or its exploding suburbs; nor did they have any say in managing growth in the Capital District, or anywhere else in the state, for that matter. This challenge to local control was not entirely new, of course; only the proposed mechanism of control was. Over the course of two centuries, the interests of outsiders had made their way into the mountains; they had become as secure as any local interests. As Chase put it so plainly, "Catskill people now have little, if any, control over their destiny." As much as his opponents might hate to hear this statement, they could hardly disagree with it. The regional organization "would help," Chase claimed, at least in giving locals some control over their own communities. In other words, Chase saw continued subdivision development as a greater threat to local autonomy than the imposition of rules that could stem the suburban tide. Seven years after Chase's comments in Leeds, a Catskills Center publication cataloged the continuing subdivision of lands in and around the mountains, especially those conducted by out-of-state land sales companies. The pamphlet, entitled *The Catskills for Sale*, included a survey of Delaware County property that found a 66 percent decrease in parcels larger than 100 acres and a similar increase in parcels between 2 and 25 acres since 1950. More relevant to the issue of local control, the survey found that nonresident landowners had shot up from 15 percent to 50 percent of all county parcels. This suburban-style, second-home development was changing what it meant to be a local resident even as it changed the rural landscape.[70]

Despite the fear of suburban encroachment, and the actual continuation of subdivision development, through the 1980s the Catskills moved no closer to regional planning and showed no signs of economic revival. Visitors continued to come, but they spent little money. Richard Ricciardella, owner of the popular Phoenicia restaurant that bore his name, complained in 1977 that business dropped as more and more tourists became "day-trippers with their thermoses and sandwich bags," rather than overnight guests who frequented restaurants. More tourists continued to "drive straight through," as Ricciardella called it, and the region's boardinghouses and hotels continued to close—as had over 400 between 1953 and 1973. At the same time, second-home owners, most of whom had money to spend, generally spent too little of it in the mountains. One Sullivan County innkeeper complained that they "never eat out or go out. Why, they won't even buy their groceries up here. They bring 'em." Meanwhile, farm families, which did spend money in the mountains, continued to give up, and as milk checks diminished, so too did part of the region's economic base.[71]

All told, the decline of agriculture and the faltering tourist industry cast a pall of failure over the mountains. A 1987 New York Times article connected the "rural blight" that crept into the mountains with the "esthetic disintegration that beset much of Appalachia." The once-proud tourist region, home to the most important American landscape imagery ever created, now looked more like the impoverished hollows of West Virginia than a recreational hinterland within easy reach of the nation's wealthiest city. The Times article did not focus on the decline, however. Rather, the article detailed the ambitions of Laurance Rockefeller, nephew of the former governor Nelson Rockefeller and heir to his family's strong conservationist ethic, who now sought to reverse the blight. Rockefeller had purchased a tract in the Town of Hardenburgh, along the Beaver Kill, deep in the mountains, where he hoped to "recycle the land back as closely as possible to what it had been a century ago." He would do this, ironically, by selling second-home sites to wealthy investors interested in returning the land "to its original state." If Rockefeller's preservationist vision privileged wilderness over agriculture and other aspects of rural culture, it also suggested that second-home development might be done well.[72]

By the time the *New York Times* publicized his efforts, Rockefeller had already been at work preserving bits of Catskills wilderness for over a decade. In collaboration with the Manhattan-based Open Space Institute, Rockefeller helped ensured the protection of sensitive lands along the Beaver Kill and further south along the Basherkill. While some locals might question the wisdom of preserving ever more land in the mountains, Rockefeller, the Open Space Institute, and the Catskill Center continued to seek out large parcels that might fall into the hands of subdivision developers. This work, especially as conducted through the Catskill Center, represented yet another phase in the long collaboration between city and local residents in shaping the mountain landscape, as both sought to protect a beloved landscape. The real difficulty in the Catskill Center's work lay not in protecting individual pieces of property, but in preserving a landscape that had been the result of an evolving Catskills culture, built over the previous two hundred years. Preserving that landscape would require preserving the culture, too, including its agriculture, tourism, and artist colonies. As the members of the Catskill Center understood, the mountains had long been much more than a wilderness; to preserve only the forests would be as destructive of the authentic, rural Catskills culture as would the continued suburbanization of the region.[73]

Epilogue

Whose Woods These Are

The peace of the hills is about me and upon me, and the leisure of the summer clouds, whose shadows I see slowly drifting across the face of the landscape, is mine. The dissonance and the turbulence and the stenches of cities—how far off they seem! The noise and the dust and the acrimony of politics—how completely the hum of the honey-bees and the twitter of swallows blot them all out!

—John Burroughs, 1913

Whose woods these are I think I know.
His house is in the village though;

—Robert Frost, 1923

A few years ago I drove up Kaaterskill Clove on Route 23A, past the trailhead to Kaaterskill Falls and through some of the most traveled scenic territory in nineteenth-century America. At the head of the clove, the village of Haines Falls showed some wear, but clearly it still attracted wealth, and, more commonly, hikers and mountain bikers, who frequent the many trails through nearby state lands. On this trip I knew enough to look out my window at just the right moment to see the entrance to Twilight Park, now a classic example of the American gated community, and well hidden from the road by large trees. Just a bit farther, the road clears another rise and then slowly descends into the head of the Schoharie Valley. There I noticed a small metal sign marking the transition with the words "Welcome to Our Watershed." It is common to see a roadside sign announcing the entrance into a municipal watershed, but I was struck by the use of the possessive pronoun "our." I was so intrigued by this phrase that I turned around, drove back to the sign, and accepted its invitation to call a toll-free number listed below the greeting. The person who answered the phone seemed just as confused about why I was calling New York City's Department of Environmental Protection Police as I was about being encouraged to call a law-enforcement office by a welcome sign. Regardless, the call cleared up the question of who had placed the sign and why, and whose watershed I had entered, though this I already knew. It is the city's. And the city wants everyone to obey the rules that protect its water.

Just a few hundred yards farther down the road a series of larger signs placed by the Village of Tannersville read "Welcome to Our Mountain Top." These signs, cloth banners hanging from telephone poles all along the road through the village, were much more inviting—real welcome signs. Tannersville welcomed tourists to what they thought they were visiting—a mountain vacationland, complete with skiing, hiking, and other outdoor activities. Tannersville was glad I had come.

Clearly these signs—one placed by New York City and the others by Tannersville—served very different purposes, but I was struck by the similarity of the signs' language. Both used the indefinite possessive pronoun "our." While the signs remained unclear as to exactly who was included in (and excluded from) either of the groups represented by the pronoun, one might easily conclude that the signs stood for the interests of two different sets of people, even if in both cases the "our" invited a sharing of possession and responsibility. These juxtaposed signs could hardly be more freighted with meaning. Even taken out of context, removed from the history that created the mountain vacationland and the city water supply, they suggested that some battle was raging over who really controlled this land and its water.

Perhaps these signs were evidence of the imperial struggle between city and country, a battle that concerned more than ownership of the land, since in this instance definition was most directly at stake. The signs invited visitors to see two different, even oppositional places. Had local residents placed corrective signs to rebuff New York City's attempt to define their mountains as its own watershed? This is *Our* Mountain Top!" While I certainly believe this struggle between urban and rural interests exists, and has existed for at least a century, to emphasize this struggle exclusively would be a distortion of the Catskills story. For the "our" found on each of these signs is remarkably inclusive; each embraces mountain and city residents, and some who are both. People from both the mountains and the city make rightful claims on the watershed and the mountain top, and both are responsible for their futures.

And thus, this drive up 23A provided an object lesson in one of the themes of this work. Over their history, the Catskills have been variously defined and redefined, especially to suit the needs of assorted city residents. Sometimes these definitions have conflicted; almost always they have limited the ability of locals to define this region for themselves. Despite the continuous influence of the great city at the end of the river, however, more than outside forces have made the mountains. The distinctive Catskills landscape and its unique culture are a product of a long collaboration between local and urban residents.

On this particular trip, I drove on through Hunter and Prattsville, recreating the type of quick auto tour that had done so much to transform the Catskills tourist industry. I turned south, toward Roxbury, and before reaching town I looked closely for signs leading to John Burroughs Memorial Field, on a hillside above the East Branch of the Delaware. Some Burroughs devotees make this trip—as I had before—a pilgrimage really, to Woodchuck Lodge and its surroundings, to see where the great writer spent the summer months of his autumn years, to be near his birthplace, and to visit his gravesite. Here they find a small wooden cabin nestled in the woods along a narrow country road; small fields allow vistas across the valley toward a modest, well-wooded mountain of the type so common in the Catskills. Visitors come a few each week, and their comments in the logbook generally connect Burroughs's love of nature to the beauty of this place—for it is truly beautiful. Many of the writers suggest that they understand how the place they now occupy could inspire Burroughs, and, showing how much they have learned from him, several of the logbook authors write a bit of prose about the birds and the trees and the shape of the mountains.

Ironically, though, when Burroughs overlooked this Catskills valley, he saw something almost entirely different than we do now. He saw farms, fields, and fences. "From Woodchuck Lodge I look out upon broad pastures," he wrote in 1913, "lands where dairy herds have grazed for a hundred years, never the same herd for many summers, but all the same habits and dispositions." One May he sat on his porch "looking out upon this broad landscape," where he saw "farmers ploughing, the cattle and woodchucks grazing on the fresh springing grass."[1] That was the Delaware County Burroughs lived in and wrote about and loved. Now, however, the forests have come down the mountains and nearly fill the valley. Trees encroach on his old house and the Memorial Field, mowed as a remnant of his farm. That so many of his admirers, even, connect Burroughs to a less populated, more wooded landscape speaks to the power of our own desire to think of the natural landscape itself as historical—a preserved past. What we see, Burroughs must have seen. The Catskills Burroughs loved and described is essentially gone, however, and is now a distant and mostly unremembered landscape. The Memorial Field, maintained so that we might remember Burroughs, should also help us remember a lost agricultural past. Unfortunately, this particular past has gone largely unmemorialized in the mountains, unlike other Catskills pasts that are well remembered and widely presented.

Woodchuck Lodge is a fine place to contemplate a second theme in this work: city residents have shaped the ideas that have helped shape the American countryside. Over the past two centuries, urbanites have traveled into the countryside from rapidly changing cities. Both the places they left behind and the means by which they did so influenced how they perceived the landscapes to which they traveled. In the mid-1800s, city travelers sought out agricultural landscapes, prizing their fresh milk and vegetables, staying in farm houses roughly converted into boardinghouses. By the late-1900s, ideas about the role of rural landscapes in urban lives had changed significantly. Most city tourists sought out deep woods rather than productive fields. Over the course of the last 150 years, ideas about nature shifted repeatedly, but throughout the modern environmental consciousness developed. This modern consciousness valued rural stasis and the preservation of natural scenes.

And so, one of the most powerful ideas to come out of urban America posits the countryside as the past—in direct contrast with the future represented by the city. There are times when this appears to be literally true, when rural America seems out of step with a rapidly evolving urban culture. I was particularly struck by the testimony of Ara Barton in 1909, who described his Olive property in an eminent domain lawsuit against the city as it prepared to build the Ashokan. Barton had been a quarry man all his life, but at age fifty-five he had to admit to the city's lawyer that he had never quarried using compressed air, then commonly used to drive power tools. However, to help give the impression that his quarrying was indeed sophisticated, Barton quickly volunteered that he had used a derrick to lift and swing heavier stones, with the aid of what he called "a horse power." "That is a real live horse, not steam?" pressed the city's lawyer. "Yes, a real live horse," Barton replied. In an era when urban Americans could begin to lose track of the etymological connections between the measure of power and actual beasts of burden, Barton's testimony provided a quaint reminder that not everyone entered the age of steam at the same time or to the same degree. In 1909, many Catskills places still moved at the pace of a real live horse.[2]

However, it is one thing to remember that changes, even those as fundamental as new systems of power, affect urban and rural places in different ways, and quite another to assume that the changes never arrive in the countryside (or even that they always initiate in the city). In one odd example, a recent *New York Times* photograph of Margaretville's relatively prosperous downtown carried a caption that called the village "reminiscent of small-town rural America in the 20s." Why the town should carry visitors back to the 1920s rather than any other decade past is unclear, but what is clear is that Margaretville will not remind urban visitors of the present. The rural landscape is where urban America goes to reminisce.[3] This "trip into the past" philosophy is so commonplace that it holds remarkable power over the shaping of particular rural places, including the Catskills, where urban visitors, so exhausted by the continuous changes that shape their metropolitan lives, seek out the constancy of the countryside, both in its small towns and its deep woods.

For many vacationers and second-home owners, like Laurance Rockefeller, who hoped to return part of the Catskills "to what it had been a century ago," trips to the mountains mean going "back to the country." Visiting the country allows tourists to return to the city and charge into the future, after having been reassured by the past—an actual, occupiable past. J. B. Jackson notes that this type of celebration of the landscape "looks back not to a specific event, but to a golden age when [our society] was at one with its environment."[4] For the Catskills to serve its purpose as a reminder of a golden age, it must remain forested, its villages tidy but small. Many urban visitors chafe at modern intrusions into their journey to the past, especially the mix of subdivisions and Main Street blight that might remind visitors of metropolitan America. (Not all of modernity's gifts are scorned in the countryside, of course—especially not those that provide amenities that make the trip more pleasurable, like air conditioning and heated pools.) In essence, this "trip to the past" philosophy holds that change belongs to the future, and thus not to the mountains.[5]

In addition to constricting the future of the mountains, this philosophy obscures the actual past of the Catskills. Clearly, Margaretville is not the same now as it was eighty-five years ago, regardless of what the editors of the *Times* might think. Those intervening years were full of people and events, of husbandry and industry. Those years are full of stories that become unimportant in understanding a place held still in time. By believing that the Catskills, and other rural places, occupy some impossible past, we must ignore the history that has actually happened there.

More fundamentally, this vision of the country as the past is simply wrong. Even the most obtuse observer, driving on asphalt roads, passing driveways with late-model cars and trucks, knows full well that the countryside holds ample evidence of modernity. The landscape confirms what physics requires: the countryside is as fully in the present as any other American place.

Why then do urbanites so frequently, so consistently, claim that their trips into the country represent a journey to the past? This trope serves several psychological needs, I think. For some visitors, the journey is personal, as they seek out a connection to their own past in the country—though this is increasingly rare. For many others, the trip to the country allows a connection to a familial past—back to the farms of ancestors, the agricultural history that runs through so many American genealogies. (Remember, this is the story of Sam Gribley in *My Side of the Mountain*.) For others, perhaps the journey into the countryside connects them to the nation's past, the myth of the frontier and the rugged individualist. In sum, the country must play the role of the past because so many Americans living in the metropolis require it—because our history as a rural nation is at the center of the mythical "golden age" Jackson described. This notion of rural America as past requires not just a misreading of the countryside, but also of history, for anyone eking out a living in the actual rural past would undoubtedly question modern romantic ideals about the simple life country living affords.[6]

At first blush, the dominance of this "trip to the past" philosophy seems remarkably imperial, but it has not developed in the city alone. Rural America, the Catskills included, has long prided itself on the survival of its way of life and its values, and, of course, the landscapes that sustain them both. Though clearly this conservative sentiment is indigenous to country communities, we may underestimate how much it draws from the urban appreciation of a static countryside and how collaborative this rural culture really is. Today, this collaboration may be most evident in the work of the Catskill Center, where preservationists from both the city and the mountains strive to keep their beloved landscape as it is. In recent decades, the preservationist impulse has affected both natural and cultural landscapes, as efforts by both locals and urbanites have led to the protection of lakes, streams, and forests, as well as the restoration of older homes, boardinghouses, and even some agricultural buildings.[7]

Currently, the preservationist impulse is strong in the mountains, but the sense of loss is perhaps just as strong. Although I was not yet born when it burned in 1965, the Grand Hotel's destruction is among my memories. I remember my mother expressing sadness at its passing, that so little remained on the hillside above my grandfather's childhood home. The hotel had gone unused for years, having long since become a ruin looming over Highmount, but I suppose that while it stood one might imagine its revival—that someone with a grand scheme and deep pockets might try to return this one Catskills hotel to its former glory. With the hotel gone, even more than this hope was lost. The building had served as a reminder of what was, the place where thousands had vacationed, where hundreds had worked. Its disappearance, along with so much of the built landscape of the grand hotel era, brought the Catskills ever closer to the historyless wilderness so often imagined of the place.

Recently I walked through the site of another lost resort—the Hotel Kaaterskill, destroyed by a fire in 1924 and never rebuilt. Though I am prone to melancholy at such places, I felt no sadness for what had been so fully removed from South Mountain. A field of goldenrod, encroaching aspens, a few stone walls, and a tangle of over-wide hiking trails mark the spot of what had been the largest mountain hotel in the world. My melancholy was kept at bay, I suppose, because I like the place as it is now: a wonderful woodland park. Within easy walking distance of the Hotel Kaaterskill site are the similarly slight remains of two other hotels, both purchased by the state of New York and intentionally burned to the ground. The Catskill Mountain House, once among the most famous hotels in America, sat in shambles for years, an eyesore and a hazard, until the state destroyed it in 1963. The Laurel House suffered the same fate in 1967. The Kaaterskill Park region, so popular among wealthy tourists in the late 1800s, now contains a state-run campground and no hotels. Unlike the Hotel Kaaterskill, at least the Mountain House is remembered by a large sign that faces out over a mowed field where the hotel had stood, at the precipice of the most famous view in nineteenth-century America. Much less frequented than in the days of the grand hotels, Kaaterskill Park is still attractive to tourists, from New York City and hundreds of other, mostly nearby, places. It is popular with those looking for a genuine outdoors experience, for wildlife encounters, wild views, and challenging trails. And, of course, that is exactly why the place looks the way it does today. The state-run campground speaks as much about the influence of urban culture over rural landscapes as did the great hotels of an earlier generation. Today's metropolitan tourists seek out different types of encounters with nature than did their urban counterparts a hundred years ago.[8]

For the moment at least, what one is unlikely to see in the mountains is something entirely new, something out of step with the past.[9] This is not to suggest that some people do not dream of a different future for the mountains. One developer, longtime Catskills resident Dean Gitter, has proposed a large development near Belleayre Ski Center, in Highmount, just across the road from the former site of the Grand Hotel and my great grandfather's home (which last I knew was owned by New York City weekenders). Gitter has proposed building 400 hotel rooms and nearly as many time-share condos and second homes, along with two eighteen-hole golf courses. Even at this size, the Belleayre Resort at Catskill Park would not be large enough to replace the capacity lost over the last generation to declining tourism in Highmount and Pine Hill. Still, opposition to the development has been fierce, both in the mountains and in the city.[10]

Obviously I cannot speak for my great-grandfather Clair, but I imagine he would have supported the plan, had it developed in his lifetime. It would have meant economic opportunity for his sons, a chance to stay in the mountains—to stay prosperous in the mountains. But once again the distinction between insiders and outsiders in the mountains has blurred. Many city folk who oppose the plan want the Catskills to stay wild, since this is what they love about the place; many locals oppose the plan because they fear the traffic it would bring to the only reasonable route from the city to Highmount. Tom Alworth, executive director of the preservation-minded Catskill Center, noted that the development would "redefine Catskill Park, and I resent that," a sentiment that undoubtedly reflects the opinion of many opponents in the city and the mountains.[11]

Alworth and the Catskill Center have a seemingly unlikely and very powerful ally in the fight to prevent the new development—the city of New York. Since 1986, the city has been struggling to meet the heightened standards of the Safe Drinking Water Act amendments. In a critical step to avoid spending billions of dollars building a filtration system for its Catskill and Delaware water supplies, in 1997 the city reached an agreement with the Environmental Protection Agency, the state of New York, the Coalition of Watershed Towns, and several private interest groups, including the Catskill Center. The Watershed Agreement attempted to balance the needs of the city with those of Catskills residents, but, of course, it did so with the primary result predetermined: that the city's watershed would be protected in perpetuity. The need to avoid building a filtration system for Catskills water has made the city all the more vigilant in policing the watershed. That means Gitter's vision for revived tourism in Highmount may well remain just a dream.

The 1997 Watershed Agreement represents a new level of municipal activism in the mountains. As part of the agreement, the city must implement a Land Acquisition Program. The watershed towns gained some protection from this program, since none of the land purchases can be made through eminent domain, and thus all acquisitions must involve willing sellers. The agreement also stipulates that individual towns can mark some lands as off-limits to city acquisition (subject to state approval), leaving space for future development. In the end, however, the agreement requires that the city commit between $250 million and $300 million for acquisition, forcing the city to become an even larger landholder. By early 2004, New York City controlled nearly 8 percent of its watershed lands in Catskills, up from less than 4 percent before the 1997 agreement. While the city must continue to pay taxes on the lands it acquires, it also can determine rules concerning recreational uses of this property, just as it has for all of its previously purchased lands.[12] Although the agreement specifies that the city not purchase lands currently occupied by residents and that the city cannot destroy viable housing, some structures can be demolished, and all purchased lands are to be held in a permanently "undeveloped" state. In sum, combined with occasional state purchases in the mountains that add to the Catskill Park lands, the city's acquisitions continue the process by which the mountains move toward a remade wilderness.[13]

The Watershed Agreement does not prevent economic development in the mountains, but it does attempt to shape it. The agreement contains a revised list of rules and regulations governing all lands inside the watersheds, the first significant updating of those rules since 1953. As one would anticipate, these rules focus on wastewater creation and water runoff, and so dictate how and to some degree where new development can occur. And so the city has confirmed its right to review all development in the Catskills watersheds, although final approval occurs at the state level, where the Department of Environmental Conservation determines if the city's interests are protected. It is in this process that the city has joined the Catskills Center in opposing the Belleayre Resort proposal, fearing that the new golf courses in particular would create objectionable runoff.[14]

To make the watershed rules and regulations more palatable to watershed residents, the city has agreed to spend over $150 million to improve sewage treatment infrastructure and septic systems, and to engage in a number of other activities that help reduce or cleanse storm-water runoff. In the process, of course, local businesses benefit from the spending of city dollars.[15] In another step to ensure local support for all of this intrusion on local sovereignty, the city has funded the creation of the Catskill Watershed Corporation, which operates out of Margaretville and is staffed primarily by local residents. In addition to publicizing the stipulations of the agreement and the progress made under it, the Watershed Corporation has several responsibilities, including oversight of the septic rehabilitation and replacement program and, more interestingly, the spending of nearly sixty million in city dollars on regional economic development through loans and grants. Called "Catskill Fund for the Future," this program has been especially supportive of preservation and restoration efforts, such as funding façade improvements on main streets in Catskills villages and grants to historical societies and local libraries. Thus, many of the grants follow the notion that this area ought to retain its historical feel. Interestingly, Catskills Fund for the Future, initially capitalized by the city but independently operated, financed a commemorative project, in which a series of roadside kiosks remember the sacrifices Catskills residents made so that the city could build its reservoirs. Thus, the city's capital has been used by local residents to memorialize the most dramatic instance of the city's reach into the mountains, or, more precisely, to memorialize the local role in the reservoir story.[16]

Outside the New York City watersheds, and thus in an entirely different Catskills, elaborate plans have been in the works to revive the fading tourist industry. In Sullivan County, where increasing Hasidic tourism has failed to offset the diminishing visitation of other New York Jews, the region has set its sights on Indian casinos to boost the economy.[17] Part of the nation's turn toward gambling as a cure-all for development woes, the call to build Catskills casinos was also part of Governor George Pataki's effort to settle the land claims of the five Iroquois tribes. The proposed casinos derive from an elaborate fiction, although not the first fiction to have an influence over the real Catskills. Following state law, developers can only build casinos on Native American lands, none of which exist in the Catskills region. Indeed, no indigenous groups have specific historical claims to the lands targeted for casino development. Thus, all of the proposed locations reflect Sullivan County's previous tourist landscape and its proximity to New York City, not its more distant Native American past.[18]

Although obviously not new, the debate over the future of the Catskills has grown more boisterous in the years during which I've researched and written this book. Opponents of casinos and the proposed Belleayre Resort have expressed grave concerns about the changes these developments might bring to their mountains. Efforts to avoid building a filtration system have also increased the city's profile in the mountains and elevated concerns about local autonomy. Perhaps more than anything, though, tensions have increased since September 11, 2001, not because the city stepped up patrols to protect its water supply, but because fear of further terrorist attacks in the city have sent thousands of New Yorkers into the countryside in search of safe and secluded second homes. The real-estate boom, felt throughout the Northeast, has been especially evident in the Catskills, where rural homesteads have sold for suburban prices. The influx of New York money has had some positive effects—the mountain economy is clearly better now than just a few years ago—but the arrival of so much city capital has increased talk of "them" and "us" and sparked fears that higher real estate values and taxes might force locals from their homes.[19]

Ongoing concerns notwithstanding, the current Catskills landscape and culture readily reveal the success of the long collaboration between city and local residents in making these mountains. Not long ago, my family and I drove up Haynes Hollow for the first time, to see the place where my ancestors had settled in the Catskills. The road along Dry Brook is beautiful, as wonderful a country road as one could hope for—fields and forests alternate along the clear, rocky stream. Well up the valley, a left turn on Haynes Hollow Road took us into the woods and past a few hunters' cabins. When we could drive no further on the steep, rutted road, we parked and walked further up, hoping to find a trail to Haynes Mountain, now part of the state forest's Big Indian Wilderness. We climbed an old road as it followed stone fences surrounding former fields that seemed impossibly high to have been worth the effort to clear. We failed to find the trail to Haynes Mountain, but we saw warblers, a woodcock, and two bright orange salamanders, and we enjoyed the walk all the same. By the time we had returned to the car, parked by a new home, still under construction, we had probably passed a hundred "Posted" signs with a dozen names, none of them Haynes. Despite the "No Trespassing" signs and the unfinished home, nothing up that road gave me concern for the future. The Catskills are beautiful and remarkably protected. The vast majority of its lands will remain forested and, if the city is successful, its waters will remain clean. The deer are back, as are the wild turkeys, black bears, and bald eagles. In sum, the Catskills ecology is as wild and complete and satisfying as it has been in over 150 years.

Just as the long relationship between the city and mountains has created a remarkable landscape, it has also given the Catskills an extraordinary history. That relationship has made the Catskill Mountains a place that has mattered, not just to the Hudson Valley but to the nation. The Catskills still contain the archetypal American wilderness, with thick woods, rounded mountains, rocky gorges, and spring-fed waterfalls— the wilderness of Thomas Cole. This is still the place that supplies the water for more than eight million New Yorkers. These mountains still represent the promise of abundance in rural America.

Notes

Preface

1. Since beginning this project, I have come to realize that the historiography of the Catskills is far richer than I had suspected. Much of the work has been written and published locally, and so has not increased the national profile of Catskills history, but collectively these works have been instrumental to me. See especially the work of Alf Evers, a long-time resident who has written extensively on the Catskills: *The Catskills: From Wilderness to Woodstock* (Woodstock, NY: The Overlook Press, 1982) and *Woodstock: History of an American Town* (Woodstock, NY: The Overlook Press, 1987). Among the prominent works that have helped elevate the Adirondacks are Roderick Nash, *Wilderness and the American Mind* (New Haven: Yale University Press, 1967); Philip G. Terrie, *Forever Wild: A Cultural History of Wilderness in the Adirondacks* (Syracuse: Syracuse University Press, 1994) and *Contested Terrain: A New History of Nature and People in the Adirondacks* (Syracuse: The Adirondack Museum, 1997); and Paul Schneider, *The Adirondacks: A History of America's First Wilderness* (New York: Henry Holt, 1997).

2. Unless otherwise noted, information on the Haynes family comes from Carliton A. Finch, *The Haynes Family (1600–1994)* (Knoxville: Tennessee Valley Publishing, 1994), and from many conversations with my mother, Gail Stradling.

3. Finch, *Haynes Family,* 233; *Pine Hill Sentinel* 27 May, 8 July 1905.

4. Letter from Glentworth Haynes to Grace Haynes, 28 March [1929], in author's possession.

5. For an introduction to this theme in American literature, at least in regard to Chicago, see William Cronon, *Nature's Metropolis: Chicago and the Great West* (New York: W. W. Norton & Company, 1991), especially 8–17. See also Timothy B. Spears, *Chicago Dreaming: Midwesterners and the City, 1871–1919* (Chicago: University of Chicago Press, 2005), for a discussion of migration narratives.

6. Letter from Glentworth Haynes to Grace Haynes, 28 March [1929]; Letter from H. F. Gunnison to Glentworth Haynes, 12 November 1928, in author's possession. On *Daily Eagle* stationary Gunnison wrote, "I have known you for many years during my stay in the summer at Highmount, and have always found you courteous and most obliging. I understand you are seeking a position in the city. I hope you will find a good position. I shall be only too glad to say a word in your behalf and you are at liberty to refer to me at any time."

7. For a good example of this approach, see J. R. McNeill, *The Mountains of the Mediterranean World: An Environmental History* (New York: Cambridge University Press, 1992), 12–67.

Introduction

John Burroughs, *My Boyhood* (Garden City, NY: Doubleday, Page & Company, 1922), 128–29.

Reverend Irenaeus Prime, letter to editor, *New York Observer* 28 August 1884, as reprinted in *The New Grand Hotel, Catskill Mountains* (New York: Stewart, Warren & Co., 1887), 21.

1. On changing American conceptions of nature, see Hans Huth, *Nature and the American: Three Centuries of Changing Attitudes* (1957; repr., Lincoln: University of Nebraska Press, 1990). On the importance of cities in creating and disseminating ideas, see Richard M. Ohmann, *Selling Culture: Magazines, Markets and Class at the Turn of the Century* (New York: Verso, 1998).

2. J. B. Beers, *History of Greene County, New York, with Biographical Sketches of Its Prominent Men* (New York: J. B. Beers & Co., 1884), 79; Henry Schile, *The Illustration of the Catskill Mountains, Sketched from Nature* (New York: Kelly & Bartholomew, 1881?), i, 36.

3. See Barbara Novak, *Nature and Culture: American Landscape and Painting, 1825–1875* (New York: Oxford University Press, 1980).

4. David M. Scobey, *Empire City: The Making and Meaning of the New York City Landscape* (Philadelphia: Temple University Press, 2002), 23. Scobey's purpose is to discuss how this growth, combined with the power of the city's economic elite, remade the city landscape. My purpose is, in part, to reveal how similarly inspired changes occurred in landscapes at some distance from the city too.

5. William Cronon, *Nature's Metropolis: Chicago and the Great West* (New York: W. W. Norton & Company, 1991). See also "Kennecott Journey: The Paths Out of Town," in *Under an Open Sky: Rethinking America's Western Past,* William Cronon, George Miles, and Jay Gitlin, eds. (New York: W. W. Norton & Company, 1992), 33.

6. William Cronon, *Changes in the Land: Indians, Colonists, and the Ecology of New England* (New York: Hill and Wang, 1983); Donald Worster, *Dust Bowl: The Southern Plains in the 1930s* (New York: Oxford University Press, 1979); Donald Worster, *Rivers of Empire: Water, Aridity, and the Growth of the American West* (New York: Oxford University Press, 1985).

7. Marjorie Hope Nicolson, *Mountain Gloom and Mountain Glory: The Development of the Aesthetics of the Infinite* (1959; repr., Seattle: University of Washington Press, 1997), 1.

8. Raymond Williams, *The Country and the City* (New York: Oxford University Press, 1973), 302.

9. Norris Hundley, Jr., *The Great Thirst: Californians and Water: A History* (Berkeley: University of California Press, 2001).

10. Gray Brechin, *Imperial San Francisco: Urban Power, Earthly Ruin* (Berkeley: University of California Press, 1999), xxi.

11. Hal K. Rothman, *Devil's Bargains: Tourism in the Twentieth-Century American West* (Lawrence: University Press of Kansas, 1998), 11.

12. Matthew Gandy, *Concrete and Clay: Reworking Nature in New York City* (Cambridge: The MIT Press, 2002), 45.

13. Max Page, *The Creative Destruction of Manhattan, 1900–1940* (Chicago: University of Chicago Press, 1999), 5.

14. David Walbert, *Garden Spot: Lancaster County, the Old Order Amish, and the Selling of Rural America* (New York: Oxford University Press, 2002), 9.

Chapter One

John Burroughs, "The Heart of the Southern Catskills," *Riverby* (New York: Houghton, Mifflin and Company, 1894), 44.
Philip Quilibet, "Drift-Wood," *The Galaxy* 24 (October 1877): 553.

1. On early nineteenth-century life in the city, see Edwin G. Burrows and Mike Wallace, *Gotham: A History of New York City to 1898* (New York: Oxford University Press, 1999).

2. Michael Kudish, *The Catskill Forest: A History* (Fleischmanns, NY: Purple Mountain Press, 2000), 47–48. Kudish's work is a remarkable study of the forest's history, with wonderfully detailed maps concerning the location of quarries, tanneries, and other industries. On Native Americans, see Edward M. Ruttenber, *History of the Indian Tribes of Hudson's River* (Albany: J. Munsell, 1872). Mark David Spence noted that "scholars and park officials" have erroneously "asserted that native peoples avoided national park areas because these places were not conducive to use or occupation." These false assertions help avoid any guilt that might come from an acknowledgement of dispossession. I have noticed a similar interest among local historians in announcing that the Catskills region had been underutilized by native peoples, probably for the same reason. See Mark David Spence, *Dispossessing the Wilderness: Indian Removal and the Making of the National Parks* (New York: Oxford University Press, 1999), 5.

3. Brian Donahue has challenged the assertion that negative environmental consequences of colonial farming, including soil exhaustion, played a critical role in the emigration of New England farmers. Instead, Donahue argues that demographic pressure in New England required some out-migration by the late 1700s and not until the second quarter of the 1800s did the influence of the capitalist market impose ecological stress on a previously sustainable mixed husbandry. See *The Great Meadow: Farmers and the Land in Colonial Concord* (New Haven: Yale University Press, 2004).

4. Ashokan Reservoir Awards, Reel 1, pp. 557, 562–63, 933–36, 943.

5. Henry E. Dwight, "Account of the Kaatskill Mountains," *The American Journal of Science and Arts* 2 (April 1820): 27.

6. "Hardenburg Patent Field Book of Great Lot No. 46 and 23," New York State Library Manuscript.

7. "Applications to Redeem Property," New York State Archives, B0847-85.

8. See John Burroughs, "Pepacton," in *Pepacton* (New York: Houghton Mifflin Company, 1881), which describes his trip down the Pepacton (the East Branch of the Delaware) and through this agricultural land. In 1886 Charles Carpenter visited the Schoharie Creek and noted, "The valley is occupied for the greater part of its length as a farming section. . . ." *Second Annual Report of the Forest Commission of the State of New York, for the Year 1886* (Albany: The Argus Company, Printers, 1887), 100.

9. Henry Schile, *The Illustration of the Catskill Mountains, Sketched from Nature* (New York: Kelly & Bartholomew, 1881?), 35. Census figures as found in Nathaniel Sylvester, *History of Ulster County, New York* (Philadelphia: Everts & Peck, 1880), 292–302, 317–24.

10. Kudish, *Catskill Forest,* 54–56.

11. Harry Albert Haring, *Our Catskill Mountains* (New York: G. P. Putnam's Sons, 1931), 72–73. Clifton Johnson's portrait of nineteenth-century Catskills farming features milk, buckwheat, and generosity. See *New England and Its Neighbors* (New York: The MacMillan Company, 1902), 240–63.

12. John Burroughs, *My Boyhood* (Garden City, NY: Doubleday, Page & Company, 1922), 13. The New York State milkshed skirted the Catskills, as better rail connections allowed farmers on the better soils of Chenango and Madison counties to send their products to the city. On the milk industry in New York, see Hal S. Barron, *Mixed Harvest: The Second Great Transformation in the Rural North, 1870–1930* (Chapel Hill: University of North Carolina Press, 1997), 83–105.

13. J. B. Beers, *History of Greene County, New York, with Biographical Sketches of Its Prominent Men* (New York: J. B. Beers & Co., 1884), 331. Beers mentions a "few engaged in dairying [in Hunter], but only to supply the hotels with milk."

14. Nathaniel Sylvester, *History of Ulster County, New York* (Philadelphia: Everts & Peck, 1880), 305–13, 326–29. New York, Ontario & Western Railway, *Annual Report* (1895), 23; "Bishop Falls House," (nd), Florence Hornbeck Collection, Town of Olive Archives.

15. Ashokan Reservoir Awards Reel 1, pp. 222–31; Reel 174, pp. 7808, 7818.

16. Judson was a cousin of James Edgar Haynes, who was then farming in an adjacent valley. See Carliton A. Finch, *The Haynes Family (1600–1994)* (Knoxville: Tennessee Valley Publishing, 1994), 59, 67.

17. Catskill Mountain Agricultural Society, "First Annual Fair of the Catskill Mountain Agricultural Society: To Be Held at Margaretville, New York . . . 1889" (Margaretville, NY: Utilitarian Print, 1889), held by Cornell University Rare Books and Manuscripts Collection.

18. Burroughs, *My Boyhood,* especially 9, 13, 114, 116.

19. Burroughs, *My Boyhood,* 13, 40, 63.

20. Jay Gould, *History of Delaware County and Border Wars of New York* (Roxbury, NY: Keeny & Gould, Publishers, 1856), 156; Maury Klein, *The Life and Legend of Jay Gould* (Baltimore: The Johns Hopkins University Press, 1986), 12–16, 21–22, 25, 263. See also Edward Renehan, *Dark Genius of Wall Street: The Misunderstood Life of Jay Gould, King of the Robber Barons* (New York: Basic Books, 2005).

21. Candace Wheeler, *Yesterdays in a Busy Life* (New York: Harper & Brothers, Publishers, 1918), 45, 61. On gender roles in New York agriculture, see Martin Bruegel, "Work, Gender, and Authority on the Farm: The Hudson Valley Countryside, 1790s–1850s," *Agricultural History* 76 (2002): 1–27.

22. Haring, *Our Catskill Mountains,* 11. On naming the Catskills, see Alf Evers, *The Catskills: From Wilderness to Woodstock* (Woodstock, NY: Overlook Press, 1982), 531–32. On the prevalence of hauntings and ghost stories in the Hudson River Valley, see Judith Richardson, *Possessions: The History and Uses of Haunting in the Hudson Valley* (Cambridge: Harvard University Press, 2003).

23. The tanning industry is described in detail by Frank W. Norcross in *A History of the New York Swamp* (New York: The Chiswick Press, 1901).

24. Haring, *Our Catskill Mountains,* 87–89.

25. Kudish, *Catskill Forest,* 158–59.

26. Evers, *Catskills,* 386.

27. *Biography of Zadock Pratt of Prattsville, New York* (no publishing information), 314. Held by the Pratt Museum, Prattsville, NY.

28. Lucius F. Ellsworth, "Craft to National Industry in the Nineteenth Century: A Case Study of the Transformation of the New York State Tanning Industry" (dissertation, University of Delaware, 1971), 247–49.

29. "The Prattsville Tannery," *Hunt's Merchants' Magazine* 17 (August 1847): 162.

30. "The Prattsville Tannery," 156–63.

31. "The Prattsville Tannery," 159. For the average number of employees per operation, I used Mortimer Strong's reporting in 1853–54. See Market Fire Insurance Company Manuscript, Library of Congress.

32. Patricia E. Millen, *Bare Trees: Zadock Pratt, Master Tanner & the Story of What Happened to the Catskill Mountain Forests* (Hensonville, NY: Black Dome Press, 1995), 91; Ellsworth, "Craft to National Industry," 255–66.

33. Ernest Ingersoll, "At the Gateway of the Catskills," *Harper's New Monthly Magazine* 54 (May 1877): 822. Haring describes the process in detail in *Our Catskill Mountains,* 87–106.

34. Charles F. Carpenter, "The Catskill Preserve," *Second Annual Report of the Forest Commission of the State of New York, for the Year 1886* (Albany: The Argus Company, Printers, 1887), 105. Michael Kudish lists forest fires in Appendix B of *Catskill Forest,* 184–85. On forest fires generally, see Stephen J. Pyne, *Fire in America: A Cultural History of Wildland and Rural Fire* (Princeton: Princeton University Press, 1982).

35. Market Fire Insurance Company Manuscript, Library of Congress; *Census of the State of New York for 1855* (Albany: Charles Van Benthuysen, 1857), 394.

36. Market Fire Insurance Company Manuscript, Dewittville quote from vol. 1, 22; Shokan Tannery, 269.

37. Market Fire Insurance Company Manuscript, Fallsburgh Tannery, 6–10

38. Market Fire Insurance Company Manuscript, Gilboa Tanneries, 257.

39. Kudish, *Catskill Forest,* 57, 60. Kudish used Pratt's figures on the number of hemlocks cut per cord and the number of acres of forest he consumed to produce his bark.

40. Millen, *Bare Trees,* 24.

41. T. Addison Richards, "The Catskills," *Harper's New Monthly Magazine* 9 (July 1854): 153.

42. Ernest Ingersoll, "At the Gateway of the Catskills," *Harper's New Monthly Magazine* 54 (May 1877): 818.

43. "The Prattsville Tannery," 163. On dairying, see "One Day's Work on the Prattsville Dairy Farm of Zadock Pratt," *Prattsville News* 1865, as found at the Pratt Museum.

44. Market Fire Insurance Company Manuscript, p. 279; Haring, *Our Catskill Mountains,* 93; population figures listed in J. B. Beers, *History of Greene County,* 63.

45. "A Used-Up Tannery District," *Shoe and Leather Reporter* (May 21, 1896): 1159–61; Charles Rockwell, *The Catskill Mountains and the Region Around* (New York: Taintor Brothers & Co., 1873), 30. The deserted tannery on the upper Kaaterskill Clove, toward Haynes Falls, also attracted the attention of T. Addision Richards as he toured the region around the Catskill Mountain House in 1854. T. Addison Richards, "The Catskills," *Harper's New Monthly Magazine* 9 (July 1854): 153.

46. John Burroughs, "A Bed of Boughs," in *Locusts and Wild Honey* (1879; repr., New York: Houghton, Mifflin and Company, 1901), 167.

47. John Burroughs, "Speckled Trout," in *Locusts and Wild Honey*, 103, 106, 112, 114.

48. John Burroughs, "A Bed of Boughs," 154.

49. John Burroughs, "Phases of Farm Life," *Signs and Seasons* (New York: Houghton, Mifflin and Company, 1886), 257.

50. Beers, *History of Greene County*, 337.

51. Haring, *Our Catskill Mountains*, 79.

52. Kudish, *Catskill Forest*, 63–67. In addition, kilns along the Ulster and Delaware route supplied charcoal to the Millerton Iron Company forges across the river, but did not export to New York City. Of course, charcoal had a limited market in the Hudson Valley, since by the late 1800s America's iron production had long since shifted toward the coal- and coke-producing Pittsburgh region.

53. Wheeler, *Yesterdays in a Busy Life*, 61–62. For a lengthy description of the rafting industry, with unfortunate racist comments concerning Native Americans, see Leslie C. Wood, *Rafting on the Delaware River* (Livingston Manor, NY: Livingston Manor Times, 1934), especially 18–30.

54. Burroughs, "Pepacton," 26–27; Evers, *Catskills*, 436–37.

55. Martial Hulce Family Papers, Box 1, Cornell University Rare Books and Manuscripts.

56. David Murray, ed., *Delaware County, New York: History of the Century, 1797–1897* (Delhi, NY: William Clark, Publisher, 1898), 39, 107. For the use of North Carolina pine in construction, see, for example, Ashokan Reservoir Awards, Reel 1, pp. 1351–53, which describes the construction of the Bishop Falls House.

57. Quilibet, "Drift-Wood," 553.

58. Beers, *History of Greene County*, 409–10. Beers describes a "great freshet" on the Batavia Kill that removed a dam at Windham in 1870, as well as a number of other floods. Leslie Wood describes the pumpkin flood in *Rafting on the Delaware*, 34.

59. The Carr story is recounted by Agnes Carr Sage, "The Christmas Greens of America," *New England Magazine* 19 (December 1895): 461–62. It also appears in Evers's *Catskills*, and he footnotes a Catskill *Examiner* reprint of a New York *Tribune* article from 1879.

60. Harold T. Dickinson, "Quarries of Bluestone and Other Sandstones in the Upper Devonian of New York State," *New York State Museum Bulletin* 61 (1903): 14–15.

61. Dickinson, "Quarries of Bluestone," 4–6.

62. *The Manufacturer and Builder* 23 (April 1891): 80.

63. *The Manufacturer and Builder* 11 (October 1879): 226.

64. Dickinson, "Quarries of Bluestone," 9–10. See also the description of the industry in John C. Smock, "Building Stone in the State of New York," *New York State Museum Bulletin no. 3* (March, 1888): 71–78.

65. Dickinson, "Quarries of Bluestone," 13–14; "Hudson River Bluestone," *The Manufacturer and Builder* 21 (June 1889): 131.

66. *The Manufacturer and Builder* 23 (April 1891): 80.

67. Ashokan Reservoir Awards, Reel 7, pp. 6203–07; Reel 5, pp. 4649–59, 4794–97.

68. Dickinson, "Quarries of Bluestone," 16.

69. Dickinson, "Quarries of Bluestone," 35, 63.

70. Quilibet, "Drift-Wood," 553.

71. Dickinson, "Quarries of Bluestone," 67.

72. Haring, *Our Catskill Mountains,* 122–31.

73. Lucy C. Lillie, "The Catskills," *Harper's New Monthly Magazine* 67 (September 1883): 522.

74. John Burroughs, "The Heart of the Southern Catskills," in *In the Catskills* (New York: Houghton Mifflin Company, 1910), 166.

75. J. B. Jackson, *The Necessity For Ruins and Other Topics* (Amherst: University of Massachusetts Press, 1980), 90 and 89–102 passim. For the fullest example of romanticizing the extractive past of the Catskills, see R. Lionel De Lisser's *Picturesque Catskills: Greene County* (Northampton, MA: Picturesque Publishing Company, 1894), a lavishly illustrated book that featured dilapidated mills and ruined dams almost as fully as waterfalls and hotels.

Chapter 2

John Burroughs, "Phases of Farm Life," *Signs and Seasons* (New York: Houghton, Mifflin and Company, 1886), 262.

Thomas Cole, "The Spirits of the Wilderness," Cole Papers, box 7, folder 3, New York State Library Manuscripts.

1. Sarah J. Hale, *Traits of American Life* (Philadelphia: E. L. Carey & A. Hart, 1835). On travel and associations, see Robert C. Bredeson, "Landscape Description in Nineteenth-Century American Travel Literature," *American Quarterly* 20 (Spring, 1968): 86–94. Eric Purchase has made a similar observation regarding the White Mountains. See *Out of Nowhere: Disaster and Tourism in the White Mountains* (Baltimore: Johns Hopkins University Press, 1999), especially 55–59.

2. Henry E. Dwight, "Account of the Kaatskill Mountains," *The American Journal of Science and Arts* 2 (April 1820): 11–12, 27.

3. On Irving in the city, see Edwin G. Burrows and Mike Wallace, *Gotham: A History of New York City to 1898* (New York: Oxford University Press, 1999), 415–19.

4. The *Sketch Book* has been published multiple times, and "Rip Van Winkle" even more often. I used Washington Irving's *The Sketch Book of Geoffrey Crayon, Gent* (New York: Dutton, 1963), 26–44. See also Judith Richardson's lengthy discussion of "Rip Van Winkle" in *Possessions: The History and Uses of Haunting in the Hudson Valley* (Cambridge: Harvard University Press, 2003).

5. Washington Irving, *Sketch Book of Geoffrey Crayon,* 27, 41.

6. Pierre M. Irving, *The Life and Letters of Washington Irving,* vol. 3 (New York: G. P. Putnam, 1864), 53–34, 26–28; Washington Irving, *Sketch Book of Geoffrey Crayon,* 27.

7. Washington Irving, "The Catskill Mountains," *Littell's Living Age* 31 (1851): 408. See also *Home Book of the Picturesque* (New York: George P. Putnam, 1852), 71–78.

8. T. Morris Longstreth, *The Catskills* (New York: The Century Company, 1918), 73.

9. On the life and career of James Fenimore Cooper and for an analysis of *The Pioneers,* see Alan Taylor, *William Cooper's Town: Power and Persuasion on the Frontier of the Early American Republic* (New York: Vintage Books, 1995), especially 406–23.

10. James Fenimore Cooper, *The Pioneers, or the Sources of the Susquehanna* (1823; repr., New York: Signet Classics, 1964), 197.

11. Cooper, *Pioneers*, 279. Like many of the famous passages concerning the mountains, this one was reprinted over and over.

12. Cooper, *Pioneers*, 279–80.

13. On the Knickerbockers, see James Grant Wilson, *Bryant and His Friends: Some Reminiscences of the Knickerbocker Writers* (New York: Fords, Howard, & Hulbert, 1886), and James T. Callow, *Kindred Spirits: Knickerbocker Writers and American Artists, 1807–1855* (Chapel Hill: University of North Carolina Press, 1967).

14. Callow, *Kindred Spirits*, 11–29.

15. On Bryant, see Parke Godwin, *A Biography of William Cullen Bryant, with Extracts from His Private Correspondence* (New York: D. Appleton and Company, 1883) and Charles H. Brown, *William Cullen Bryant* (New York: Charles Scribner's Sons, 1971), especially 132.

16. Cooper, *Pioneers*, 281.

17. Parke Godwin, ed., *The Poetical Works of William Cullen Bryant*, vol. 1 (New York: Russell & Russell, 1967; reissue of 1883 original), 130–34, 223–24, 268–72. On Bryant's nature writings, see Hans Huth, *Nature and the American: Three Centuries of Changing Attitudes* (Berkeley: University of California Press, 1957), and Roderick Nash, *Wilderness and the American Mind* (New Haven: Yale University Press, 1967).

18. William Cullen Bryant, ed., *Picturesque America, or, The Land We Live In* (New York: D. Appleton & Co., 1872).

19. The "publicity" these writers provided for the Catskills can be starkly contrasted with the relative paucity of early attention paid to Pennsylvania's Pocono Mountains, which are about the same distance from Manhattan, but remained much more difficult to reach until better rail connections made access easier. See Lawrence Squeri, *Better in the Poconos: The Story of Pennsylvania's Vacationland* (University Park: Pennsylvania State University Press, 2002), 4–7.

20. "Editor's Easy Chair," *Harper's New Monthly Magazine* 13 (July 1856): 272. On the sense of dislocation caused by rapid change, see David M. Henkin, *City Reading: Written Words and Public Spaces in Antebellum New York* (New York: Columbia University Press, 1998), 27–38.

21. For a fuller discussion of the sublime, see William Cronon, "The Trouble with Wilderness; or, Getting Back to the Wrong Nature," in Cronon, ed., *Uncommon Ground: Toward Reinventing Nature* (New York: W. W. Norton & Company, 1995), 73–75; and, Marjorie Hope Nicolson, *Mountain Gloom and Mountain Glory: The Development of the Aesthetics of the Infinite* (Seattle: University of Washington Press, 1997; reprint of 1957 original), passim.

22. Lewis Gaylord Clark, ed., *The Literary Remains of the Late Willis Gaylord Clark* (New York: Stringer & Townsend, 1851), 132, 210.

23. Park Benjamin, "Cattskill Mountain House," *The New World* 7 (August 12, 1843): 183.

24. Charles Lanman, *Adventures in the Wilds of the United States and British American Provinces* (Philadelphia: John W. Moore, 1856), 179.

25. T. Addison Richards, "The Catskills," *Harper's New Monthly Magazine* 9 (July 1854): 148.

26. *The Scenery of the Catskill Mountains* (New York: D. Fanshaw, 1843); *The Scenery of the Catskill Mountains, As Described by Irving, Cooper, Bryant, Willis Gaylord Clark . . .* (Catskill, NY: Joseph Joesbury, Printer, 1864); *The Scenery of the Catskill Moun-*

tains (Catskill: J. B. Hall & Sons, 1872); Charles Rockwell, *The Catskill Mountains and the Region Around* (New York: Taintor Brothers & Co., 1873).

27. Callow, *Kindred Spirits*, 3–8. For Cole's biography, see Ellwood C. Parry III, *The Art of Thomas Cole: Ambition and Imagination* (Newark: University of Delaware Press, 1988), and Louis L. Noble, *The Life and Works of Thomas Cole, N. A.* (New York: Sheldon & Company, 1860).

28. Barbara Novak, *Nature and Culture: American Landscape and Painting, 1825–1875* (New York: Oxford University Press, 1995), 228–31.

29. John Ruskin, *Modern Painters*, vol. 4 (New York: John Wiley & Sons, 1878; originally published in 1856), 337.

30. For the fullest discussion of Hudson River art and the Catskills, see Kenneth Myers, *The Catskills: Painters, Writers, and Tourists in the Mountains, 1820–1895* (Yonkers: The Hudson River Museum of Westchester, 1987; distributed by Hanover, NH: University Press of New England, 1987). Other helpful works on the Hudson River School include *American Paradise: The World of the Hudson River School* (New York: Metropolitan Museum of Art, 1987) and Andrew Wilton and Tim Barringer, *American Sublime: Landscape Painting in the United States, 1820–1880* (Princeton: Princeton University Press, 2002).

31. Asher B. Durand, "On Landscape Painting," *The Crayon* 1 (January 3, 1855): 2. For another example of how art shaped a tourist region, see Pamela J. Belanger, *Inventing Acadia: Artists and Tourists at Mount Desert* (Rockland, ME: The Farnsworth Art Museum, 1999).

32. Thomas Cole to Robert Gilmore, December 25, 1825, as quoted in Noble, *Life and Works of Thomas Cole*, 93; Novak, *Nature and Culture*, 265.

33. Myers, *Catskills*, 40; Allan Nevins, ed., *The Diary of Philip Hone, 1828–1851*, vol. 2 (New York: Dodd, Mead and Company, 1927), 838–39; "A Review of the Gallery of the American Academy of Fine Arts," *New York Review and Atheneum Magazine* 2 (January 1826): 153.

34. Cole spent the winter of 1834–35 at 520 Broome Street. Thomas Cole to J. Alexander, 1 September 1834; Thomas Cole to William Adams, 29 October 1834, Thomas A. Cole Papers, box 1, folder 1, New York State Library (hereafter cited as NYSL); Thomas Cole, "Journal: 1834–1848," November 8, 1834, box 4, folder 7, NYSL. As early as 1826, Cole expressed dissatisfaction with the "noise and bustle" of New York City, and, stuck in the city in early June 1828, Cole lamented that he was "wasting these precious moments in the barren City." See J. Bard McNulty, ed., *The Correspondence of Thomas Cole and Daniel Wadsworth* (Hartford: The Connecticut Historical Society, 1983), 1, 42.

35. "The Clove Valley," Cole Papers, box 5, folder 8, NYSL.

36. For an essay on the freezing and thawing of the Hudson, see John Burroughs, "A River View," *Signs and Seasons* (New York: Houghton, Mifflin and Company, 1886), 203–20.

37. Thomas Cole to Luman Reed, (about) 13 January 1836, Cole Papers, box 1, folder 2, NYSL. Thomas Cole to Asher B. Durand, 18 December 1839, Asher B. Durand Papers, box 3, folder 8, New York Public Library (hereafter cited as NYPL); and Cole Papers box 1, folder 4, NYSL.

38. Thomas Cole to Asher B. Durand, 12 September 1836. Durand Papers, box 3, folder 5, NYPL. Cole is always very apologetic for his favors. "Now I think I ought to be ashamed of my self for filling a letter with errands for you to do," he wrote on November 2, 1837. Durand Papers, box 3, folder 6, NYPL. See also Thomas Cole to Asher B. Durand, 17 September 1836, Cole Papers, box 1, folder 2, NYSL.

39. "Journal: 1829," Cole Papers, box 4, folder 8, NYSL. On Luman Reed, see Lillian B. Miller, *Patrons and Patriotism: The Encouragement of the Fine Arts in the United States, 1790–1860* (Chicago: University of Chicago Press, 1966), 152; J. Bard McNulty, ed., *The Correspondence of Thomas Cole and Daniel Wadsworth* (Hartford: The Connecticut Historical Society, 1983), 1–4 ; Gilmore quoted in Miller, *Patrons and Patriotism,* 151; A. N. Skinner to Thomas Cole, 17 September 1840, Cole Papers, box 3, folder 1, NYSL. On Skinner and Cole, see Kenneth J. LaBudde, "The Rural Earth: Sylvan Bliss," *American Quarterly* 10 (Summer 1958): 149–50.

40. Quoted in Novak, *Nature and Culture,* 107.

41. July 6, 1835, "Journal: 1834–1838," Cole Papers, box 4, folder 7, NYSL. On the mill, see Alf Evers, *The Catskills: From Wilderness to Woodstock* (Woodstock, NY: The Overlook Press, 1982), 489, and Myers, *Catskills,* 41–42.

42. Novak, *Nature and Culture,* 15–17.

43. LaBudde, "The Rural Earth," 152–53.

44. Myers, *Catskills,* 70–71; T. Addison Richards, *Appleton's Illustrated Hand-Book of American Travel* (New York: D. Appleton & Co., 1857), 147; John I. H. Baur, ed., *The Autobiography of Worthington Whittredge, 1820–1910* (New York: Arno Press, 1969), 59.

45. T. Addison Richards, *American Scenery, Illustrated* (New York: Leavitt and Allen, 1854), 258–59.

46. *Autobiography of Worthington Whittredge,* 42, 59, 63.

47. *Autobiography of Worthington Whittredge,* 63; Ila Weiss, *Poetic Landscape: The Art and Experience of Sanford R. Gifford* (Newark: University of Delaware Press, 1987), 64–65.

48. Franklin Kelly, *Frederic Edwin Church and the National Landscape* (Washington, DC: Smithsonian Institution Press, 1988).

49. The State of New York and the Olana Partnership have preserved this wonderful estate, where one can enjoy very informative tours.

50. "American Painters.—Frederic Edwin Church, N. A.," *Art Journal* 4 (1878): 65–66.

51. Miller, *Patrons and Patriotism,* 100–102, 154–55; "Exhibition of the Paintings of the Late Thomas Cole," Cole Papers, box 7, folder 2, NYSL.

52. Myers, *Catskills,* 46.

53. Myers, *Catskills,* 53, 58; Hans Huth, *Nature and the American,* 48. The lithograph market was much more diverse than that of landscape painting, with engravings covering everything from current events and city street scenes to critical historical moments, topics New York's landscapists rarely covered. In addition, rural scenes regularly focused on farmsteads and other domestic or agricultural topics, and few offered the wild scenes that dominated Hudson River art. On lithographic art, see Bryan F. LeBeau, *Currier & Ives: America Imagined* (Washington, DC: Smithsonian Institution Press, 2001), 170–77.

54. A discussion of narrative movement and Emerson's quote are found in Novak, *Nature and Culture,* 93–94.

55. Doreen Bolger Burke and Catherine Hoover Voorsanger, "The Hudson River School in Eclipse," in *American Paradise* (1987): 71–90; "National Academy of Design," *New York Times,* 23 May 1867.

56. Novak, *Nature and Culture,* 266.

57. For a similar relationship between city and country, see Nicholas Green's work on Paris and the French countryside as created by the Barbizon painters, *The Specta-*

cle of Nature: Landscape and Bourgeois Culture in Nineteenth-Century France (Manchester: Manchester University Press, 1990).

58. Candace Wheeler, *Yesterdays in a Busy Life* (New York: Harper & Brothers, 1918), 91.

59. Thomas Bender, "Spirited Away," *New York Times,* 9 May 2005. In the spring of 2005, the New York Public Library auctioned off *Kindred Spirits* to raise money. Walmart heiress Alice L. Walton purchased the painting. See *New York Times,* 13 May 2005.

Chapter 3

John Burroughs, "Footpaths," *Pepacton* (New York: Houghton, Mifflin and Company, 1881), 177.

George William Curtis, *Lotus-Eating: A Summer Book* (New York: Harper & Brothers, Publishers, 1852), 12–13.

1. On Rip Van Winkle generally, see Roland Van Zandt, *The Catskill Mountain House: America's Grandest Hotel* (1966; repr., Hensonville, NY: Black Dome Press Corp., 1991), 88–99. Thomas Cole described this area as "Rip Van Winkle's Hollow" in 1835, as quoted in Charles Rockwell, *The Catskill Mountains and the Region Around* (New York: Taintor Brothers & Co., 1867), 281. *Van Loan's Catskill Mountain Guide,* (New York: The Aldine Publishing Company, 1879), labels this stretch "Sleepy Hollow." R. Lionel De Lisser, *Picturesque Catskills: Greene County* (1894; facs. repr., Cornwallville, New York: Hope Farm Press, 1967), 58. On the use of Rip in marketing, see the Catskill Chamber of Commerce's series of pamphlets, "Greene County Catskills: Amid the Haunts of Rip Van Winkle," by Richard Barrett, produced in the late 1910s and early 1920s, two of which are held at the New York Public Library. On the lasting influence of Irving's story, see Judith Richardson, *Possessions: The History and Uses of Haunting in the Hudson Valley* (Cambridge: Harvard University Press, 2003), 64–83.

2. A. E. P. Searing, *When Granny Was a Little Girl* (New York: Doubleday, Page & Company, 1927), especially 148–53; Richardson, *Possessions,* 68–69. See Alf Evers on the importance of legends like "Rip Van Winkle" and local attempts to place these legends specifically (*The Catskills: From Wilderness to Woodstock* [Woodstock, NY: The Overlook Press, 1982], 520–29).

3. John F. Sears, *Sacred Places: American Tourist Attractions in the Nineteenth Century* (New York: Oxford University Press, 1989); Cindy S. Aron, *Working at Play: A History of Vacations in the United States* (New York: Oxford University Press, 1999); Jon Sterngass, *First Resorts: Pursuing Pleasure at Saratoga Springs, Newport & Coney Island* (Baltimore: The Johns Hopkins University Press, 2001). On the role of travel in changing ideas of nature, see Hans Huth, *Nature and the American: Three Centuries of Changing Attitudes* (1957; repr., Lincoln: University of Nebraska Press, 1990), 71–86.

4. On the Grand Tour, see Dona Brown, *Inventing New England: Regional Tourism in the Nineteenth Century* (Washington, DC: Smithsonian Institution Press, 1995), 23–40.

5. Huth, *Nature and the American,* 82. For examples of popular tourist books, see Caroline Gilman, *The Poetry of Traveling in the United States* (New York: S. Colman,

1838), and Harriet Martineau, *Retrospect of Western Travel,* vol. 1 (London: Saunders and Otley, 1838).

6. On Niagara Falls, see Sears, *Sacred Places,* 12–30.

7. On early spas, see Sterngass, *First Resorts,* 7–39.

8. George William Curtis, *Lotus-Eating,* 12–13.

9. Brown, *Inventing New England,* 4. On the theme of "taking the city with us," see Sterngass, especially in his discussion of Saratoga, *First Resorts,* 6–39.

10. For an extensive history of the Mountain House, see Van Zandt, *Catskill Mountain House.*

11. "Travels from Home," *New York Tribune,* 12 July 1860.

12. Journal entry, July 23, 1891, Burroughs Papers, box 2.17, Vassar College.

13. Tyrone Power, *Impressions of America, During the Years 1833, 1834 and 1835,* vol. 1 (London: Richard Bently, 1836), 426; Robert Vandewater, *The Tourist, or Pocket Manual for Travelers on the Hudson River. . . .* (New York: Harper & Brothers, 1836), 33–34.

14. See, for example, *The River Hudson, Together with Descriptions and Illustrations* (New York: Ross & Tousey, 1859), 34.

15. Allan Nevins and Milton Halsey Thomas, eds., *The Diary of George Templeton Strong,* vol. 1 (New York: The MacMillan Company, 1952), 213–14.

16. Nevins and Thomas, *Diary of George Templeton Strong,* 214. Martineau, *Retrospect of Western Travel,* 89–90; J. S. Buckingham, *America: Historical, Statistic, and Descriptive,* vol. 2 (London: Fisher, Son, & Co., 1841), 257.

17. Park Benjamin, "Cattskill [sic] Mountain House," *The New World* 7 (August 12, 1843): 183. On changes in New York City, see Edwin G. Burrows and Mike Wallace, *Gotham: A History of New York City to 1898* (New York: Oxford University Press, 1999), especially 429–51, 587–602, 735–60.

18. "Journal: 1834–1838," 6 July 1835, Cole Papers, box 4, folder 7, New York State Library.

19. T. Addison Richards, "The Catskills," *Harper's New Monthly Magazine* 9 (July 1854): 148. On "pilgrimage" and tourism, see Sterngass, *First Resorts,* 68–69.

20. *Guide to Rambles from the Catskill Mountain House; By A Visitor* (Catskill, NY: J. Joesbury Book & Job Printer, 1863).

21. Bradford Torrey and Francis H. Allen, eds., *The Journal of Henry D. Thoreau,* vol.1 (Boston: Houghton Mifflin Company, 1949), 361; Rockwell, *Catskill Mountains,* 328. On Thoreau's visit, see Evers, *Catskills,* 488–90; on Laurel House, see Van Zandt, *Catskill Mountain House,* 142–43.

22. Evers, *Catskills,* 498–502; West Shore Railroad, *Summer Homes and Excursions Embracing Lake, River, Mountain and Seaside Resorts* (New York, 1887), 36.

23. Henry Schile, *The Illustration of the Catskill Mountains, Sketched from Nature* (New York: Kelly & Bartholomew, 1881?), 29.

24. *Kaaterskill Park: Scenery, Walks, Drives, Geology, Etc.* (Kaaterskill Publishing Company, 1881), 5–6; *The Kaaterskill* 2 (August 1, 1883): 2.

25. Francis R. Kowsky, *Country, Park, & City: The Architecture and Life of Calvert Vaux* (New York: Oxford University Press, 1998), 7, 64–65. On Central Park, see Roy Rosenzweig and Elizabeth Blackmar, *The Park and the People: A History of Central Park* (Ithaca: Cornell University Press, 1992).

26. Frederick Law Olmsted, Sr., *Forty Years of Landscape Architecture: Central Park,* ed. Frederick Law Olmsted, Jr., and Theodora Kimball (1928; repr., Cambridge: The

MIT Press, 1973), 46; J. K. Larke, *Davega's Handbook of Central Park* (New York: Baldwin & Co., 1866), 19, 38; *Kaaterskill Park: Scenery, Walks, Drives*, 4.

27. Schile, *Illustration of the Catskill Mountains*, 31, 33.

28. *Catskill Mountain Breeze and Tourist's Guide* 2 (21 August 1884): 4; Rockwell, *Catskill Mountains*, 327. For cuisine, see menus from the Catskill Mountain House, July 4, 1905, 1919, and 1923, Catskill Mountain House Manuscript, box 31, folder 1, Greene County Historical Society.

29. *The New Grand Hotel, Catskill Mountains*, (New York: Stewart, Warren & Co., 1887), 3–4, 8, 10.

30. *New Grand Hotel*, 11, 15; Richard S. Barrett, *The Eagle Guide to the Catskill Mountains* (New York: Brooklyn Eagle, 1902), 23.

31. West Shore Railroad, *Summer Homes and Excursions*, 33.

32. *Catskill Mountain House, Eighty-Third Season* (Catskill, NY: Recorder Print, 1905), unpaginated; "Tanner House, J. W. Tanner, Prop.," (188?), as found in S. B. Champion Scrapbook, 1825–1903, New York State Historical Association. In 1887, a train from New York City took twelve hours to arrive at the center of the White Mountains, at a time when the Grand Hotel promised a trip of four and a half or five hours. The Saranac Inn in the Adirondacks was ten hours from New York in 1896, more than twice as far as most Catskills resorts. On the travel time to the White Mountains, see Eric Purchase, *Out of Nowhere: Disaster and Tourism in the White Mountains* (Baltimore: Johns Hopkins University Press, 1999), 46; on the Adirondacks, see New York Central & Hudson River Railroad, "Health and Pleasure on 'America's Greatest Railroad,'" (New York: New York Central Passenger Department, 1896), 487.

33. See Gerald M. Best, *The Ulster and Delaware: Railroad Through the Catskills* (San Marino, CA: Golden West Books, 1972), 33 and passim.

34. Julia Olin called Round Top the tallest Catskills peak in "The Overlook," *Ladies Repository* 23 (December 1863): 708. French geographer Arnold Guyot produced a more accurate map of the Catskills in 1879, which correctly identified Slide as the highest mountain. Arnold Guyot, "Map of the Catskill Mountains," 1879, held by the New York Public Library.

35. Barrett, *Eagle Guide,* 7. Note, however, that Barrett did not include Sullivan County in his expansive definition of the Catskills.

36. "The Catskill Mountains, Pine Hill and Summit Mountain," (Rondout, NY: Kingston Freeman Company, 1883); "Souvenir of Stamford: 'Queen of the Catskills,'" (Middleburgh, NY: Pierre W. Danforth, Publisher, 1905).

37. Hudson River Day Line, *Summer Tours* (1907); Charles Taintor, *Hudson River Route: New York to West Point, Catskill Mountains, Saratoga, Lake George, Lake Champlain, Adirondacks, Montreal, and Quebec* (New York: Taintor Brothers & Co., 1888). For a more complete history of early tourist guides, see Marguerite S. Shaffer, *See America First: Tourism and National Identity, 1880–1940* (Washington, DC: Smithsonian Institution Press, 2001), 172–80.

38. Washington Irving, *The Kaaterskill Region: Rip Van Winkle and Sleepy Hollow* (Kaaterskill Publishing Company, 1884).

39. Ulster and Delaware Railroad, *Catskill Mountains* (1892): 6–12.

40. *Rand McNally & Co's Handy Guide to the Hudson River and Catskill Mountains* (New York: Rand McNally, 1905), 155; Sylvanus Lyon, *Outing in the Catskills: Cairo and Greene County, New York* (1889), held by New York State Library.

41. "Economy in the Catskills," *The Catskill Mountain Breeze* 3 (June 25, 1885): 4.

42. New York Central & Hudson River Railroad, *Health and Pleasure on 'America's Greatest Railroad'* (New York: New York Central Passenger Department, 1890), 75.

43. De Lisser, *Picturesque Catskills,* 66–67.

44. Barrett, *Eagle Guide,* 15.

45. Ulster and Delaware annual guide (1908), 9, 109.

46. The falls, and the mills on either side of them, even gained the attention of famed travel writer Ernest Ingersoll, who described them at length in "At the Gateway of the Catskills," *Harper's New Monthly Magazine* 54 (May 1877): 818–20. This same prose reappeared in Rand McNally's *Handy Guide to the Hudson River,* 159–60.

47. Ashokan Reservoir Awards (hereafter cited as ARA) Reel 115, pp. 34, 38, 68, 199; Reel 174, p. 7950, Ulster County Clerk's Office.

48. ARA Reel 174, pp. 7808, 7818–20, 7822.

49. On flirtations and relaxed gender norms, see Sterngass, *First Resorts,* 2, 132–39.

50. Lucy C. Lillie, "The Catskills," *Harper's New Monthly Magazine* 67 (September 1883): 533. Betsy Blackmar and Elizabeth Cromley, "On the Verandah: Resorts of the Catskills," in *Victorian Resorts and Hotels: Essays from a Victorian Society Autumn Symposium,* ed. Richard Guy Wilson (Philadelphia: The Victorian Society in America, 1982), 51–57.

51. Julia M. Olin, "The Overlook," 706–8.

52. Samuel E. Rusk, *Rusk's Illustrated Guide to the Catskill Mountains; With Maps and Plans* (Catskill, NY: Samuel E. Rusk, 1879), 55, 101; Lyon, *Outing in the Catskills,* 29.

53. The *Tribune* article appeared in the *Pine Hill Sentinel,* 29 April 1905; *Catskill Mountain Breeze* 2 (July 10, July 17, and August 28, 1884).

54. Brown, *Inventing New England,* 3; Olin, "The Overlook," 708.

55. De Lisser, *Picturesque Catskills,* 34. Note that the hotels and shops didn't provide the only means of making money from the tourist trade. Rusk (*Rusk's Illustrated Guide*) includes a reference to a furniture factory, D. B. Baldwin and Company, in Hunter: "We make a specialty of furnishing hotels and boarding houses" (123). In addition, salesmen toured the mountains, visiting boardinghouses along the route, selling any number of items. Some less scrupulous businessmen even took to advertising on the scenery itself, much to the chagrin of the *Catskill Mountain Breeze,* which editorialized against patent-medicine ads painted on rocks along the highways. See "Disfigurement of the Mountains," *The Catskill Mountain Breeze* 2 (June 26, 1884): 4.

56. Paul Shepard, *Man in the Landscape: A Historic View of the Esthetics of Nature* (1967; repr., Athens: The University of Georgia Press, 2002), 127.

57. James Fenimore Cooper, *The Pioneers, or the Sources of the Susquehanna* (1823; repr., New York: Signet Classics, 1964), 281; Bryant reprinted in Rockwell, *Catskill Mountains,* 332.

58. See Evers, *Catskills,* 489. Barbara Novak, *Nature and Culture: American Landscape and Painting, 1825–1875* (New York: Oxford University Press, 1995), 160.

59. Nevins and Thomas, *Diary of George Templeton Strong,* 213; Calvert Vaux, *Villas and Cottages* (1857; repr., New York: Harper & Brothers, Publishers, 1872), 167.

60. Rusk, *Rusk's Illustrated Guide,* 71.

61. Curtis, *Lotus-Eating,* 48; Annie Searing, *The Land of Rip Van Winkle: A Tour Through the Romantic Parts of the Catskills; Its Legends and Traditions* (New York: G. P. Putnam's Sons, 1884), 44.

62. T. Morris Longstreth reported that the falls were still operated by the Hotel in 1918, *The Catskills* (New York: The Century Company, 1918), 90.

63. Schile, *Illustration of the Catskill Mountains,* 29.

64. T. Addison Richards, *Appletons' Illustrated Hand-Book of American Travel* (New York: D. Appleton & Company, 1857), 146.

65. Dona Brown goes so far as to claim that vacation communities would become "far more segregated than most urban neighborhoods" (Brown, *Inventing New England,* 7). Perhaps the ultimate example of physical segregation by class at tourist destinations was the development of exclusive Newport, Rhode Island, in the late 1800s. See Sterngass, *First Resorts,* 182–228.

66. Joel Benton, *Memories of the Twilight Club* (New York: Broadway Publishing Co., 1910), 17.

67. *Twilight Park in the Catskills,* (New York: Albert B. King, Printer, 189?), 7–8.

68. *Twilight Park in the Catskills,* 39; John A. MacGahan, *Twilight Park: The First Hundred Years, 1888–1988* (South Yarmouth, MA: Allen D. Bragdon, Publishers, Inc., 1988). In 1935, Twilight Park merged with neighboring Santa Cruz Park.

69. *Handy Guide to the Hudson River,* 165–66; Clara Barrus, *The Life and Letters of John Burroughs,* vol. 1 (New York: Houghton Mifflin Company, 1925), 316. On the founding of Onteora, see Candace Wheeler, *Yesterdays in a Busy Life* (New York: Harper & Brothers Publishers, 1918), especially 268–89. On the private parks generally, see Evers, *Catskills,* 538–44.

70. *Van Loan's Catskill Mountain Guide,* 74. See advertisements in *In the Catskills: Devoted to Boarding-houses and Hotels of the Catskills, Shawangunks and Mountains of Sullivan County* (Catskill, NY: Catskill Daily Mail?, 1929), 38–47; Evers, *Catskills,* 688–91.

71. *New York Times,* 20 June 1877.

72. *The Courier,* 23 August 1879, as found in scrapbooks of G. H. Hastings, Lexington, New York State Library MSS, SC16495.

73. Alice Hyneman Rhine, "Race Prejudice at Summer Resorts," *The Forum* 3 (July 1887): 524; "The Anti-Hebrew Crusade," *New York Times,* 7 May 1889; "Bishop Falls House," Florence Hornbeck Collection, Town of Olive Archives.

74. De Lisser, *Picturesque Catskills,* 62, 154.

75. Reproduced in Kenneth A. Johnson, "Origins of Tourism in the Catskill Mountains," *Journal of Cultural Geography* 11 (1990): 15. For subtler, coded warnings against Jews, see advertisements in *In the Catskills* (1932).

76. William F. Helmer, *O&W: The Long Life and Slow Death of the New York, Ontario and Western Railway* (Berkeley, CA: Howell-North, 1959). The Ontario and Western formed in 1880, after the failure of its predecessor, the New York and Oswego Midland Railroad, which actually completed the line in 1873.

77. *Summer Homes of the Midland for New York Business Men* (1879), 5–6.

78. *Summer Homes among the Mountains on the New York, Ontario & Western Railway* (1881), 7. At this point, the O&W had the distinct disadvantage of reaching only to Middletown, New York, where passengers had to transfer from the Erie Railroad. Interestingly, the guide did not privilege the Sullivan County stations, offering descriptions of stops all along the O&W route up to Oswego, even in Central New York communities like Earlville and Eaton that had no hope of attracting summer guests.

79. *Summer Homes* (1894), 11.

80. *Summer Homes* (1894), 72. On tuberculosis in Liberty, see Evers, *Catskills,* 668–76.

81. *Summer Homes* (1911).

Chapter 4

John Burroughs, *Wake-Robin* (1871; repr., New York: Hurd and Houghton, 1877), 60.
Theodore Gordon, "American Trout Fishing," in Arnold Gingrich, ed., *American Trout Fishing* (New York: Alfred A. Knopf, 1966), 15.

1. Roderick Nash, *Wilderness and the American Mind* (New Haven: Yale University Press, 1982), 141–60.

2. On the definition of "wilderness," see Nash, *Wilderness,* especially 1–7.

3. Louis L. Noble, *The Life and Works of Thomas Cole, N.A.* (New York: Sheldon & Company, 1860), 217–18; Thomas Cole, "Essay on American Scenery," *American Monthly Magazine* 1 (January 1836): 1–12; see especially 5, 9, 12.

4. Cole, "Essay on American Scenery," 5; Charles Lanman, *Adventures in the Wilds of the United States and British American Provinces* (Philadelphia: John W. Moore, 1856), 172–75, 181.

5. For Burroughs's biography, see Edward J. Renehan, Jr., *John Burroughs: An American Naturalist* (Hensonville, NY: Black Dome Press, 1998) and Clara Barrus, *The Life and Letters of John Burroughs,* vol. 1 (New York: Houghton Mifflin Company, 1925). For a narrower portrait of Burroughs, see Ralph H. Lutts, *The Nature Fakers: Wildlife, Science & Sentiment* (Charlottesville: University of Virginia Press, 1990).

6. Barrus, *Life and Letters,* 107–13.

7. Barrus, *Life and Letters,* 368. Burroughs also worked as a bank examiner from 1873 to 1886, a job that required frequent travel.

8. Journal entry, March 26, 1878, John Burroughs Papers, box 2, folder 1, Vassar College. Burroughs continued to farm for income, however, proudly selling grapes and other produce.

9. Journal entry, November 18, 1877, Burroughs Papers, box 2, folder 1.

10. Ibid.

11. Quoted in Barrus, *Life and Letters,* 342. See also Burroughs's journal entry in January 1884: "It still seems at times as if I must go back there to live; as if I should find shelter there; as if I should find the old contentment and satisfaction in the circle of those hills; but I know I should not." As quoted in Barrus, *Life and Letters,* 271–72.

12. Journal entry, November 27, 1877, Burroughs Papers, box 2, folder 1. On the sublime and wilderness, see William Cronon, "The Trouble with Wilderness; or, Getting Back to the Wrong Nature," *Uncommon Ground: Toward Reinventing Nature* (New York: W. W. Norton & Company, 1995), 72–76.

13. Burroughs, "Pepacton," in *Pepacton and Other Sketches* (1881; repr., New York: Houghton, Mifflin Company, 1895), 8–9. See Philip Marshall Hicks, *The Development of the Natural History Essay in American Literature* (thesis, University of Pennsylvania, 1924). Hicks points to the significant contrast between Thoreau and Burroughs, noting, "To Burroughs, man is part of nature" (125–26).

14. John Burroughs, *Birds and Bees: Sharp Eyes and Other Papers* (Cambridge: Riverside Press, 1887); see Barrus, *Life and Letters,* 285, 333.

15. Quote found in Barrus, *Life and Letters*, 346. On the nature-study movement, see Anna Botsford Comstock, *Handbook of Nature-Study: For Teachers and Parents* (Ithaca: Comstock Publishing Company, 1911), and Clifton F. Hodge, *Nature Study and Life* (Boston: Ginn and Company, Publishers, 1902). Both Comstock and Hodge quote Burroughs on birds. For an overview of the nature-study movement, see Liberty Hyde Bailey, *The Nature-Study Idea* (New York: The Macmillan Company, 1913).

16. Cronon, "Trouble with Wilderness," 79.

17. On the conservation movement, see Samuel P. Hays, *Conservation and the Gospel of Efficiency* (1959; repr., Pittsburgh: University of Pittsburgh Press, 1999).

18. Karl Jacoby, *Crimes Against Nature: Squatters, Poachers, Thieves, and the Hidden History of American Conservation* (Berkeley: University of California Press, 2001), 13–16; Philip G. Terrie, *Forever Wild: A Cultural History of Wilderness in the Adirondacks* (Syracuse: Syracuse University Press, 1994), 92–97.

19. "Communication From the Comptroller Submitting Report of the Forestry Commission," State of New York Assembly, Document no. 36, 23 January 1885, 14–15.

20. Norman J. Van Valkenburgh, *Land Acquisition for New York State: An Historical Perspective* (Arkville, NY: The Catskill Center, 1985), 18. See also Norman J. Van Valkenburgh and Christopher W. Olney, *The Catskill Park: Inside the Blue Line, The Forest Preserve and Mountain Communities of America's First Wilderness* (Hensonville, NY: Black Dome Press, 2005), especially 38–44. The state added Delaware County to the Forest Preserve in 1888.

21. This includes the fine works I reference here, such as Roderick Nash's *Wilderness and the American Mind* and Philip Terrie's *Forever Wild*. In *Crimes Against Nature*, Karl Jacoby mentions the three Catskills counties in a footnote.

22. *Second Annual Report of the State of New York, for the Year 1886* (Albany: The Argus Company, Printers, 1887), 92–142. Carpenter's report is also reprinted in full in Van Valkenburgh and Olney, *Catskill Park*, 149–201.

23. Forest, Game and Fish Commission, *Annual Reports, 1904, 1905, 1906*, 111; Association for the Protection of the Adirondacks, "The Adirondack Appropriation Bill of 1906: Reasons Why the State Should Make Liberal Provisions. . . ." (New York: Association for the Protection of the Adirondacks, 1906), 11.

24. "Special Report of the Forest Commission," State of New York Assembly, Document no. 22, 16 January 1894, 19; *Annual Report of the Forest Preserve Board* (1898), 69; "Adirondacks for the Rich," *New York Times*, 6 April 1904.

25. Association for the Protection of the Adirondacks, "A Special Plea for the Adirondack and Catskill Parks," (1903?), 27–29.

26. Reports of Occupancy of Lands, B0943-85, New York State Archives.

27. Harry Albert Haring, *Our Catskill Mountains* (New York: G. P. Putnam's Sons, 1931), 75.

28. Chapter 283, *Laws of New York, 1885*, 482; Jacoby, *Crimes Against Nature*, 197–98; Mark David Spence, *Dispossessing the Wilderness: Indian Removal and the Making of the National Parks* (New York: Oxford University Press, 1999), 88.

29. On legislation, see Norman J. Van Valkenburgh, *Land Acquisition*; *Laws of New York* (Albany: J.B. Lyon Company, Printers, 1893), 642–44. See also Van Valkenburgh and Olney, *Catskill Park*, 58–61.

30. "Deer Park in the Catskills," *New York Times*, 28 March 1891. On state management of the Adirondacks in this era, see Philip Terrie, *Contested Terrain: A New History*

of Nature and People in the Adirondacks (Syracuse: The Adirondack Museum/Syracuse University Press, 1997), 134–58.

31. Roland Van Zandt, *The Catskill Mountain House: America's Grandest Hotel* (Hensonville, NY: Black Dome Press, 1991), 305; Norman Van Valkenburgh, "The Forest Preserve—A Chronology," *The Conservationist* 39 (May–June 1985): 5–9; Lisbeth Brooks and Lisa Jensen, "All-In-One Family Fun: Camping at North-South Lake," *The Conservationist* 59 (June 2005): 6–9.

32. Chapter 283, *Laws of New York, 1885*, 482–87; Forest, Fish and Game Commission, "Fire! Fire! Fire! An Appeal to the Citizens of the Adirondack and Catskill Regions" (Albany: Evening Union Co., 1904).

33. "Jewett Items," *The Windham Journal* 4, 18 September 1879, as found in "Scrapbooks of G. H. Hastings, Lexington," New York State Library MSS.

34. Michael Kudish, *The Catskill Forest: A History* (Fleischmanns, NY: Purple Mountain Press, 2000), 75.

35. Kudish, *Catskill Forest*, 73–74.

36. Edgar A. Mearns, "Notes on the Mammals of the Catskill Mountains, New York, with General Remarks on the Fauna and Flora of the Region," *Proceedings of the United States National Museum*, vol. 21 (1899): 341–60. Catskills bear hunting, almost entirely engaged in by locals, gained remarkable attention in the *New York Times*. See, for example, "Bears in the Catskills," 4 November 1892; "Big Game in the Catskills," 17 December 1893. Through this period the state still paid a $10 bounty on every bear killed, as part of an effort to protect livestock from wild predators.

37. This should not indicate that Adirondack waterfowl attracted many urban hunters, since prime duck season fell after the peak of tourist season (as I was reminded in a personal correspondence from Philip Terrie, 19 January 2004).

38. Jacoby, *Crimes Against Nature*, 60–61.

39. *Second Annual Report of the Forest Commission of the State of New York, for the Year 1886* (Albany: The Argus Company, Printers, 1887), 116.

40. Forest Commission, *Annual Report* (1890), 33; Forest Commission *Annual Report* (1894), 7; Alf Evers, *The Catskills: From Wilderness to Woodstock* (Woodstock, NY: Overlook Press, 1982), 588–89. "Game in the Catskills," *New York Times*, 9 February 1890; *Rand McNally & Co's Handy Guide to the Hudson River and Catskill Mountains* (New York: Rand McNally, 1905), 169. See also "May Lose All the Deer," *New York Times*, 30 June 1894. For a discussion of how game management played a central part in creating "Romantic Landscapes of Tourism," see Richard Judd, *Common Lands, Common People: The Origins of Conservation in Northern New England* (Cambridge: Harvard University Press, 1997), 197–228. One wealthy summer resident, Julius Fleischmann of Cincinnati, took it upon himself to increase the region's deer population. Fleischmann created his own private deer park, though a release of deer from his property in 1908 did not turn out as planned when several of the animals starved to death (*Pine Hill Sentinel*, 28 March 1908).

41. A rich literature describes the importance of the Catskills to American trout fishing. See particularly Austin M. Francis, *Catskills Rivers: Birthplace of American Fly Fishing* (New York: Lyons & Burford, 1983), and Ed Van Put, *The Beaverkill: The History of a River and Its People* (Guilford, CT: The Lyons Press, 1996). On American fly fishing more generally, see Paul Schullery, *American Fly Fishing: A History* (New York: Nick Lyons Books, 1987).

42. "Little Talks About Fly-Fishing," *Forest and Stream* 70 (June 27, 1908): 1020. See also John McDonald, ed., *The Complete Fly Fisherman: The Notes and Letters of Theodore Gordon* (New York: Charles Scribner's Sons, 1947).

43. Emlyn M. Gill, *Practical Dry-Fly Fishing* (New York: Charles Scribner's Sons, 1913); George M. LaBranche, *The Dry Fly and Fast Water* (New York: Charles Scribner's Sons, 1914). In addition, Anthony W. Dimock published a series of autobiographical sporting and travel books, including *Wall Street and the Wilds*, which described his purchase of a retreat in "Happy Valley" near Peekamoose Mountain. As the title of his book suggests, Dimock made his money in New York, and, as was not at all uncommon, sought the quietude of the mountains, where his fortune could purchase an extensive buffer from the city and also convey him frequently back and forth to the metropolis. See Anthony W. Dimock, *Wall Street and the Wilds* (New York: Outing Publishing Company, 1915).

44. *Anglers' Club Bulletin* 1 (Spring, 1922); 2 (June 1924); 5 (October 1926).

45. See Judd, *Common Lands*, especially 180–81; and Jacoby, *Crimes Against Nature*, 59–60.

46. On the conflict between local farmers and vacationing sport fishermen, see Judd, *Common Lands*, 206–9.

47. As early as 1838, the first American sporting magazine, *American Turf Register and Sporting Magazine*, published in Baltimore, made mention of a fishing trip to the rivers of Sullivan County. The report called the Willowemoc, Calicoon, and Beaver Kill rivers "three of the finest trout streams in this country; they are comparatively unknown to city anglers, and are less fished than any others of like pretensions within our knowledge." "Fly and Bay Fishing," *American Turf Register and Sporting Magazine* 9 (August 1838): 368.

48. *Forest and Stream* 2 (July 9, 1874): 346. On the Ontario and Western, see William F. Helmer, *O&W: The Long Life and Slow Death of the New York, Ontario & Western Railway* (Berkeley: Howell-North, 1959), and Manville B. Wakefield, *To the Mountains by Rail: People, Events and Tragedies . . . the New York, Ontario and Western Railway and the Famous Sullivan County Resorts* (Grahamsville, NY: Wakefair Press, 1970).

49. Robert Barnwell Roosevelt, *The Game Fish of the Northern States and British Provinces* (1862; repr., New York: Orange Judd Company, 1884), 37.

50. "Fishing in the Catskills," *New York Times*, 23 April 1901.

51. C. Van Brunt, Letter to the Editor, *Forest and Stream* 2 (April 23, 1874): 173.

52. Van Put, *Beaverkill*, 33–35.

53. *Forest and Stream* 10 (April 4, 1878): 162.

54. Theodore Gordon notes this fishing "technique" in "Little Talks About Fly-Fishing," *Forest and Stream* 70 (June 27, 1908): 1020.

55. Francis, *Catskills Rivers*, 32.

56. Clarence M. Roof, Letter to the Editor, "Leasing the Trout Streams," *New York Times*, 27 March 1885.

57. Theodore Gordon, *Fishing Gazette*, 12 October 1912, as found in John McDonald, ed. *The Complete Fly Fisherman*, 297. On Gordon's fishing at private clubs, none of which he apparently joined, see Francis, *Catskills Rivers*, 175.

58. Van Put, *Beaverkill*, 93–94.

59. "The Leasing of Trout Streams," *New York Times*, 3 April 1885.

60. "The Orchard Lake Club," *Forest and Stream* 80 (May 3, 1913): 567.

61. Van Put, *Beaverkill*, 62–63; Commission of Fisheries, Game and Forests, *Annual Report, 1897*, 146–66.

62. Samuel E. Rusk, *Rusk's Illustrated Guide to the Catskill Mountains; with Maps and Plans* (Catskill, NY: Samuel E. Rusk, 1879), 24, 33.

63. *Summer Homes on the New York, Ontario and Western Railway* (1887), 10; *Summer Homes* (1894), 14. The popularity of fishing in the southern Catskills convinced the state that a regional hatchery would be advisable, and so a state facility opened near Rosco on the Beaver Kill in 1895. Unfortunately, the poor location of the hatchery led to its early closure in 1904, and the region continued to import from hatcheries in Caledonia or Cold Spring. See Van Put, *Beaverkill*, 161–65.

64. "Trouting in the Catskills," *New York Times*, 2 May 1892.

65. Van Put, *Beaverkill*, 99–104; "Midseason Beaverkill Fishing," *New York Times*, 15 July 1894.

66. Van Put, *Beaverkill*, 64–65. On rainbows in the Esopus, see Jim Capossela, *Good Fishing in the Catskills* (Tarrytown, NY: Northeast Sportsman's Press, 1989), 25.

67. Van Put, *Beaverkill*, 107–11.

68. "Angling Notes," *Forest and Stream* 55 (September 1, 1900): 166; Van Put, *Beaverkill*, 151–60.

69. Van Put, *Beaverkill*, 267–72.

70. Haring, *Our Catskill Mountains*, 203; State of New York Conservation Department, *A Biological Survey of the Delaware and Susquehanna Watersheds* (Albany: J. B. Lyon Company, Printers, 1936), 10, 14, 19–44.

71. Terrie, *Forever Wild*, especially 150–65; Van Valkenburgh and Olney, *Catskill Park*, 93–94. The Department of Environmental Conservation publishes guides to the preserve, including separate brochures for the Slide Mountain and Big Indian Wilderness areas.

72. Jean Craighead George, *My Side of the Mountain* (1959; repr., New York: Puffin Books, 1988), 10, 76.

73. George, *My Side of the Mountain*, xii, 172–77.

74. John R. Stilgoe, *Common Landscape of America, 1580–1845* (New Haven: Yale University Press, 1982), 206.

Chapter 5

John Burroughs, "The Heart of the Southern Catskills," *Riverby* (New York: Houghton, Mifflin and Company, 1894), 40.

Andrew Dresser, conversation with author at Zadock Pratt Museum, Prattsville, 12 July 2001.

1. Ulster and Delaware Railroad, *Catskill Mountains* (Rondout, NY: 1892), 13.

2. Henry E. Dwight, "Account of the Kaatskill Mountains," *The American Journal of Science and Arts* 2 (April 1820): 27.

3. John Burroughs, "Speckled Trout," as found in *In the Catskills* (New York: Houghton Mifflin Company, 1910), 188–89. Originally published in John Burroughs, *Locusts and Wild Honey* (New York: Houghton Mifflin Company, 1879).

4. Los Angeles's taking of the Owens Valley has garnered the most attention as an

example of a city's arrogant exploitation of a rural region. For perhaps the most complete telling of the Owens Valley story, see William L. Kahrl, *Water and Power* (Berkeley: University of California Press, 1982). On water in the West generally, see Donald Worster, *Rivers of Empire: Water, Aridity, and the Growth of the American West* (New York: Oxford University Press, 1985), and Norris Hundley, Jr., *The Great Thirst: Californians and Water: A History* (Berkeley: University of California Press, 2001).

5. Donald Pisani has encouraged scholars to expand their studies to include hydrological issues in the East. See "Beyond the Hundredth Meridian: Nationalizing the History of Water in the United States," *Environmental History* 5 (October 2000): 466–82. For a comparison of Eastern and Western water supply battles, see Sarah S. Elkind, *Bay Cities and Water Politics: The Battle for Resources in Boston and Oakland* (Lawrence: University Press of Kansas, 1998).

6. On nineteenth-century cholera epidemics, see Charles E. Rosenberg, *The Cholera Years: The United States in 1832, 1849, 1866* (1962; repr., Chicago: University of Chicago Press, 1987). On early New York water supply problems, see Gerard T. Koeppel, *Water for Gotham: A History* (Princeton: Princeton University Press, 2000).

7. Koeppel, *Water for Gotham,* 139–217.

8. *Kaaterskill Park: Scenery, Walks, Drives, Geology, Etc.,* (Kaaterskill Publishing Company: 1881?), 6; *The New Grand Hotel, Catskill Mountains,* (New York: Stewart, Warren & Co., 1887), 3, 8.

9. For fuller discussions of New York City's Catskills water supply, see Charles H. Weidner, *Water for a City: A History of New York City's Problem from the Beginning to the Delaware River System* (New Brunswick: Rutgers University Press, 1974), and Diane Galusha, *Liquid Assets: A History of New York City's Water System* (Fleischmanns, NY: Purple Mountain Press, 1999). Galusha's work contains a handy appendix that describes the entire water supply system (265–73). Of less value is Matthew Gandy's *Concrete and Clay: Reworking Nature in New York City* (Cambridge: The MIT Press, 2002). Gandy's sixty-page discussion of New York's water supply offers a brief summary of its expansion, but the relationship between city and country comes in and out of focus here; apparently without irony, he even calls the Catskills "the city's watershed" while discussing the displacement of locals. Calling the delivery of Croton water to the city a "democratization of nature" probably would not have sat well with many nineteenth-century Westchester County residents. See Gandy, *Concrete and Clay,* 35, 46–47.

10. The Adirondack idea was debated through the early 1900s. See John R. Freeman, *Report upon New York's Water Supply with Particular Reference to the Need of Procuring Additional Sources and Their Probable Cost with Works Constructed Under Municipal Ownership* (New York: Martin B. Brown, Co., 1900), 475–89. The Merchants' Association of New York finally dismissed the Great Lakes, Lake George, and Lake Champlain in its exhaustive 1900 report, *An Inquiry into the Conditions Relating to the Water-Supply of the City of New York.* See pp. 93–94.

11. R. D. A. Parrott, "The Water Supply for New York City," *Scientific American Supplement* 22 (September 4, 1886): 8890–92.

12. The city's population fell by nearly a million in the 1970s, but has slowly recovered. The city surpassed the eight-million mark for the first time in the 2000 census.

13. A previously organized company had also proposed supplying water to the city in 1884. See Ramapo Improvement Company, *Proposal to the Sinking Fund Commission for a Supplementary Supply of Water to the City of New York* (New York: Martin B.

Brown, Printers, 1884). For a brief history of the two Ramapo companies, see Merchants' Association of New York, "Reasons for Revoking the Excessive Powers of the Ramapo Water Company" (February 13, 1901), held by the New York Public Library.

14. Merchants' Association, *Inquiry into New York's Water Supply* (1900), 17–21; *New York Times* 19, 21, and 23 August 1899. Nostrand eventually testified for the city in the Ashokan takings proceedings, revealing the figures on several contracts he signed and the process by which he secured them. See Ashokan Reservoir Awards, Reel 1, pp. 861–907.

15. John R. Freeman, *New York's Water Supply*, 3–5; *New York Times*, 8 April 1900.

16. Freeman, *New York's Water Supply*, 7.

17. Freeman, *New York's Water Supply*, 8.

18. Merchants' Association, *Inquiry*, 5, 14–15.

19. Merchants' Association, *Inquiry*, 86. The *New York Times* also reacted favorably to the Merchants' Association report. See 20 and 22 August 1900.

20. *New York Times*, 9 August 1901.

21. New York Commission on Additional Water Supply, *Report of the Commission on Additional Water Supply for the City of New York* (New York: M. B. Brown Co., Printers, 1904), 42, 187, 470, 493–98.

22. *New York Times*, 4 December 1902; for *New York Times* editorials on waste, see, for example, 11 October and 22 November 1902; Municipal Government Committee of the City Club of New York, *Why the Citizens of New York Should Resist and Defeat the Ramapo Water Scheme; Present Supply Ample; Stop the Waste* (August 1899). Although Freeman had recommended finding a new source quickly, the *Times* accepted only the notion that eliminated waste would dramatically, quickly, and, most important, economically diminish the need for a new supply. Organizations such as the City Club called for increased metering and stepped-up enforcement to limit waste and put off the date when a new supply would have to be found. The City Club published a pamphlet arguing that the city wasted two-thirds of its water and that its current supply ought to last until the city reached a population of six million. The City Club of New York, *The Useless Loss of Water by Preventable Waste and Leakage in the Boroughs of Manhattan and the Bronx* (December 1902), held by the New York Public Library.

23. *New York Times*, 9 October 1909; 28 March 1909; 15 May 1910; 28 and 31 January 1912; *Second Annual Report of the Board of Water Supply of the City of New York* (December 31, 1907), 165. Even as the *Times* questioned the necessity of the Catskills project, it glorified the new Croton dam, declaring, "Excepting the Pyramids, it is the Greatest Piece of Masonry in the World" (1 February 1905). Evidence of the need for a new system, beyond simply adding to the Croton supply, fluctuated with the weather. As the plan moved forward in the summer of 1907, the city had so much water—more than a 200-day supply—that some people advocated using the surplus to flush the streets. Just four years later, however, a drought left the water supply perilously low, with the Croton waters so diminished that photographs revealed old roads inside the reservoir once again exposed to view. Though such droughts were fleeting, periods of low water determined the real need for expansion, for the Catskills system would be insurance against drought, at least at first. *New York Times*, 27 July 1907 and 27 August 1911.

24. *New York Times*, 20 April 1908 and 22 August 1909.

25. *New York Times*, 14 March 1901; 8 June 1904; 7 August 1905; 1 April 1907; and 22 May 1907. Almost 100 years passed before the construction of a filtration plant for Croton waters began.

26. "Crystal Spring Water from the Catskill Mountains" (Pine Hill Crystal Spring Water, 1901?), 3, 11, 13, held by the New York Academy of Medicine Library; *Pine Hill Sentinel*, 18 March 1905; "Sunset Spring Water," postcards held by the Haines Falls Public Library.

27. Weidner, *Water for a City*, 176–80. Earlier, Suffolk County had also achieved protection through state law, which effectively put fine Long Island waters off-limits to Brooklyn, the borough most in need of new supplies.

28. Board of Water Supply of the City of New York, *Annual Report* (1906), 222–49. Actually, the city had to clear two hurdles. The first was cleared in the November 1904 election, when voters amended the state's constitution to allow the city to take on debt to build a new water supply system.

29. *Report of the Board of Water Supply of the City of New York to the Board of Estimate and Apportionment, October 9, 1905*, held by the New York Municipal Reference Library. This report also contains "Decision of State Water Supply Commission, Dated May 14, 1906," 22–36.

30. *Pine Hill Sentinel*, 4 March 1905; *Kingston Daily Freeman*, 28 January and 15 February 1905.

31. *Daily Freeman*, 15, 16, 23, and 28 February 1905.

32. The original plan also included a smaller reservoir on Rondout Creek, though construction there would be delayed for decades.

33. *Daily Freeman*, 1 March 1905.

34. *Daily Freeman*, 16 March 1905.

35. Board of Water Supply, *Report to George B. McClellan, Mayor*, April 9, 1906, p. 12.

36. *New York Times*, 27 January 1904, 9 February 1905, and 5 February 1906. *Kingston Daily Freeman*, 20 March 1905. The *Daily Freeman* reported on March 23, 1905, that the *Tribune*, *Herald*, *Sun*, and *American* all claimed that Ulster opposition to the McClellan Bill resulted from connections to Ramapo. The *Freeman* noted that it "only seems necessary to cry Ramapo to scare ordinarily level-headed men into spasms."

37. *Sentinel*, 1 and 8 April 1905.

38. *Sentinel*, 6 May 1905.

39. New York Commission on Additional Water Supply, *Report* (1904), 175–81; *Sentinel*, 6 May 1905.

40. "Three More Villages to Go," *New York Times*, 2 July 1905.

41. *Daily Freeman*, 17 March 1905.

42. ARA, Reel 4, pp. 3071–73, 3124–47. Shockingly, the city's lawyer, John Linson, argued that the commission ought to consider the diminished value of the properties as they existed in 1907, because the law required only compensation of market value at the time of the first takings. In other words, Linson argued that the city should have to pay less and thereby benefit from the long deterioration in the valley caused by their own proposed reservoir. ARA, Reel 3, pp. 2155–57.

43. *Catskill Water Supply: A General Description and Brief History* (New York: New York City Board of Water Supply, 1917), 27; *Illustrated and Descriptive Account of the Main Dams and Dikes of the Ashokan Reservoir* (Brown Station, NY: E. G. Nimgern, 1909?), 10, 26, 29, 33. For a more complete description of building the Ashokan, see Bob Steuding, *The Last of the Handmade Dams: The Story of the Ashokan Reservoir* (Fleischmanns, NY: Purple Mountain Press, 1985).

44. *New York Times,* 9 January 1910.

45. *Daily Freeman,* 16 and 29 March 1909; *New York Times,* 4 April 1909.

46. *Catskill Water Supply,* 27; "Clearing and Grubbing the Site of the Ashokan Reservoir," *The Catskill Water System News,* 20 March 1913, 169–70.

47. ARA, Reel 1, pp. 143–44.

48. ARA, Reel 6, p. 5430; Reel 3, p. 2945.

49. See, for example, ARA, Reel 1, p. 143; Reel 4, pp. 3220–51.

50. ARA, Reel 116, pp. 646–47.

51. ARA, Reel 1, pp. 492–94.

52. The Commissions dismissed another 515 claims totaling nearly $2.3 million.

53. Board of Water Supply, *Twenty-Seventh Annual Report,* January 1, 1933, 12.

54. Board of Water Supply, *Eighth Annual Report,* December 31, 1913, 23–30.

55. See, for example, "Lies Passed in Plumland," *Daily Freeman,* 29 April 1909.

56. Edward S. Brownson, Jr., to Joseph Haag, 28 April 1908, Mayor George McClellan Papers, MGB 21 #6, New York Municipal Archives. Though not necessarily a good comparison, a 1905 report contained a list of properties acquired by the state for the Catskills Forest Preserve, which also included the prices paid, usually at tax sale. As the city noted, the state paid on average just over $3 per acre. See ARA, Reel 5, 4078.

57. *Daily Freeman,* 9 May 1908; ARA, Reel 115, p. 67; Ashokan Orders Depositing Money, Reel 205, p. 5.

58. Board of Water Supply, *Fifth Annual Report,* December 31, 1910, 8; Board of Water Supply, *Sixth Annual Report,* December 31, 1911, 5; Board of Water Supply, *Ninth Annual Report,* December 31, 1914, 105.

59. *The Catskill Water System News,* 20 May 1912, 89–90; 5 June 1912, 96; ARA, Reel 4, p. 3544.

60. Board of Water Supply, *Minutes of Meetings,* June 9 to December 27, 1905, 42, held at the New York Public Library.

61. ARA, Reel 115, pp. 235, 245, 272.

62. Letter from George G. Honness, Board of Water Supply, to C. A. Haynes, 26 February 1913, in author's possession.

63. *The Catskill Water System News,* 5 October 1913, 227.

64. Board of Water Supply, *Nineteenth Annual Report,* January 1, 1925, 15.

65. On the Croton celebration, see Koeppel, *Water for Gotham,* 281–84.

66. This book has been edited by Richard Frisbie and republished as Edward H. Hall, *Water for New York City* (Saugerties, NY: Hope Farm Press, 1993).

67. *New York Times,* 12 and 14 October 1917.

68. *New York Times,* 12 October 1917.

69. Board of Water Supply, *Sixth Annual Report,* December 31, 1911, 3; *Kingston Daily Freeman,* 4 and 25 February 1915; and especially "New York Tax Dodgers Begin a New Campaign," *Kingston Daily Freeman,* 26 June 1915.

70. Board of Water Supply, *Ninth Annual Report,* December 31, 1914, 129; Board of Water Supply, *Eleventh Annual Report,* December 31, 1916, 106; *Catskill Water Supply,* 55; *The Catskill Water System News,* 20 June 1912, 97.

71. Board of Water Supply, *Petition, Memorandum and Approval of the City's Maps, Profiles and Plan for Securing a Supply of Water from the Schoharie Watershed,* September 1914, 8; Board of Water Supply, "Catskill Water Supply: A General Description" (1922), 26–29, 36.

72. "Reservoir Evicts Many from Homes, "*New York Times,* 4 June 1949. For a much fuller discussion of the Delaware System, see Galusha, *Liquid Assets,* 187–226.

73. Alice H. Jacobson, *Beneath Pepacton Waters* (Andes, NY: Pepacton Press, 1988), 55, 70–72; *New York Times,* 4 June 1949.

74. Board of Water Supply, *Thirty-Third Annual Report,* January 1, 1939, front matter.

75. Board of Water Supply, *Report to George B. McClellan, Mayor,* April 9, 1906, 43, held by New York Public Library; Department of Water Supply Gas & Electricity, "Rules and Regulations for the Protection of the Water Supply from Contamination" (1917), held by New York City Municipal Reference Library.

76. *New York Times,* 1, 15, and 29 March 1950; ibid., 8 April 1950; ibid., 1 May 1950; New York City Water Supply Bureau, *Annual Report of the Chief Engineer* (1950), 108.

77. Slutsky v. City of New York, 1950 N.Y. Misc. Lexis 1633; *New York Times,* 27 July 1950.

78. *New York Times,* 22 December 1951 and 19 February 1952. In the end, Howell claimed that his rainmaking efforts had probably increased rainfall by about 14 percent in the target area. See Theodore Steinberg, *Slide Mountain: or, The Folly of Owning Nature* (Berkeley: University of California Press, 1995), for a fuller discussion of the problems of cloud seeding, relating particularly to the 1964 case of Fulton County, Pennsylvania.

79. Tobie Geertsema, "The City's Cup of Water . . . Was Ulster's Bitter Draught," *Daily Freeman,* 30 September 1967, as found in the Vera Sickler Collection, Town of Olive Archives. Department of Environmental Protection rules require the storage of rowboats in specific "boat areas" along certain reservoir shores. In some places, such as along the Pepaction Reservoir, these hull-up, metal boats occupy significant stretches of shoreline. For current DEP watershed recreation rules, see the NYC Department of Environmental Protection Web site. Rules have always prohibited swimming in the reservoirs. Tourist guides have for some time featured images of the region's reservoirs, especially the Ashokan, the expanse of which provides wonderful reflections of partly cloudy skies and the peaks beyond. See, for example, Catskill Association for Tourism Services, "Catskill Region Travel Guide" (circa 2000). For an earlier use of the Ashokan Reservoir in tourist advertising, see Department of Environmental Conservation—Advertising portfolio of state tourism promotions during 1939 World's Fair, New York State Archives, A3324–78.

80. Dresser quote from conversation with author, 12 July 2001; Sylvia Rozzelle quoted in *Kingston Sunday Freeman,* 28 March 1999, as found at www.town.olive.ny.us/175th/celebrationnewsclips.htm; *New York Times,* 15 May 1910.

Chapter 6

John Burroughs, "Phases of Farm Life," *Signs and Seasons* (New York: Houghton, Mifflin and Company, 1886), 244–45.
David Boroff, "The Catskills: Still Having Wonderful Time," *Harper's* 217 (July 1958): 56.

1. Abraham Cahan, *The Rise of David Levinsky* (New York: Grosset & Dunlap, Publishers, 1917).

2. Cahan, *Rise of David Levinsky*, 403–4.

3. Thanks to Peggy Shaffer for making this connection for me.

4. Cahan, *Rise of David Levinsky*, 406, 437, 440–41.

5. On the importance of the Lower East Side to American Jewry, see Hasia Diner, *Lower East Side Memories: A Jewish Place in America* (Princeton: Princeton University Press, 2000).

6. The phrases "summer world" and "Catskills culture" come from the titles of two popular works on Jews in the Catskills, both of which reflect on the importance of the mountains to New York Jewish identity. See Stefan Kanfer, *A Summer World: The Attempt to Build a Jewish Eden in the Catskills, From the Days of the Ghetto to the Rise and Decline of the Borscht Belt* (New York: Farrar, Straus & Giroux, 1989), and Phil Brown, *Catskill Culture: A Mountain Rat's Memories of the Great Jewish Resort Area* (Philadelphia: Temple University Press, 1998).

7. Esterita "Cissie" Blumberg, *Remember the Catskills: Tales by a Recovering Hotel-keeper* (Fleischmanns, NY: Purple Mountain Press, 1996), 7, 12, 27. Indeed, the relationship worked both ways, for surely when anyone in Sullivan County referred to "the city," there could hardly be confusion about which one.

8. The Williamsburg Bridge opened in 1903 and the Manhattan Bridge in 1909, joining the Brooklyn Bridge in linking the two largest boroughs. The Queensboro Bridge connected Manhattan to Queens in 1909. In 1905, the subway reached the Bronx via tunnel, and by 1915 subways linked Queens and Manhattan. On the development of New York's transportation infrastructure, see Clifton Hood, *722 Miles: The Building of the Subways and How They Transformed New York* (Baltimore: Johns Hopkins University Press, 1993).

9. C. Morris Horowitz and Lawrence J. Kaplan, *The Jewish Population of the New York Area, 1900–1975* (New York: Federation of Jewish Philanthropies of New York, 1959), 15. On Jews and urban life, see Eli Lederhendler, *New York Jews and the Decline of Urban Ethnicity, 1950–1970* (Syracuse: Syracuse University Press, 2001), 1–35.

10. A rich literature describes the Lower East Side. See especially Irving Howe's seminal *World of Our Fathers* (New York: Harcourt Brace Jovanovich, 1976) and Moses Rischin, *The Promised City: New York's Jews, 1870–1914* (Cambridge: Harvard University Press, 1962).

11. See Leonard Dinnerstein, *Antisemitism in America* (New York: Oxford University Press, 1994), especially 35–57.

12. Alf Evers, *The Catskills: From Wilderness to Woodstock* (Woodstock, NY: The Overlook Press, 1982), 545. For a biography of Charles Fleischmann, see Charles Frederick Goss, *Cincinnati: The Queen City*, vol. 4 (Chicago: The S. J. Clarke Publishing Company, 1912), 324–26. See also Christina Haderup Flisser's "History of the Village of Fleischmanns," a brief memoir held by the Skene Memorial Library in Fleischmanns.

13. Ernest Ingersoll, *Rand, McNally & Co.'s Illustrated Guide to the Hudson River and Catskill Mountains* (New York: Rand, McNally & Company, Publishers, 1900), 165; Cahan, *Rise of David Levinsky*, 423. As was common for the genre, Rand, McNally published its guide in slightly altered form year after year. Individual hotel listings and advertisements changed, but the descriptive prose changed very little over time. The language relating to Jews in Tannersville appeared for perhaps twenty years unchanged.

14. Howe, *World of Our Fathers*, 218. *Forward* translation found in Howe, *World of Our Fathers*, 217.

15. Manville B. Wakefield, *To The Mountains by Rail: People, Events and Tragedies . . .*

the New York, Ontario and Western Railway and the Famous Sullivan County Resorts (Grahamsville, NY: Wakefair Press, 1970), 395, 397.

16. New York, Ontario & Western Railway, *Summer Homes*, (Middletown: The Ontario & Western Railway Historical Society, Inc., 1994 facsimile reproduction of the 1881 original).

17. "Mount Meenahga House and Cottages, Season of 1909," held by the Town of Shandaken Historical Society.

18. For a fuller description of the rise of the Borsht Belt, see Kanfer, *Summer World*. Also of value is Phil Brown's collection of key sources, *In the Catskills: A Century of the Jewish Experience in "The Mountains"* (New York: Columbia University Press, 2002). A number of former owners and residents of the resorts have written a wealth of material concerning the Jewish Catskills, but most of it is nostalgic and uncritical, lamenting the passage of a golden era. At this point, the Jewish resorts have yet to be the subject of scholarly, monographic treatment. For the best of the reminiscences, see Irvin Richman, *Borscht Belt Bungalows: Memories of Catskill Summers* (Philadelphia: Temple University Press, 1998), and Phil Brown, *Catskill Culture*, which is much more than a personal reminiscence. Brown also includes material gathered from dozens of interviews and available written sources. See also a wonderful collection of material at the Catskill Institute's website: http://www.brown.edu/Research/Catskills_Institute/.

19. Mountain Top Historical Society, *Kaaterskill: From the Catskill Mountain House to the Hudson River School* (Hensonville, NY: Black Dome Press, 1993), 78–79, 84, 87; Evers, *Catskills*, 688.

20. The *New York Times* used "Borscht Belt" in a headline as early as September 18, 1949, and had used the phrase "Borscht Circuit" in the late 1930s.

21. For an example of this expansive definition, see Joey Adams's *The Borscht Belt* (New York: The Bobbs-Merrill Company, Inc., 1959). The dust jacket reads in part: "The resort hotels scattered through the Catskill and Adirondack Mountains in New York, the Poconos in Pennsylvania, and the Berkshires in New England make up the legendary stretch of land called the Borscht Belt—the 'old country' of American show business, where so many of today's great entertainers got their start." Note also that Stefan Kanfer felt comfortable quoting Arthur Kober's 1937 play *Having Wonderful Time* to illustrate points regarding the Catskills, despite the fact that the play was set at the fictional Camp Kare-Free in the Berkshires. Camp Kare-Free was part of this flexible Borscht Belt that expanded beyond the Catskills. See Kanfer, *Summer World*, 138–39, 172. Arthur Kober, *Having Wonderful Time* (New York: Random House, 1937).

22. David M. Gold, "Jewish Agriculture in the Catskills, 1900–1920," *Agricultural History* 55 (January 1981): 31–49; Abraham D. Lavender and Clarence B. Steinberg, *Jewish Farmers of the Catskills: A Century of Survival* (Gainesville: University Press of Florida, 1995), especially 27–83.

23. Wakefield, *To The Mountains by Rail*, 78–80; Jewish Agricultural and Industrial Aid Society, *Annual Report* (1905): 8–9; *American Hebrew* 123 (August 31, 1928): 460, 463.

24. Lavender and Steinberg, *Jewish Farmers of the Catskills*, 54–55, 71, 170; Kanfer, *Summer World*, 254–55; Bob Spitz, *Barefoot in Babylon: The Creation of the Woodstock Music Festival, 1969* (New York: W. W. Norton & Company, 1989), 277–78.

25. *Summer Homes* (1881), 53; Wakefield, *To The Mountains by Rail*, 140–42.

26. Myrna Katz Frommer and Harvey Frommer, *It Happened in the Catskills: An Oral History in the Words of Busboys, Bellhops, Guests, Proprietors, Comedians, Agents,*

and Others Who Lived It (New York: Harcourt Brace Jovanovich Publishers, 1991), 4–5; Brown, *Catskill Culture,* 31.

27. Frommer and Frommer, *It Happened in the Catskills,* 8–9.

28. The history of Grossinger's has been told many times. See in particular Harold Jaediker Taub, *Waldorf in the Catskills: The Grossinger Legend* (New York: Sterling Publishing Co., Inc., 1952), and Joel Pomerantz's more detailed *Jennie and the Story of Grossinger's* (New York: Grosset & Dunlap, 1970). See also Tania Grossinger, *Growing Up at Grossinger's* (New York: David McKay Company, Inc., 1975).

29. Brown, *Catskill Culture,* 50; Richman, *Borscht Belt Bungalows,* 9–11.

30. Herbert Tobin, "New York's Jews and the Catskill Mountains, 1880–1930," in Ronald A. Brauner, ed., *Jewish Civilization: Essays and Studies,* vol. 1 (Philadelphia: Reconstructionist Rabbinical College, 1979), 169–70.

31. Evers, *Catskills,* 671–75; Tobin, "New York's Jews," 165.

32. N. B. Fagin, "East Siders in "the Mountains," *The Survey* 50 (July 15, 1923): 443–44.

33. "The Ghetto and the Summer Resorts," *American Israelite* 50 (August 20, 1903): 8; "Catskill, Playground of Jewish Masses," *American Hebrew* 123 (August 31, 1928): 460, 463. The title of this piece speaks to the looseness with which New Yorkers could use the term "Catskills"—here perhaps inadvertently truncated to "Catskill," an actual town nowhere near the resorts discussed in the article.

34. Lavender and Steinberg, *Jewish Farmers of the Catskills,* 54, 88.

35. *Mountain Hotelman* 1 (May 9, 1930); William F. Helmer, *O&W: The Long Life and Slow Death of the New York, Ontario & Western Railway* (Berkeley, CA: Howell-North, 1959), 115, 136.

36. The Lincoln Tunnel opened in 1937.

37. Wakefield, *To The Mountains by Rail,* 60–61. On travel to the mountains see also Adams, *Borscht Belt,* 25–27. On Moses and parkway bridges, see Robert Caro, *The Power Broker: Robert Moses and the Fall of New York* (New York: Vintage Books, 1975), 951–54.

38. Nearly all works on the Jewish Catskills discuss tummlers. See in particular Phyllis Deutsch, "Theater of Mating: Jewish Summer Camps and Cultural Transformation," *American Jewish History* 75 (March 1986): 307–21.

39. Martin Gottfried, *Nobody's Fool: The Lives of Danny Kaye* (New York: Simon & Schuster, 1994), especially 13, 25, 39.

40. *New York Times,* 18 September 1949.

41. Sid Caesar, *Where Have I Been? An Autobiography* (New York: Crown Publishers, 1982), especially 94–95.

42. Herman Wouk, *Marjorie Morningstar* (Garden City, NY: Doubleday, 1955). Other Catskills novels include Harvey Jacobs, *Summer on a Mountain of Spices* (New York: Harper & Row, 1975), and Martin Boris, *Woodridge, 1946* (New York: Crown, 1980).

43. Frommer and Frommer, *It Happened in the Catskills,* 94–141.

44. Boroff, "Catskills," 56.

45. On Americanization, abundance, and the Catskills, see Andrew R. Heinze, *Adapting to Abundance: Jewish Immigrants, Mass Consumption, and the Search for American Identity* (New York: Columbia University Press, 1990), especially 128–32.

46. Lederhendler, *New York Jews,* 28–29; Grossinger, *Growing Up at Grossinger's,* 34–35. On American Jews and the postwar world, see also Debra Dash Moore, *To the Golden Cities: Pursuing the American Jewish Dream in Miami and L.A.* (New York: The Free Press, 1994), 1–20.

47. Lederhendler, *New York Jews,* especially 81, 87.

48. *New York Times,* 10 May 1953; Richman, *Borscht Belt Bungalows,* 64.

49. Boroff, "Catskills," 62.

50. For the best description of daily life in bungalow colonies, see Irwin Richman, *Borscht Belt Bungalows,* especially 74–75, 80–82, 104–8.

51. Taub, *Waldorf in the Catskills*; Pomerantz, *Jennie and the Story of Grossinger's.*

52. Gilbert Burck, "Pleasure Dome in the Catskills," *Fortune* 52 (August 1955): 106–9, 144, 146, 148; Frommer and Frommer, *It Happened in the Catskills,* 144–47; Kanfer, *Summer World,* 166–70.

53. Boroff, "Catskills," 59; Grossinger, *Growing Up at Grossinger's,* 204.

54. Frommer and Frommer, *It Happened in the Catskills,* 51–53; *New York Times,* 27 September 1955.

55. Frommer and Frommer, *It Happened in the Catskills,* 37, 122–25; Grossinger, *Growing Up at Grossinger's,* 117, 130. On the 1951 scandal, see Stanley Cohen, *The Game They Played* (New York: Carroll & Graf Publishers, Inc., 1977), especially 97–100.

56. Boroff, "Catskills," 61.

57. Horowitz and Kaplan, *Jewish Population,* 17, 21–22. In 1957, a total of 2.1 million Jews still lived in the city: 854,000 in Brooklyn, 493,000 in the Bronx, 423,000 in Queens, and 339,000 in Manhattan. Nassau County counted 329,000 Jews, while Westchester held 116,000.

58. Frommer and Frommer, *It Happened in the Catskills,* 31; Richman, *Borscht Belt Bungalows,* 69.

59. Brown, *Catskill Culture,* 128, 147; Richman, *Borscht Belt Bungalows,* 37.

60. *Literary Digest* 109 (May 9, 1931): 7–8; Frommer and Frommer, *It Happened in the Catskills,* x, 117, 130; Richman, *Borscht Belt Bungalows,* 69.

61. Richman, *Borscht Belt Bungalows,* 69, 94; Frommer and Frommer, *It Happened in the Catskills,* 16–17. Richman uses the terms "goy" and "goyim" throughout in his reminiscences, and, though he may mean no disparagement, their presence in his work clearly reveals the distance between his family and most local Christians. Unlike the majority of Jews who appear in his wonderfully detailed work, most Christians are not referred to by name here, only as "the goy." See *Borscht Belt Bungalows,* especially 38–39.

62. The growing importance of Miami Beach to New York Jews is evidenced in the involvement of several Catskills hotel owners in the booming Florida market. In 1940, Grossinger's constructed its own Miami Beach resort, and in 1946 purchased another, called Grossinger's-Pancoast. By 1940 the Androns owned two hotels—the old Mountain House in Greene County and the new Hotel Senator in Miami Beach. The success of Miami Beach gave some owners and workers off-season opportunities, but, more important, it signaled the beginning of the end for the Catskills. The Androns advertised their hotels together. See "Andron's Mountain House presents Hotelevision" (1940), Catskill Mountain House Manuscript, Greene County Historical Society. On the growth of Jewish resorts in Miami Beach, which some Jews apparently dubbed "the southern borscht belt," see Moore, *To the Golden Cities,* 32–33 and passim.

63. Not everyone who performed regularly in the Catskills was Jewish, obviously. For example, Lionel Hampton played several summers at Grossinger's in the 1940s. Frommer and Frommer, *It Happened in the Catskills,* 44.

64. Blumberg, *Remember the Catskills,* 108.

65. Richman, *Borscht Belt Bungalows,* 105, 182. Upon her return to Grossinger's in

1974, after a nearly ten-year absence, Tania Grossinger noticed how much the guests had changed, how they "seemed so much older." Grossinger, *Growing Up at Grossinger's*, 208.

66. On ruins, see Brown, *Catskill Culture*, 5–6; Richman, *Borscht Belt Bungalows*, 39. My own observations of the region were much informed by Irwin Richman, who led a bus tour of the area as part of the History of the Catskills Conference, August 23–25, 2002.

67. Eileen Pollack, *Paradise, New York* (Philadelphia: Temple University Press, 1998), 60. Other novels include Allegra Goodman, *Kaaterskill Falls* (New York: Dial, 1998); Ellen Pall, *Among the Ginzburgs* (Cambridge, MA: Zoland Books, 1996); and my favorite, Terry Kay, *Shadow Song* (New York: Pocket Books, 1994).

68. This phrase appears repeatedly in Catskills Institute literature. See http://catskills .brown.edu.

69. George Kranzler, *Hasidic Williamsburg: A Contemporary American Hasidic Community* (Northvale, New Jersey: Jason Aronson Inc., 1995). In 2003, as the Catskills Institute gathered to remember and praise the golden era of the Jewish Catskills at Kutsher's, one of the few remaining hotels, the continuing change became all the more evident. Part of the hotel has now been given over to Hasidic clientele, bringing with it the structural changes that their traditions require. See Irwin Richman, "Bus Tours, Blintzes, & Memories," *In the Mountains* (November 2003): 1.

70. Harvey Jacobs, *Summer on a Mountain of Spices* (New York: Harper & Row, Publishers, 1975), 17.

Chapter 7

John Burroughs, "Phases of Farm Life," *Signs and Seasons* (New York: Houghton, Mifflin and Company, 1886), 243.

"Woodstock," written by Joni Mitchell, apparently while in a New York City hotel, unable to attend the festival. "Woodstock" became a hit for Crosby, Stills, Nash, and Young when it appeared on their *Déjà vu* album (Atlantic Records, 1970). Their recording used slightly different lyrics. That same year, Mitchell's own version appeared on *Ladies of the Canyon* (Reprise Records, 1970).

1. T. Morris Longstreth, *The Catskills* (New York: The Century Company, 1918), 31.

2. Longstreth, *Catskills*, 42.

3. Arthur C. Mack, *Enjoying the Catskills: A Practical Guide to the Catskill Region for the Motorist, Camper, Hiker, Hunter, Fisherman, Skier, and Vacationer* (New York: Funk & Wagnalls Company, 1950), 4; Gerald M. Best, *The Ulster & Delaware; Railroad Through the Catskills* (San Marino, CA: Golden West Books, 1972), 164–78.

4. Paul S. Sutter, *Driven Wild: How the Fight Against Automobiles Launched the Modern Wilderness Movement* (Seattle: University of Washington Press, 2002). On suburbanization and the growth of environmentalism, see Adam Rome, *The Bulldozer in the Countryside: Suburban Sprawl and the Rise of American Environmentalism* (New York: Cambridge University Press, 2001). On exurbanites, see Auguste C. Spectorsky, *The Exurbanites* (New York: Lippincott, 1955).

5. Department of Environmental Conservation—advertising portfolio of state tourism promotions during 1939 World's Fair, A3324–78, New York State Archives; *Time* 34 (August 14, 1939): 4. Not wanting to give up on the Switzerland comparison alto-

gether, the radio ad declared that the Mountain House overlook contained a perpendicular drop "like the Matterhorn-in-miniature."

6. Cathy Newman, "The Lure of the Catskills," *National Geographic* 182 (November 1992): 112. On the definition of suburb and on suburbanization generally, see Kenneth Jackson, *Crabgrass Frontier: The Suburbanization of the United States* (New York: Oxford University Press, 1985), especially 4–8.

7. For auto ownership number, see "Popular Routes for Summer Tours," *New York Times*, 4 August 1907. For highway miles, see Hal S. Barron, *Mixed Harvest: The Second Great Transformation in the Rural North, 1870–1930* (Chapel Hill: University of North Carolina Press, 1997), 33. On the transformation of the countryside brought about through auto travel, see also Michael L. Berger, *The Devil Wagon in God's Country: The Automobile and Social Change in Rural America, 1893–1929* (Hamden, CT: Archon Books, 1979). On early highways, see John B. Rae, *The Road and Car in American Life* (Cambridge: The MIT Press, 1971), especially 23–83.

8. Warren James Belasco, *Americans on the Road: From Autocamp to Motel, 1910–1945* (Baltimore: The Johns Hopkins University Press, 1997), 7–18.

9. "June Rush in the Catskills," *New York Times*, 25 June 1905. For an example of an early national auto tour, see Mary Crehore Bedell, *Modern Gypsies* (New York: Brentano's, Publishers, 1924). For analysis, see Sutter, *Driven Wild*, especially 19–38, and Marguerite S. Shaffer, *See America First: Tourism and National Identity, 1880–1940* (Washington, DC: Smithsonian Institution Press, 2001), especially 131–68.

10. Roy Lewis, "Side-Car Scenics," *Outing* 78 (April 1921): 13. Lewis recommended the Conservation Commission map in 1921. On the bond act, see "New York State Road Organization," *Engineering News* 70 (November 13, 1913): 982. Road conditions in the Catskills (and other parts of the state) gained considerable attention in the *New York Times*. See 12 June 1904, 4 August 1907, and 29 July 1913.

11. *New York Times*, 4 August 1907 and 4 September 1910. See also *New York Times*, 30 August 1908.

12. Frank C. Hill, "Discovering the Catskills," *Outing* 72 (May 1918): 112–13.

13. Lewis, "Side-Car Scenics," 12.

14. Lewis, "Side-Car Scenics," 12; Belasco, *Americans on the Road*, 41–69.

15. *New York Times*, 31 August 1909 and 14 July 1912.

16. *New York Times*, 14 July 1912.

17. *New York Times*, 14 July 1912.

18. Belasco, *Americans on the Road*, especially 23; Jackson, *Crabgrass Frontier*, 253–63.

19. On early road building, see Bruce E. Seely, *Building the American Highway System: Engineers as Policy Makers* (Philadelphia: Temple University Press, 1987).

20. *New York Times*, 28 August 1927; *Palisades Interstate Park, 1900–1960* (Bear Mountain, NY: Palisades Interstate Park Commission, 1960).

21. William Copeman Kitchin, *A Wonderland of the East* (Boston: The Page Company, 1920).

22. Kitchin, *Wonderland of the East*, especially 75, 80.

23. Kitchin, *Wonderland of the East*, 78–80, 84.

24. Sutter, *Driven Wild*, 35. Perhaps the most lasting of these rituals is the lighting of a campfire, even when campers expect to do no cooking and the weather requires no fire for warmth. The country simply became the place where people could sit around an open fire, a ritual that had long since become impractical or illegal for most urban residents.

25. Kitchin, *Wonderland of the East*, 82–87, 91–92.

26. "Catskill Mountain Region Popular for Motor Tours," *New York Times*, 28 August 1927; "Catskill Tour Suggested Now," *New York Times*, 26 August 1928. See also "In the Green Catskills," *New York Times*, 1 June 1930. Early highways around the country took on names that spoke to the nation's history, including the proposed Lincoln Highway, designed to run from coast to coast. See Shaffer, *See America First*, 137–60.

27. "Open New Bridge over the Hudson," *New York Times*, 3 July 1935. See also "Week-End Auto Trips," *New York Times*, 12 October 1947; and, Mack, *Enjoying the Catskills*, passim.

28. "Along the Rip Van Winkle Trail," *New York Times*, 10 June 1951; "The Vacationland Rip Van Winkle Built," *New York Times*, 14 June 1953.

29. "Tame Deer on a Farm," *New York Times*, 3 August 1941. For a very brief history of the game farm, see www.catskillgamefarm.com.

30. Michael Kudish, *The Catskill Forest: A History* (Fleischmanns, NY: Purple Mountain Press, 2000), 150–51; "First Snow Train Ever to Come into Catskills Made Phoenicia History Sunday," *Stamford Mirror-Record*, 30 January 1936.

31. "Winter Sports in Phoenicia and Woodstock is Doing All Sorts of Good for Business," *Stamford Mirror-Record*, 13 February 1936; "Catskill Winter Plans," *New York Times*, 14 November 1937.

32. "Ski Slopes and Trails," *New York Times*, 25 December 1949; Kudish, *Catskill Forest*, 105; Rip Van Winkle Ski Association, "Preliminary Progress Report on Possible Major Ski Areas in the Catskill Mountains on Plateau Mountain and Hunter Mountain in Greene County, NY," 15 March 1957, Department of Environmental Conservation Papers, Box 36, "Skiing—Catskills," New York State Archives; "Doing it up Greene," *New York Times*, 5 May 1963.

33. "Catskill Ski Picture," *New York Times*, 16 January 1955.

34. "The Vacationland Rip Van Winkle Built," *New York Times*, 14 June 1953; "Builders of the Great Thruway," *New York Times*, 17 December 1950. See also "Thruway Magic," *New York Times*, 8 May 1966.

35. Central Catskills Association, "Central Catskill Area Guide, 1955" (Pine Hill, NY: The Pine Hill Press, 1955), 74–75. The 1956 edition contains the update concerning the completion of the Tappan Zee Bridge.

36. Ulster & Delaware Railroad, "Catskill Mountains" (Rondout, NY, 1892), held by New York Public Library.

37. These "suburban neighborhoods" included many areas in the city itself, including nearly all of Queens and most of the northern Bronx.

38. Alf Evers, *Woodstock: History of An American Town* (Woodstock, NY: The Overlook Press, 1987), 626; "A Dutchman in the Catskills," *Fortune* 53 (May 1956): 204.

39. United States Bureau of the Census, *Census of Population, 1970, v. 1, part 34, New York*, table 10.

40. Evers, *Woodstock*, 662–64, 668.

41. "Artists at Woodstock," *New York Times*, 19 July 1914. On the founding of Byrdcliffe and Maverick, see Evers, *Woodstock*, 412–19, 429–30, and 452–54. On the Arts and Crafts movement, see T. J. Jackson Lears, *No Place of Grace: Antimodernism and the Transformation of American Culture, 1880–1920* (Chicago: University of Chicago, 1981), 60–96.

42. Longstreth, *Catskills*, 19.

43. Harry Albert Haring, *Our Catskill Mountains* (New York: G. P. Putnam's Sons, 1931), 320; *The Woodstock Festival of Music and Art, Summer 1960*, held by the Woodstock Public Library strike). See also other festival pamphlets held by the library, including 1959, 1964, and 1966.

44. "The Catskills Greenwich Village," *New York Times*, 18 August 1963.

45. "Hippy Festival Upstate Is Cool amid the Bonfires," *New York Times*, 4 September 1967. Inadvertently, Mack reveals how effectively Central Park has assumed the role of countryside inside the city. Seemingly all it lacked was camping.

46. See Dylan's description of the Greenwich Village scene in *Chronicles, Volume One* (New York: Simon and Schuster, 2004), especially 9–22.

47. With essentially no official news concerning the accident, or Dylan's condition, rumors abounded, some even suggesting Dylan was paralyzed or near death. Apparently, Dylan's recuperation was as much psychological as physical, however, and his seclusion in Woodstock kept him away from hectic New York and the stresses of the road. There are half a dozen Dylan biographies, all of which cover in some detail his Woodstock years. I found Howard Sounes's work as complete and accessible as any. See Sounes, *Down the Highway: The Life of Bob Dylan* (New York: Grove Press, 2001), especially 73–87, 139–41, 177–78, and 216–18.

48. Ostensibly, Dylan invited the band members to aid his work in editing a documentary film. For a concise recounting of The Band's stay in Woodstock, see Rob Bowman's liner notes on the rereleased *Music from Big Pink* (Capital Records, 2000). See also Levon Helm (with Stephen Davis), *This Wheel's on Fire: Levon Helm and the Story of the Band* (Chicago: A Capella Books, 2000), 155–56, 157, 165–69. For a more complete history of The Band, see Barney Hoskyns, *Across the Great Divide: The Band and America* (London: Pimlico, 2003).

49. Bowman, liner notes.

50. "Woodstock's a Stage, but Many Don't Care for the Show," *New York Times*, 9 July 1969.

51. In describing the growing buzz surrounding the approaching festival, Ellen Willis wrote, "back on St. Marks Place, Woodstock was rapidly evolving into this year's thing to do." See "Musical Events," *New Yorker* 45 (Sept 6, 1969): 121. On the Woodstock festival, see Bob Spitz, *Barefoot in Babylon: The Creation of the Woodstock Music Festival, 1969* (New York: W.W. Norton & Company, 1989).

52. Andrew Kopkind, "Coming of Age in Aquarius," in *Decade of Crisis: America in the '60s* (New York: World Publishing, 1972), 254–56; "Bethel Farmers Call Fair a Plot 'to Avoid the Law,'" *New York Times*, 20 August 1969; "200,000 Thronging to Rock Festival Jam Roads Upstate," *New York Times*, 16 August 1969. On Yasgur's small farming empire in Sullivan County, see "Yasgur's—Land of Milk and Honey," *Upper Delaware Drummer* (Narrowsburg, NY: Snug Harbor Country Store, 1965), 19–20.

53. The *Times* editorial page reacted in horror to initial reports from Bethel (see "Nightmare in the Catskills," *New York Times*, 18 August 1969), but after the festival, the *Times* gave a more judicious account (see "Woodstock: Like It Was," *New York Times*, 25 August 1969). See also Richard Reeves, "Mike Lang (Groovy Kid from Brooklyn) Plus John Roberts (Unlimited Capital) Equals Woodstock," *New York Times*, 7 September 1969.

54. Sounes, *Down the Highway*, 244–54; Dylan, *Chronicles*, 118; Peter Moscoso-Gongora, "Woodstock Was," *Harper's* 245 (September 1972): 40–44. See also "Woodstock Up Tight as Hippies Drift In," *New York Times*, 19 June 1970.

55. Evers, *Woodstock*, 662–64; "Woodstock's a Stage," *New York Times*, 9 July 1969; "Nude-Swimming Issue Leads to 3d Political Party in Woodstock," *New York Times*, 2 November 1971.

56. One early acquisition of land came in the spring of 1976, when the struggling Balsam Lake Club, a nearly century-old fly-fishing club, gave its 3,600-acre property to the Catskill Center after falling behind on property taxes. The Catskill Center sold the land to the state in 1979. See Norman J. Van Valkenburgh and Christopher W. Olney, *The Catskill Park: Inside the Blue Line, The Forest Preserve and Mountain Communities of America's First Wilderness* (Hensonville, NY: Black Dome Press, 2004), 80–81.

57. Sherret S. Chase, "The Catskills of Tomorrow," *American Forests* (December 1975): 41–44; Sherret S. Chase, "The Founding of the Catskill Center: A Personal Account of the Early Years," *The Hudson Valley Regional Review* 6 (March 1989): 20–31. See also www.catskillcenter.org.

58. Peter R. Borreli, ed., *The Catskill Center Plan: A Plan for the Future Conservation and Development of the Catskill Region* (Hobart, NY: Catskill Center for Conservation and Development, Inc., 1974), 14, 16.

59. In describing his role in the Catskill Center, Chase noted, "A few years ago a newspaper account referred to me as a 'member of an old-time Catskill Family'"—an assumption the writer may have made because of Chase's devotion to the mountains or perhaps because his family name had already attached itself to the landscape, including Chase Road in Shokan. Chase, "Founding of the Catskill Center," 20.

60. Another early member, John Adams, had been a cofounder of the Natural Resources Defense Council in 1970 and then a founding member of the Open Space Institute a few years later. Adams and wealthy conservationist Laurance Rockefeller worked together on the preservation of lands in the Beaver Kill Valley. Adams, the Open Space Institute, and the Natural Resources Defense Council were all based in Manhattan. "OSI's Past, Present and Future in the Catskills," *Open Space* 3 (Fall 2004): 9.

61. Chase, "Catskills of Tomorrow," 43; Chase, "Founding of the Catskill Center," especially 25–26. Kingdon Gould, Jr., is the great-grandson of Catskills native Jay Gould. Jay's son George had purchased Furlow Lake and built Furlow Lodge in the late 1880s. Alf Evers, *The Catskills: From Wilderness to Woodstock* (Woodstock, NY: The Overlook Press, 1982), 546.

62. Philip G. Terrie, *Contested Terrain: A New History of Nature and People in the Adirondacks* (Syracuse: Syracuse University Press, 1997), 159–73.

63. Those four hailed from Hunter, Margaretville, DeLancey, and South Fallsburg. "The Catskill Study Commission," *The Conservationist* 27 (April–May, 1973): 34. Chase quotes the legislative charge, "Catskills of Tomorrow," 43.

64. "While Rip Van Winkle Sleeps," *The Conservationist* 27 (April–May, 1973): 3.

65. Joseph Marcogliese and Mary Allison Farley, "The Catskills Today and Tomorrow," *The Conservationist* 27 (April–May, 1973): 34–35, 38.

66. *The Future of the Catskills* (Stamford: Temporary State Commission to Study the Catskills, 1975), 5.

67. "Land Resources Management in the Catskills: Assessment and Recommendations," *Catskill Study Report #1* (New York State Department of Environmental Conservation, 1976). "Catskill Study," Department of Environmental Conservation Collection (13063–81), box 11, New York State Archives.

68. "Land Resources Management in the Catskills," 3.

69. "Statement of Sherret S. Chase, President, The Catskill Center for Conservation and Development before the Assembly Committee on Environmental Conservation in Support of a Regional Commission for the Catskills, February 23, 1977, Leeds, N.Y.," 10–11, Department of Environmental Conservation Collection (13063–83), Box 23, "The Catskills Center" Folder, New York State Archives.

70. "Statement of Sherret S. Chase," 19; Tim Hauserman and Tom Miner, *The Catskills For Sale: A Report of the Catskill Center for Conservation and Development, Inc. on the Land Sales Activities of Patten Realty and Timber Land Consultants* (Arkville, NY: Catskill Center for Conservation and Development, 1984), 3.

71. Quotes found in John G. Mitchell and Charles D. Winters, *The Catskills: Land in the Sky* (New York: The Viking Press, 1977), 83–84. Viking Press published this book for the Catskills Center.

72. "Reversing Rural Blight in the Catskills," *New York Times*, 11 October 1987.

73. "OSI's Past, Present and Future in the Catskills," 9.

Epilogue

John Burroughs, "In 'The Circuit of the Summer Hills,'" *The Summit of the Years* (New York: Houghton Mifflin Company, 1913), 25.
Robert Frost, "Stopping by Woods on a Snowy Evening," *New Hampshire* (New York: Henry Holt & Company, 1923), 87.

1. John Burroughs, "In 'The Circuit of the Summer Hills,'" 31–32; as quoted in Clara Barrus, *The Life and Letters of John Burroughs*, vol. 1 (New York: Houghton Mifflin Company, 1925), 160.

2. Ashokan Reservoir Awards, Reel 6, p. 5764.

3. "Weekender: Margaretville, N.Y.," *New York Times*, 18 April 2003.

4. *New York Times*, 11 October 1987; J. B. Jackson, *The Necessity for Ruins, and Other Topics* (Amherst: University of Massachusetts Press, 1980), 100.

5. See David Walbert, *Garden Spot: Lancaster County, the Old Order Amish, and the Selling of Rural America* (New York: Oxford University Press, 2002).

6. Like many others, I would also suggest that the journey serves a simple human need to connect us to the land, to nature, in contrast to the unnatural concentration of humanity in cities, though this journey does not require believing the country exists as a remnant of a past unavailable in the city. For a discussion of upstate New York settlers' decidedly unromantic notions of nature, see Alan Taylor, "'Wasty Ways': Stories of American Settlement," *Environmental History* 3 (July 1998): 291–310.

7. "A Catskills Renaissance," *Catskill Center News* (Winter 2000/2001): 3–4. In some instances, replicas have replaced what has been lost, including a handmade wooden bridge over the Platte Clove, designed to replicate one that stood on the site nearly a century ago. See "To Build a Bridge . . . ," *Catskill Center News* (Fall 2001): 8.

8. On the end of the Mountain House, see Roland Van Zandt, *The Catskill Mountain House: America's Grandest Hotel* (Hensonville, NY: Black Dome Press, 1991; New Brunswick: Rutgers University Press, 1966), 322–40.

9. There are a few obvious exceptions, including the wastewater facilities New York City has built to protect the city's water supply, discussed below.

10. "A Boon for the Catskills, or Something in the Water?" *New York Times,* 8 February 2004; "Water Woes Put Catskills Golf Resort in Doubt," *New York Times,* 24 April 2004.

11. Ibid. Unsurprisingly, given its size, the proposed Belleayre Resort has sparked a great deal of controversy in the region. See coverage in *The Phoenicia Times* at www.phoeniciatimes.com/e28/br.html.

12. The agreement allows the city to purchase conservation easements in addition to outright purchases of property. In both cases, the land must remain undeveloped in perpetuity.

13. See "Summary Guide to the Terms of the Watershed Agreement" (Arkville, NY: The Catskill Center for Conservation and Development, Inc., 1997), 1–12; "Acquisition Update," *The Watershed Advocate* (Winter 2004): 6. For a similar outcome, see Thomas Conuel, *Quabbin: The Accidental Wilderness* (Amherst: The University of Massachusetts Press, 1990). See also William L. Kahrl, *Water and Power: The Conflict over Los Angeles' Water Supply in the Owens Valley* (Berkeley: University of California Press, 1982), in which he notes that Los Angeles has "reversed the [Owens] valley in time" in a process that "might be applauded from a preservationist point of view as being in some vague sense an environmental good" (443).

14. "Summary Guide," 14–16; "Water Woes Put Catskills Golf Resort in Doubt."

15. "Summary Guide," 20–22. In one prominent, if perhaps obtrusive, example, the city has funded the upgrading of a now massive wastewater facility for the village of Pine Hill, in what is surely the single largest construction project in that area for decades.

16. See for example, "From Meat to Movies: CWC Awards $425,000 in Economic Development Grants," *The Watershed Advocate* (August 2001).

17. Efforts to bring gambling to Sullivan County date back to at least 1978. See Laventhol & Horwath, "Projected Impact of Casino Gaming on the Catskills Resort Area" (Catskills Resort Association, Inc., 1979). Many locals oppose the proposed casinos, which still face many hurdles. See "Setback for Legislation to Allow Indian Casinos in Catskills," *New York Times,* 16 April 2005.

18. "Against All Odds, a Complicated Casino Proposal Advances," *New York Times,* 17 April 2000. In anticipation of the casinos, wealthy outsiders have snapped up lands in the vicinity, gambling themselves that the developments will come and, of course, that tourists will follow. One of these outsiders, Louis Cappelli of Westchester County, purchased both the Concord and Grossinger's in hopes of profiting from the reincarnated Catskills. See "Tribe Wins Federal Approval for Casino in the Borscht Belt," *New York Times,* 7 April 2000; "Gold Rush in New York: Companies Vie for a Stake in the Untapped Gambling Market," *New York Times,* 17 December 2001. The shifting plans have projected several casinos in Sullivan County, including one at Monticello Raceway and another at the faltering Kutsher's Country Club.

19. See Martha Frankel's "Them & Us . . . Again," *The Phoenicia Times,* 21 July 2005, at www.phoeniciatimes.com/phoenicia/phoenicia.html.

Bibliographical Essay

The endnotes contain the details regarding sources I have relied upon to write this book, so I intend this essay to describe only the most important sources, those I turned to repeatedly and those that shaped my thinking about the mountains and their relationship to the city. Thus, this essay does not make reference to all the sources I consulted, nor even all that appear in the notes. Rather, it contains the primary and secondary sources that guided my work and should be sought out by those interested in knowing more about these topics.

General Catskills Histories

I began this project under the mistaken assumption that scholars had largely overlooked Catskills history, in part because so many important works address the Adirondacks without making so much as a reference to the smaller New York mountain range. I soon discovered, however, that a rich literature describes the region's history, with many of the important works having been locally published, especially by Black Dome Press, Purple Mountain Press, and The Overlook Press, small operations that have done much to keep the region's rich history alive.

The most comprehensive history of the region, Alf Evers's *The Catskills: From Wilderness to Woodstock*, was first published by Doubleday & Company, Inc., in 1972, but the revised and updated edition came from The Overlook Press (Woodstock, NY) ten years later. Evers penned a similarly detailed history of Woodstock, entitled *Woodstock: History of An American Town* (Woodstock, NY: The Overlook Press, 1987). Both of these books are encyclopedic in their approach, and so provide rich information on their topics. Evers also wrote a shorter collection of essays, *In Catskill Country: Collected Essays on Mountain History, Life and Lore* (Woodstock, NY: The Overlook Press, 1995), and though these were of less importance to my work, they are more accessible than the books. Field

Horne's *The Greene County Catskills: A History* (Hensonville, NY: Black Dome Press, 1994) offers a nicely illustrated, accessible narrative. Bob Gildersleeve and the Mountain Top Historical Society also published a brief collection of essays entitled *Kaaterskill: From the Catskill Mountain House to the Hudson River School* (Hensonville, NY: Black Dome Press, 1993), which illuminates the long history of that area. In *The River and the Mountains: Readings in Sullivan County History* (South Fallsburg, NY: Marielle Press, 1994), David M. Gold has gathered a number of essays and excerpts on the history of Sullivan County, some of which are difficult to find outside this collection.

I have also relied on a number of other comprehensive works on the Catskills, though they are old enough to function as primary sources as much as secondary reference works. Harry Albert Haring's *Our Catskill Mountains* (New York: G. P. Putnam's Sons, 1931) offers both a brief history and a valuable portrait of the region in the 1930s. T. Morris Longstreth's *The Catskills* (New York: The Century Company, 1918) is equally valuable in its description of the mountains a little more than a decade earlier, and also offers brief commentary on the region's past, while Charles Rockwell's *The Catskill Mountains and the Region Around* (New York: Taintor Brothers & Co., 1867) offers a snapshot of the mountains as tourism began its rapid expansion. Several nineteenth-century county histories are useful, including J. B. Beers' *History of Greene County, New York, with Biographical Sketches of Its Prominent Men* (New York: J. B. Beers & Co., 1884) and Nathaniel Bartlett Sylvester's *History of Ulster County, New York* (Philadelphia: Everts & Peck, 1880). Jay Gould's earlier work on a neighboring county, *History of Delaware County and Border Wars of New York* (Roxbury, NY: Keeny & Gould, Publishers, 1856), was of interest to me largely because of the author's later fame.

John Burroughs's many writings on the Catskills provide special insight into the region. I made use of his published essays, including those that appeared in *Wake-Robin* (New York: Hurd and Houghton, 1871), *Locust and Wild Honey* (1879), *Pepacton and Other Sketches* (1881), *Signs and Seasons* (1886), *Riverby* (1894), *The Summit of the Years* (1913), all published by Houghton, Mifflin and Company in New York, and *My Boyhood* (Garden City, NY: 1922), published by Doubleday, Page & Company. I also made use of his largely unpublished diaries held by Vassar College, and Clara Barrus's *The Life and Letters of John Burroughs* (New York: Houghton Mifflin Company, 1925). Edward J. Renehan, Jr., has also published a valuable biography, *John Burroughs: An American Naturalist* (Hensonville, NY: Black Dome Press, 1998).

The City-Country Relationship

General works on the Catskills region helped provide a basic narrative for my own Catskills history, but most of them all but ignore the relationship between the mountains and the city, even skirting the issue when discussing tourism and the water supply. Several works on the city-country relationship that do not discuss the Catskills were instrumental in shaping the theme of this work. William Cronon's *Nature's Metropolis: Chicago and the Great West* (New York: W. W. Norton & Company, 1991) has most deeply influenced my thinking about the city-country relationship, convincing me that no history of the Catskills could claim accuracy if it did not also discuss changes in the city down the river. Raymond Williams' classic, *The Country and the City* (New York: Oxford University Press, 1973), influenced me more than I thought it might upon first reading, but it convinced me just how powerful even diffuse urban cultural influence can be in the country. Gray Brechin's *Imperial San Francisco: Urban Power, Earthly Ruin* (Berkeley: University of California Press, 1999) and Matthew Gandy's *Concrete and Clay: Reworking Nature in New York City* (Cambridge: The MIT Press, 2002) both influenced my thinking, though in the end I moved away from the imperial model for describing the city-country relationship. David Walbert's *Garden Spot: Landcaster County, the Old Order Amish, and the Selling of Rural America* (New York: Oxford University Press, 2002) contains important arguments about the role of the past in shaping urban thoughts about rural places, and J. B. Jackson convinced me of the importance of ruins in American culture. See *The Necessity for Ruins, and Other Topics* (Amherst: The University of Massachusetts Press, 1980).

Natural Resources and Agriculture

Since the Catskills' history of natural resource extraction and agriculture is so diverse, I have made use of a wide variety of primary sources. Portraits of early settlement can be drawn from "Hardenburg Patent Field

Book of Great Lot No. 46 and 23," held at the New York State Library, and "Applications to Redeem Property" (B0847–85) held at the New York State Archives. Henry E. Dwight's "Account of the Kaatskill Mountains" (*The American Journal of Science and Arts* 2 [April 1820]) is a valuable firsthand account of the region around Hunter. To describe the region's agricultural history, I relied on a few personal accounts, including those of John Burroughs, listed above, and Candace Wheeler, whose *Yesterdays in a Busy Life* (New York: Harper & Brothers Publishers, 1918) is a fine autobiography of a Delaware County childhood. The Ashokan Reservoir Awards trial transcripts, held on microfilm by the Ulster County Clerk's Office, offer unbelievable detail on agricultural life in Olive in the late 1800s and early 1900s.

The Market Fire Insurance Company Manuscript, held at the Library of Congress, offers incomparable detail on the state of the tanning industry just as it was waning in the Catskills. The Pratt Museum in Prattsville contains a number of items related to Zadock Pratt, including an unpublished biography, but the most valuable single source on his business is "The Prattsville Tannery," a lengthy article published in *Hunt's Merchants' Magazine* 17 (August 1847). The tanning industry in the city itself is thoroughly described in Frank W. Norcross's *A History of the New York Swamp* (New York: The Chiswick Press, 1901), and the industry throughout the state is well described in Lucius F. Ellsworth, "Craft to National Industry in the Nineteenth Century: A Case Study of the Transformation of the New York State Tanning Industry" (dissertation, University of Delaware, 1971). Patricia E. Millen's *Bare Trees: Zadock Pratt, Master Tanner & the Story of What Happened to the Catskill Mountain Forests* (Hensonville, NY: Black Dome Press, 1995) is the most complete secondary source on Catskills tanning, despite its focus on Pratt.

Michael Kudish's *The Catskill Forest: A History* (Fleischmanns, NY: Purple Mountain Press, 2000) is an immensely useful text, complete with details on every manner of forestry and natural resource extraction. Also of interest is Robert P. McIntosh, "Forests of the Catskill Mountains, New York," *Ecological Monographs* 42 (Spring 1972): 143–61. The Martial Hulce Family Papers, held at Cornell University Rare Books and Manuscripts, offer insight into Delaware County's lumber market, as does Leslie C. Wood's *Rafting on the Delaware River* (Livingston Manor, NY: Livingston Manor Times, 1934).

The bluestone industry is thoroughly described by Harold T. Dickinson in "Quarries of Bluestone and Other Sandstones in the Upper

Devonian of New York State," *New York State Museum Bulletin* 61 (1903). The Ashokan Reservoir Awards trial transcripts also contain wonderful detail of the bluestone industry.

Catskills in Literature

Throughout the nineteenth century a great number of writers published pieces concerning the Catskills, both fictional stories and travelogs. The most important Catskills story was among the first, "Rip Van Winkle," published by Washington Irving in *The Sketch Book of Geoffrey Crayon, Gent*, first published in 1819 and dozens of times since. Pierre M. Irving's *The Life and Letters of Washington Irving* (New York: G. P. Putnam, 1864) is a good place to begin research on Irving's career. On the lasting influence of Irving, and especially "Rip Van Winkle," see Judith Richardson, *Possessions: The History and Uses of Haunting in the Hudson Valley* (Cambridge: Harvard University Press, 2003). James Fenimore Cooper's *The Pioneers, or the Sources of the Susquehanna* (1823; repr., New York: Signet Classics, 1964) has also been reprinted many times since appearing in 1823. Alan Taylor's *William Cooper's Town: Power and Persuasion on the Frontier of the Early American Republic* (New York: Vintage Books, 1995) places Cooper and his novel in context and offers a compelling portrait of settlement in upstate New York, just beyond the Catskills.

Less famous writers also wrote oft-reprinted prose on the Catskills. See Lewis Gaylord Clark's collection of his brother's work, *The Literary Remains of the Late Willis Gaylord Clark* (New York: Stringer & Townsend, 1851). Much of the well-known prose first appeared in periodicals, including Benjamin Park's "Cattskill [sic] Mountain House," *The New World* 7 (August 12, 1843) and T. Addison Richards, "The Catskills," *Harper's New Monthly Magazine* 9 (July 1854). Perhaps the most important collection of nineteenth-century prose concerning American places is William Cullen Bryant's two-volume *Picturesque America, or, The Land We Live In* (New York: D. Appleton & Co., 1872, 1874), which contains an essay on the Catskills as well as a series of wonderful lithographs by Harry Fenn.

The secondary literature on New York's early literary scene includes James Grant Wilson, *Bryant and His Friends: Some Reminiscences of the Knickerbocker Writers* (New York: Fords, Howard, & Hulbert, 1886), and James T. Callow, *Kindred Spirits: Knickerbocker Writers and American*

Artists, 1807–1855 (Chapel Hill: University of North Carolina Press, 1967), the latter of which I found especially helpful. Parke Godwin's *A Biography of William Cullen Bryant, with Extracts from His Private Correspondence* (New York: D. Appleton and Company, 1883) is still a useful introduction to one of the most important New York authors. Godwin also published a valuable edited volume, *The Poetical Works of William Cullen Bryant* (1883; repr., New York: Russell & Russell, 1967). On the changing role of mountains in Western literature and the development of the sublime, see Marjorie Hope Nicolson's classic, *Mountain Gloom and Mountain Glory: The Development of the Aesthetics of the Infinite* (Ithaca: Cornell University Press, 1959).

The Hudson River School

I made use of the New York Public Library's Thomas Cole and Asher B. Durand Papers, as well as the larger collection of Cole papers at the New York State Archives. Cole's life is well described in two works, Ellwood C. Parry III, *The Art of Thomas Cole: Ambition and Imagination* (Newark: University of Delaware Press, 1988), and, more important, Louis L. Noble's *The Life and Works of Thomas Cole, N.A.* (New York: Sheldon & Company, 1860). Other artists' biographies are important to understanding the development of the American style of landscape painting, including *The Autobiography of Worthington Whittredge, 1820–1910* (New York: Arno Press, 1969), edited by John I. H. Baur; Ila Weiss, *Poetic Landscape: The Art and Experience of Sanford R. Gifford* (Newark: University of Delaware Press, 1987); and Franklin Kelly, *Frederic Edwin Church and the National Landscape* (Washington, DC: Smithsonian Institution Press, 1988).

Barbara Novak's classic *Nature and Culture: American Landscape and Painting, 1825–1875* (New York: Oxford University Press, 1980) shaped my thinking about mid-nineteenth century art and several individual artists. Novak's book remains among the most influential works in American art history. John Ruskin's *Modern Painters*, vol. 4 (New York: Wiley & Halsted, 1856) reveals the importance of mountains to nineteenth-century landscape painting. On the development of the Barbizon School, see Nicholas Green's *The Spectacle of Nature: Landscape and Bourgeois Culture in Nineteenth-Century France* (Manchester, VT: Manchester University Press, 1990).

Obviously the Hudson River School has attracted the attention of a great number of scholars, including Kenneth Myers, whose *The Catskills: Painters, Writers, and Tourists in the Mountains, 1820–1895* (Yonkers: The Hudson River Museum of Westchester, 1987; distributed by Hanover, NH: University Press of New England) may be the best place to start a study of the Catskills in art. Among the many other works on the Hudson River School, I found *American Paradise: The World of the Hudson River School* (New York: Metropolitan Museum of Art, 1987) most helpful. On how New York's art world functioned, see *Patrons and Patriotism: The Encouragement of the Fine Arts in the United States, 1790–1860* (Chicago: University of Chicago Press, 1966) by Lillian B. Miller.

Tourism and the Grand Hotels

The New York Public Library houses an important collection of pamphlets related to the growing tourist industry, including *The New Grand Hotel, Catskill Mountains* (New York: Stewart, Warren & Co., 1887), *Catskill Mountains Summer Resorts* (New York: American Resort Association, 1902), and *Catskill Mountain House, Eighty-Third Season* (Catskill, NY: Recorder Print, 1905). New York Public also holds a series of pamphlets published by the Hudson River Day Line, including *The Most Charming Inland Water Trip on the American Continent* (1903), *Summer Tours* (1907), and *Hudson River by Daylight* (1912). Other works on Hudson River tourism include Robert Vandewater's *The Tourist, or Pocket Manual for Travellers on the Hudson River* . . . (New York: Harper & Brothers, 1836) and Charles Taintor's *Hudson River Route: New York to West Point, Catskill Mountains, Saratoga, Lake George, Lake Champlain, Adirondacks, Montreal, and Quebec* (New York: Taintor Brothers & Co., 1888). See also *The Hudson River by Daylight* (New York: American News Company, 1875, 1884) and *The Hudson* (New York: Bryant Union, Temple Court, 1894), both by Bruce Wallace.

The Ontario & Western Archives in Middletown contain annual tourist guides, titled *Summer Homes*, published by the O&W in the late 1800s and early 1900s. Several of the Ulster and Delaware Railroad's annual guides are held at the New York Public Library, under a variety of titles, many of which contain the phrase "The Haunts of Rip Van Winkle." The library holds issues from 1892, 1899, 1908, and 1912. The New York Public Library also holds a number of other railroad tour guides, including New York Central and Hudson River Railroad, *Health and Pleasure on "Amer-*

ica's Greatest Railroad" (New York: New York Central Passenger Department, 1890, 1896), The West Shore Railroad's *Summer Homes and Excursions Embracing Lake, River, Mountain and Seaside Resorts* (New York: 1887) and Kirk Munroe's *Summer in the Catskill Mountains*, published by the Passenger Department of the New York, West Shore and Buffalo Railway Company in 1883.

New York Public Library also holds three valuable sources on the Twilight Club, the best known of the private second-home developments in the Catskills. See *Twilight Park in the Catskills* (New York: Albert B. King, Printer, 189?), Joel Benton, *Memories of the Twilight Club* (New York: Broadway Publishing Co., 1910), and John A. MacGahan, *Twilight Park: The First Hundred Years, 1888–1988* (South Yarmouth, MA: Allen D. Bragdon, Publishers, Inc., 1988).

The Library of Congress holds a brief run of the *Catskill Mountain Breeze and Tourist's Guide* (1884–85), which contains important material on who vacationed in the mountains and what they did there. New York State Historical Association in Cooperstown holds a cluster of material on Stamford, including the S. B. Champion Scrapbook, 1825–1903. The Greene County Historical Society holds a Catskill Mountain House Manuscript, though much of the valuable material concerns the twentieth century.

Early tour books contain insight into what nineteenth-century vacationers expected to find in the mountains, including Samuel E. Rusk's *Rusk's Illustrated Guide to the Catskill Mountains; With Maps and Plans* (Catskill, NY: Samuel E. Rusk, 1879), Richard S. Barrett's *The Eagle Guide to the Catskill Mountains* (New York: Brooklyn Eagle, 1902, 1905), and Ernest Ingersoll's *Rand, McNally & Co.'s Illustrated Guide to the Hudson River and Catskill Mountains* (New York: Rand, McNally & Company, 1897, 1900, 1905). Some literature published by the hotels themselves has survived, including *K!tterskill Park: Scenery, Walks, Drives, Geology, Etc.* (New York: Kaaterskill Publishing Company, 1881?) and *The Kaaterskill Region: Rip Van Winkle and Sleepy Hollow* (New York: Kaaterskill Publishing Company, 1884), which the Hotel Kaaterskill published with Washington Irving listed as author. Perhaps my favorite guide is Henry Schile's *The Illustration of the Catskill Mountains, Sketched from Nature* (New York: Kelly & Bartholomew, 1881?).

More widely available are a number of other primary sources, such as R. Lionel De Lisser, *Picturesque Catskills: Greene County*, originally published in 1894, but reprinted in 1967 in a facsimile edition by Hope Farm

Press (Cornwallville, NY). See too *A Catskill Souvenir: Scenes on the Line of the Ulster and Delaware Railroad*, originally published in 1879 and reprinted in 1969, also by Hope Farm Press. Hope Farm Press has also reproduced the popular *Van Loan's Catskill Mountain Guide* (New York: The Aldine Publishing Company, 1879).

Local guides, in addition to Van Loan's, include Annie Searing's entertaining *The Land of Rip Van Winkle: A Tour Through the Romantic Parts of the Catskills; Its Legends and Traditions* (New York: G. P. Putnam's Sons, 1884); the instructive *Guide to Rambles from the Catskill Mountain House; By a Visitor* (Catskill, NY: J. Joesbury Book & Job Printer, 1863); *The Scenery of the Catskill Mountains, As Described by Irving, Cooper, Bryant, Willis Gaylord Clark* . . . (Catskill, NY: Joseph Joesbury, Printer, 1864, 1872), which is really just a collection of Catskills literature; and J. G. Butler's *The Catskill Mountains, Pine Hill and Summit Mountain* (Rondout, NY: Kingston Freeman Company, 1883).

Tourist literature became quite popular in the mid-1800s, and dozens of autobiographies recounted vacation trips that included the Catskills. Among the most important are Caroline Gilman's *The Poetry of Travelling in the United States* (New York: S. Colman, 1838), Harriet Martineau's *Retrospect of Western Travel*, vol. 1 (London: Saunders and Otley, 1838), Tyrone Power's *Impressions of America, During the Years 1833, 1834 and 1835* (London: Richard Bentley, 1836), George William Curtis's *Lotus-Eating: A Summer Book* (New York: Harper & Brothers, Publishers, 1852), and Charles Lanman's *Adventures in the Wilds of the United States and British American Provinces* (Philadelphia: John W. Moore, 1856).

The secondary literature on tourism has expanded rapidly in the last two decades. Among the early influential works are John A. Jakle's *The Tourist: Travel in Twentieth-Century North America* (Lincoln: University of Nebraska Press, 1985) and John F. Sears's *Sacred Places: American Tourist Attractions in the Nineteenth Century* (New York: Oxford University Press, 1989), the latter of which I found to be especially helpful. Roland Van Zandt's *The Catskill Mountain House: America's Grandest Hotel* (New Brunswick: Rutgers University Press, 1966) is the best work focused on nineteenth-century tourism in the Catskills. I also learned from works that focus on other areas, including Dona Brown, *Inventing New England: Regional Tourism in the Nineteenth Century* (Washington, DC: Smithsonian Institution Press, 1995), Cindy S. Aron, *Working at Play: A History of Vacations in the United States* (New York: Oxford University Press, 1999), Eric Purchase, *Out of Nowhere: Disaster and Tourism in the White*

Mountains (Baltimore: The Johns Hopkins University Press, 1999), and Jon Sterngass, *First Resorts: Pursuing Pleasure at Saratoga Springs, Newport & Coney Island* (Baltimore: The Johns Hopkins University Press, 2001). On later tourism, especially the turn toward automobiles, see Marguerite S. Shaffer, *See America First: Tourism and National Identity, 1880–1940* (Washington, DC: Smithsonian Institution Press, 2001).

Railroads

Aside from the many railroad tour guides, all of which describe routes, timetables, and destinations, the company histories themselves are instrumental in describing the city-country relationship. The regional railroads of the Catskills have received considerable attention. See William F. Helmer, *O&W: The Long Life and Slow Death of the New York, Ontario & Western Railway* (Berkeley, CA: Howell-North, 1959); Gerald M. Best, *The Ulster and Delaware: Railroad Through the Catskills* (San Marino, CA: Golden West Books, 1972); Gertrude Fitch Horton, *The Delaware and Northern and the Towns It Served* (Fleischmanns, NY: Purple Mountain Press, 1989); and, most important, Manville B. Wakefield's *To the Mountains by Rail: People, Events and Tragedies . . . the New York, Ontario and Western Railway and the Famous Sullivan County Resorts* (Grahamsville, NY: Wakefair Press, 1970), which is much more than a history of the railroad in Sullivan County.

Wilderness, the Forest Preserve, and Catskill Park

The recently published *The Catskill Park: Inside the Blue Line, The Forest Preserve & Mountain Communities of America's First Wilderness* (Hensonville, NY: Black Dome Press, 2004) contains Norman J. Van Valkenburgh's fine essay on the founding of the park and a full reprint of Charles Carpenter's 1886 "Report to the State Forest Commission on the Catskill Preserve," one of the most important primary sources on the condition of the Catskills forest as state conservation began. The Association for the Protection of the Adirondacks published a number of important documents, including *A Plea for the Adirondack and Catskill Parks* (1903?), held by the Adirondack Museum. The New York State Forest Commission *Annual Reports* are also instructive, especially in revealing the relative unimportance of the Catskills to state officials more concerned with the Adirondacks. Later the Forest Commission became the Forest, Game and Fish Commission. Edgar A. Mearns's "Notes on the Mammals of the Catskill Mountains, New York, With General Remarks on the Fauna and Flora of the Region," *Proceedings of the United States National Museum* vol. 21 (1899): 341–60, also contains some valuable detail.

Catskills trout fishing has attracted the attention of dozens of authors. See especially Emlyn M. Gill, *Practical Dry-Fly Fishing* (New York: Charles Scribner's Sons, 1913), and George M. L. LaBranche, *The Dry Fly and Fast Water* (New York: Charles Scribner's Sons, 1914). *Forest and Stream* magazine also contains regular references to Catskills fishing, as does the *New York Times*. Arnold Gingrich edited a fine collection of Theodore Gordon's essays, published under the title *American Trout Fishing* (New York: Alfred A. Knopf, 1966), and John McDonald has done the same for Gordon's letters, published under the title *The Complete Fly Fisherman: The Notes and Letters of Theodore Gordon* (New York: Charles Scribner's Sons, 1947). Among the valuable secondary sources are Austin M. Francis, *Catskill Rivers: Birthplace of American Fly Fishing* (New York: Lyons & Burford, 1983), and Ed Van Put, *The Beaverkill: The History of a River and Its People* (Guilford, CT: The Lyons Press, 1996). For a fuller history of fly fishing, see Paul Schullery's *American Fly Fishing: A History* (New York: Nick Lyons Books, 1987).

Several secondary sources helped shape my thinking on wilderness preservation generally and in New York specifically. Most important, Roderick Nash's *Wilderness and the American Mind* (New Haven: Yale University Press, 1967, 1982) was the first work of environmental history I ever read, and it is still among the most important. William Cronon's article "The Trouble with Wilderness; or, Getting Back to the Wrong Nature" offers a good summary of the power of the sublime and a valuable critique of the role of wilderness in modern environmentalism. See *Uncommon Ground: Toward Reinventing Nature* (New York: W. W. Norton & Company, 1995). Mark David Spence's groundbreaking work on Native Americans and preservation, *Dispossessing the Wilderness: Indian Removal and the Making of the National Parks* (New York: Oxford University Press, 1999), taught me a great deal about mythmaking's role in setting aside wild lands. Philip G. Terrie has provided a thorough analysis of the Adirondacks' important story in two works: *Forever Wild: A Cultural His-*

tory of Wilderness in the Adirondacks (Syracuse: Syracuse University Press, 1994) and *Contested Terrain: A New History of Nature and People in the Adirondacks* (Syracuse: The Adirondack Museum/Syracuse University Press, 1997). Karl Jacoby's *Crimes Against Nature: Squatters, Poachers, Thieves, and the Hidden History of American Conservation* (Berkeley: University of California Press, 2001) influenced my thinking about the Adirondacks and conservation more generally. Paul Schneider's *The Adirondacks: A History of America's First Wilderness* (New York: Henry Holt and Company, 1997) is also a highly accessible and informative history of the other New York mountain range. On the conservation movement more generally, see Samuel P. Hays, *Conservation and the Gospel of Efficiency* (1959; repr., Pittsburgh: University of Pittsburgh Press, 1999). Richard Judd's *Common Lands, Common People: The Origins of Conservation in Northern New England* (Cambridge: Harvard University Press, 1997) and Paul S. Sutter's *Driven Wild: How the Fight Against Automobiles Launched the Modern Wilderness Movement* (Seattle: University of Washington Press, 2002) have also influenced my thinking on conservation politics.

New York City Water Supply

The New York Public Library holds the three important engineering studies that led to the rejection of the Ramapo water plan and the acceptance of the Catskills as the future water source for the city: Merchants' Association of New York's *Inquiry into the Conditions Relating to the Water-Supply of the City of New York* (1900), John R. Freeman's *Report Upon New York's Water Supply with Particular Reference to the Need of Procuring Additional Sources and Their Probable Cost with Works Constructed Under Municipal Ownership* (New York: Martin B. Brown, Co., 1900), and William H. Burr, Rudolph Hering, and John R. Freeman, *Report of the Commission on Additional Water Supply for the City of New York* (New York: M. B. Brown, Co., Printers, 1904).

The most valuable source on the consequences of the construction of the Catskills supply is the Ashokan Reservoir Awards transcript, held by the Ulster County Clerk. These lengthy transcripts reveal the excruciating process navigated by those removed from the Ashokan basin and painstakingly catalogue what they lost. New York Public Library and the New York Municipal Library hold a wide variety of publications from the New York City Board of Water Supply, including annual reports and the occasional progress report on the work undertaken in the mountains or along the aqueduct. Of particular interest is a semi-monthly publication devoted to the interests of the employees of the Board of Water Supply, published from June 1911 to December 1913 under the title *The Catskill Water System News*. A similar newspaper accompanied the building of the Delaware system, *The Delaware Water Supply News*, published from August 1938 until October 1965.

The New York Public Library contains a number of other valuable publications related to the city's supply, including Edward Nimsgern's *Illustrated and Descriptive Account of the Main Dams and Dikes of the Ashokan Reservoir* (Brown Station, NY: E.G. Nimgern, 1909) and George Frederick Kunz's *Catskill Aqueduct Celebration Publications* (New York: The Mayor's Catskill Aqueduct Celebration Committee, 1917). The *New York Times* also contains thorough coverage of the water supply controversy and the move into the Catskills, as does the *Kingston Daily Freeman*, the editors of which grew quite concerned when the city sets its sites on the mountains.

Gerard T. Koeppel's *Water for Gotham: A History* (Princeton: Princeton University Press, 2000) is a very entertaining narrative of the city's early efforts to secure a satisfactory water supply. Charles H. Weidner's *Water for a City: A History of New York City's Problem from the Beginning to the Delaware River System* (New Brunswick: Rutgers University Press, 1974) is less engaging but more complete. Diane Galusha's *Liquid Assets: A History of New York City's Water System* (Fleischmanns, NY: Purple Mountain Press, 1999) is well illustrated and contains critical details. Bob Steuding's *The Last of the Handmade Dams: The Story of the Ashokan Reservoir* (Fleischmanns, NY: Purple Mountain Press, 1985) offers a fine narrative history of that aspect of the water supply story. See also Alice H. Jacobson's touching *Beneath Pepacton Waters* (Andes, NY: Pepacton Press, 1988).

The secondary literature on the construction of water supplies is very rich. I have been especially influenced by William Kahrl, *Water and Power: The Conflict over Los Angeles' Water Supply in the Owens Valley* (Berkeley: University of California Press, 1982); Norris Hundley, Jr.'s classic, *The Great Thirst: Californians and Water: A History* (1992; repr., Berkeley: University of California Press, 2001); and Sarah Elkind's *Bay Cities and Water Politics: The Battle for Resources in Boston and Oakland* (Lawrence: University Press of Kansas, 1998).

The Jewish Catskills

Abraham Cahan's *The Rise of David Levinsky* (New York: Grosset & Dunlap, Publishers, 1917) contains a fictionalized visit to the thriving Jewish resorts of turn-of-the-century Greene County and might serve as an introduction to Jews in the Catskills. The most comprehensive work on Jewish tourism is Stefan Kanfer's *A Summer World: The Attempt to Build a Jewish Eden in the Catskills, From the Days of the Ghetto to the Rise and Decline of the Borscht Belt* (New York: Farrar, Straus & Giroux, 1989). See also Herbert Tobin's essay, "New York's Jews and the Catskill Mountains, 1880–1930," in Ronald A. Brauner, ed., *Jewish Civilization: Essays and Studies,* vol. 1 (Philadelphia: Reconstructionist Rabbinical College, 1979).

My study of the Jewish resort region of Sullivan County has been largely reliant on the many memoirs written by former hotel and bungalow owners and visitors. Among the most important are Phil Brown's *Catskill Culture: A Mountain Rat's Memories of the Great Jewish Resort Area* (Philadelphia: Temple University Press, 1998) and Irwin Richman's *Borscht Belt Bungalows: Memories of Catskill Summers* (Philadelphia: Temple University Press, 1998). See also the lavishly illustrated Myrna Katz Frommer and Harvey Frommer, *It Happened in the Catskills: An Oral History in the Words of Busboys, Bellhops, Guests, Proprietors, Comedians, Agents, and Others Who Lived It* (New York: Harcourt Brace Jovanovich Publishers, 1991), and the personal account of Esterita "Cissie" Blumberg, *Remember the Catskills: Tales by a Recovering Hotelkeeper* (Fleischmanns, NY: Purple Mountain Press, 1996). Of some interest are Joey Adams (with Henry Tobias), *The Borscht Belt* (New York: The Bobbs-Merrill Company, Inc., 1959); and three works on Grossinger's: Harold Jaediker Taub, *Waldorf in the Catskills: The Grossinger Legend* (New York: Sterling Publishing Co., Inc., 1952); Joel Pomerantz, *Jennie and the Story of Grossinger's* (New York: Grosset & Dunlap, 1970); and Tania Grossinger, *Growing Up at Grossinger's* (New York: David McKay Company, Inc., 1975). For a sense of the changing nature of Jewish tourism in the Catskills, see *Oscar Israelowitz's Catskills Guide* (New York: Israelowitz Publishing, 1992).

On Jews in the city, see Irving Howe's classic *World of Our Fathers* (New York: Harcourt Brace Jovanovich, 1976); Moses Rischin, *The Promised City: New York's Jews, 1870–1914* (Cambridge: Harvard University Press, 1962); Hasia Diner, *Lower East Side Memories: A Jewish Place in America* (Princeton: Princeton University Press, 2000); and Eli Lederhendler's *New York Jews and the Decline of Urban Ethnicity, 1950–1970* (Syracuse: Syracuse University Press, 2001). On anti-Semitism, see Leonard Dinnerstein, *Antisemitism in America* (New York: Oxford University Press, 1994), and on Americanization, see Andrew R. Heinze, *Adapting to Abundance: Jewish Immigrants, Mass Consumption, and the Search for American Identity* (New York: Columbia University Press, 1990).

Jewish farmers in the Catskills have received some scholarly attention. See David M. Gold, "Jewish Agriculture in the Catskills, 1900–1920," *Agricultural History* 55 (January 1981): 31–49, and, more importantly, Abraham D. Lavender and Clarence B. Steinberg, *Jewish Farmers of the Catskills: A Century of Survival* (Gainesville: University of Florida Press, 1995). I also made use of several years of the Jewish Agricultural and Industrial Aid Society *Annual Report*, available at the Klau Library of Hebrew Union College.

A wave of new Catskills fiction is part of the growing nostalgia for a time and place that have disappeared. See Terry Kay, *Shadow Song* (New York: Pocket Books, 1994); Eileen Pollack, *Paradise, New York* (Philadelphia: Temple University Press, 1998); and Allegra Goodman, *Kaaterskill Falls* (New York: Dial, 1998).

Automobiles and Suburbanization

The complex effects of the increasing usage of automobiles on tourism can be traced through articles in the *New York Times* and through the changing tourist literature. See especially Arthur C. Mack, *Enjoying the Catskills: A Practical Guide to the Catskill Mountain Region for the Motorist, Camper, Hiker, Hunter, Fisherman, Skier, and Vacationer* (New York: Funk & Wagnalls Company, 1950); Eric Posselt and Arthur E. Layman, *Guide to the Catskills: The Rip Van Winkle Trail* (New York: Arrowhead Press, Publishers, 1949); and Carl Ratsch *Return to the Catskills* (Oak Hill, NY: Big Acorn Press, 1946). See also William Copeman Kitchin's very entertaining *A Wonderland of the East* (Boston: The Page Company, 1920). For scholarly treatment of the automobile and tourism, see Paul Sutter, *Driven Wild*, and Marguerite S. Shaffer, *See America First*, both noted above, and Warren James Belasco, *Americans on the Road: From Autocamp to Motel, 1910–1945* (Cambridge: The MIT Press, 1979).

On the growing threat of suburbanization in the mountains, see the

New York State Department of Environmental Conservation's *Catskill Study Reports* (1976) and the various articles on the Catskills that appear in the DEC's periodical, *The Conservationist*. See also the many publications of the Catskills Center for Conservation and Development, including *Catskill Center News*, its periodical; Tim Hauserman and Tom Miner, *The Catskills for Sale: A Report of the Catskill Center for Conservation and Development, Inc. on the Land Sales Activities of Patten Realty and Timber Land Consultants* (Arkville, NY: Catskill Center for Conservation and Development, 1984); and *The Catskill Center Plan: A Plan for the Future Conservation and Development of the Catskill Region* (Hobart, NY: Catskill Center for Conservation and Development, Inc., 1974), edited by Peter R. Borrelli.

For scholarly treatment of autos, roads, and changing rural culture, see Hal S. Barron, *Mixed Harvest: The Second Great Transformation in the Rural North, 1870–1930* (Chapel Hill: University of North Carolina Press, 1997) and Michael L. Berger, *The Devil Wagon in God's Country: The Automobile and Social Change in Rural America, 1893–1929* (Hamden, CT: Archon Books, 1979). Many fine works on suburbanization now exist, but I am still most influenced by Kenneth Jackson's classic, *Crabgrass Frontier: The Suburbanization of the United States* (New York: Oxford University Press, 1985).

Woodstock, Dylan, and The Band

In addition to Alf Evers's monograph on Woodstock, noted above, several fine secondary sources on the music and arts scene in Woodstock exist. See the collection of pamphlets describing the early Woodstock Festivals held by the Woodstock Public Library. On Bob Dylan, see his beautifully written autobiography, *Chronicles, Volume One* (New York: Simon and Schuster, 2004), and Howard Sounes's *Down the Highway: The Life of Bob Dylan* (New York: Grove Press, 2001), which I found to be the best of the several Dylan biographies. On The Band, see Barney Hoskyns, *Across the Great Divide: The Band and America* (London: Pimlico, 2003), and Levon Helm (with Stephen Davis), *This Wheel's on Fire: Levon Helm and the Story of the Band* (Chicago: A Cappella Books, 2000). On the 1969 festival, see Bob Spitz, *Barefoot in Babylon: The Creation of the Woodstock Music Festival, 1969* (New York: W.W. Norton & Company, 1989), and the ample coverage in the *New York Times*.

New York City

The literature on New York City is remarkably rich. In addition to the many works listed above under specific topics, I made frequent use of Edwin G. Burrows' and Mike Wallace's encyclopedic *Gotham: A History of New York City to 1898* (New York: Oxford University Press, 1999). I was especially influenced by David M. Henkin's *City Reading: Written Words and Public Spaces in Antebellum New York* (New York: Columbia University Press, 1998); Max Page's *The Creative Destruction of Manhattan, 1900–1940* (Chicago: University of Chicago Press, 1999); and David M. Scobey's *Empire City: The Making and Meaning of the New York City Landscape* (Philadelphia: Temple University Press, 2002). On Central Park, see Roy Rosenzweig and Elizabeth Blackmar, *The Park and the People: A History of Central Park* (Ithaca: Cornell University Press, 1992), and a wonderful, brief guidebook, J. K. Larke's *Davega's Handbook of Central Park* (New York: Baldwin & Co., 1866). On the career of Calvert Vaux, see Francis R. Kowsky, *Country, Park, & City: The Architecture and Life of Calvert Vaux* (New York: Oxford University Press, 1998).

Index

Adirondack Mountains, xvi, 32, 64, 212; creating wilderness in, 121; development pressure in, 233–34; Forest Preserve in, 117–20; forest regulations in, 123; hunting in, 125; as potential source of water, 144, 148

agriculture, 20, 22–28, 43; Forest Preserve and, 120–21; Jews and, 186–87; John Burroughs on, 115, 242–43; road building and, 214; tourism and, 95, 106, 109

Alworth, Tom, 247

Angler's Club of New York, 127

anti-Semitism, 104–6, 181–82, 184–85, 203

Ashokan Reservoir, 150, 152, 157; construction of, 159–60, 166–69; as "Lake Ashokan," 220; takings trials for, 161–66

Association for the Preservation of the Adirondacks, 119–20

automobiles, 210–11; recreated roadsides and, 217, 221; road building and, 213–15; in Sullivan County, 192, 204; touring and, 214–20

The Band, 228–29

Barlow Advertising Agency, 211–12

Barton, Ara, 243

Beaver Kill, 127–29, 134, 239

Belleayre Ski Center, 222–23, 247

Bender, Thomas, 75

Benjamin, Park, 57–58, 82

Bethel, 187, 230

Bierstadt, Albert, 72

Bishop Falls, 22, 94, 162, 168–69

Bishop Falls House, xv, 25, 94–95, 164, 166–67

bluestone, 24, 40–43, 162

Blumberg, Cissie, 180

boardinghouses, 94–96, 103–4

Board of Water Supply, 152, 155–60 passim, 167–68; and land management, 170

Boice, John I., 162

Borscht Belt, xxii, 184–85, 201; decline of, 203–6; national reputation of, 203. *See also* Jews: in the Catskills

Brodhead's Bridge, 41, 42, 94

brook trout, 133, 134–35. *See also* fishing

Brown, Arthur, 161

Brown's Station, 124, 164, 168

brown trout, 133, 134–35. *See also* fishing

Bryant, William Cullen, 53–55, 99; and *Kindred Spirits*, 74–75

bungalows, 188–89, 197

Burr, William, 149, 152, 155

Burroughs, John, 5–6; on bark roads, 35–36; on Catskills water, 141; on Catskills wilderness, 43–44; childhood of, 26–27, 112; early career of, 113; ideal landscape of, 114–15; Memorial Field and, 242; at the Mountain House, 80; popularity of, 115–16; Riverby and, 113–14; romanticism and, 114–15; tramping and, 112

busses, 193, 210

Byrdcliffe, 226, 228

Caesar, Sid, 194, 195

Cahan, Abraham, 177–79

camping, 123, 218–19, 246–47

Cantor, Eddie, 199

Carpenter, Charles F., 118, 125

casinos, 249–50

Catskill, 29, 50, 63
Catskill Aqueduct, 152, 160, 169
Catskill Center for Conservation and
    Development, 232–34, 237, 239, 247
Catskill Game Farm, 221–22
Catskill Mountain Association, 80.
    See also Mountain House
Catskill Mountain Breeze, 93–94, 98
Catskill Park, 122
Catskills Preserve. *See* Forest Preserve
Catskill Watershed, 141, 172–73
Catskill Watershed Corporation, 249
Central Park, 85, 88, 127, 228
Chase, Sherret, 232–33, 237
Christmas trees, 39–40
Church, Frederic, 70, 72
city-country relationship, 7–8, 10–11;
    agriculture and, 26; deforestation
    and, 39; environmental conscious-
    ness and, 243–45; fishing and, 127–
    28, 130; as imperialism, 12–16, 142,
    241; Jewish tourism and, 178–79,
    200–201, 206–7; reservoirs and, 169–
    70, 175–76; tourism and, 96, 98–99,
    108, 209–10; water and, 141–43, 156,
    173; wilderness and, 109–10, 121–22,
    139; Woodstock Music Festival and,
    231
Civilian Conservation Corps, 123, 124,
    222
Clark, Willis Gaylord, 57, 58
Claude Lorrain, 60
Clearwater, Alfonso, 154–55, 161
Cole, Thomas, 10, 11–12, 15, 58, 99; early
    success of, 62; Frederic Church and,
    70; Hudson River School and, 59–63;
    in *Kindred Spirits,* 74–75; landscape
    style of, 65–67; New York City and,
    62–65; popularity of, 71; tourism
    and, 82–83; wilderness and, 110–12
Coler, Bird, 147
Commission on Water Supply, 149–50
Concord Hotel, 195, 198, 205
Cooper, James Fenimore, 11, 58, 79, 99,
    212; and *The Pioneers,* 51–54; quoted
    in tourist literature, 92
Coykendall, Samuel, 155

Cronon, William, 10–11, 116
Croton water supply, 143–44, 151–52, 154,
    157–58
Crystal Spring Water Company, 151–52
Curtis, George, 79, 100

dairying, 23–25, 187
deforestation, 28, 31, 39
Delaney, John, 154–55
Delaware River, 25; timber rafting and,
    37–38
Delaware Watershed, 171, 173
DeLisser, Richard, 76, 94, 99, 105
Denning Township, 180
Department of Environmental Protec-
    tion, 172–73
Deposit, 38
Downing, Andrew Jackson, 85
Dresser, Andrew, 176
Durand, Asher, 15, 61, 62, 68; *Kindred
    Spirits* and, 74–75; Thomas Cole and,
    64–65
Dwight, Henry, 22–23, 47–48, 141
Dylan, Bob, 213, 228–29

eminent domain, 152–53, 163–66
Erie Canal, 43, 50
Erpf House, 233
Esopus Creek, 34, 94–95, 219; Shandaken
    Tunnel and, 170–71; as water source,
    145–50 passim, 157, 162, 168
Evers, Alf, 234

Fallsburg, 106, 187
Fisher, Eddie, 199
fish hatcheries, 132
fishing, 126–35; conservation and, 134
Flagler House, 187–88
Fleischmann, Charles, 182
Fleischmanns, 90, 182
flooding, 39
folk music, 227
forest fires, 32; prevention of, 123–24
Forest Preserve: Adirondacks and, 118–
    20; creation of, 117–18; expansion
    through tax sale, 120–21; making
    wilderness in, 121–23

Freeman, John R., 147–48, 155
Fuertes, James, 148
furniture factories, 37

George, Jean Craighead, 135, 138
Gifford, Sanford, 15, 69–70
Gilboa, 34, 170
Gitter, Dean, 247
Gordon, Nathan H., 164–65
Gordon, Theodore, 126
Gottfried, Herman, 175
Gould, Jay, xxiii, 27, 31
Grand Hotel (Highmount), xvi, xx, 89,
    144, 246
Green, Seth, 132
Greene County, 29, 32–33
Greenwich Village, 62–63, 228
Griffin's Corners, 182
Grossinger's Hotel, 188, 195, 198–99, 205
Guyot, Arnold, 180

Haines Falls, 28, 240
Hale, Sarah, 47, 73
Hardenburgh, 23
Harding, George, 84
Haring, Harry, 24, 28, 120–21, 134, 227
Haynes, Glentworth, xv–xviii, xxiii
Haynes Hollow, xv–xvii, 26, 250–51
hemlocks, 28, 31, 34, 38
Highmount, xvi, xviii, xx
hiking, 96–97
historic preservation, 211
hoop making, 36–37
Hotel Kaaterskill, 84, 88, 144, 185, 246
hotels, 79–90; automobiles and, 216–
    19; entertainment in, 193–95; as
    intensification of urban life, 195;
    in Sullivan County, 185–88, 197–
    200
Housatonic River, 147–49
Howell, Wallace E., 174
Hudson, Henry, 47, 49
Hudson River, 50–51, 64; as potential
    water source, 142, 145, 148–49, 155;
    tourism and, 80–81
Hudson River School, 15, 59–62, 178;
    Catskills Aqueduct and, 169; decline

of, 72–74; as defining the Catskills,
    72–75; Kaaterskill Clove and, 68–69;
    Kindred Spirits and, 74–75; popular-
    ity of, 70–71; Thomas Cole's influ-
    ence on, 66–68. See also names of
    individual painters
Hunter, 23, 29, 35, 37, 182; anti-Semitism
    and, 104–5; David Levinsky in, 177–
    78, 183; early description of, 47; and
    skiing, 223
hunting, 124–26
Hurley, 225
Huth, Hans, 78

IBM, 225
Ingersoll, Ernest, 182
Irving, Washington, 11, 48–50, 56, 58–59,
    178; quoted in tourist literature, 92

Jackson, J. B., 44, 244–45
Jacobson, Alice, 172
Jacoby, Karl, 121
Jewett, 23
Jews: agriculture and, 186–87; Ameri-
    canization and, 196, 207; in the Cats-
    kills, 177–207 passim; Holocaust and,
    196; nature and, 183, 207; in New
    York City, 180–81; Russian pogroms
    and, 181; stereotypes of, 181–82

Kaaterskill Clove, 22, 29, 58; as artists'
    destination, 68–69; Rip Van Winkle
    and, 76; tanning and, 35; Thomas
    Cole and, 66–67
Kaaterskill Falls, 54–55, 58, 62, 65;
    changes to, 99–101
Kaaterskill Park, 84–85, 86–87 (map),
    88–89, 246
Kaye, Danny, 193–94
Kindred Spirits, 74–75
Kingston, xvi, 32, 218; Ashokan Reser-
    voir and, 153–54, 156, 167–69; subur-
    banization and, 225
Kitchin, William Copeman, 218–20
Kopkind, Andrew, 230
Kornfeld, Artie, 230
Kuchaleins, 191–92

Kudish, Michael, 34, 43
Kutsher's Hotel, 199–200

Lake Kiamesha, 198
Lake with Dead Trees, 67
landscape paintings, 15, 60–62, 67–68;
   of Barbizon School, 72–73. *See also*
   Hudson River School; *names of indi-*
   vidual painters
Lang, Michael, 230
Lanman, Charles, 111–12
Laurel House, 83, 100, 185
Levinsky, David, 177–79, 183, 196
Lewis, Jerry, 194
Liberty, xxii, 106, 183, 188; tuberculosis
   and, 190
Lillie, Lucy C., 43–44, 96
Loomis Sanitarium, 189–90
Longstreth, T. Morris, 209–10, 224
Lower East Side, 177, 179, 181, 190
Lyon, Sylvanus, 93, 97

Malden, 43
Marjorie Morningstar, 195
Marsh, George Perkins, 117
Martineau, Harriet, 81
McClellan Act, 152, 154, 156
McEntee, Jervis, 68, 69, 85
McGrath, John, 164
Merchants' Association of New York,
   147–48
Mohican Trail, 220
Mohonk House, 25
Monticello, xxii, 183, 206–7
Mountain House, 76, 79–84, 111–12, 184,
   185, 246
Muir, John, 114, 116
Music from Big Pink, 12, 229
My Side of the Mountain, 135, 138–39,
   245

Nash, Roderick, 109
National Academy of Design, 69, 71, 73,
   110
Native Americans, 21
Nevele Country Club, 175, 188, 200
Neversink Club, 131

Neversink River, 33; fishing in, 127, 129,
   131, 134; Jewish tourists and, 187, 197
Newburgh, 85
New York City, xix–xx, 6–7, 9, 20; anti-
   Semitism and, 104; art market in,
   59–60, 65; art studios in, 61–63, 69;
   Central Park and, 85, 88; as "the
   city," 16–17; consolidation of, 145;
   fishing and, 126–28; Forest Preserve
   and, 119; growth of, 50–51; immigration and, 101–2; Jews in, 180–
   82, 190–91, 196, 200–201; John Burroughs in, 113–14; leather industry
   in, 29–30; literary scene in, 51, 53–
   59; rainmaking and, 174–75; romanticism and, 56–57; segregation in, 102;
   water supply of, 142–74, 247–49;
   Woodstock and, 227
New York, Ontario and Western Railway, 91, 192; decline of, 192; fishing
   and, 128, 130; fish stocking and, 132;
   tourism and, 106–8, 184
New York State Thruway, 223–24, 226,
   234
Niagara Falls, 78–79
Nicolson, Marjorie Hope, 13
Nostrand, Peter, 146
Novak, Barbara, 60, 100

Olana, 70
Olin, Julia, 97
Olive, 24, 176
Olmsted, Frederick Law, 85
Ontario and Western Railroad. *See* New
   York, Ontario and Western Railway
Onteora Park, 80, 102, 103
Open Space Institute, 239

Palenville, 63, 68; and Rip Van Winkle,
   77, 221
Paradise, New York, 205–6
Paulding, James K., 53
Pepacton Reservoir, 171–72
Philadelphia, Pennsylvania, 38, 42
Phoenicia, 216, 222, 238
Picturesque America, 55
Pine Hill, xviii, 32, 89, 91, 151

Pine Hill Sentinel, 156–57
Pine Orchard, 52, 58, 80, 84, 218
Plattekill Clove, 58
Pratt, Zadock, 29–31, 33
Prattsville, 30, 35
preservationism, 8, 17–18, 139, 235, 238–39, 245–46
private parks, 102–4. *See also* Onteora Park; Twilight Park

quarrying, 24, 40–42. *See also* bluestone

railroads, 91, 128, 192, 210. *See also* New York, Ontario and Western Railway; Ulster and Delaware Railroad
rainmaking, 174–75
Ramapo Water Company, 146–49, 156
Reed, Luman, 64–65, 71, 111
reforestation, 124
reservoirs, 142, 176, 236. *See also individual reservoirs*
Rhine, Alice Hyneman, 105
Ricciardella, Richard, 238
Richards, T. Addison, 34, 58, 68; in Kaaterskill Park, 83, 101
Richfield Springs, 79
Richman, Irwin, 202–3, 204–5
"Rip Van Winkle," 48–49, 59, 76–77, 138, 178, 212
Rip Van Winkle Bridge, 221
Rip Van Winkle Trail, 220
Riverby, 5, 113–14
Rockefeller, Laurance, 238–39
Rockwell, Charles, 35, 59, 83, 89
romanticism, 8–9, 56–58; John Burroughs's critique of, 114–15; wilderness and, 116–17
Rondout Reservoir, 171
Roosa, Albert, 168
Roosevelt, Robert Barnwell, 128
Roslyn, 54, 74
Rothman, Hal, 14
Rotron, 225
Roxbury, 27, 31
Rozzelle, Sylvia, 176
Rusk, Samuel, 97, 100
Ruskin, John, 60, 226

Samsonville, 35
Saratoga Springs, 79; anti-Semitism in, 104
Sargent, Charles S., 117
Saugerties, 42, 225
Schile, Henry, 9, 23–24, 84; Kaaterskill Falls and, 101; Kaaterskill Park and, 88
Schoharie Creek, 22, 29, 145, 147, 149, 170–71
Schroon Lake, 64–65
Scribner, Silas, 67, 68, 99
Searing, Annie, 101
Shandaken, 24, 120, 157, 235
Shavertown, 172
Shawangunk Mountains, 184
Shepard, Paul, 99
Shokan, 25, 33, 147, 167
skiing, 222–23
Slabsides, 113
Slide Mountain, 43, 122, 124, 135; deer park on, 125
Slosson, Harrison, 161, 165, 167–68
Slutsky, Charles, 188
Smith, J. Waldo, 155
South Lake, 62, 66–68, 83
Stamford, 91, 218
Strong, George Templeton, 81
sublime nature, 57, 80–82, 99, 101, 209
suburbanization, 200–201, 223–25; as threat to Catskills, 210–11, 213, 225–26, 232–38
Sullivan County, 33; casino plans in, 249–50; economy of, 201–2, 203; moving the Catskills to, 179–80; organized crime in, 202; reputation of, 204; segregation in, 202–3; suburbanization in, 235; tourism in, 106–8, 183–207 passim
Summer Homes, 106–8, 184, 186, 192
Summer on a Mountain of Spices, 206–7
Sutter, Paul, 211, 219

Tammany Hall, 146
Tannersville, 29, 68, 94, 241; anti-Semitism and, 104–5; Jewish tourism in, 182
tanning industry, 24, 29–34; collapse of, 35–36; water pollution and, 34

Taylor, Bayard, 53, 80, 218
Temporary State Commission to Study the Catskills, 233–35
Thoreau, Henry David, 83
timber industry, 37–38
Tobin, Leslie, 229
tourism, 8, 12, 14; agriculture and, 25, 95, 106; anti-Semitism and, 104–6; automobiles and, 214–21; boardinghouses and, 94–96; decline of, 209–10; fishing and, 130–31; health and, 92, 107; ideas of nature and, 77–78; Kaaterskill Falls and, 99–101; local residents and, 97–99; Mountain House and, 79–84; peak of, 93–94, 140; railroads and, 89–92; remade landscape and, 98–99, 101, 108; segregation and, 102–6; spas and, 79; in Sullivan County, 106–8, 183–207 passim; tramping and, 109–12; wilderness and, 111; women and, 96–97; urban tastes and, 79. *See also* hotels
tourist literature, 78–79, 91–94
tramping, 109–12, 115, 216
Trumbull, John, 62
tuberculosis, 107, 148, 189–90
tummlers, 193–94
Twilight Park, 102–3, 108, 240

Ulster and Delaware Railroad, xvii, 25, 32, 77, 225; Ashokan Reservoir and, 147, 155; bluestone and, 40–42; decline of, 210; Snow Train and, 222; and tourism, 89, 90–94

Van Etten, Amos, 158–59
Vaux, Calvert, 85; and Kaaterskill Falls, 100

Walbert, David, 18
water, 14, 140–41, 150. *See also* New York City: water supply of
Watershed Agreement, 247–49
West Saugerties, 229
Wheeler, Candace, 28, 75
White, Hervey, 226
Whitehead, Ralph, 226
Whittridge, Worthington, 69
wilderness, 108; defined, 110; making of, 121–22, 134, 248, 251; in *My Side of the Mountain*, 135, 138–39; state protection of, 117, 120–21, 135–36; Thomas Cole and, 66–67, 110–12, 116; tramping and, 109–12
wilderness cult, 109–10, 135
Williams, Raymond, 12–13
Willis, Nathaniel Parker, 53
Willowemoc Club, 129
Willowemoc Creek, 127–29, 134
Winchell, Mary, 158
Winchell Hill, 159
Windham, 223
Wingate, Charles, 102–3
A Wonderland of the East, 218–19
Woodchuck Lodge, 242–43
Woodridge, 186
Woodstock, 24, 225; as arts community, 226–28; Bob Dylan and, 228–29, 231; suburbanization and, 232
Woodstock Music Festival, 229–31
wool, 27
Wordsworth, William, 114–15
Workmen's Circle, 189–90
Worster, Donald, 11

Yasgur, Max, 187, 230

WEYERHAEUSER ENVIRONMENTAL BOOKS

The Natural History of Puget Sound Country by Arthur R. Kruckeberg

Forest Dreams, Forest Nightmares: The Paradox of Old Growth in the Inland West by Nancy Langston

Landscapes of Promise: The Oregon Story, 1800–1940 by William G. Robbins

The Dawn of Conservation Diplomacy: U.S.-Canadian Wildlife Protection Treaties in the Progressive Era by Kurkpatrick Dorsey

Irrigated Eden: The Making of an Agricultural Landscape in the American West by Mark Fiege

Making Salmon: An Environmental History of the Northwest Fisheries Crisis by Joseph E. Taylor III

George Perkins Marsh, Prophet of Conservation by David Lowenthal

Driven Wild: How the Fight against Automobiles Launched the Modern Wilderness Movement by Paul S. Sutter

The Rhine: An Eco-Biography, 1815–2000 by Mark Cioc

Where Land and Water Meet: A Western Landscape Transformed by Nancy Langston

The Nature of Gold: An Environmental History of the Alaska/Yukon Gold Rush by Kathryn Morse

Faith in Nature: Environmentalism as Religious Quest by Thomas R. Dunlap

Landscapes of Conflict: The Oregon Story, 1940–2000 by William G. Robbins

The Lost Wolves of Japan by Brett L. Walker

Wilderness Forever: Howard Zahniser and the Path to the Wilderness Act by Mark Harvey

On the Road Again: Montana's Changing Landscape by William Wyckoff

Public Power, Private Dams: The Hells Canyon High Dam Controversy by Karl Boyd Brooks

Windshield Wilderness: Cars, Roads, and Nature in Washington's National Parks by David Louter

Native Seattle: Histories from the Crossing-Over Place by Coll Thrush

The Country in the City: The Greening of the San Francisco Bay Area by Richard Walker

Drawing Lines in the Forest: Creating Wilderness Areas in the Pacific Northwest by Kevin R. Marsh

Making Mountains: New York City and the Catskills by David Stradling